24⁹⁹
₁6⁵¹

MW00682847

BOOM
TOWN
BLUES

Elliot Lake
Collapse and Revival in a Single Industry Community

Edited by
Anne-Marie Mawhiney
&
Jane Pitblado

DUNDURN PRESS
TORONTO · OXFORD

Copyright © Institute of Northern Ontario Research and Development 1999

All rights reserved. No part of this publication may be reproduced, stored in a retrieval system, or transmitted in any form or by any means, electronic, mechanical, photocopying, recording, or otherwise (except for brief passages for purposes of review) without the prior permission of Hounslow Press. Permission to photocopy should be requested from the Canadian Copyright Licensing Agency.

Design: Scott Reid
Printer: Webcom

Canadian Cataloguing in Publication Data

Boom town blues — Elliot Lake: collapse and revival in a single-industry community
ISBN 1-55002-291-1

1. Elliot Lake (Ont.) — History. 2. Uranium mines and mining — Ontario — Elliot Lake. 3. Retirement, Places of — Ontario — Elliot Lake. I. Mawhiney, Anne-Marie, 1953– . II. Pitblado, Jane.
FC3009.E417B66 1999   971.3'132   C97-931819-X
F1059.5.E417B66 1999

1   2   3   4   5   03   02   01   00   99

THE CANADA COUNCIL | LE CONSEIL DES ARTS
FOR THE ARTS | DU CANADA
SINCE 1957 | DEPUIS 1957

We acknowledge the support of the **Canada Council for the Arts** for our publishing program. We also acknowledge the support of the **Ontario Arts Council** and the **Book Publishing Industry Development Program** of the **Department of Canadian Heritage.**

Care has been taken to trace the ownership of copyright material used in this book. The author and the publisher welcome any information enabling them to rectify any references or credit in subsequent editions.

Printed and bound in Canada.

Printed on recycled paper.

Dundurn Press
8 Market Street
Suite 200
Toronto, Ontario, Canada
M5E 1M6

Dundurn Press
73 Lime Walk
Headington, Oxford,
England
OX3 7AD

Dundurn Press
2250 Military Road
Tonawanda NY
U.S.A. 14150

To the people of Elliot Lake — especially the laid-off mining families —
whose spirit has kept Elliot Lake alive in the face of enormous challenges

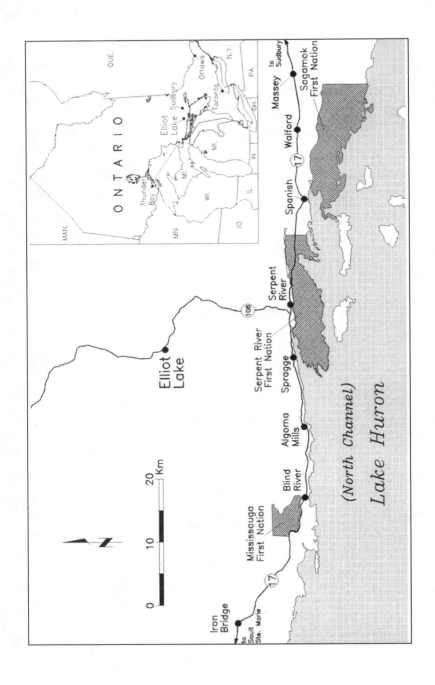

Contents

Acknowledgements

Many people and organizations contributed to the development of this book. First, we thank those from Elliot Lake who were participants in and interviewers for the various research projects reported on here. In addition to the contributors to this book, several staff members of the Elliot Lake Tracking and Adjustment Study (one of INORD's projects) — Patrick Barnholden, Judy Lynn Malloy, Suzanne Dansereau, Jan Lewis, Mike Mallette, Tim Boston, and Linda Liboiron — provided assistance and feedback on a number of the papers. The new director of INORD, Brian MacLean, has been supportive. Thanks are also due to Jane Holland of Lewis Carroll Communications, to Léo Larivière of the geography department at Laurentian University for the maps used in the book, to Mary Roche of Laurentian's Instructional Media Centre for help in processing the photographs, and to copy editor Doris Cowan for her many valuable suggestions. Several people in Elliot Lake assisted us in finding photographs for the book — in particular, Carrie Chenier of the Steelworkers, City Councillor Fred J. Mann, Carmaine McCallum of the Economic Development Office, Ian Ludgate and Roy Morrell of Denison Mines Limited, and Darla Hennessey of the Nuclear and Mining Museum — and we thank all of them for their help.

We are grateful for the contributions by INORD's sister research institutes at Laurentian University, both to the book and to the conference out of which the book grew. Researchers and staff associated with the Elliot Lake Research Field Station and its Environmental Rehabilitation Group (now Environmental Services), the Northern Health Human Resources Research Unit (now the Centre for Rural and Northern Health Research), and the Centre for Research in Human Development have all conducted research projects in Elliot Lake.

The eloquence of community-based authors makes the realities of the people in Elliot Lake come alive, and we wish to acknowledge their special contributions to the book.

INORD Books

Boom Town Blues — Elliot Lake: Collapse and Revival in a Single-Industry Community is the sixth in a series of publications sponsored by INORD and deriving from INORD conferences and symposiums. Many of the papers in *Boom Town Blues* were first presented at INORD's sixth conference, "Elliot Lake: Northern Community in Transition," held in Elliot Lake in January 1997. The previous INORD books are *Changing Lives: Women in Northern Ontario* (1996), edited by Margaret Kechnie and Marge Reitsma-Street; *Hard Lessons: The Mine Mill Union in the Canadian Labour Movement* (1995), edited by Mercedes Steedman, Peter Suschnigg, and Dieter K. Buse; *Rebirth: Political, Economic, and Social Development in First Nations* (1993), edited by Anne-Marie Mawhiney; *At the End of the Shift: Mines and Single-Industry Towns in Northern Ontario* (1992) edited by Matt Bray and Ashley Thomson; and *Temagami: A Debate on Wilderness* (1990), edited by Matt Bray and Ashley Thomson. All of these books have addressed issues of particular importance to Northern Ontario, and all have fostered dialogue between academics from a variety of disciplines and interested members of the relevant communities (including activists for women's issues, labour leaders, mayors, Aboriginal leaders, and environmentalists). The efforts to produce these books, all published by Dundurn Press, have been liberally supported by both the Social Sciences and Humanities Research Council of Canada and the Ontario Heritage Foundation.

Anne-Marie Mawhiney and Jane Pitblado
Sudbury, February 1998

Elliot Lake's nuclear symbol being fabricated at Rio Algom Limited in Elliot Lake. The symbol now stands in the city's Westview Park.

City of Elliot Lake

Introduction

Since the days of early contact between its original inhabitants and European newcomers, the development of the land now known as Northern Ontario has centred primarily on the extraction of natural resources — furs, timber, and minerals. Unlike sister communities in the south with their diversified economies and strong population base, our northern communities have experienced repetitive boom-and-bust cycles that have had major impacts on the day-to-day life of their inhabitants. Not that long ago — for the post-contact history of Northern Ontario is relatively young — pioneers carved small resource-based communities from forests, around lakes, and out of rocks. In the early days, lumber companies followed the forests, with the result that communities were temporary, and those involved in the forest industries moved from place to place. Likewise, mining company towns were not always seen as permanent sites. Communities such as Creighton, Dome Extension in South Porcupine, and Matachewan — once small yet viable mining town sites — have all but disappeared, except for the memories of the people who once lived there. In similar fashion, we have lost single-industry communities in other parts of Canada as well, such as Uranium City, Saskatchewan, and Bralorne, British Columbia. Little is known about the impact on families of the dislocation from these dying communities, nor about the ways the bust phase of the cycle for single-resource communities affected the wider socio-economic fabric of the surrounding area or region. What we do know is that the survival of Northern Ontario depends on these communities, even after their resource industries have shut down.

In the last ten years, several communities throughout Northern Ontario have faced major economic and social crises as companies have shut down or threatened to shut down because of high production costs, poor markets, low prices, and even wider, more global economic forces. Decisions to shut down have often been made in southern Ontario or in the United States, where many of the corporate headquarters are far removed from the realities faced by those for whom

11

the shutdowns and mass layoffs would have the most immediate effect: those supporting the industry within the communities — the industry's workers, their families, local government and service workers, and local business owners and operators.

Some communities have pulled together to formulate effective strategies to prevent the most devastating effects of the impending shutdowns. For instance, the employee buy-out of Algoma Steel in Sault Ste. Marie has been highly successful in revitalizing that company and in maintaining the community's economic vitality.[1] The strategies used in Kapuskasing to maintain the Spruce Falls Power and Paper Company have similarly stabilized that community. Sudbury's economic diversification strategy was relatively successful until the recent provincial cutbacks and downsizing. The stories of these and other similar communities are important stories and ones that need to gain wide audience so that we learn from each other.

In *Boom Town Blues: Elliot Lake — Collapse and Revival in a Single-Industry Community*, we look at the struggle to revive Elliot Lake's economy after the collapse of its mining industry following announcements in 1990 by Denison Mines Limited and Rio Algom Limited of mass layoffs. In January 1997, the Institute of Northern Ontario Research and Development (INORD) held its sixth conference, "Elliot Lake: Northern Community in Transition," in Elliot Lake. Community representatives and researchers were invited to present their perspectives and findings on the effects on the community of Elliot Lake of the collapse of the mining industry there. *Boom Town Blues* is a compilation of the papers presented at the conference, with the addition of a few other valuable perspectives.

Elliot Lake, a city with a population in 1996 of 13,588 (according to the census), is situated roughly halfway between Sudbury and Sault Ste. Marie.[2] This remote northern city is about 40 kilometres north of the Trans-Canada Highway, along which lie several small towns and two First Nations, dotting the north shore of Lake Huron (see map, p. 4). The city was formed in 1955, and its economy over the following 35 years depended almost exclusively on the extraction of uranium from large nearby deposits under the management of Denison Mines Limited and Rio Algom Limited. Strong demand for the ore first came from the U.S. military, but when this contract was not renewed in 1959, the city experienced its first bust; the population declined from a high of nearly 25,000 to 6,600 by 1965. The expansion of the nuclear power industry in the late 1960s led to a renewed boom that peaked in the 1980s with the signing of long-term purchasing contracts between Ontario Hydro (a public utility) and the two firms.

Uranium production from the Elliot Lake mines climbed to a high of 6.1 million pounds for Denison in 1982 and 7.6 million pounds for Rio Algom in 1984. At these peak production levels, employment at Denison's Elliot Lake operations stood at just over 2,300 (1981–82) and at about 3,000 (1983–84) for Rio Algom. These employment expansions raised the population of the town to about 18,000 in the mid-1980s. Indeed, the future looked rosy for Elliot Lake. A promotional brochure for the town in the late 1980s talked of long-term contracts for uranium and stability for the town into the next century (brochure photos are reproduced below with their original captions). Denison extracted ore from a single mine, while Rio operated three mines at Elliot Lake. Both firms, with investments in a number of other mineral deposits in other communities in Canada and around the world, have head offices in Toronto. The majority of the workforces at Denison's and Rio Algom's Elliot Lake operations were represented under collective agreements by the United Steelworkers of America.

Original late-1980s caption: "Uranium mines in Elliot Lake, such as Denison (#2 mine shaft shown), have long-term contracts to supply ore that extend well into the next century."
City of Elliot Lake

Towards the end of the 1980s, extraction of uranium in Saskatchewan had expanded to account for 48.3 percent of Canadian output. The Saskatchewan ore was a higher grade of uranium and thus supposedly less costly than that from Elliot Lake. (The reported costs of the ore were disputed, especially by the Steelworkers, for not taking into account different safety requirements necessary in the higher-grade mines.) This

Original late-1980s caption: "Strong projections for uranium markets ensure both the community of Elliot Lake, and nearby mines such as Rio Algom Quirke II shown here, a stable future."

City of Elliot Lake

competition eventually led Ontario Hydro to attempt to renegotiate its Elliot Lake contracts in 1991; when this failed, Hydro's purchasing arrangements for uranium were revised. Since 1992, the Crown corporation's policy has been to buy uranium through a competitive bidding process (flexible sourcing) and thus to acquire the mineral from various firms and countries. Hydro's decision to terminate its contracts with Denison and Rio Algom — and the competition from apparently less expensive uranium production — ultimately resulted in the closure of all mines in Elliot Lake.

The corporate exit from the community began with the announcements in the spring of 1990 that Denison planned to reduce its 1,800-employee workforce by 450 workers and that Rio was to lay off 1,600 of its 2,400 employees. By September, over 400 Denison production and maintenance workers and about 1,300 Rio production, maintenance, office, and technical employees had been permanently laid off. Rio closed its main administrative office by the end of 1990, and by then another 300 or so workers had been laid off. In addition, some workers left their jobs shortly after the layoffs were announced (before receiving official notice of termination), and some accepted voluntary layoff or early retirement. As of the end of December 1990, Rio had closed two of its mine operations in Elliot Lake and had shifted all remaining workers to Stanleigh Mine. At both companies the layoffs were governed by the seniority provisions of the respective collective agreements. Between July 1 and December 31, 1990, then, employment in the town's mining industry had nearly been halved. Over the next several years, the layoffs continued: Denison stopped production at the end of February 1992 and closed its last mine by the end of April the same year; Rio's Stanleigh operations came to a halt at the end of June 1996. A very small number of administration workers remain in Elliot Lake until the company closes its local operations. (For a graphical representation of these employment patterns, see Figure 1 of Chapter 8 in this volume, p. 108.)

The mine closures have obviously had a significant impact on the local economy, both in Elliot Lake and along the North Shore. All levels of government stepped in offering a number of adjustment programs, from special provisions under the then Unemployment Insurance Fund to the Elliot Lake and North Shore Corporation for Business Development (ELNOS) economic development fund, which was created mainly with Hydro compensation payments. An Employee Assistance Committee was established by Rio Algom to help laid-off workers locate jobs (see Ferguson, Chapter 9 in this volume).

Nevertheless, by 1991 unemployment had risen to 60 percent and the city's population began to decline. In response, the municipality developed a scheme to attract retirees to the area to live in homes vacated by the laid-off workers. These homes (single detached houses, duplexes, and apartments) had been constructed by the mining firms and were subsequently sold to, or rented by, employees. Of course, the housing market crashed and many laid-off workers and their families suffered major losses in investment. It is still possible to purchase a detached home in Elliot Lake for under $30,000. The Retirement Living Program has in many ways been successful: Elliot Lake's population has stabilized at around 13,500 and a small service industry has remained afloat. Unfortunately, the arrival of seniors has not generated sufficient employment for the former mine workers, and unemployment among laid-off workers and their family members remains high. The mining firms have not fared as badly. Both Rio Algom and Denison continue their mining operations outside Elliot Lake. Although Denison experienced a corporate downsizing as a result of the mine closure in Elliot Lake, it is now developing a new uranium mine in Saskatchewan.

In *Boom Town Blues: Elliot Lake — Collapse and Revival in a Single-Industry Community*, we trace some of the stories of mining families as they struggled to recover from the far-reaching consequences of the layoffs. We also present stories from local labour leaders, business owners, service providers, and politicians, who talk about the collapse and revival from the perspective of the community of Elliot Lake itself. The mass layoffs directly or indirectly affected every person in the city in one way or another, and undermined the viability of the community as well. These witnesses, representing different perspectives on what has happened in Elliot Lake, speak from the heart and soul of the struggles, successes, and failures of the community and its people.

In addition to the chapters written by community members who lived the experience first-hand, *Boom Town Blues* contains — as have all of the books in the INORD series — chapters by academic researchers. They have followed the case study of Elliot Lake as it has gone through transitions during the last seven years and provide an understanding of what has happened in that community. They use a variety of research strategies and focus on different aspects of the collapse and revival of the people, the community, and the environment.

There are three inextricable threads to the story about Elliot Lake's collapse and revival, which we have gathered into the three main sections of the book. The first thread, in "Part One: The Uphill Climb," weaves together the stories of the people of Elliot Lake who were most directly affected by the collapse of the uranium mining industry in Elliot Lake — the workers and their families. Before the layoffs, mining families had relatively high wages that afforded a good standard of living for the vast majority of them. Mining families had built the social fabric of Elliot Lake and had a strong attachment to their community, their neighbours, and friends. Our stories start after the layoffs were announced and relate what has happened since 1990.

Intertwined with the first thread is the second, in "Part Two: Refusing to Become Another Ghost Town." This thread tells us about the community's efforts to survive after the collapse of the industry. Community leaders, local politicians, business owners, entrepreneurs, and outside experts pulled together to formulate strategies that would revive the local economic viability of the community.

The third thread, in "Part Three: Reclaiming the Land," looks at the wider environmental impact of the uranium mines and at experiments to restore the environment to its former natural splendour. Uranium mining presents some unique challenges to ensuring that environmental integrity is maintained during and after mining production. In particular, uranium tailings need to be stored forever in such a way as to protect the physical safety of local residents as well as those living on waterways linked to the Elliot Lake area. The mining decommissioning process needs to ensure that the local ecosystem is safe and that mining sites are returned to nature in appropriate ways.

Framing these three sections in the book are a prologue and an epilogue. In the prologue, Alex Berthelot's song "Boom Town Blues" — which gives our book its title — provides a compact history of the cyclical exploitation of northern resources. This is followed by Shawn Heard's background paper tracing the history of the community of Elliot Lake prior to the 1990 shutdown announcements. In the epilogue, Anne-Marie Mawhiney stands back from the stories of adjustment that form the main part of the book and suggests a possible policy strategy for other communities that face mass layoffs and plant closures, one that could lessen the blow to both individuals and the communities. The book closes with a second song by Alex Berthelot, Jr., "Mystère économique," which calls on northerners to join together to ensure that more of the wealth gained through northern resource exploitation stays in the North and enriches the communities and the people of the North.

It is our belief that people from other communities, especially single-industry communities elsewhere in Northern Ontario and across Canada, will see similarities between their experiences and those described in parts of the story of Elliot Lake's collapse and revival. In Chapter 17, Alex Berthelot, Jr. states that "when our particular crisis struck, there was precious little in the way of documentation of the experiences of other single-industry towns in crisis and of their efforts to redesign themselves."*Boom Town Blues* helps to meet that need. Armed with a better understanding of the immense challenges an economic crisis such as this presents to people and their community, we hope they will be better prepared to meet those challenges.

Boom Town Blues does not represent all aspects of the story of Elliot Lake. There are still many stories left to be told, and many stories still unfolding. However, we have tried to capture some of the emotions and debate about Elliot Lake's transition from a mining community to one that is trying to survive in other ways. Will Elliot Lake survive as a vital and dynamic community? Or has the inevitable end merely been postponed? Is there life after layoffs for the mining families? Will the mining decommissioning process and ecological experiments be successful in providing a safe and healthy environment for the local area? Many would say that the verdict is not yet in.

Our subtitle for this book is provocative, and likely to cause debate. Was there a collapse after the layoffs were announced in 1990? Some authors in this book, as well as others living in the community of Elliot Lake, would say no. Equally important, however, are the views of those who assert that the layoffs have had devastating effects on the mining families, the service workers and business community, and the overall well-being of the community of Elliot Lake itself. Has Elliot Lake revived? For those who argue that there was no collapse, revival is a misnomer. For those who argue that Elliot Lake did experience a serious socio-economic crisis, there are at least two points of view. One suggests that the negative and debilitating effects of the layoffs are still being felt in the community and therefore neither the people nor the community has "revived." Others would support the idea that the people and community are reviving and that Elliot Lake has effectively avoided disaster through effective and thoughtful interventions targeting people and community. As you read through the book, you will experience the various standpoints on this question of collapse and revival. We leave to you, the reader, the verdict on the questions that we have raised. Do you think the people, the community, and the local environment collapsed? Do you think they have revived, or has the inevitable collapse of the community been merely postponed?

Anne-Marie Mawhiney, Monica Neitzert, and Jane Pitblado

Notes

[1] See Mick Lowe (1995), "Steel resolve," *Financial Post Magazine*, April: 20-31

[2] The section of the introduction that describes the Elliot Lake context relies heavily on David Leadbeater (1998), "Report on the Elliot Lake Tracking Study Population (1990)." ELTAS Report Series #2R1. Sudbury, ON: INORD, Laurentian University.

Prologue

Boom Town Blues
Lyrics by Alex Berthelot, Jr.
Sung to the tune of "The Wabash Cannonball"

Some four hundred years ago, the French came to explore,
The rich and rugged woodlands, of Huron's great North Shore,
They traded with the natives for furs and pelts galore,
Then they left the Jesuit Fathers and said, "We'll come back for more."
And then you'll hear…

Chorus: The jingle, the rumble and the roar,
Riding through the woodlands, through the hills and by the Shores,
We'll take all those resources, even rocks right to the core,
Then the CPR and CNR won't run here any more.

Well, the King of France, he did not care, so to England we did go,
She needed timber for her ships and to make the empire grow,
So we cut down all the big trees, and shipped them out you know,
Then we watched the growth of England and the Town of Toronto.
And then we heard… (chorus)

With the big trees gone, the little trees were all that still remained,
So in Espanola we built a mill, our stature was regained.
We shipped out pulp and paper, our future seemed assured,
Our economic woes were sure forever to be cured.
And again we heard… (chorus)

But soon there were more sources than the market could endure,
And once again we realized our future's insecure.
With the furs 'n timbers, little trees gone, it was our darkest hour,
Until we found those special rocks that cities burn for power.
And again we heard… (chorus)

19

But now the needed wonder fuel comes from Saskatchewan,
And once again the way we made our living was all gone,
But our home is just too beautiful to simply walk away,
So now we share the way we live to help us pay our way.
'cause we need to hear…

Chorus: The jingle, the rumble and the roar,
Riding through the woodlands, through the hills and by the Shores.
This time we'll take that CPR and turn that train around,
We've gotta find a way to get resources Northward Bound!

So to seniors from across the land we made our message clear,
There is no better way to live than the way we do it here.
And with the richness that they represent, once again we're pioneers,
So if you think we've gone and died, my friends please dry your tears.
And listen for…

Chorus: The jingle, the rumble and the roar,
Riding through the woodlands, through the hills and by the Shores,
We've found brand new resources, but unlike days of yore,
Now the CPR and CNR bring riches to our door!

Mining machinery welcomed visitors to Elliot Lake in
the past.

City of Elliot Lake

Chapter 1
The City of Elliot Lake to 1991:
Before the Roof Fell In
Shawn Heard

E lliot Lake has had a brief but fascinating historical development. It began with the intrigue of a cloak-and-dagger staking bee, quickly dwindled into Canada's "most modern ghost town," boomed during its days of providing much of the uranium for the secretive "Uranium Cartel," and now has been reborn as a very successful retirement community.

As a community, Elliot Lake did not exist until the 1950s, but the area had seen a variety of uses long before that. Today's Mississagi Provincial Park, about 15 miles north of the City of Elliot Lake, has provided archaeological evidence of an aboriginal (Ojibwa) population dating back 10,000 years.[1]

When the Hudson's Bay Company established operations in the Algoma region, the Elliot Lake area certainly played a part in the fur trade, with both the North West Company and the Hudson's Bay Company operating posts just south of the area near the present-day community of Blind River. The Elliot Lake townsite itself was the site of a seasonal Ojibwa village, and a number of trappers gathered furs from what is now the Elliot Lake region. Logging companies in Northern Ontario did not bypass the Elliot Lake region either. Blind River operators logged the Elliot Lake district early in the 1900s, and by the 1920s the logging trail that would become Highway 108 to Elliot Lake was being used by the industry.

With World War II and the development of the atomic bomb came renewed interest in uranium. Its immense destructive power had been demonstrated, but the peaceful uses of uranium were also being investigated, especially in the areas of energy and medical research. Prospectors began exploration work in areas where uranium deposits had been suspected in earlier years, and then fogotten. The Elliot Lake region had been briefly prospected at various times, and in 1931 a sample of uranium-bearing rock from the area was assayed at the Sault Ste. Marie assay office. Never picked up, the rock sat in the assayer's office until 1949, when Karl Gunterman found it.[2] Gunterman took it to the respected geologist Franc Joubin,[3] who was very interested but thought that radioactive readings were likely the result of thorium. Joubin did go to Long Township with Gunterman to investigate various claims, but they eventually lapsed when Joubin was unable to find further evidence of uranium, despite strong surface readings.[4]

Four years later, after reviewing similar South African fields, Joubin went back to the Elliot Lake area. This time he was successful. Long Township was, in fact, the southwest tip of the fabulous "Big Z" uranium field, a track that runs from Highway 17 north to Ten Mile Lake in a rough "Z" pattern. Joubin had discovered a 100-square-mile corridor, rich in uranium.[5]

With the backing of Joe Hirshhorn,[6] Joubin's financial partner, a great "back-door staking bee" began immediately in June 1953. Eighty prospectors, geologists, lawyers, cooks, accountants, clerks, and secretaries were assembled near the middle of the "Big Z" and told to stake quickly and quietly.[7] By working so quickly, Hirshhorn and Joubin found themselves in control of 1,500 claims in one of the world's largest uranium discoveries. Only one other significant claim was staked: Art Stollery, a young mining engineer, heard rumours of the staking and was able to claim what later became the Denison Mines holdings.[8] Joubin and his associated discoveries were eventually financed by the Rio Tinto Company of England,[9] becoming the Rio Algom properties, and Stollery's discoveries were sold to Stephen B. Roman and the Denison Mines Company.[10]

The future of the mines seemed secure. Uranium was plentiful, and by 1957 the Canadian government had negotiated contracts with the Atomic Energy Commission of the United States for more than $1.5 billion worth of uranium oxide, with more than two-thirds of that total to be produced by the Elliot Lake mines.[11] In their first full year of production, 1958, the mines earned $200 million,[12] milling 34,000 tons of ore per day; Consolidated Denison's 6,000-ton plant was the largest of its kind in the world.[13] By 1959, Canada's uranium oxide output had reached the 31,784,000-pound mark, worth roughly $331 million. Approximately 80 percent of this total came from Ontario, the majority from the Elliot Lake mines.[14]

At the prompting of the mine owners, who hoped to avoid some of the costs associated with establishing a new town, federal and provincial help was enlisted in the development of a community to service the mines and their employees. The Ontario government, through an order-in-council on October 13, 1955, formed the Improvement District Committee for the Elliot Lake Area, consisting of Franc Joubin, E.B. Gillanders, W.E. Willoughby, and Percy Lorne Brown. Once the site was chosen, a bush camp was quickly set up, with access provided by the old logging road, which was expanded and became Highway 619 (later 108) to allow easier access. Marshall Macklin Monaghan Limited were hired as the town's engineering consultants.

Elliot Lake, the Ontario government decided, would be a well-planned permanent community, a role model for other towns.[15] The project combined the efforts of the federal and provincial governments, four mining groups, and twelve contracting firms,[16] and the town plan was designed by architectural students at Cornell University.[17]

By the late 1950s, Elliot Lake was complete.[18] Neighbourhoods of from 300 to 1,500 single-family residences had been built, each with schools, churches, parks, recreational facilities, shopping, and other services. There was a central downtown core for the entire community. All roads were planned on a circular pattern, to reduce speeding and allow for the eventual return to the main thoroughfares. By 1956, downtown Elliot Lake had a theatre, billiard hall, church, school, and banks, and construction continued. By 1958, the town was near completion, with a solid downtown business core, schools staffed and churches opening, streets being paved, street lights being installed, and the population nearing 18,000.[19] With mine bunkhouses and trailer parks taken into account, the population was actually closer to 25,000.[20]

Sooner than most single-industry communities, Elliot Lake faced the pressures of dependence on mines and world markets. The same high prices and incentives that had encouraged exploration in Canada were also at work in other areas of the world. The U.S. government was considering protecting the American uranium industry, and was cutting back on military purchases. On November 6, 1959, the Canadian government announced that it was unable to convince the Atomic Energy Commission in Washington to extend its uranium contracts. After 1963, the U.S. would not be stockpiling uranium. As a single-industry community, Elliot Lake experienced a dramatic downturn in its fortunes with this news. From a high of almost 25,000, the population dropped to 6,664 by 1966.[21] Five mines closed in 1960 alone, although the Diefenbaker government was able to persuade the Americans to soften the blow by stretching out previously agreed-to contracts to 1966. Residents, disheartened by the hard luck they felt they were experiencing, erected signs declaring Elliot Lake "the world's most modern ghost town," and a delegation of housewives visited Ottawa to plead with Prime Minister John Diefenbaker to save their town. Town officials were faced with a dilemma, because repayment of the loans that had built the town's infrastructure was required to begin in 1960, just as revenues plummeted. Deeply in debt, the town would find it very difficult to attract secondary industry.

Banner on display in the Algo Centre for 1997–1998 homecoming. In 1960, the Elliot Lake Women's Emergency Committee organized 135 members in a motorcade to Ottawa to urge the government to save Elliot Lake. They carried this banner on Parliament Hill, and some draped sheets over their heads as ghosts.

Jane Pitblado

The population of Elliot Lake was drastically reduced, but the town did not disappear. In January 1960, town leaders met and formed an emergency committee, consisting not only of politicians, but also of priests, ministers, leaders of service clubs, and representatives of women's groups.[22] The committee pressured the federal and provincial governments to provide relief for the unemployed and was directly responsible for the relocating of a planned nuclear research centre from Manitoba to Elliot Lake. The worst time for a town to attempt to diversify its economic base is during a time of crisis, but the town did manage to attract some alternatives. In 1961, a penal institute was located on mine property just north of town, and the inmates built the ski hill that residents still use. Various attempts were made to promote tourism, and several tourist camps were built in 1961.

By a stroke of very good luck for the residents of Elliot Lake, their representative in Parliament, Lester B. Pearson, became Prime Minister in 1963 and began to play a more active role in aiding the community.[23] Visiting the town, Pearson stated, "Elliot Lake deserves help, because it refuses to accept defeat."[24] The following year, local citizens, the federal government, and the provincial department of education founded the Elliot Lake Centre, a residential centre for continuing education, to "retrain residents of Northern Ontario whose jobs had become redundant through automation in industry and others who wanted to upgrade their artistic abilities."[25] The centre would help the workforce develop further skills and make the region more attractive to industry. It also met the cultural needs of the changing society and became a busy arts centre. Interestingly, the Elliot Lake Centre continues to be active in the 1990s and has become an important part of Elliot Lake's present diversification, spearheading projects like the Elliot Lake Community Complex and Performing Arts Theatre, the White Mountain Academy of the Arts, and the Great Canadian Mine Show.

It should be noted here that none of the solutions presented in the 1960s were meant to be permanent, nor were they designed to create many jobs or any real secondary industry in the area. There seems to have been little, if any, coordinated planning; the townspeople were just scrambling to survive. The ideas and initiatives that came into being through either local work or government grants were stopgap measures, designed to last only until the mines re-opened, as they eventually did.

In 1966 the Canadian government announced that it would stockpile uranium for the next five years in order to help strengthen the ailing mining industry.[26] The original impetus for this came from Stephen Roman; it represented little more than the government artificially keeping the mines alive. This stockpiling continued through the early 1970s.[27]

February 15, 1972, was an extremely important date for residents of Elliot Lake, especially for those who worked in the uranium mines. It was on this day that federal Energy, Mines and Resources Deputy Minister Jack Austin met secretly with top-ranking uranium officials to see if they could establish a private cartel among world producers, thus artificially inflating prices and ensuring profits for everyone. It was not until August 1976 that news of this cartel became public when classified documents were stolen by an employee at Mary Kathleen Uranium in Australia. In the meantime, uranium producers, with the support of their governments and led by the Canadian government of Pierre Trudeau, were able to cause a general panic among worldwide uranium users and raise the price of uranium by 700 percent.[28] With the advent of nuclear power as the "solution" to the energy crisis, uranium producers could drastically raise prices and still have buyers. By setting artificial base rates, and with the cartel controlling the majority of the world's known uranium, a trend towards increased prices that had nothing to do with production costs occurred.[29]

This period of the early 1970s was the beginning of Elliot Lake's comeback. Denison Mines signed an $800-million contract with Japanese Electric Utilities through to 1994, and Rio Algom agreed to a $400-million contract with British Nuclear Fuels.[30] Other contracts followed, including Rio Algom's sale of 17 million pounds of uranium concentrate to the Tennessee Valley Authority.[31] The mines looked for customers at home, too, and were able to secure an advance contract with Ontario Hydro indexed at 1975 prices, with world-price clauses, open-ended escalation clauses, guaranteed profits, and large cash advances. Ontario Hydro agreed to a 126-million-pound contract with Denison and a 72-million-pound contract with Rio Algom, guaranteeing the two companies a combined profit of $2.2 billion.[32]

As the mines grew, so did the town. Mine expansions were scheduled for the late 1970s and early 1980s, and in 1976, in preparation for the arrival of successive waves of new workers, the Township of Elliot Lake became the Town of Elliot Lake. New housing subdivisions went up as more than 4,000 people came to Elliot Lake between 1976 and 1978; during this time, 251 housing units were built, with an additional 1,500 finished by 1981.[33] Also in 1976, 31 new businesses opened their doors, as the marketplace shifted to meet growing demand. A new arena, a French-language high school, hotels, and shopping areas continued to appear almost on a daily basis.

Elliot Lake Heritage Quilt, made by the Elliot Lake Arts Club and presented to the Town of Elliot Lake in September 1980 to mark the town's twenty-fifth anniversary. It hangs in the Elliot Lake Nuclear and Mining Museum.
Jane Pitblado

Once again, Elliot Lake's future seemed secure. However, by the late 1980s, miners who were promised jobs for the rest of their lives were dismayed at the news that cutbacks and layoffs would be reducing the mines' labour force, and the town began a second decline that sharpened with contract cancellation.

As the mines' production levels rose in the early 1970s to meet the demands of new contracts, Elliot Lake had become preoccupied with expansion rather than diversifying. Despite the town's experience in the 1960s, no one was preparing for the time when the mines would no longer be able to produce enough quality ore to remain economically viable. This state of affairs continued until the mid-1980s, when some of the problems associated with dependence on a single industry began to be recognized. In 1986, the Elliot Lake Economic Development Committee (ELEDC) was established, and the Tourism Development Study Committee began its report. With the mines still producing and employment at full capacity, diversification planning, this time, was not a reaction to crisis, but a solid and ambitious plan for the future.

At the time of the creation of the ELEDC, the community was heavily dependent on the industry; the uranium mines in the area employed over 4,500 workers, and the 1986 ratio of mine employees to Elliot Lake residents was roughly one to four.[34] A statement prepared for *The Town of Elliot Lake Economic Development Strategy,* by Marshall Macklin Monaghan Limited, examined the problems of this dependence:

> The Town has recognized the *importance of diversifying its economy* as it is presently almost completely dependent on the uranium mining industry. Diversification is critical as control over the well being of the community needs to be returned to its residents; a major reversal from the current situation.... Elliot Lake's population and economic well being have always been dependent on the level of mining activity at Rio Algom and Denison Mines. Immediate action is required as Elliot Lake is no longer the dominant world force in uranium production it once was. Large uranium deposits of a higher grade have been discovered in Saskatchewan and Australia which can be mined for less than Elliot Lake's lower grade uranium ore.[35]

Rio Algom's announcement on January 26, 1990, that it would be closing two of its three existing Elliot Lake mines, had been anticipated for many months, but it was still a shock to the citizens of Elliot Lake. The closing affected 1,600 miners in 1990 — about 25 percent of Elliot Lake's workforce: the Quirke and Panel Mines were to be closed, while Stanleigh Mine would stay open to fill existing contracts with Ontario Hydro. About 500 Rio Algom miners remained in Elliot Lake; in all, 1,700 were laid off.

More bad news followed on February 16, 1990, when Leo Gerard, president of District 6 of the United Steelworkers of America, reported that Denison Mines would be laying off 650 workers because of low uranium prices. At this point, Denison appeared to be in a slightly stronger position than Rio Algom, because Ontario Hydro was to begin receiving all of Denison's Elliot Lake production beginning in 1994.[36]

However, Ontario Hydro was no longer happy with its Elliot Lake contracts,[37] and renegotiations began in January 1991 between Ontario Hydro and both Rio Algom and Denison. Unable to agree on a new price with Denison, Ontario Hydro informed the company that as of 1992 it would no longer be buying uranium from its Elliot Lake operations. It would continue to buy from Rio Algom in order to give Elliot Lake time to diversify and adjust its economy.[38] Following this announcement, Denison Mines decided to close its Elliot Lake operations in 1991, permanently releasing 1,060 miners.

Needless to say, the loss of over 3,000 mining jobs had a major impact on Elliot Lake's economy. Stores closed, workers turned to Unemployment Insurance and retraining packages once their severance pay ran out, then to welfare. The city's infrastructure was also in trouble, since the mine closures meant a huge tax loss for the city (see Robinson and Bishop, Chapter 16 in this volume).[39]

In March 1991, the new provincial government, under the leadership of the New Democratic Party, formed a working group to develop an aid package for the City of Elliot Lake that would allow the city to diversify and recover from the mine closures.[40] After meeting and negotiating with all of the parties involved, the group was able to suggest some possibilities. On June 17, 1991, the Ministry of Northern Development and Mines announced a $250-million economic aid package for the Elliot Lake area, to be funded by Ontario Hydro.[41] Under the agreement, Ontario Hydro would continue to buy uranium from Rio Algom until 1997, maintaining about 775 jobs at the Elliot Lake operations. This would provide some stability for the community while it was diversifying. In addition, Hydro would provide $90 million to aid in developing long-term diversification and short-term economic adjustments, including $9.6 million for short-term job creation to increase Unemployment

Insurance allowances for workers about to have their benefits run out. Ontario Hydro was also to use $25 million to develop energy-efficient programs in the area. This package was to ensure that economic diversification and development had a sure base to work from for several years, and it eliminated some worries about how to fund certain economic development programs.

Marshall Macklin Monaghan Limited, in the process of preparing an economic development strategy for Elliot Lake, met with the ELEDC, the town's economic development officer, council, and business leaders, and with 17 community groups.[42] Workshops were held with roughly 150 of Elliot Lake's citizens, in order to gain as much input as possible from an interested cross-section of community members.[43] In these discussions, the advantages and disadvantages of various methods of attracting industries were explored, and Marshall Macklin Monaghan formulated their report on the basis of the information thus gathered. The draft report was presented at a public meeting attended by approximately 70 people.

The final report, called *The Town of Elliot Lake Economic Development Strategy,* was presented to the Elliot Lake City Council by the ELEDC in March 1990, and Council passed a resolution at that meeting to adopt both the plan and the methods of implementation provided in the strategy. A further public meeting was held in June, at which about 175 people were given an update and asked questions about the plan.

The *Strategy* identified several possible courses of action for attracting industry, diversifying existing economic opportunities, and establishing new ones. It also provided a base for the expansion of programs that had begun prior to the writing of the *Strategy* and fostered an atmosphere conducive to the development of any new ideas that might be offered.

According to the *Strategy,* three main action objectives had emerged from the citizen workshops: the development of training and support programs; the enhancement of the Elliot Lake Retirement Living Program; and the retention, expansion, and attraction of businesses.[44] These three areas were the focus of the strategies proposed in the report.

Perhaps the most successful of Elliot Lake's diversification sectors has been the Retirement Living Program.[45] The plan, created in 1987 by Claire Dimock, a town councillor who was then vice-president for community relations and housing for the Elliot Lake operations of Denison Mines, was to attract retired people to live in houses built by Denison and Rio Algom to supply a housing market that had never materialized.[46] Originally under the auspices of the mining companies in tandem with the Town of Elliot Lake, Retirement Living was funded by a $10,200 grant from the Ministry of Northern Development and Mines to market the program.[47]

Elliot Lake did not seem to be ideally situated for a popular retirement community, but Dimock realized that even though it was a small community in comparison to many, and isolated from large population centres, it could make one extremely attractive offer to seniors: inexpensive housing. When the program began in 1987, rents were as low as $250 a month for a one-bedroom apartment, with three-bedroom houses renting through the program for about $400 a month. House prices ranged from $38,000 to $58,000.[48] Prices have remained much lower than the provincial average. The inexpensive housing allowed retirees to liquidate more expensive real estate and realize a cash profit, giving them an opportunity to enjoy a better lifestyle than was previously possible for them.[49] As well, for seniors in a weakened financial situation, the affordable housing meant that a better lifestyle could still be possible.[50]

In 1990, the Retirement Living Program was reorganized as a not-for-profit corporation, as recommended in a report by the Redma Group on ways to improve the program.[51] A $7-million grant to the corporation from the Ministry of Northern Development and Mines for the purchase of houses from the mines assured the success of the program. Shortly thereafter, Rio Algom gave 574 houses to the corporation as a charitable donation, and Denison Mines arranged for the sale of 938 homes to the program.[52] This provided Retirement Living with a healthy inventory with which to attract new seniors, and plans call for another 2,000 seniors to be attracted as soon as possible.

Elliot Lake's economic revival continues. This chapter has provided an outline of the evolution of the community to 1991; the story of the Elliot Lake of the 1990s will be told in the other chapters in this volume. Our community has responded, on several levels, to the serious threats posed by the mine closures, and the early attempts at diversification during the 1960s pointed the way to the renewed, more successful efforts currently under way in the community.

Notes

[1] This information comes from Reginald Eveleigh, *Elliot Lake: A Northern Mosaic* (Elliot Lake: Woodland Printers, 1984), a booklet produced through an Experience '84 grant. Eveleigh, a Trent University history student at the time, sifted through endless source materials over two summers to produce his work. It was among his findings that "Recent archaeological work ... has unearthed artifacts which prove that Mississagi Park was a centre of activity for several bands as far back as 10,000 years" (pages unnumbered).

[2] Gunterman was in possession of a Geiger counter that he had been passing over old rock samples.

[3] Joubin is a world-respected geologist and discovered, in addition to the Elliot Lake field, important mineral deposits on five continents. He was one of the 12 charter members of Canada's Mining Hall of Fame, and his life is chronicled in his autobiography, co-authored with D. McCormack Smyth, *Not for Gold Alone: Memoirs of A Prospector* (Toronto: Deljay Publications, 1986).

[4] This story can be found in Joubin and Smyth, *Not for Gold Alone*, 169–71; and in Paul McKay, *The Roman Empire: The Unauthorized Life and Times of Stephen B. Roman* (Toronto: Key Porter Books Ltd., 1990), 26–27. Gunterman himself was drowned in a canoeing accident on the Montreal River before the importance of the find was discovered.

[5] It was unknown in Canada at the time, but uranium leaching had been found to happen in South Africa. In certain conglomerates, rain water can dissolve the iron segment of the conglomerate, and then the uranium leaches underground, with traces of its passing left on the surface. Thus, the "Big Z"'s strong surface readings were actually evidence of uranium that had leached underground and shafts had to be sunk in order to find the actual uranium. See Joubin and Smyth, *Not for Gold Alone*, 203–04.

[6] Joubin discusses his relationship with Hirshhorn throughout *Not for Gold Alone*. See also Barry Hyams, *Hirshhorn: Medici from Brooklyn* (New York: E.P. Dutton, 1972); and for Hirshhorn's rivalry with Stephen Roman, see McKay, *The Roman Empire*.

[7] The story of the "secret" staking can be found in Joubin and Smyth, *Not for Gold Alone*, 208–21.

[8] See Joubin and Smyth, *Not for Gold Alone*, 216–17; and McKay, *The Roman Empire*, 30–35, which also discusses Stollery's selling to Roman.

[9] For a history of Rio Tinto prior to their Elliot Lake acquisitions, see Charles E. Harvey, *The Rio Tinto Company: An Economic History of a Leading International Mining Concern 1873–1954* (Cornwall: Alison Hodge, 1981).

[10] See McKay, *The Roman Empire*; and Joubin and Smyth, *Not for Gold Alone*, 236–42.

[11] Town of Elliot Lake, *Community Profile*, 5.

[12] Town of Elliot Lake, *Community Profile*, 5.

[13] Morris Zaslow, *The Northward Expansion of Canada, 1914–1967* (Toronto: McClelland and Stewart, 1988), 241.

[14] Zaslow, *Northward Expansion*, 242. There were also mines operating in Bancroft that were part of the 80 percent.

[15] See R.G. Bucksar, "Elliot Lake," in *Little Communities and Big Industries*, ed. Roy T. Bowles, 175–81; N. Pearson, "Elliot Lake: the best-planned mining town," *The Canadian Architect* 3, 11 (November 1958); Gilbert A. Stelter and Alan F.J. Artibise, "Canadian resource towns in historical perspective," *Plan Canada* (March 1978): 7–16; and Robert Robson, "Building resource towns: a decade of government intervention," unpublished, 1990. For a contrary

opinion, Paul McKay, *The Roman Empire*, makes good points in stating: "Despite grander expectations, the emerging town of Elliot Lake was the quintessential frontier company town. Its beginnings were marked by panic planning, profiteering, violence, disease, primitive living conditions, and a social stratification encouraged by absolute dependence on the uranium mines" (53). What McKay is not discussing is the fact that Elliot Lake was one of the few towns in Canada to have any kind of centralized plan.

[16] Elliot Lake Secondary School 455.02 Class, *Jewel in the Wilderness: A History of Elliot Lake* (Elliot Lake: Inter-Collegiate Press, 1980), 49.

[17] Eveleigh, *Elliot Lake: A Northern Mosaic.*

[18] Obviously, there would be discomfort in the time between the mines' opening and the town's completion. Paul McKay, *The Roman Empire*, describes the situation: "Jammed into helter- skelter trailer sites with no plumbing and poor heating, the families of miners suffered badly. Mothers, wives, and girlfriends were forced to make daily treks down to the lake, where they chopped holes in the metre-thick ice with axes to obtain drinking and bathing water. There were no schools for their children.... Everything took place in a quagmire of mud and slush. Predictably, in the spring of 1957, an epidemic of dysentery broke out....Three hundred cases were reported, and ninety victims were sent to the hospital in Blind River" (57). As well, a high crime rate, fitting to the 1:100 female/male ratio, was also a great problem. It was not until the town was completed and families arrived that the scene started to settle down. Nevertheless, the short amount of time it took to complete the townsite was in itself remarkable.

[19] Joubin and Smyth, *Not for Gold Alone*, 256. According to the assessed population of the Corporation of the Town of Elliot Lake, the population in 1958 was 22,177.

[20] ELSS 455.02 Class, *Jewel in the Wilderness*, 53.

[21] Corporation of the Town of Elliot Lake assessed population figure for 1966.

[22] ELSS 455.02 Class, *Jewel in the Wilderness*, 55.

[23] Pearson appears to be a bit of an odd figure in this debate. A former Nobel Peace Prize winner, he condemned the nuclear arms race; yet in his own home riding, the Elliot Lake mines produced uranium that went exclusively to American and British weapons races until 1965. See McKay, *The Roman Empire*, 107.

[24] Pearson, quoted in ELSS 455.02 Class, *Jewel in the Wilderness*, 104.

[25] L. Carson Brown, "Elliot Lake — the world's uranium capital," *Canadian Geographical Journal* 75, 4 (October 1967): 120–33.

[26] Eveleigh, *Elliot Lake: A Northern Mosaic.*

[27] McKay, *The Roman Empire*, 111–15. From 1971 to 1975, the Trudeau government promised to stockpile 6.4 million pounds in order to maintain employment in Elliot Lake and build a stockpile in order to attract customers for the CANDU reactors.

[28] See McKay, *The Roman Empire*, especially chapter 7, "Cartel blanche"; and Earle Gray, *The Great Uranium Cartel* (Toronto: McClelland and Stewart,

1982). Because of its classification by governments, it is unlikely that the whole story of this affair has yet been told, although McKay has researched painstakingly. As McKay explains, "the exposure of the cartel in 1976 led to sensational media coverage around the globe, a high-powered U.S. congressional inquiry and Justice Department investigation, more than a dozen criminal and civil court actions, and a series of political firestorms in Canada, Australia, France, and Britain. These in turn prompted the federal governments in Canada, Australia, and Britain to invoke draconian gag laws aimed at preserving a seal of secrecy around the cartel" (117–18). In fact, the Trudeau government made it a criminal offence to publish or release cartel documents, punishable by fine or imprisonment.

[29] As usual, this price push would result in problems later, as exploration increased and new, high-grade deposits were found in Saskatchewan and Australia.

[30] Eveleigh, *Elliot Lake: A Northern Mosaic.*

[31] In contrast, the Denison Mines Japanese contract was for 40 million pounds, and the Rio Algom British contract called for a 20-million-pound delivery.

[32] These figures come from McKay, *The Roman Empire*, 138–39. However, with the cancelling and cutback of contracts announced in the 1990s, it must be realized that these figures represent only the original worth of the contract.

[33] According to the assessed populations of the Corporation of the Town of Elliot Lake, the following rates were found: 8,779 (1976); 10,729 (1977); 12,893 (1978); 14,230 (1979); 15,524 (1980); 17,245 (1981); 18,670 (1982); 19,619 (1983).

[34] Marshall Macklin Monaghan Limited, *The Town of Elliot Lake Economic Development Strategy*, undated (1990), 1–5 and 1–6.

[35] Marshall Macklin Monaghan, *Economic Development Strategy*, 1–1. This was written prior to the announcements of mine closures.

[36] This was to amount to about 5.4 million pounds annually. See Peter Gorrie, "450 Denison workers to lose jobs, union says," *Toronto Star*, 1990 02 16, C1–2.

[37] According to Marc Eliesen, Chair of Ontario Hydro's Board of Directors, buying Elliot Lake uranium for another ten years would cost the utility $1.5 billion above market prices (Marc Eliesen, "Hydro's not in the bail-out business," *Toronto Star*, 1991 09 12, A22). The letter to the editor was in response to an editorial by *Star* staff writer David Crane, "It's not Ontario Hydro's job to bail out one-industry towns," *Toronto Star*, 1991 08 17, D2.

[38] The Rio Algom contracts were for less uranium than the Denison Mines contracts had been for.

[39] In fact, welfare costs rose to the highest levels ever. See "Welfare costs highest ever," *The Standard* (Elliot Lake), 1992 01 25, A6. In addition, millions of tax dollars were lost with the closing of the mines, making upkeep and maintenance of the town a huge problem, especially with loans

that financed the expansion of the 1970s coming due. Mayor George Farkouh has stated that 1970s expansion "left Elliot Lake with a capital debt burden of $11 million at 17 percent (which was reduced to $8.5 million) and a shrinking tax base in danger of becoming incapable of serving the debt" from George Farkouh, "Elliot Lake," in *The End of the Shift: Mines and Single-Industry Towns in Northern Ontario*, ed. Matt Bray and Ashley Thomson (Toronto: Dundurn Press, 1992), 145–48.

40 The group included Dave Mellor, United Steelworkers Elliot Lake Staff Representative; Lois Miller, Algoma-Manitoulin NDP riding president; Floyd Laughren, Treasurer of Ontario; Shelley Martel, Northern Development Minister; Bud Wildman, Natural Resources Minister; Jenny Carter, Energy Minister; Ruth Grier, Environment Minister; Bob McKenzie, Labour Minister; and Leo Gerard, United Steelworkers of America director.

41 Mayor George Farkouh, letter to the residents of Elliot Lake, 1991 07 05. According to Eliesen, this would still result in a $1.25-billion saving to Ontario Hydro (*Toronto Star*, 1991 09 12, A22).

42 Included among the groups consulted were band councils, Chamber of Commerce, local council, government agencies, Labour Council, The East Algoma Partners in Occupational Training (TEAPOT), and community groups representing the following interests of the population: tourism, education, media, seniors, arts, women's groups, health, service sector, forestry, religion, and youth (Marshall Macklin Monaghan, *Economic Development Strategy*, 4–1).

43 Marshall Macklin Monaghan, *Economic Development Strategy*. In each workshop, participants were asked to identify their perception of Elliot Lake's future and to identify advantages and disadvantages. They were also asked how they would be able to aid in the economic development of the community, how they wished to aid the economic development, and what assistance they would need in order to aid in the economic development.

44 Marshall Macklin Monaghan, *Economic Development Strategy*, 6–1.

45 Out of 9.4 million residents in Ontario in 1990, an estimated 1 million were over the age of 65. See Claire Pilon, "More seniors in Ontario," *Sudbury Star*, 1990 01 31.

46 Carol Jerome, "CBC Radio's Sunday Morning," 1990 03 11. The program had taken on a new importance. According to Redma Group, *Elliot Lake Retirement Living: Executive Summary* (September 1990), "while the initial objective of Elliot Lake Retirement Living was to fill vacant housing units owned by the Mining Companies, the significance of the program has become much greater. Retirement Living is now a key economic initiative to assist the recovery of Elliot Lake from its historical dependence upon cyclical uranium based industries and an opportunity to provide the Province's seniors with an improved quality of life" (i).

47 Redma Group, "Backgrounder," *Elliot Lake Retirement Living: Executive Summary*, 2.

[48] Retirement Living Program Statistics, 1989 10 10.

[49] Redma Group, "Backgrounder," 3.

[50] Redma Group, "Backgrounder," 3. This would include seniors on government assistance, including Old Age Security and Canada Pension Plan, and other minimal pensions. Affordable housing means there will be an excess of money for other expenditures.

[51] Redma Group, *Elliot Lake Retirement Living: Executive Summary*, iv. Shares in the corporation are non-voting and are held in trust for the participants of the program, 70 percent for the Ministry of Northern Development and Mines and 30 percent for the City of Elliot Lake.

[52] Bill Morris, "Security and independence," *Life and Times* 1, 3 (September 1991): 2.

Part One

The Uphill Climb
Monica Neitzert and Anne-Marie Mawhiney

Various perspectives on the people of Elliot Lake are reflected in the first section of the book, each filling in a part of the story of the people's experiences as they started the uphill climb after the layoffs. Narratives from local people have been included as well as reports from researchers of the Elliot Lake Tracking and Adjustment Study (ELTAS), a longitudinal study of the impact of the layoffs on workers and their families (generously funded in 1994 for three years by Human Resources Development Canada).

"A Salute to the Miners, 1956–1996." Wall-hanging donated to the City of Elliot Lake by the Elliot Lake Quilt Guild in recognition and appreciation of forty years of uranium mining in Elliot Lake. According to the plaque beside it in the Elliot Lake Nuclear and Mining Museum, the Guild wished to "pay tribute to the miners and focus the attention on their lifestyle."

Jane Pitblado

The first three chapters of Part One of the book give voice to the hopes and concerns of the people of the community. In the aftermath of the layoffs, services were developed to try to offset their far-reaching effects and to provide support to mining families. Peggy Quinn, a social service worker with strong roots in the community, discusses the programming and supports needed by families and individuals to help them cope with major transitions. Garry Romain and Stephen Withers describe the efforts of the Elliot Lake Men's Support Centre to provide needed services to men who were laid off. Literacy programs were identified as a need for many of the laid-off workers, and Jan Lewis, a local literacy advocate, details the struggles involved in establishing a workforce program to address this.

Chapters 4 through 7 were written by ELTAS researchers. Monica Neitzert, Anne-Marie Mawhiney, and Elaine Porter describe how the spouses of the miners assisted in the process of seeking alternative ways to support their families. Derek Wilkinson and David Robinson discuss the strategies that have been and are being used by those who were laid off as they look for alternative work and where those who were laid off have found new work.

ELTAS began as the Elliot Lake Tracking Study (ELTS) in 1990 and has been a major research project of the Institute of Northern Ontario Research and Development (INORD) since then.[1] The relative size and potential consequences of the layoffs in Elliot Lake led an interdisciplinary group of researchers at Laurentian University to undertake a tracking study of the laid-off workers and their families. This group initially included David Leadbeater and David Robinson from the Department of Economics, Peter Suschnigg and Derek Wilkinson from the Department of Sociology and Anthropology, and Matt Bray from the Department of History. ELTS received a small grant to assess the costs of adjustment for workers, their families, and communities, and to contribute to the policy response process for workers and communities in similar circumstances.

The researchers set out to survey all the workers on August employment lists from both companies, regardless of their employment status. The first round of the study began in September of 1990, at which time a subset of employees on the lists had already been laid off or had retired. Those still employed were a control group. Interviewers attempted to reach each person on the list by telephone at least three times in order to arrange an interview. A total of 1,174 interviews — that is, with more than half of the employees on the August employee lists — were completed. A second round of interviews was held with the same respondents between January and March of 1992, the third round from January to March of 1994, the fourth round from January to March of 1995, and the final round from January to March of 1996. Very few respondents were lost over the course of the five survey rounds, so that in the final year more than 1,000 of the original group of continuing or former employees were interviewed.

In the first year (1990), most of the workers lived in Elliot Lake or Blind River (a North Shore town of 3,500, approximately 60 kilometres from Elliot Lake), and so 87 percent of the interviews were conducted in person. As more families emigrated from Elliot Lake, the proportion of interviews that were conducted by telephone rose. The interviews generally lasted 45 minutes to one hour and covered a wide range of social, economic, and political topics including: work and education; household income, budget, and assets; relocation; individual and family health; family structure and status; and community and neighbourhood attachment. Although the survey instrument was refined over the years, the basic structure of most questions was left unchanged, so that comparisons of individuals and families over time would be possible.

When new funding was received in November 1994 from Human Resources Development Canada, the project expanded to become the Elliot Lake Tracking and Adjustment Study (ELTAS) and included not only the original ELTS, but also a spousal project, called the Elliot Lake Spousal Project (ELSP), and several related sub-projects. ELSP was directed by Elaine Porter, Anne-Marie Mawhiney, and Monica Neitzert, and together with the ELTS group formed the directorate of the Elliot Lake Tracking and Adjustment Study. In 1995 and 1996, separate interviews were held with the currently cohabiting spouses of all respondents, as part of ELSP. A number of papers have been produced or are planned on topics studied by ELTS, ELSP, and the sub-projects. Further information can be obtained by contacting INORD at Laurentian University.

The final chapter in this section, again written by a person from the community (Barry Ferguson), gives a company perspective suggesting a relatively successful conclusion to the adjustment process by the last 553 miners who were laid off when Stanleigh Mine closed in 1996.

Note
[1] This section, dealing with the Elliot Lake Tracking Study, relies on David Leadbeater and David Robinson (1991), "Mass layoffs in a remote single-industry mining town: the Elliot Lake Tracking Study," mimeo, available from the authors.

Chapter 2
Bringing the People Through Life Transitions
Peggy Quinn

Transition is defined as passing from one condition, form, stage, activity, or place to another. There are different life transitions that we all go through. We move from childhood to young adulthood, then to parenthood, the empty nest, and finally retirement. The transition from one life stage to another can be very traumatic, or it can occur without any severe effects.

Transition is about change, and whether an individual is pleased to have a new challenge or frightened about the future, change brings stress, and these stressors need to be understood and managed.

In every community there are people who have supportive families and friends. Many that have this support system see major change as a challenge and a learning experience, and move quickly from being in denial and angry about the situation to looking for options for their future. Every community also has others who for any number of reasons do not have developed support systems, and many of these individuals tend to have great difficulty working through problems with a healthy, positive attitude.

Rio Algom Limited, Denison Mines Limited, and the unions worked closely with community organizations in Elliot Lake and developed their own adjustment services so that there were supports available to those who needed them during the major downsizing and closure periods. In preparing employees for the downsizing and then closure of the mines, professionals from financial-planning institutions, job-search experts, teachers of healthy life-styles, and personal counsellors provided educational information to all employees. The main goal of the seminars and information was to normalize some of the feelings and effects, and also to help individuals and families identify their strengths and challenges in different areas of their lives.

Some of the supports were geared to helping them understand that most people facing layoff will go through a grieving process. The information provided normalized their response to their job loss. The employees facing unemployment needed to understand that denial, anger, and fear about the situation were normal and they needed to identify these feelings and work through them. People's identity and self-esteem are closely related to the job they do, and their confidence in their ability to provide for their families, so with the loss of employment fear and feelings of inadequacy surface.

Laid-off employees were also encouraged to examine their problem-solving style, so that they could decide whether they needed to develop more effective skills given the situation. Individuals who cope with their problems by using alcohol or drugs, or those who have serious difficulty identifying and expressing their feelings, often have problems coming through a major life transition.

Many employees, particularly during the downsizing transition, tried to make future decisions in isolation. They didn't want to "worry" their loved ones by discussing the situation. Such individuals were encouraged to communicate and plan for the future with the others affected. Employees needed to understand that the whole family goes through the transition, not just the person laid off.

Other alterations in the family situations were role changes. More women were going into paid employment, and the challenge for the couple and family was to decide who took responsibility for childcare and housework when the man was unemployed. Other families had to adjust to the husband and father commuting home for limited amounts of time from a new job in another community. This transition continues to be a challenge as women take on the role of a part-time single parent, carrying the majority of the family and home responsibilities.

People were encouraged not only to build on their individual and family strengths but also to identify unresolved areas, because those would almost inevitably surface or accelerate during such a stressful time. It became evident early on that individuals with unresolved past issues — such as grief, sexual assault, or childhood experiences in a home with an alcoholic parent — or present concerns — such as marital conflict or living with a challenging teenager — were going to need support to cope with and resolve the multiple problems facing them and their families.

One of the healthy coping methods that individuals learned was to plan the ways they would fill their time during the unemployment period. For a short time, individuals often enjoyed the relaxation, but when the unemployment period was for months at a time or even into its second year, planning positive activities was very important. Many found a new hobby, volunteered their time, or increased their skills and knowledge by taking a course. Those who kept active were better able to cope with the disappointments of not getting a job or of having only a part-time or contract position.

The two major transitions in Elliot Lake — first, the layoff of the majority of miners, and second, the closure of the last mine — presented different challenges and responses. The initial layoff had a different dynamic, including a denial period, when people could still hope that the Government of Ontario would reverse its decision about purchasing uranium elsewhere for Ontario Hydro, and that they would get their jobs back. This period was made more difficult by the poor job market in general, and specifically because there were few employment opportunities in the mining sector in Canada.

The second major transition presented different types of issues, often related to the age of the person being laid off. Individuals in their forties and fifties were anxious about whether companies would hire them, because of their age. There were also serious concerns by others whose children were in secondary school, once they realized that a move to another community could be very traumatic for them.

Service providers were better prepared to deal with the second transition, the closure of Stanleigh Mine, because of the experience they had gained during the initial change. There was a better understanding of the common issues faced by those laid off during the first transition, and there was a more proactive approach to helping the Stanleigh miners and their families. An example of this was the placement of adjustment workers on the mining site. This provided an opportunity to monitor individual and group situations, as well as to give a quick response to those in need.

If a community, the families, and the individuals going through a major workplace adjustment are to make a healthy transition, they need the companies and unions to plan the programming and supports together. Families need to use their strengths and develop skills, including the ability to communicate and solve problems together. Individuals need to be able to ask for support, and to create a vision of a new future. The road through this transition has many potholes, blind corners, and crossroads, and sometimes the map seems faded, but a healthy transition means reaching that new place in your life, with the anger, fear, and discouragement worked through.

Chapter 3
The Elliot Lake Men's Support Centre
Garry Romain and Stephen Withers

The Elliot Lake Men's Support Centre was established to provide drop-in services for men who needed peer support, crisis counselling, and sometimes a place to go where they could talk together, play cards, or shoot pool. The need for such a centre in Elliot Lake had been identified even before the announcement of the mass layoffs in 1990. Since then, the need for these support services has increased significantly.

From the time of the first announcements of mining cutbacks, there have been approximately 4,000 unionized workers and staff employees who have lost their jobs. In addition to these losses, 850 employee positions in the service sector disappeared. Since men held the vast majority of these mining positions, effect on the male population and their families in Elliot Lake has been serious.

During the 1980s, the families in Elliot Lake were financially secure, with mining positions having an average annual salary of about $60,000. Now, many of these same families are struggling to survive on welfare benefits that range from $12,000 to $14,000 a year. In addition to the obvious financial stress being experienced, many of the services previously available to the men through the workplace no longer exist. For example, the employee assistance program ceased operations in August 1992, which created further problems, as this program had been the main source of support for workers experiencing personal difficulties. At that point, the United Steelworkers of America sought assistance from the federal government to deal with these concerns. A $6,000 grant from the Social Service Programs sector of Health and Welfare Canada was allocated for a needs survey of this target group and the recommendation of appropriate program responses. Completed in February 1991, the survey established that the men had no support when they were in crisis. Disputes and conflicts with family members were identified as primary issues that resulted in the need for crisis services. With no end in sight to the unemployment situation, there was an urgent need for services that could provide some relief for individuals and their families.

The result of this research was the recommendation of three initiatives: 1) that a men's service centre be established where, in a safe environment, men could be assisted to resolve crises and stressful situations; 2) that a peer support service be developed; and 3) that a men's residential centre be established to provide emergency accommodation to men in crisis situations.

In 1993 the Elliot Lake Men's Support Centre opened. We now have four mandates: peer support, accommodation, social leisure, and short-term counselling and referrals.

Peer support, in our case, means men helping men. Sometimes the men just need someone to talk to. For some who come to our centre, the difficulty may be that they are no longer the principal breadwinner. For others, it may be that they are having a hard time paying their mortgage or various bills. Still others, faced with a move, may not want to leave Elliot Lake, or they may be unable to leave because they own a home in town. Perhaps they are just five or six years away from retirement and can't get a job. While at the centre, the men can see other men, sometimes fellow workers who are in the same predicament as they are, and know they are not alone. Many of our users are men who have just moved to our community and are sometimes finding it hard to cope with the new environment. At the centre, they meet with others in the same situation.

The centre offers the services of two qualified counsellors as well as several trained volunteers who work with men 18 years or older who come to the centre. The two counsellors are at the centre from 10 a.m. to 5 p.m. five days a week, and they are on call 24 hours a day, seven days a week. The welfare of the client is always the primary concern of these counsellors. If a counsellor is not immediately available, the volunteers at the centre are prepared to act in any given situation. The volunteers are on a continuous training course. They are trained to deal with marriage problems, separation, divorce, grief, cultural changes, job loss, and so on. The Elliot Lake Men's Support Centre is equipped with three pool tables that are available to everyone who comes to the centre. There are weekly pool leagues, one for snooker players and one for eight-ball players. A few times a year, the centre holds a pool tournament where prizes are awarded. We also have cards, and chess and dart competitions every Wednesday night. All our leisure activities — such as our chess, pool leagues, and darts — are organized and run by our patrons and volunteers. The centre also has a computer that is available to the users, where they can work on a résumé or whatever else they may want to do.

Throughout the year, the centre holds family activities such as camp-outs and car rallies. Although the centre is for the men of Elliot Lake and the North Shore, we also provide a safe environment where a father can bring his children every Saturday for our Father and Child Day, and every fourth Saturday we hold a Family Day.

We have monthly volunteer meetings so that the staff can update and assess our volunteers. At these meetings, we try to have guest speakers who keep our volunteers and users up to date on events happening in our community. They also give talks on various activities that the men enjoy, such as hunting and fishing.

The Elliot Lake Men's Support Centre provides emergency accommodation to clients in distress who are aged 18 years or older. We have an emergency two-bedroom apartment that offers a secure environment for a period of from three to five days. During such a stay the men will be provided with meals and supplies paid for by fund-raising efforts of staff and volunteers, or donated by the Knights of Columbus and our local food bank. At the apartment, the clients have bathing facilities, bedding, and entertainment such as TV and radio. We expect the occupants to clean up, wash dishes, do laundry, vacuum, and leave the apartment as they found it. There are no women, alcohol, or drugs allowed in the apartment. Smoking is permitted on the balcony only. The stay can be extended beyond five days, if necessary, and if the apartment is available. Staff would bring the matter up with the executive director and work out the best solution for the client.

Although the apartment has only two bedrooms, with three beds, we have had as many as five clients in residence at one time. Of the 401 people who occupied the apartment during 1996, 62.5 percent were self-referred from Elliot Lake and the North Shore, and 37.5 percent were referrals from other local social services, such as Detoxification Services and the Camillus Centre (both in the Oaks Centre), and Algoma District Social Services (welfare).

We provide this service 24 hours a day. Once the user contacts us directly, or through referrals, we do an intake to get some background information. Next we do an assessment with the user to see if a referral to another service or organization is necessary. For example; at times we refer the user to Detoxification Services, the Camillus Centre, East Algoma Mental Health, or the Family Life Centre. Our centre also requests that new arrivals sign consent forms, giving us permission to seek information and services needed to support the client.

We encourage seniors to get involved by volunteering at the centre. Their participation not only helps them to stay independent, it also eases their adjustment to new environments with which they are faced. Seniors also have a lifetime of knowledge and experience, and their input helps the centre operate more efficiently.

The Elliot Lake Men's Support Centre has become an important service for men in our community. When there is a crisis, men know they can come to the centre and be sure of getting help. If necessary, we may suggest they go to one of the other local counselling centres, but for many, we are able to offer all the support they need, including peer interaction and short-term crisis housing. We believe that many of these men would not seek help from other services on their own. Our accessibility and our reputation for providing help and support in a non-threatening environment are our greatest strengths in this success story.

Chapter 4
Development of the Workforce Literacy Program After the First Mass Layoffs in Elliot Lake
Jan Lewis

One of the more dramatic episodes to arise after the first mass layoffs in Elliot Lake occurred during the development of the Training Access Centre, a program developed in 1990 to help laid-off workers improve their basic literacy skills. Established in response to an acute crisis in the workplace, the centre was the first workforce literacy program in the province and it rapidly evolved into, quite possibly, the largest adjustment literacy program ever created in the country. Unfortunately, its existence was marred by political infighting and truncated by student insurrection. In this paper, I present a brief history of the Training Access Centre and try to identify some of the factors that led to the crisis. I offer only my own interpretation of the events that took place; others hold different views, which you may find equally valid.

Initial Planning, July 1990 to December 1990

In July 1990, I was hired by the North Channel Literacy Council to assess the need for workplace literacy programs in the Elliot Lake area. However, the social dislocation and distress in the aftermath of the mass layoffs convinced us that our efforts should be redirected to those in greatest need — the laid-off illiterate and semi-literate workers of Elliot Lake. The Literacy Council and the Ministry of Education approved this revised initiative, and my new objectives were now to respond to the immediate crisis by developing, marketing, and delivering a training program in basic literacy skills to meet the urgent upgrading needs of the laid-off workers.

Many hours were spent during the fall of 1990 welcoming the first clients. It was a highly emotional time. The trauma inflicted by sudden permanent layoffs falls most harshly on laid-off workers with literacy problems. Profound uncertainty about the future exacerbated old wounds. Many wept openly as they talked of difficult pasts frequently marked by abuse and, almost always, by failure. As one man phrased it, "To be 49 years old, out of work, and unable to read — it is my worst nightmare come true."

By November 1990, a classroom model supplemented with one-on-one tutoring was chosen to address student needs. Delivery partnerships were developed — the North Shore Board of Education agreed to provide instructors and the North Channel Literacy Council to provide tutors. An intensive search for funding partners was finally rewarded when the Labour Adjustment Branch of the Ministry of Labour listened to our pleas, recognized the problem, and set aside $5 million for the literacy training of displaced workers in Ontario.

Implementation and Continued Growth, January 1991 to November 1991

On 7 January 1991, the first literacy classes for 44 displaced workers began in a single classroom at the Learning Centre in Elliot Lake. By May the burgeoning numbers, and the need to allow displaced workers as many upgrading hours as possible, resulted in the decision to move the whole program to the New Life Assembly Building. By this time there were five instructors and nine classes, addressing all levels of literacy and numeracy instruction. Seventy-two students participated in the program since its inception; forty-six were at that time enrolled in full-time day classes.

In the fall of 1991, I was asked by Employment and Immigration Canada to prepare a proposal requesting 52 weeks of project-based training to provide a second year of literacy programming and income support for displaced workers with literacy problems. The purpose of this proposal was to provide a more realistic upgrading timetable, since unemployment insurance claimants, at that time, were only allotted one year to acquire the basic skills required for further vocational training. I responded by spending the next two months designing a complex program that would offer the pre-employability training courses needed for project approval. The basic literacy and numeracy programming was expanded to include self-assessment, career exploration and job-search skills, life skills, labour market information, essential workplace and computer skills, and a work placement. At a meeting on 21 November 1991, Employment and Immigration officials indicated that they liked the proposal and told me that "the eyes of the province" would be on us, as this was the only literacy program that Employment and Immigration had ever funded.

Political Infighting Begins, December 1991 to October 1992

I prepared a formal presentation of the proposal to make to the North Channel Literacy Council board for their meeting on 9 December 1991. Unexpectedly, the council closed the board meeting to me, and turned down the proposal. Some of the reasons given for this surprising decision were that the program was not based solidly enough on provincial assessment criteria, and that it was too risky and might put the directors into a "liability" situation if the money was not used properly.

At this same meeting, the North Shore Board was asked to start its own Adult Basic Skills program and a decision was made to move the whole program from its present location into a more neutral space because, in the Literacy Council directors' view, the Training Access Centre was funnelling students into the North Shore Board of Education's Adult Education Centre, which was located in the same building as the Training Access Centre. Surprised by this unexpected development and its implications for the people we were trying to help, I contacted Employment and Immigration officials. They were also surprised that the board had turned down the proposal. I then spoke to the Steelworkers and they got in touch with the Labour Adjustment Branch, which, in turn, contacted the Literacy Branch at the Ministry of Education. In the end, sufficient political pressure was generated to turn the tide. The Literacy Council finally approved the $157,000 proposal and submitted it to Employment and Immigration, who officially accepted it on 6 February 1992.

By the spring of 1992, the Training Access Centre had become a large, complex program with a $400,000 budget, five administrative staff, and five instructors with access to an exceptional range of resources (including a lab with 14 computers). It offered a complex mix of programming designed to try to satisfy the requirements of the five different funders. The amount of day-to-day work involved in managing a startup program of this magnitude and complexity was staggering.

Relations between the Training Access Centre and the North Channel Literacy Council became strained as more and more board meetings were closed, and decisions were made arbitrarily, without consultation with management. For instance, at a closed meeting in May 1992, the board made a number of painful staff and space cuts, which in my view were unnecessary and harmful to the continued operation of the program. New students were barred from entering the program, and a statement was issued that the Training Access Centre would cease to exist in its current form, on or before February 1993. When the Workers' Compensation Board, impressed with the quality of the programming offered, agreed to fund their students at the Training Access Centre in June of 1992, the Literacy Council pre-empted the money. They planned to use the money to hire an executive director for the organization as a whole, they said.

Impasse and Insurrection, September 1992 to December 1992

By September, our differing views on the continued management and direction of the Training Access Centre had diverged too greatly to be reconciled. When asked if the Literacy Council would consider letting the Training Access Centre obtain another local sponsor, one who would be more supportive of our efforts to address the needs of the low-skilled, displaced workers of Elliot Lake in more varied and creative ways, the Literacy Council refused. In the face of this opposition, the entire administrative staff at the Training Access Centre resigned.

On October 28, 1992, the administrative staff met with the students to tell them what had happened. The students responded with an immense outpouring of support for the program and quickly put together a committee of nine students to see if they could obtain another local sponsor. By 4:30 p.m. that day, they had arranged a meeting with the mayor that was to become the first of many such meetings designed to garner the political support needed to enable the students to move the program to an alternate sponsor. It was an extremely tense time for everyone involved with the program. Many emotionally charged meetings were held. In the end, the North Channel Literacy Council finally agreed to allow the students to leave their sponsorship *if* a secret student ballot underscored that desire. At the end of November 1992, the future of the Training Access Centre was changed when every student voted in a secret ballot to leave the North Channel Literacy Council.

On December 2, 1992, approximately 40 battle-weary but triumphant students gathered at the Adult Education Centre on Roman Avenue to resume classes in a new location, under a new sponsor, the Elliot Lake Centre, and under a new name, the Workforce Development Centre.

Factors Contributing to the Crisis at the Training Access Centre

In my opinion, a number of factors were responsible for this disturbing chain of events. One important element was the early success of the Training Access Centre. The size of the community's economic crisis (the single largest worker dislocation in the country) and the depth of need (the laid-off workers we sought to help were among the most vulnerable) enabled us to marshal assistance that might not have been forthcoming to those laid off in smaller downsizings. Access to people in positions of influence and power, who had connections and could and did lobby on our behalf, was critical to our success. Other important factors were the huge amounts of time and energy devoted to the development of the program, the willingness of others to assist us by sharing their expertise, and the overall strength and loyalty of the Training Access Centre staff, which met regularly as a team to provide quality solutions to our ongoing start-up problems.

The reactive nature of government and the political processes also contributed to the difficulties that overwhelmed the Training Access Centre. Throughout the 1970s and 1980s, it was recognized that the basic educational requirements for successful re-employment were growing at an exponential rate. Many displaced workers in resource industries lacked the basic skills and educational requirements to obtain even the most menial jobs outside their resource sector. Low-skilled workers were left stranded without the skills to secure another job, or even to succeed in vocational retraining programs. Their difficulties had not been foreseen, and no provision had been made to deal with this problem.

"Government unwillingness to set up straight-line response mechanisms equipped with sufficient resources and autonomy"[1] to make a real difference in the area of basic skills retraining led directly to our attempt to try to use existing government structures whose funding and mandates were already preset in other directions. This set the stage for project failure. The North Channel Literacy Council was a volunteer organization with a mandate to set up and manage community literacy programs for a huge geographical region. With the best will in the world, the volunteer members of the board did not have the time to invest hours trying to understand the complexities of a an adjustment literacy program set up for a specific group of displaced workers in Elliot Lake. As the Training Access Centre grew rapidly in size, complexity, and resources, the need to address the centre's concerns frequently came to dominate North Channel Literacy Council meetings. Although this added to the chagrin of more distant members who had no stake in these proceedings, it was still an inadequate amount of time and effort to address the multitude of problems stemming from a start-up situation.

In addition, the hierarchical style of management practised by most governing structures serves to block rapid, innovative response. Instead of adopting the more democratic flat management approach, now recognized and practised by many private enterprises as the most flexible and creative means of responding to rapidly changing situations, most bureaucracies still adhere to an authoritarian style that favours control over creativity and perceives criticism as a threat, not an opportunity to learn. When asked to adapt to new conditions, the North Channel Literacy Council became increasingly controlling, until decisions made behind closed doors, usually without consultation with management, became the norm. Ironically, this increasing effort to assert their authority finally resulted in complete loss of control, and sapped the very initiative and loyalty that they tried to require of their administrative staff.

In the absence of a previously agreed-upon mandate or any negotiated agreement with other organizations about how that mandate might affect them, the rapid success of the Training Access Centre upset the apple cart of expected outcomes and created fear and jealousy both inside and outside the North Channel Literacy Council. When institutions are forced to compete for student dollars, the rapid rise of newcomers can be perceived as a threat.

The herculean efforts needed to release the kind of funding required to develop the Training Access Centre would not have been successful without the right political connections. Intensive local lobbying by influential people released the resources needed. Unfortunately, the very influence that made the Training Access Centre possible also led to its demise. In my opinion, my relationship with "the influential" posed a continuing threat to the local governing body and led them to redouble their efforts to retain complete control.

Finally, the practice of tying funding dollars to artificial program and service boundaries designed by technocrats in distant places led to a situation in which students were inundated with overlapping program criteria, criteria that were not necessarily in the best interests of the students and that were too time-consuming and demanding for teachers to be able to implement in a start-up program. Every Training Access Centre funder had different service criteria. This became an administrative nightmare and made it very difficult for the North Channel Literacy Council directors to know which dollar was attached to which criterion. Pilot adjustment projects need far more flexibility in this regard and far more input from those on the front lines as to what actually meets the needs of those for whose benefit the program exists.

The story of the Training Access Centre is a cautionary tale of how little can be accomplished in an adjustment scenario — no matter how great the need, and no matter how well-intentioned all of the parties concerned may be — if there are no previously agreed-upon solutions to the political problems that are certain to arise. That said, it is important to realize that there are limits to what small communities, particularly those under great stress, can achieve if the competition for empire and influence is such that no agreement can be reached. Optimism must also be restrained by awareness that political infighting is fostered by the very nature of our technocratic, highly specialized, multi-stakeholder society, which makes it very difficult for individuals and institutions to integrate their thinking sufficiently to see the larger picture. Without a common vision, it is difficult to develop the political will to promote the co-operation and the co-ordination needed to respond accurately, rapidly, and flexibly to the needs arising from an acute adjustment crisis. It is often said that failure is a more fertile learning ground than success. Perhaps greater understanding of the issues underlying the conflict at the Training Access Centre may help to develop policies with the potential to prevent an adjustment crisis of similar proportions from ever occurring again.

Note

[1] R.E. Michels, *The Atikokan Story* (Atikokan: Quetico Centre, 1980). I am indebted to Michels for identifying many of the barriers to successful adjustment that I have listed. Unfortunately, barriers identified 17 years ago are still with us today.

Chapter 5
Life After Layoff: Women in a Remote Single-Industry Community[1]
Monica Neitzert, Anne-Marie Mawhiney, and Elaine Porter

High and persistent unemployment rates in Canada since the mid-1970s have fuelled a debate about labour adjustment and its policy treatment. Part of the debate revolves around the treatment of workers who have been permanently displaced as a consequence of structural change.[2] Previous research uncovered much about the causes of permanent layoff (Picot, Lin, and Pyper 1996), the process of industrial restructuring (Shaiken and Hertzenberg 1992) and the changing labour market (Jackson 1996), but we still know little about what happens to workers and their families and communities after a massive permanent layoff occurs. The purpose of this paper is to inform public policy by means of a micro-economic study of the adjustment experiences of women workers in a remote northern mining community.

Policy interest in the group of permanently laid-off workers is warranted for both equity and efficiency reasons. Structural change resulting in shocks in labour demand by industry could eventually benefit society by raising social welfare, but without government intervention the costs of adjustment are borne inequitably (Jackson 1996, MacDonald 1995, Fudge 1996). Furthermore, due to gender segregation and discrimination in the labour market, it is likely that the consequences of permanent layoff differ systematically for women and men, yet few studies separately consider the adjustment process of women employees.[3] This is a serious gap in the literature, since a male-dominated workforce can no longer be considered the norm: women now represent 45 percent of the Canadian labour force. Some may argue that the focus on male displacement is warranted because of the higher permanent layoff rates in male-dominated industries, such as construction and mining. However, in 1988 the highest shares of permanent layoffs were to be found in construction (18.2 percent of all permanent layoffs), consumer service (17.4 percent), manufacturing (15.1 percent), retail trade (14.6 percent), and public administration (7.6 percent). Three of these industries — retail trade, consumer services, and public administration — are significant employers of women. We focus on displaced women workers in a sample of observations on men and women for two reasons. First, the labour market imperfections referred to above require that we study adjustment of male and female workers separately. Second, the number of women in the sample is small enough to provide a very detailed account of their adjustment experience.

Previous studies of permanent layoffs have emphasized the highly variable labour market outcomes of adjustment: unemployment duration tends to be longer for older and less educated workers, wage gains are registered for one-half of displaced workers whereas losses ensue for almost one-third (Picot and Pyper 1993). A number of causal factors have been linked to these outcomes. Youth, occupational switching, duration of unemployment, wage level in lost job, and previous layoff are negatively correlated with post-adjustment wages, while education, size of firm, and skill level are positively correlated with post-adjustment wages (Picot and Pyper 1993). Region of layoff has also been found to affect post-adjustment wages (Picot and Pyper 1993).

These studies focus on the outcome of the adjustment process: wage change or exit from unemployment by displaced workers. Indicators of adjustment include the duration of unemployment (the speed of adjustment), occupational switching, migration, and bouts of unemployment between spells of employment. The cost (or benefit) of adjustment is measured in terms of the loss (or gain) in wages upon exit from unemployment. Successful adjustment is considered to occur when the worker has found permanent employment and is earning a stable income. Assuming that adjustment benefits all of society, policy makers informed by these studies will design programs that reduce the duration of unemployment and that redistribute income to displaced workers. Thus we see the public provision of income support for displaced workers' job search, retraining, and educational upgrading.

These findings are based, however, on a narrow definition of adjustment in terms of fluctuations in displaced workers' wages and on employment occurring in the formal labour market. Apart from potential underestimation of adjustment costs and benefits that result from non-wage fluctuations, this narrow view of adjustment also fails to recognize the impact of permanent layoff on others who rely on the worker's income and who in turn provide support to the worker. Inter-household labour supply adjustments are not considered; adjustments in wages or employment in informal, unpaid, non-market, and reproductive activities undertaken by the worker or members of the worker's family are ignored and thus implied to be costless (MacDonald 1995). These oversights may lead to poorly designed labour adjustment policies if, for example, longer unemployment for some workers is supported by increasing labour market hours on the part of another household member or by more home production. In these instances, efficiency may not be improved by attempting to reduce the length of unemployment for it may only encourage poor job matching and greater turnover. Furthermore, tying the receipt of income support for job search to the displaced worker may create disincentives for the efficient reallocation of labour market work among household members.[4]

Another shortcoming of existing studies of labour adjustment is that they implicitly assume that the individual worker's objective is to maximize income. This is a standard assumption of neoclassical economists who tend to equate income with (indirect) utility. The assumption simplifies the analysis because the researcher can then easily compare pre-displacement earnings with post-adjustment earnings to approximate the cost (or benefit) of adjustment that is borne by the worker. It may mislead public policy because it does not take into account that the objective of the household is to provision itself, rather than simply to raise the income of one of its members (Nelson 1993). As an example, consider the fact that this method will indicate that a family with a very high wage earner who finds a moderately paying job after displacement bears a higher cost of adjustment than a worker in another family who switches from one low-paying job to another. Families with the characteristics of the former may then be entitled to larger transfers if income support is determined on the basis of wage loss even if the second family is unable, after adjustment, to meet its needs.

Our argument is that the design of efficient and equitable adjustment policies requires that researchers consider changes in families' ability to provide for their members' needs as the measure of adjustment costs, and that adjustments undertaken by any member of a displaced worker's family are eligible for policy treatment. We develop this argument in the next section by providing a broader definition of successful adjustment and proposing a series of indicators of adjustment that can be used to measure costs and benefits. Then we describe the data and set out our findings, followed by a discussion of the policy implications of these findings and a conclusion.

For ten years, the United Steelworkers of America sponsored the Santa Claus float in Elliot Lake's Santa Claus parade. In 1992, shrinking membership forced the union to donate the float to the city. Steelworkers asked that the tradition of having the local 5417 banner carried in front of the float (shown here in 1985) be continued by the local Boy Scouts.

United Steelworkers of America, Local 5417

Children enjoying a Denison Mines picnic.

City of Elliot Lake

Defining and Measuring Successful Adjustment

We define labour adjustment as changes in provisioning work undertaken by family members in response to the permanent layoff of one or more members. Provisioning work is labour that furnishes the means for people to fulfil their objectives, and may be subdivided into productive and reproductive activities. Production involves the creation of output (goods and services), regardless of whether that output is exchanged on the open market. The important criterion, according to Stone and Chicha (1993), is the existence of one or more consumers whose well-being can be assumed to increase from consumption of the output. This broad definition of productive work includes child and elder care, meal preparation, laundry, house cleaning, yard maintenance, paid employment and self-employment, volunteer work, emotional support, and the like. Reproduction involves activities that result in the expansion of human productive capacity and includes endeavours such as childbearing, education, training, job search, activism, and supporting friendships.[5] Thus adjustment involves "wage" and employment fluctuations in these "markets." A successful adjustment occurs if a family has regained the ability to provide for its members in the post-adjustment period. Adjustment costs (benefits) can be measured in terms of reductions (increases) in provisioning capability relative to some social minimum-level provisioning criteria. Consistent reductions in particular areas of provisioning would indicate the need for government intervention.

To evaluate the family's capability to provide for itself before and after adjustment, we establish the needs of the family and then propose measures of the family's achievements in providing for these needs at a given point in time. We have argued elsewhere (Neitzert, Mawhiney, and Porter 1996) that needs can be subdivided into four categories: productivity, equity, sustainability and empowerment. Productivity is required for individuals to support themselves independently and jointly, equity ensures that every citizen has the opportunity to be productive and to contribute to social well-being, sustainability is necessary so that current and future generations can continue to be self-reliant, and empowerment is needed to ensure that all individuals have a voice in shaping their destiny. Although each need category is required at the individual level, few human beings directly provide all of these needs for themselves in each time period. Rather, individuals choose to live in groups, and needs are provided through a process of cooperative conflict (Manser and Brown 1980) by members of households, communities and nations.

It is possible to suggest a minimum requirement within each category of need that must be met before the need can be adequately satisfied. If households fall below these minimum requirements, government intervention is warranted. The minimum will depend upon the relative achievements in the community and nation in which the household resides at the time period under consideration. We may then assess adjustment with reference to this minimum requirement level, acknowledging that some capable households may choose to achieve beyond the minimum in some categories of need. In theory some part of these surpluses may be available for redistribution to less advantaged households on the assumption that achievement of at least the minimum in every category is a benefit to the whole of society.[6] We now propose measures and minimum requirements for each need category.

We can measure the degree to which a household is meeting its productivity needs by assessing the household's per adult equivalent gross household product.[7] Gross household product is the sum of earned income (before taxes and excluding transfers) plus the value of home production undertaken in the household. Home production includes cooking and washing up, housekeeping, maintenance and repair of home and vehicles, shopping, child and elder care. We distinguish between home production and market production to show the level of cash income that the household is generating. In addition, the average duration of spells of unemployment for the year and the unemployment rate indicate the household's access to productive opportunities, and average weekly wage (before deductions, for those with jobs) indicates labour market productivity.

At a minimum, the household requires cash income equivalent to the relevant low income cutoff (or poverty line) plus one-third the national average per adult equivalent value of home production. In addition, the relative contribution of home production should not exceed two-thirds of gross household product in today's income-based society. A minimum of one-third of the national average for home production is arbitrary, but corresponds to the division of society into three classes, the bottom third of which is considered to be disadvantaged. Furthermore, a minimum for home production recognizes that some needs cannot be met through market purchases. In terms of the duration of unemployment, we argue that the number of weeks experienced in the community should not rise above the national average, and the same should hold for the unemployment rate. Average weekly wages should at minimum correspond to the low income cutoff.

We propose three measures of equity: one, the ratio of household income in the poorest 20 percent to that in the richest 20 percent of households; two, the share of households whose expenditures on basic necessities (food, shelter, and clothing) amount to 56.2 percent or more of net household labour income; and three, the relative poverty gap.[8] The first is a measure of relative income equity, while the second and third measure the degree of poverty in the population of interest. In each case we present estimates of the measures without government transfer payments to assess the need for government intervention. The minimum requirement in the case of equity is arbitrary, but we argue that the rich to poor income ratio in the mass layoff community should not fall below the national average.[9] The share of households spending more than 56.2 percent of income on basic necessities should be no greater than the national average. In terms of the poverty gap, our minimum requirement that every household achieve at least the poverty-line level of income implies that the poverty gap should remain at least equal to zero throughout the period of adjustment.

We limit the measurement of sustainability to the ability of the family to sustain the current and next generation. To measure the ability of the household to sustain the current generation, we measure the level of education and health of (one of) the head(s) of the household (that is, the worker) and the average nightly hours of sleep of the workers. Education is measured in terms of the percentage of the sample with completed high school education, while health is measured by the proportion of the population reporting excellent or very good health status.[10] These measures provide information on the household's ability to sustain its current level of measured productivity. We also assess sustainability of the current relationship by way of an index of the quality of the relationship for those who are married or living common-law, and by changes in marital status among the group of workers.[11] These measures indicate the sustainability of the household as the unit that provides members' needs. Finally, to measure sustainability of the next generation we evaluate household wealth per child for those households with children. The minimum required to sustain the current generation should follow the national average rule for level of education and health and for hours of sleep. For sustaining the provision unit, we propose that in households with laid-off workers there be no increase in divorced and separated couples over the period of adjustment relative to the national average and that relationship quality not decline. Finally, at a minimum, households should be able to generate sufficient wealth to provide the equivalent of half of college tuition and half of poverty-line subsistence for each child.[12]

To provide a measure of empowerment, we estimate the value of volunteer labour provided by household head(s) to professional, union, recreational, political, or church groups and organizations. We also estimate the federal voter turnout rate among displaced workers at various points in the adjustment process. Participation in community organizations and in national politics indicates that individuals perceive themselves to have a voice in institutions that shape their future. The minimum level of empowerment is set at the national average value of volunteer labour and voter turnout rate to indicate that empowerment in the community affected by layoff should not fall below national empowerment levels.[13]

Table 1 displays the minimum provisioning levels for each of the indicators described above. We monitor fluctuations in each of these indicators for displaced and non-displaced workers and their families every two years over the period of adjustment. This allows us to evaluate fluctuations during and after adjustment, relative to the minimum requirements and relative to the level achieved on the eve of displacement. We isolate the effect of the layoff by comparing, at each point in time, the households of displaced workers with households in which no member is displaced.

We consider the direction of changes in each of the indicators as well as the distance from the minima. Our sample size is not large enough for us to conduct rigorous quantitative analysis of the determinants of successful adjustment, although we are able suggest some qualitative conclusions about correlates. We leave the question of rigorous tests to a future paper, along with the comparison of outcomes in which male workers are displaced.

Table 1. Minimum provisioning levels 1990-1996

	1990	1992	1994	1996
Productivity				
• Low income cutoff per adult ($)[1]	11,072	11,870	12,108	12,652
• ⅓ mean per adult home product value ($)[2]	--	4,977	--	--
• Maximum per adult home production ($)[3]	7,418	7,953	8,112	8,477
• Average (weeks) duration of unemployment[4]	18.5	21.3	25.6	24.2
• Unemployment rate (Ontario) (%)[5]	6.3	10.9	9.6	9.2
• Weekly $ wage (40 hours at minimum wage)	274.0	280.0	280.0	280.0
Equity				
• Income ratio of top 20% to bottom 20%[6]	--	7.1	--	--
• % of persons spending more than 56.2% of income on necessities[7]	14.6	16.1	16.6	--
• Relative poverty gap (%)[8]	--	--	22.6	--
Sustainability				
• % of 15+ population completed high school[5]	21.7	22.3	21.2	--
• % of women 25-44 completed high school[9]	--	18.5	--	--
• % reporting excellent or very good health[10]	62.4	--	62.0	--
• % of women aged 18-64 divorced, separated or widowed[11]	11.0	--	--	--
• National average hours of sleep per night[12]	--	7.9	--	--
• ½(college tuition + poverty line) ($)[13]	12,072	12,870	13,308	14,452
Empowerment				
• Value of mean annual volunteer labour ($)[14]	--	931	--	--
• Voter turnout rate—federal (%)	--	75.0	--	--

[1] Low income cutoffs for communities with less than 30,000 population (National Council of Welfare 1996)

[2] One-third of average 1992 value measured by the gross opportunity cost method (Chandler 1993)

[3] Two-thirds of low income cut-offs

[4] For women in Ontario; figure reported under 1996 column is the 1995 annual average. Statistics Canada (1995a)

[5] Statistics Canada (1995a) estimates for Ontario

[6] United Nations Development Programme (1995) reports the average income ratio for 1980–1992 for Canada.

[7] National Council of Welfare (1996)

[8] Average percent by which income falls below the low income cutoff in poor households (National Council of Welfare 1996)

[9] Statistics Canada (1995c) estimates for Canada for 1991

[10] 1990 for 15–65 Ontario women from Ministry of Health (1990); 1994 figure for 15 and older population of Canada from Statistics Canada (1995b)

[11] McDaniel (1994)

[12] Average for married mothers aged 25–44 and employed full-time (Frederick 1995)

[13] Half the two-year cost of tuition and half of single adult poverty line income for two years

[14] National average annual hours of civic and voluntary activity for women aged 25–44 and employed full time, valued at average hourly gross opportunity cost (Chandler 1993, Frederick 1995)

Our Study

In this paper we focus on the 38 women included in the Elliot Lake Tracking Study sample who had been employed by either Rio Algom Limited or Denison Mines Limited at the time of the layoff announcements.[14] The small number of women in the sample reflects the fact that few women have been employed as mining production workers (in 1994, 21.3 percent of workers in primary occupations were women). Although 13 percent of the women in our sample were or had been production employees, the majority held clerical positions in these two companies (see Table 2). Because the Elliot Lake operations were production sites, clerical positions were relatively few in number. In the following section, we describe the adjustment experience of the 38 women in our sample and their families over the six years of the study.

Table 2. Workers' occupational distribution

	Number	Percent
Mineral production	5	13.2
Administration	3	7.9
Technical	3	7.9
Health	4	10.5
Service	2	5.3
Clerical	21	55.3
Total	**38**	**100.0**

The Adjustment Experience in Elliot Lake

In this section we first describe the family composition and status of our sample on the eve of the layoffs in 1990. We then go on to discuss the changes that occurred among the group of displaced and not-displaced families over the ensuing six years. At the time of the first interviews from September to November 1990, 32 respondents were married, two were single and had never been married, and four were divorced; in 1990 none were widowed or separated. Among those married or living common-law, the mean length of the union was 14.4 years. Eight women in the sample had no children, and eleven had no dependent children living at home. Among all of the respondents there were 67 children, of whom 48 were dependent children living with the women respondents. Interestingly, only 38 percent of child members of households were daughters. The average

age of the women was 38 in 1990, the average age of spouses (where present) was 42, and the average age of children living at home was 11. Of those with spouses (32 women), 20 husbands were employed and six husbands were looking for work. On the eve of the layoff, 16 households in the sample (42 percent) depended solely on the labour income of the respondent, 21 households (55 percent) had two earners, and one household had three earners. Mean annual gross employment earnings for respondents was $36,050 before layoff and average tenure with the firm was 11.2 years. No one in the sample of households received government transfer payments in 1990 up to the time the interviews were held. By the end of 1990, 23 of the women in the sample had been laid off; one of these women had accepted voluntary retirement in 1988, another had been laid off in 1989, and another quit (that is, took voluntary layoff) in 1990. Table 3 details changes in the adjustment indicators from 1990 to 1996 for the group of workers who were displaced.

Table 3. Changes in provisioning levels, 1990-1996, households with displaced workers

	1990	1992	1994	1996
Productivity				
• Household income per adult equivalent ($)[1]	33,688	16,088	19,123	26,243
• Mean per adult home product ($)	23,845	19,337	26,748	23,319
• Home production % of household product (%)[2]	41.4	54.6	58.3	47.1
• Mean weeks of unemployment since layoff	14.9	41.8	85.6	106.3
• Average weekly $ wage (working respondents)[3]	680.0	528.0	548.0	644.0
• Unemployment rate at time of survey (%)	43.5	41.4	35.5	34.4
Equity				
• Income ratio of top 20% to bottom 20%	2.5	30.6	∞[4]	7.1
• Share of persons spending more than 56.2% of Income on necessities (%)	44.4	47.8	--	9.4
• Relative poverty gap (%)	0	64.9	81.2	43.3
Sustainability				
• % completed high school	34.8	40.0	41.9	40.6
• % reporting excellent or very good health	81.8	76.7	77.4	81.3
• % of respondents divorced, separated or widowed	17.4	20.0	29.0	18.8
• % relationship quality[5]	67.4	61.0	72.0	72.0
• Average hours of sleep per night	7.1	6.9	8.4	7.2
• Average wealth per child ($)	38,377	40,281	21,112	59,577
Empowerment				
• Value of mean annual volunteer labour ($)	1,990	879	1,028	1,000
• Voter turnout rate—federal (%)	95.7	96.7	90.3	87.5
Number of displaced workers	23	30	31	32
Number of children in workers' families	41	56	52	53

[1] Income for the year before the survey
[2] Row 2 as a percentage of the sum of rows 1 and 2
[3] Wage at the time of the interview, among those employed
[4] Bottom 20 percent of households have no income before government transfers.
[5] Relationship quality is measured as a percentage score from the respondent's response to three questions about her relationship with her partner.

Overall, the table shows that this sample started out being an advantaged group relative to the minima established in Table 1. According to Table 3, 1992 to 1994 were the worst years from the perspective of the displaced workers and their families. In these years, household income per adult equivalent dropped to the lowest in the period, equity indicators deteriorated seriously among displaced families, health levels declined, divorce rates increased, and empowerment as measured by participation in community organizations declined. The number of displaced workers rose by 30 percent between 1990 and 1992, and by 6.7 percent between 1992 and 1996. The number of children in families with displaced workers rose by 36.3 percent between 1990 and 1992, and declined somewhat thereafter. The decline was due to the departure of some children to start families of their own, and to the reduction in the number of foster children that had been members of these families. Wealth levels among families with displaced workers dropped off significantly by 1994. The most important determinant of wealth is the value of the principal residence, but the data also indicate that many families ran down some of their other assets or increased indebtedness during these difficult years.

By 1996, substantial improvements in the indicators are evident, although most had not returned to their pre-layoff levels. It is important to note in particular that the polarization among families with displaced workers had not abated by 1996, although there was some improvement. A significant minority (15.6 percent) of the families still had incomes below the poverty line (before government transfers) and were spending more than 56.2 percent of income on basic necessities (food, shelter, and clothing). Unemployment among these workers still stood at 34.4 percent (about 10 percentage points below the 1990 post-layoff level). Thus, the increase in those indicators measured at means does not imply that there was an improvement for all families. In fact, the indicators did not improve at all for a small number of families. Whether those families who had not experienced an improvement by 1996 will do so eventually remains to be seen; most of the disadvantaged group in 1996 had been laid off in 1990 or 1991.

Comparing the results presented in Table 3 with the minimum indicator levels established in Table 1, we make several noteworthy observations. In terms of productivity, the mean income per adult equivalent was more than twice the poverty line in 1990, 36 percent above the line in 1992, 56 percent higher in 1994, and double the poverty line in 1996. The mean value of home production fell, but remained above the minimum level among this group over the study period, and it stayed below two-thirds the value of gross household product.[15] Average weekly wages remained well above minimum wage for those who had jobs. The problem for productivity was one of finding work. The unemployment rate was substantially above the Ontario average throughout the period, and the duration of unemployment was much longer than the average duration for women in Ontario.[16] Access to employment is especially problematic in remote single- industry communities, although a number of those in the least desirable categories have migrated.

With respect to equity, Elliot Lake families with displaced workers fell substantially behind the national averages by 1992. Income disparity — measured without government transfers — peaked in 1994, when none among the poorest 20 percent of families had income above zero. The relatively high level of expenditure on basic necessities in 1990 and 1992 was substantially above the national average for those years, and the relative poverty gap reached dangerous levels in 1992 and 1994. The poverty gap remained above the national average in 1996. Clearly government intervention to assist these families to meet their productivity and equity needs is warranted (a number of the families did receive transfer payments in these years).

It is interesting to compare sustainability and empowerment indicators for the sample of displaced workers with the minimum indicator levels. The results indicate that the sample of displaced workers continues to meet basic needs in these areas. Compared with the average among women in Canada, a larger proportion of women in the Elliot Lake sample of displaced women workers completed high school as their highest level of education. This reflects two facts: Elliot Lake women are more likely to have completed secondary education (7.9 percent of our sample have incomplete secondary education compared to 18.1 percent of Canadian women aged 25–44), and are less likely to have university education than average Canadian women (5.3 percent of women in the sample have a university degree compared to 15.3 percent of Canadian women aged 25–44). Compared with the average among women in Ontario, a much higher proportion of women in the Elliot Lake sample report their health to be excellent or very good. This may be related to living in a small community in a natural setting. The divorced, separated, and widowed rate among displaced women workers in Elliot Lake was higher than the national average throughout the period. This may be a reflection of the age of our sample (average age was 38 in 1990) compared to the age group over which the national divorce rate is calculated (18–64). The estimated wealth per child in the sample of families with displaced workers remains substantially above the minimum that was established in Table 1 (half the amount of college tuition plus half the poverty line income level per child). The indicators of empowerment show that women in the sample continued to be active in the community despite their displacement from employment, although we do note that these indicators decline over the period.

Table 4 reports the indicator levels for families in which the respondent was not laid off before 1996 (by June 1996, all workers would have been laid off). The table provides us with another relative comparison with which to evaluate the adjustment of displaced workers and their families. Although the number of non-displaced workers is small, the results displayed in the table can assist in isolating the direct effects of the layoffs. The comparison between displaced and non-displaced corroborates what we have learned from comparing the displaced women in our sample with our minimum criteria: displaced families' capability of meeting their productivity and equity needs were substantially undermined for a significant period after the permanent layoff of an income earner, but their ability to meet sustainability and empowerment needs were not as heavily affected in the short to medium term. Thus, although the largest impact of the layoff was to affect productivity, there were important effects on equity, sustainability, and empowerment at the family and community levels.

Perhaps the most noteworthy finding from this second comparison is that in a small community, non-displaced workers — or workers who are displaced at a later date — do not escape being immediately affected by the displacement of their colleagues. In particular, the incomes of non-displaced families declined significantly between 1992 and 1994, their wages stagnated, home production declined, income disparity within the still employed group increased, and wealth declined substantially. The decline in many of these variables indicates the community impact of the mass layoffs: market wages declined and property values diminished. In relative terms, however, the non-displaced are always better off, except perhaps in terms of the value of home production, and the health and hours of sleep of continuing workers.

Table 4. Changes in provisioning levels, 1990–1996, households with no displaced workers

	1990	1992	1994	1996
Productivity				
• Household income per adult equivalent ($)[1]	39,358	21,080	23,587	43,136
• Mean per adult home product ($)	21,865	13,839	16,166	17,087
• Home production % of household product (%)[2]	35.7	39.6	40.7	28.4
• Average weekly $ wage (of respondents)[3]	744.0	740.0	736.0	840.0
Equity				
• Income ratio of top 20% to bottom 20%	2.7	2.8	3.5	2.7
• Share of persons spending more than 56.2% of income on necessities (%)	0.0	20.0	--	0.0
• Relative poverty gap (%)	0.0	6.7	0.0	0.0
Sustainability				
• % completed high school	33.3	50.0	42.9	50.0
• % reporting excellent or very good health	76.9	62.5	85.7	33.3
• % of respondents divorced, separated or widowed	0.0	12.5	0.0	16.7
• % relationship quality[4]	70.8	78.0	73.0	76.0
• Average hours of sleep per night	7.0	6.6	6.9	6.0
• Wealth per child ($)	63,375	22,495	46,525	86,848
Empowerment				
• Value of mean annual volunteer labour ($)	1,542	5,498	529	902
• Voter turnout rate—federal (%)	100	100	100	16.7
Number of non-displaced workers	15	8	7	6
Number of children in workers' families	26	11	12	9

[1] Income for the year before the survey
[2] Row 2 as a percentage of the sum of rows 1 and 2
[3] Wage at the time of the survey among those employed
[4] Relationship quality is measured as a percentage score from the respondent's response to three questions about her relationship with her spouse.

Comparing the post-layoff situation of families with displaced workers and non-displaced workers also sheds light on the experience of adjustment. Comparing Tables 3 and 4, one can identify the indicators that were initially affected by the layoff. Income and unemployment were immediately affected, but relationship quality and divorce rates followed soon after. Equity and wealth were affected immediately following layoff and seemed to continue to decline for a substantial period thereafter. In the years subsequent to the layoff, health at first improved for displaced relative to non-displaced workers, but then the relative gain diminished. The initial health gain for displaced workers may reflect the decline in stress from working, whereas the subsequent relative deterioration in health may be associated with a gradual increase in stress due to continuing unemployment. The significant decline in self-reported health among non-displaced workers in 1996 may indicate the stress associated with the impending displacement of these workers in June 1996. Empowerment also appears to be affected by the layoff, although not as severely as income.[17] In particular, note the divergent reaction in volunteer contributions among displaced and non-displaced groups in 1992.

Discussion and Conclusion

Our analysis and comparison of displaced workers with their non-displaced peers and with minimum needs levels provide some insight into the process of adjustment experienced by displaced workers and their families. Adjustment may be broken into two separate stages that are not necessarily consecutive: reconciliation and reform.[18] During reconciliation, the family must adapt to the fact that an income earner is, possibly temporarily, out of work. At a minimum, the family must reconcile current expenditures with the new income level. In the reform phase, the family must design and institute a new provisioning strategy. We previously argued that a successful adjustment has occurred when the family is once again able to provide for the needs of its members. Our results suggest that certain variables figure importantly in the reconciliation phase, and that families choose different reform strategies.

Since permanent layoff most directly affects productivity, reconciliation largely involves the adjustment of expenditures given the new income level. This reconciliation can include running down assets or raising indebtedness, reducing expenditures, raising home production, or reducing the number of dependent family members. Our results show that the families of displaced workers engage in all of these techniques of reconciliation. Factors determining which of these techniques are chosen likely include education, number and age of children, and pre-existing wealth level (itself a function of age, marital status, education, and occupation). Government intervention aimed at maintaining a basic level of household income will be especially important for those families who started the adjustment process with lower levels of education, younger children, or lower wealth, and who had only the displaced worker earning income. Government assistance at this stage, and with clear guidelines as to its purpose and duration, is likely to encourage families to move to the reform stage of adjustment. Other reasons government intervention at this stage is important are that once productivity has been affected many other needs follow suit, and that in small communities the productivity effects are not limited to the families of the displaced workers. This assistance should be accompanied by aid to identify and implement effective reform strategies.

In the long run, it is not possible for families to continue to run down assets or to maintain expenditures below minimum needs levels. Reform strategies for families adjusting to the permanent layoff of a member include: migration (geographic or occupational), role change (switching responsibilities among family members), education or training, and family reconstitution (marriage, divorce, children). The choice and effectiveness of any of these strategies will be influenced by the age of the displaced worker, employment status of family members, marital status, the age of the children, and the worker's level of education and training, occupation, experience, and previous wage.

We found examples of successful adjustment based on each of these strategies. Among the most successful were displaced workers who quickly found new jobs that made use of their existing skills, those who migrated early on in the crisis period, those who were able to search for a new job for a longer period of time, those whose partners took up paid employment, and those who found new, income-earning partners.

In our sample, the workers who found new jobs making use of their existing skills had migrated to new communities. Migration poses a dilemma for many families with adolescent children: whether to move the family and risk the well-being of the children or whether to reduce expenditures and hold off migration until the children have completed high school (Dansereau 1996). Those workers who took a longer time to find a new job had the benefit of a second income in the household. Some workers with high scores on the adjustment indicators had changed marital status (some divorcées remarried, some unions dissolved). These changes resulted in an improvement in well-being for the worker, but our data do not indicate whether the well-being of other members of the original household increased or not, and thus we remain somewhat agnostic as to whether family reconstitution is truly a strategy for successful adjustment or not. This strategy may be more commonly adopted by women workers who have fewer income-earning opportunities than men, particularly in isolated single-industry communities.

Some families in our sample appear to be caught at the reconciliation phase, seemingly unable to develop a reform strategy. The age of children and the employment status of the partner can be barriers to reform. The group of most disadvantaged families had more children (2.4) than the sample average (1.6). If the partner has little previous experience, or little opportunity to find paid employment, the displaced worker may be forced to accept whatever paid work can be found quickly. Of the most disadvantaged families, none had partners with long-term employment, and no workers who found several short spells of employment could be considered successful. In addition, almost half of those who were still struggling with adjustment in 1996 were divorcées in 1990, and more than half of these households had no partner (were either single, divorced or separated) in 1996. The only divorcées in 1990 who did successfully adjust to permanent layoff were married or living common-law by 1995.

Our conclusion from this analysis is that although productivity characteristics identified in the literature are important determinants of the degree of success in adjustment to permanent layoff, family characteristics may be equally important, especially for women workers. In particular, marital status and age and presence of children are significant factors in determining the ability of families to cope with layoffs. These have been overlooked in the standard economics literature on permanent layoffs.

The importance of these variables for policy is that they influence the choice of adjustment strategy and affect the distribution of the costs of adjustment. On the one hand, a supportive family can be an aid in the development and implementation of a successful adjustment strategy. On the other hand, the existence of others directly affected by the layoff may mean that the costs of adjustment (or non-adjustment) are felt by more individuals and potentially across generations. The policy implication is that programs to aid workers must not hinder workers' families, for it is the family that appears to be one of the most important factors in determining the outcome of the adjustment.

Notes

[1] We wish to thank our colleagues David Leadbeater, David Robinson, and Derek Wilkinson in the Elliot Lake Tracking and Adjustment Study for releasing the data on which this paper is based. In addition, we appreciate the research provided by our associate Suzanne Dansereau, and we are grateful to the participants of the Elliot Lake Tracking Study for the information they provided in responding to the ELTS questionnaires. This study has benefited from the generous support of Human Resources Development Canada, the Ministry of Northern Development, and the Institute of Northern Ontario Research and Development.

[2] We use the terms "permanently laid-off workers" and "displaced workers" interchangeably in this paper.

[3] Many of the more recent studies include women and men workers, but these studies tend to consider gender as one of many independent variables that affect the outcome of adjustment (for example, Gray and Grenier 1996). Some studies separately analyze women and men (for example, Picot and Pyper 1993) workers but fail to incorporate occupational segregation by gender or wage discrimination.

[4] We use the terms "household" and "family" interchangeably in this paper in

recognition of the fact that not all individuals in society live in traditionally constituted families. For our purposes, a family or a household can comprise any group of individuals sharing accommodations and income.

5 Production and reproduction are not precise and mutually exclusive categories. The categories are introduced here to reconcile two alternative views of human labour. Provisioning is a concept originally introduced by Adam Smith and revived by Julie Nelson (1992) to describe the economic value of human labour. The division of provisioning work into productive and reproductive aspects corresponds more closely to Marxian traditions and has merit in its explicit recognition of the economic value of reproduction.

6 It is easy to see this in the case of productivity, for example.

7 In calculating adult equivalencies, we give the first adult in the household a weight of 1, and each additional adult a weight of 0.4. Each child is assigned a weight of 0.3, except in single-parent families in which the first child is weighted at 0.4 and subsequent children receive a 0.3 weighting (Picot and Myles 1995).

8 The poverty gap is given by $\text{í}N(y^*-Y)/Ny^*$ where N is the number of people whose incomes (Y) fall below the poverty line y^*.

9 This minimum requirement has the unfortunate corollary that if the national average income ratio increases, then an equivalent increase in equity in the community in which displaced workers reside meets the minimum requirement. Although this is consistent with the concept of successful relative adjustment, it does not amount to successful absolute adjustment if the decline in equity in the community is related to the layoffs. A stricter rule would set the minimum in absolute terms.

10 In response to the question, "In general, for your age, would you describe your health as: (1) excellent (2) good (3) average (4) poor or (5) very poor?"

11 The inclusion of a measure of relationship quality reflects our belief that — in spite of the social benefit of the family unit as a provider of needs — the partners in a union cannot be expected to sacrifice their own well-being in order to sustain the family unit.

12 We assume that children will be able to generate incomes sufficient for the other half.

13 Some displaced workers in our survey migrated to other communities as a part of their adjustment. In these cases it might be preferable to measure equity and empowerment relative to the new community. Our argument in using the original community as the base is that a reduction in equity or sustainability there, all else constant, implies a reduction in the national average.

14 Another six interviewees, for whom the variable indicating gender is missing from the dataset, have been identified as female on the basis of their names and/or the presence of a husband or male partner. We have not incorporated these six individuals into our analysis in this paper.

15 Part of the reason the value of home production declines is that the average

wage (opportunity cost) declines.

[16] Obviously, the Ontario average duration of unemployment includes many unemployed who were not permanently displaced and also excludes people who were not searching for work during the reference week. These two facts will reduce the average duration of a spell. All women in this sample who were out of work looked for work some time during the six months before the interview. We therefore consider all of them to be "unemployed."

[17] The seemingly small impact on empowerment may be due to a poor choice of indicators.

[18] Alternatively, we could label the stages with more typical economics jargon: stabilization and restructuring.

References

Bakker, Isabella. (1993). "Through a feminist lens: macroeconomic restructuring in Canada." Paper prepared for the Economic Equality Workshop sponsored by Status of Women Canada, Ottawa, November 29–30.

Chandler, William. (1993). "The value of household work in Canada, 1992," in Statistics Canada, *National Income and Expenditure Accounts*, Fourth Quarter 1993, Catalogue Number 13–001, Ottawa: Ministry of Industry, Science and Technology.

Dansereau, Suzanne. (1996). *How Miners Plan to Face the Future: Early Adjustment of Stanleigh Miners and Their Spouses*. ELTAS Analysis Series #1A3. Sudbury, ON: INORD, Laurentian University.

Day, Tanis. (1992). "Women's economic product: unmeasured contributions to measured output or the perils of woman-blindness," Paper prepared for CEA meetings in Charlottetown, PEI, June.

Dooley, Martin. (1994). "Women, children and poverty in Canada," *Canadian Public Policy* 20, 4: 430–43.

Ellis, Diana. (1986). *An Overview of Women's Involvement in the Economic Development Process*. Vancouver: Women's Research Centre.

Frederick, Judith A. (1995). *As Time Goes By ... Time Use of Canadians*, Statistics Canada Catalogue Number 89–544E, Ottawa: Ministry of Industry.

Fudge, Judy. (1996). "Fragmentation and feminization: the challenge of equity for labour-relations policy" in *Women and Canadian Public Policy*, ed. Janine Brodie. Toronto: Harcourt, Brace.

Ghalam, Nancy Zukewich. (1993). *Women in the Workplace*, 2nd edition. Statistics Canada Catalogue Number 71–534, Ottawa: Ministry of Industry, Science and Technology.

Gray, David and Gilles Grenier. (1996). "Jobless durations of displaced workers: a comparison of Canada and the United States." Presented at the Canadian Economics Research Forum/Canadian Labour Market and Productivity Centre Conference in Ottawa. February. Mimeo.

Jackson, Andrew. (1996). *The Future of Jobs: A Labour Perspective*. Research Paper No. 4. Ottawa: Canadian Labour Congress.

La Novara, Pina. (1993). *A Portrait of Families in Canada.* Statistics Canada Catalogue Number 89–523E, Ottawa: Ministry of Industry, Science and Technology.

MacDonald, Martha. (1995). "The empirical challenges of feminist economics: the example of economic restructuring," in *Out of the Margin: Feminist Perspectives on Economics*, ed. Edith Kuiper and Jolande Sap with Susan Feiner, Notburga Otta and Zafiris Tzannatos. New York: Routledge.

Manser, Marilyn and Murray Brown. (1980). "Marriage and household decision-making: a bargaining analysis," *International Economic Review* 21, 1: 31–44.

McDaniel, Susan A. with Carol Strike. (1994). *Family and Friends.* General Social Survey Analysis Series, Catalogue Number 11–612E, Number 9, Ottawa: Ministry of Industry, Science and Technology.

National Council of Welfare. (1996). *Poverty Profile 1994.* Ottawa: National Council on Welfare.

Neitzert, Monica, Anne-Marie Mawhiney, and Elaine Porter. (1996). *Stitching the Equilibria: A Feminist Tapestry of Labor Adjustment.* ELTAS Analysis Series #1A1. Sudbury, ON: INORD, Laurentian University.

Nelson, Julie A. (1993). "The study of choice or the study of provisioning? Gender and the definition of economics" in *Beyond Economic Man: Feminist Theory and Economics*, ed. Marianne A. Ferber and Julie A. Nelson. Chicago: University of Chicago Press. 23-36.

Ontario Ministry of Health. (1990). *Ontario Health Survey.* Toronto: Ministry of Health.

Picot, Garnett, Zhengxi Lin, and Wendy Pyper. (1996). *Permanent Layoffs in Canada: Overview and Longitudinal Analysis*, Analytical Studies Branch, Research Paper #103. Ottawa: Statistics Canada.

Picot, Garnett and John Myles. (1995). *Social Transfers, Changing Family Structure, and Low Income among Children.* Ottawa: Ministry of Industry.

Picot, Garnett, and Wendy Pyper. (1993). *Permanent Layoffs and Displaced Workers: Cyclical Sensitivity, Concentration, and Experience Following the Layoff.* No. 55. Statistics Canada, Analytical Studies Branch.

Shaiken, Harley and Steven Hertzenberg. (1992). *Automation and Global Production: Automobile Engine Production in Mexico, the United States and Canada.* University of California, San Diego: Center for US-Mexican Studies.

Statistics Canada. (1995a). *Labour Force Survey Annual Averages 1990–1994.* Catalogue Number 71–001, Ottawa: Ministry of Industry.

Statistics Canada. (1995b). *National Population Health Survey Overview 1994–95*, Catalogue Number 82–567, Ottawa: Ministry of Industry.

Statistics Canada. (1995c). *Women in Canada: A Statistical Report*, 3rd edition. Ottawa: Ministry of Industry.

Statistics Canada. (1996). *Consumer Prices and Price Indexes January–March 1996.* Catalogue Number 62–010–XPB, Ottawa: Ministry of Industry.

Stone, Leroy O. and Marie-Thérèse Chicha. (1993). *The Statistics Canada Total Work Accounts System*, Statistics Canada Catalogue No. 89–549–XP, Ottawa: Ministry of Industry, Science and Technology.

United Nations Development Programme (UNDP). (1995). *Human Development Report 1995*. New York: Oxford University Press.

Wilkinson, Derek and David Robinson. (1993). "Neighbourhood cohesion: level of analysis and determinants," mimeo.

Carrie Chenier, the last Steelworker in Elliot Lake, gets help from Peter Vintinner, a former local member, to take down the USWA Local 5417 sign from the Steelworkers' Union Hall in Elliot Lake, October 1997.

Jane Pitblado

Chapter 6
Search, Succour, and Success: Looking for Jobs from Elliot Lake
Derek Wilkinson and David Robinson

Once upon a time, people in single-industry towns could almost automatically get well-paying work in local factories or mines (Lucas 1971). That time is gone. More people are now spending more time, more effort, and more money searching for work, and people expect to have to apply many places in order to get a job.

In this chapter, we present new empirical data for three topics that interface between economics and sociology in a Canadian, specifically Northern Ontario, labour-market context. The first major interest is job-search effort. Who searches for work? The second area of interest is succour. Who gets help when they are job-searching? From whom do they get this help? What kinds of help do they get? The third area of interest is success in finding work. Who actually got a job in the past five years? How did they find out about the job? Here we attempt an assessment of the relative importance of different social chains. Do direct methods work better than social connections? Are kin more important than friends?

The subject of search has not found a clear scientific home. Economics, psychology, and sociology each has its own perspective and the practical literature on counselling has been divorced from theory. As a result, research is scattered across a large number of journals and employs theoretical and empirical frameworks that are entirely unrelated. We begin by describing a few of the more interesting approaches.

An important sociological work specifically related to job search is that of Granovetter (1974), entitled *Getting a Job*. Granovetter's account looks at the roles of friends and relatives in job search. His work was done with technologists in eastern United States. He emphasizes (also in Granovetter 1985) the "strength of weak ties." Individuals with whom a person has less contact will be more useful for finding jobs because the overlap of their knowledge with that of the respondent will be less. Thus their information will be different from that of the person seeking work and will more likely be useful.

Grieco (1987), a British researcher, strongly criticized Granovetter's conclusion. She showed that the connections of relatives were very important in finding jobs in her study of manual labourers in England and Scotland. An important aspect of her argument is that employers have an interest, themselves, in supporting peer connections: "Lads of dads can be controlled better because they have kin sanction operating on them, but the sponsoring worker also faces a control because the ability to sponsor is granted on the basis of past success and past performance — thus dads of lads are equally well controlled." (176) These types of mechanisms are not available with weak ties. Nevertheless, although she rejected Granovetter's emphasis on weak ties, she shared his perception of the importance of social ties in job search.

In Canada, Grayson (1985) and found that the most important way people got jobs after four waves of layoffs at SKF Canada Limited in Toronto was through friends (with percentages of 36, 42, 27, and 36 respectively). This compares with 12, 26, 37, and 30 percent for those getting jobs from direct contacts after the same four waves of layoffs. Holzer (1988) found the same, that using multiple methods led to more success, as did relying on friends and relatives and using newspapers.

Also in Canada, Wellman (for example, Wellman and Wortley 1990, Wellman and Tindall 1993) has done extended studies on a group of working-class individuals from East York. His research shows the durability of relationships with relatives compared to those with friends. In his recontact study of East Yorkers, only relatives survived as major contacts ten years later (Wellman et al. 1995). It is not clear that this supports their importance in job finding; however it does present a counter-argument to those who would emphasize the role of long-term friendships. Unfortunately, his recontact sample was relatively small and he did not select it to include primarily job seekers.

The role of assistance from friends as well as family members remains an important topic for sociologists. However, Wellman's and Grieco's research would appear to imply that family members are the most helpful in job search in the long run. There may well be geographical and temporal variations in the relative importance of family and friends that remain to be explored.

In both Canada and the U.S., only those who are actually searching are officially defined as unemployed. This distinction is built into both Canada's Labour Force Survey and the U.S. Current Population Survey. Since those surveys are used to calculate unemployment rates, slight differences in the definition can influence the level of measured unemployment. Reading newspaper help-wanted ads is classified as active search in Canada but not in the U.S. As a result, Canadian unemployment rates are automatically higher than in the U.S. We have calculated unemployment rates for our sample varying from 12 percent to over 30 percent, depending in part on the definition of search that we used. Beginning in the 1970s, some studies began to make other distinctions. The earliest of these distinguish "systematic" versus "random" search, with the latter defined as one involving direct contact with a potential employer (Krahn and Lowe 1988).

The goal of most studies of search is to identify effective job-search methods. To accomplish this, some way of measuring "success" is required. Many criteria have been used, but with high rates of unemployment in recent years, getting a job is one of the most common criteria.

Help comes in different forms and is provided by various people and organizations. Some comes from government and government-supported agencies. Some is provided by friends or relatives. From the point of view of policy, it is important to look at the help people get in job-search and job finding because understanding what kinds of help actually work can point to ways that government can facilitate the job search process.

Holzer (1988), found that males aged 16 to 23 used methods with the following frequencies: 85 percent asked friends and relatives, 80 percent contacted employers directly, 58 consulted newspapers, and 54 percent went to state employment agencies. Of the one-third receiving a job offer in the month prior to the study interview, 82 percent reported using either friends and relatives or direct contact.

Some economic and policy research has focused on official government-sponsored programs. For example, the U.S. Department of Labour (1995) cites experimental evidence on the usefulness of job-search training. Leigh (1995) suggests that training in job search may represent the most cost-effective public investment. Search training has been an important component of public sector employment agencies. Osberg (1993) contrasts public employment agencies (Canada Employment Centres) with informal methods of search. He concludes that public employment agencies only help the most difficult clients and that assistance seems more valuable during more severe recessions.

Methods

The Elliot Lake Tracking Study (ELTS) is a large-scale longitudinal study of 1,182 individuals who were laid off from Rio Algom Limited and Denison Mines Limited in Elliot Lake between 1990 and 1996. Of the 1,006 who were interviewed for the fifth round of the study in 1996, 829 had been laid off. Interviews in person or by telephone were conducted from January to March of 1996 with trained interviewers. Details of the methodology are available elsewhere (Wilkinson, Suschnigg, Robinson, and Leadbeater 1993).

Many early studies measure "search intensity" by looking at the number of contacts with employers (see Devine and Kiefer 1991). Our measure is somewhat different. All ELTS interviews have had a few questions concerned with search. On each occasion of our survey (1990, 1992, 1994, 1995, and 1996), we asked if the respondent was looking for work. From 1994 to 1996, we also asked about search activities four weeks and six months prior to the interview. Those who had not looked at all in the previous six months were not asked about their more recent activities.

Our account of help comes from two questions asked in the 1996 ELTS questionnaire. First, we asked:

How exactly did you find out about the most recent job?

1. Through a friend, workmate, neighbour
2. Through a relative
3. Through an advertisement
4. I applied directly to the company
5. I became self-employed
6. Through an agency
7. Through someone I didn't know
8. Through a previous employer
9. Other (specify)

Some of the respondents circled more than one possibility.

The other question on more general help with job search was a multi-stage question asking, "In the last five years did anybody help you in preparing a résumé, job application letter, or form, or point out job openings to you?"[1] We used this question to consider the subjectively perceived roles of different groups in the process (see Figure 3 for the categories).

Some variables like age and gender are self-explanatory. For occupational characterizations, we have used the National Occupational

Classification (NOC) described in detail in Robinson and Wilkinson (1997). Employment status in 1996 and geographical mobility over the five-year period are interesting variables, since they have not been presented in previous Elliot Lake Tracking Study reports. They provide the essential background for much analysis of the effects of layoffs, and we present figures for them here. Of the retired, and the retired and disabled, all but one in each category were in the not-employed group. However, there were a number of disabled individuals who were working in new jobs or who were still at Rio. A brief breakdown is presented in Figure 1.

Figure 1. Occupational status at time of 1996 interview

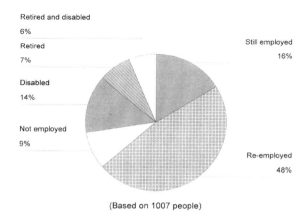

Retired and disabled
6%

Retired
7%

Disabled
14%

Not employed
9%

Still employed
16%

Re-employed
48%

(Based on 1007 people)

If we consider only those who were laid off and neither disabled nor retired in 1996, we have 56.4 percent of the sample. In this group, 14 percent were not employed.

Moving to find work is one alternative for workers that have been laid off and it is likely to affect a variety of variables. We expect the proportion moving to decline with time because those who were not laid off until 1996 had the most seniority and therefore tended to be older than those who had been previously laid off, and because those most willing to move tended to go early, leaving behind those most resistant or unable to move. Figure 2 shows that the number leaving the Elliot Lake and North Shore area was initially quite high. It was lower between 1992 and 1994 and increased again after 1994. Nonetheless, 62.7 percent were still living in the community in 1996.

Figure 2. Moving out of the Elliot Lake and North Shore area

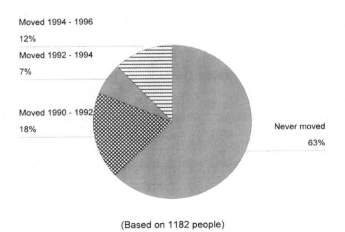

(Based on 1182 people)

Search

In 1996 the job seekers constituted 34 percent of those who had not yet been laid off, 17 percent of those who had new jobs, 80 percent of those without jobs who were neither disabled nor retired, 14 percent of the disabled only, 5 percent of the retired only, and none of those who were both retired and disabled. Clearly the non-employed who were not retired or disabled were the most engaged in job search. Those who were both retired and disabled searched less than did the others.

There is a noticeable and significant increase in the last year in search intensity for those who were still working at Rio Algom in 1996 compared to the previous five years. This is interesting because it was well known in the community that Stanleigh Mine would close in 1996, but few looked for alternative work until the closing date of the mine approached. In 1996, 34 percent were looking for work, compared to 18 percent in 1990, 4 percent in 1992, 2 percent in 1994, and 8 percent in 1995.

Age was also a very important factor in determining searching. There was an age-related trend where the younger workers were more involved in search than older workers for every time period. For those still at Rio, age was by far the most important variable determining searching.[2] It was also very important for those without work. Age was less related to search for those who had found a new job.

Women who had no job were more likely to be searching for work than were men with no job. On the other hand, for those still employed at Rio Algom, men were more likely to be searching than women. Among those who were still working at Rio Algom, married people, both men and women, were more likely to search than those not married. This accords with Leigh's (1995) finding that in general in the United States men married to full-time homemakers search more than other men. But among those not still working at Rio Algom, those who were not married searched most. Those workers in the sample with children under 18 in 1990 searched more in each period. Search levels appear to be highest initially for those with a degree. Over the long term, those without a high school diploma appear to have had successively lower search levels.

Among the 217 people searching for work, 94 were searching in both mining and other industries. We expected a large number of people to search in Elliot Lake only. While many (60) were indeed searching in Elliot Lake, only eight were searching exclusively in Elliot Lake. Those eight who were searching only in Elliot Lake were searching in non-mining industries only. Our initial expectation that there would have been a large number unwilling to move turned out to be quite wrong. The remaining 209 were searching outside Elliot Lake. In fact, most (157) were searching only elsewhere. Most (155) were searching outside mining.[3] The 62 people searching only in mining were searching only outside Elliot Lake.

We have used retirement and disability to separate out those who might not have searched or got help because they did not want to be in the labour market. For the most part, we found that those who were retired were not searching. However we found a number of disabled workers were either still working or had new jobs. Apparently, disability is a complicated status that may need further investigation.

Succour

A slight majority said they did not receive any help with job-search activities. For 48.1 percent of the 1,006 who were asked the question, however, job search was not a purely individual action. However, since these are retrospective reports, it is important to note that some individuals may have forgotten about the help they received. It is likely that more than half of our respondents did receive help in their job search.

For those who did have help, it is important to look at the network and the type of help. We asked about four types and nine sources of help. The numbers of individuals who received each of the four types of help are as follows: assistance with résumés (335), letters (265), forms (174), and information about job openings (204). The most frequent types of help were those given for résumés and letters.

The sources of help were: Community Adjustment Centre (175), friends (105), spouse/partner (including former) (93), Canada Employment Centre (71), other relatives (46), union (40), teacher/former teacher (22), books (3), Men's Centre/Women's Centre (2), and others (to be specified by respondent) (170).

There was some correlation between source and type. The formal public agencies had a much higher involvement in assistance with résumés, letters, and forms than they did with information about job openings. On the other hand, friends, spouses, and relatives helped more with information about job openings.

Figure 3 shows responses in the 1996 interview to the question: "Who provided the most help?" The most frequently mentioned were the Community Adjustment Centre and spouses.[4] The division is almost equal between the "public" sources of support (CAC, CEIC, men's and women's centres, union) and the "private" sources of support (spouse, other relatives, friends, teacher). Among the most frequently mentioned other sources were the Employee Adjustment Committee (43), a company or business other than Rio or Denison (25), Rio or Denison (22), college (20), and some branch of the government (16).

Figure 3. Who helped you most? (1996 interview)

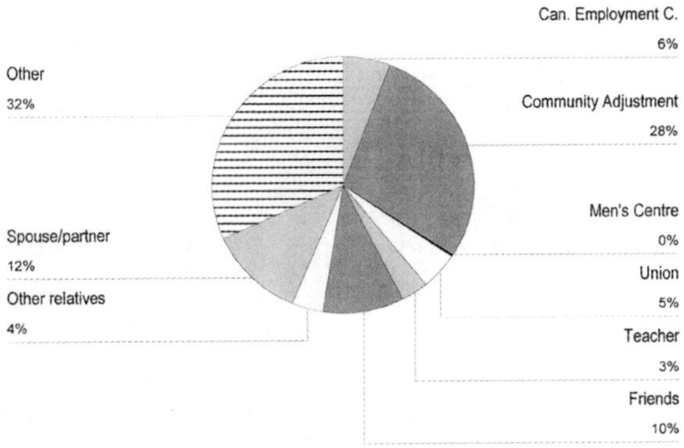

Can. Employment C.
6%

Other
32%

Community Adjustment
28%

Men's Centre
0%

Spouse/partner
12%

Union
5%

Other relatives
4%

Teacher
3%

Friends
10%

(Based on 472 people)

Success

In 1996, we asked who had found a job in the previous five years. Of those who answered, 72.9 percent or 597 had done so. Men were slightly less likely to have found re-employment than women. There was no difference between married and non-married individuals. However, age made a significant difference, as Figure 4 shows. Clearly, there is a different distribution for those who had found jobs and for those who had not. Generally the older one gets, the lower the probability of getting a job.

Figure 4. Successful job search in past five years, controlling for age

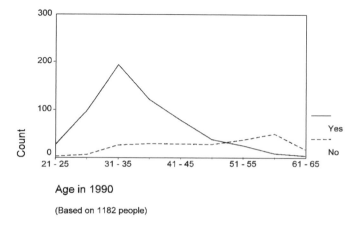

How did our respondents who had obtained jobs within the previous five years find out about the opening for their most recent job? The results are presented in Figure 5. The use of direct application was high, perhaps due to the combination of a low population density and the relative isolation of Elliot Lake. Nevertheless, 30 percent found work through personal ties. Friends were more likely to be sources of information than were relatives.

Figure 5. Sources of information for job obtained in past five years

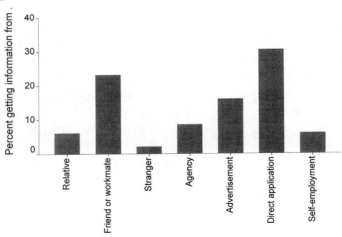

If it was a friend who had helped, we asked how they knew the friend. The friends who provided information about job openings were generally workmates; the workplace is an important source of contacts. Furthermore, as people age, workmates become more important as sources of job information. Employers (including supervisors) are more important for the middle-aged group than for the youngest group. Combining workmates and employers accounts for 66.7 percent of the information leading to jobs for the middle-aged group. If those who are laid off become isolated and have more difficulty connecting with these friends from work as time goes by, we should expect that people will have increased difficulty in finding jobs as time elapses following layoffs.

We asked who the relative was that helped, and because kinship terms tend to be gender-specific, we were able to estimate the gender balance among the relatives who helped. We found that most of the relatives who assisted were men. Perhaps these jobs are part of a male information network.

Those people in our sample who got information about a job from a friend or relative were asked how that friend or relative had found out about the job. The friend's or relative's own knowledge was itself based on work contacts in 66.1 percent of the cases. Not only are the friends who give information known from the workplace, as we have previously seen, but the knowledge which the friends have is also gained primarily through work relationships. We get information from a workmate who got information from their workplace. The workplace plays an important role in two separate steps in the information transfer process.

We had a particular interest in the question of whether jobs would be found through weak ties or strong ties. We measured tie strength by the frequency of contact. We asked our respondents how frequently they were seeing their relative or friend at the time they heard about the job from them. The exact question was: "Around the time when your friend/relative told you about this job, how much communication did you have in general with him/her? We were seeing each other: 1. pretty often 2. occasionally 3. seldom. If seldom, did you speak on the phone? 1. pretty often 2. occasionally 3. seldom." The question provides a five-point scale measuring the strength of the "tie." We find that 68.8 percent of the ties with relatives that led to jobs were strong ties in Granovetter's sense, while only 32.8 percent of productive ties with friends were strong. Help comes through strong ties with relatives and weak ties with friends.

Summary and Conclusions

There is no general "theory of job search." We have approached the issue by looking at three questions: who searches; the help, or succour, that searchers receive; and their success in finding work. In this final section we pull the three strands together. The picture of job search that emerges from our work is consistent with the results reported for other samples, but we have added important details that should be of value in shaping labour-market policy.

Our results broadly support Granovetter's weak ties hypothesis: friends predominate as the source of job contacts, and most of the friends are not seen very often. To this picture we add the essential observation that the friends providing job information are generally friends from employment. We also found that older workers rely more on acquaintances from employment. Our finding that jobs are found through friends has implications for job-search training. Job-search training should emphasize the importance for the search process of getting assistance from close relatives and the importance of informing occasional friends and soliciting information from them. Work contacts are a main resource and will decline over time, so it is best to use workplace contacts as soon as possible. Because work ties tend to weaken after a layoff, it should be suggested to workers before the layoff that they begin their job search as soon as possible, and without taking an interim vacation.

Providing support for personal networks might reduce job-search costs for many individuals. Mutual support is not a substitute for public agencies, however. The workers who get information about jobs from friends are relying on private information: by definition not everyone has access to information that is private. Young workers and women re-entering the labour market are among those who lack contacts from employment and will be forced to rely more on other sources of information.

Our data supports the view that public agencies should provide information and services, as Osberg suggested, to those who have not found work by directly approaching employers or through their own networks. It appears, therefore, that an important role of public employment agencies is to complement personal networks and provide support where these are insufficient.

Our work suggests that weak ties are used primarily for information while stronger ties, such as family or close friends, are relied on for more costly kinds of assistance. We also find that public employment agencies provide clerical and other time-consuming assistance similar to that provided by family and close friends.

One of the most important observations, in our view, is that local adjustment committees are cited as the most helpful in providing assistance in preparing for search and as the most common formal source of information. These organizations were community-based, with intense union participation, and they employed laid-off miners as counsellors. They exploited existing networks and operated as extensions of those existing networks, which explains both their success in working with the people in our sample and their relatively large informational role. We would argue that they provide a model for public employment agencies. They complement and reinforce existing networks; they have a strong, industry-specific component; and representatives of workers have a significant role in designing and delivering the services.

The role of the unions in the adjustment committees is significant, in our view. They provided the main mechanism for taking advantage of the contacts throughout the industry and of the private knowledge of workers. The lack of sector-wide unions may actually be a significant barrier to effective employment policy in an industry like mining, since it limits the institutional support for broad workplace-based networks.

We found that older workers and disabled workers were less likely to be re-employed than others. The organization of the mining industry is such that both older and injured workers tend to be discarded through layoffs. This is consistent with the findings of Yelin and Katz (1994) that, during periods of recession in the U.S., disabled workers were more likely to be laid off than healthier workers. In addition, disabled workers were not so likely to be rehired during subsequent periods of expansion. Therefore, their work prospects were linked more directly and profoundly to economic cycles than were those of other workers. This consequence is more severe in mining because mining has higher disability rates. Only legislation at the industry level or higher will prevent companies in a free labour market from refusing employment to potentially high cost or low productivity workers, even when the industry itself creates the disability and the health liabilities. In the absence of general legislation, programs to provide smoother transition to retirement should be supported.

We believe that the workers in our sample are typical of mining-industry workers in peripheral communities in terms of age, skill levels, and marital status. They may also resemble workers in other resource industries. To the extent that it is possible to generalize from a sample in a single industry, our work leads us to stress the importance of personal contacts in the job-search process and the role of public agencies as a complement to these private resources. Public employment policy should move towards investing in community resources and even lead unions to reinforce existing networks, which are often based on work association. At the same time, it is important to keep in mind that personal resources are unequally distributed. It has been the role of the public sector in Canada to support in their search for work those who are disadvantaged, whether by age, lack of experience, sex, location, or training. The need for these compensating services will not go away.

Our respondents have dealt with the problems arising from the layoffs with forbearance and fortitude. Even so, experiencing a layoff is highly stressful. It causes important problems for the individuals concerned, for other members of their households, and for the community they reside in. Providing more effective help is not charity; it is good social management. Our research suggests that the way to help people in the labour market may be through augmenting the social network they already have.

Notes

[1] We would like to thank Anne-Marie Mawhiney for suggesting this question, and for her recommendations about possible revisions to improve the paper.

[2] In the remainder of this paragraph, we present a general description of the results but space does not permit showing the tables from which the results were derived. These tables are available on request from the authors.

[3] However, our questions for the first three surveys allowed alphanumeric responses for searching outside mining and outside Elliot Lake. Further analysis would require these responses to be recoded. Nevertheless, we can

state that there was some decline in the number searching in mining over the 1990 to 1994 interval followed by a rise in 1996.

⁴ The large number of others was related to the fact that the question had a write-in section.

References

Devine, T. J., and N.M. Kiefer. (1991). *Empirical Labor Economics: The Search Approach.* New York: Oxford University Press.

Granovetter, M. S. (1974). *Getting a Job: A Study of Contacts and Careers.* Cambridge, MA: Harvard University Press. See also the second edition, Chicago: University of Chicago Press, 1995.

Granovetter, M. (1995). *Getting a Job: A Study of Contacts and Careers* (2nd ed.). Chicago: University of Chicago Press.

Grieco, M. (1987). *Keeping It in the Family: Social Networks and Employment Chance.* London: Tavistock.

Grayson, J. P. (1985). "The closure of a factory and its impact on health," *International Journal of Health Services* 15, 1: 69–93.

Holzer, H. J. (1988). "Search method use by unemployed youth," *Journal of Labour Economics* 6: 1–20.

Krahn, H., and G. Lowe. (1988). *Work, Industry and Canadian Society.* Scarborough: Nelson.

Leigh, D. (1995). *Assisting Workers Displaced by Structural Change: An International Perspective.* Kalamazoo, MI: W.E.Upjohn Institute.

Lucas, R.A. (1971). *Minetown, Milltown, Railtown: Life in Canadian Communities of Single Industry.* Toronto: University of Toronto Press.

Osberg, L. (1993). "Fishing in different pools: job-search strategies and job-finding success in Canada in the early 1980s," *Journal of Labour Economics* 11, 2: 348–86.

U.S. Department of Labour. (1995). *What's Working (and What's Not): A Summary of Research on the Economic Impacts of Employment and Training Programs.* Washington DC: Office of the Chief Economist.

Wellman, Barry, and David B. Tindall. (1993). "How telephone networks connect social networks," *Progress in Communication Sciences*, 12: 63–93.

Wellman, Barry and Scot Wortley. (1990). "Different strokes from different folks: community ties and social support," *American Journal of Sociology* 96 (November): 558–88.

Wellman, B., R.Y. Wong, D. Tindall, and N. Nazer. (1995). *A Decade of Network Change: Turnover, Persistence and Stability in Personal Communities.* Toronto: Centre for Urban and Community Studies, University of Toronto.

Wilkinson, D., P. Suschnigg, D. Robinson, and D. Leadbeater. (1993). *Elliot Lake Tracking Study Phase Two: 1992, Interim Community Report.* Sudbury, ON: INORD, Laurentian University.

Yelin, E.H., and P.P. Katz. (1994). "Labor force trends of persons with and without disabilities," *Monthly Labor Review* 117, 10: 36–42.

Chapter 7
Women's Deployment with Husbands' Unemployment: Women's Labour in the Balance[1]

Elaine Porter

The types of work that women do within and outside of households share several characteristics; both tend to be socially significant but are either unpaid or undervalued. The unpaid work that takes place within the household consists of housework, which is geared towards physical maintenance of the household members. Childcare activities, the other major component of unpaid household work, is an aspect of caring labour, which contributes to social reproduction. However, it should be taken into consideration that women's caregiving extends beyond child-rearing to provision of social support for partners, other relatives, and in the broadest terms, it includes the immense variety of volunteer community and organizational work in which women also engage (Baines, Evans, and Neysmith 1991).

Women's reproductive labour is just beginning to attract the research and theoretical attention it deserves. Its characteristics of being unpaid and privatized in the household have meant that its significance for the larger economy has been generally overlooked. Because women perform such labour out of social responsibility and find satisfaction in providing it, reproductive labour is often not considered as work. Nevertheless, as Folbre (1994) has cogently argued, one of the consequences of undervaluing women's labour is to put in jeopardy its continued existence because there is very little consideration given to the support that is needed so that women can continue to perform these important activities. Apart from the fact that women often do not receive direct economic benefits from the fruits of their household and caring labour, they may also suffer from the stress and poor health that a disproportionately heavy workload brings.

This chapter describes the parameters of women's work within and outside the household in the wake of massive layoffs in Elliot Lake. It also examines the level and composition of work through the lens of the life-course approach, which takes into account the demands of family responsibilities, as well as the ways in which these might interact with wives' "mopping-up" tasks after their husbands' layoffs.

One facet of the life-course approach is to acknowledge that each stage of the family life cycle has its own set of demands. With children of preschool years in the household, women are somewhat less likely to work for pay outside the home than when their children are older. Nonetheless, many women still work during this time period. Some do so on a part-time basis to accommodate the needs of their children, or because of the lack of available daycare, or both. School-age children also require parental care that supports their children's growing involvement in social organizations outside the family (Bronfenbrenner 1979).

Much has been written of the caregiving demands on women with elderly parents (Brubaker 1990). The term "sandwich generation" refers to parents whose children are in their teen years and whose parents are at the same time reaching older age and needing more care. These are the women whose "kin work" adds caring labour from two generations.

In this chapter, the family life cycle is used as a heuristic device, in the context of the life- course approach, to set out the kinds of tasks that may structure women's lives through child-rearing. A family's stage in the life cycle is measured in terms of whether there are children in the family, and the age of the youngest child regardless of the ages of older children, so that the defining feature of each category is for the families with children to have at least one child of a specific age. Various life-cycle stages also capture other kinds of social behaviour and attitudes, given that wives from certain birth cohorts fall into specific family life-cycle categories. Wives were grouped by age into cohorts because it is likely that the messages each cohort received about paid work and women's roles in family life varied from one time period to another. For example, women from the baby-boom cohort (1947–1967) were exposed to conflicting messages about women's paid work outside the home. Women born before or during World War II were more consistently exposed to standards that emphasized women's role within the family and the breadwinner responsibilities of men, while younger women (in the post-baby-boom era, born after 1967) were influenced by the women's movement and were more likely encouraged to consider paid work as a normal life-course event.

The life-course perspective requires that we take into consideration the effects of the larger social context to which families are responding. The kinds of changes taking place in Elliot Lake are not confined to this community but are part of economic restructuring, in response to global competition.

In the terminology of the life-course approach, unemployment caused by mass layoffs results in a disorderly transition from one part of the life cycle to the next (Rindfuss, Swicegood, and Rosenfeld 1987). Adaptation to this unanticipated, untimely, and non-normative transition is significantly different from adjusting to normative family transitions such as marriage and childbearing. Like another disorderly family transition, divorce, unemployment calls into question the taken-for-granted assumptions underlying a host of social relationships inside and outside the family. By their nature, all social status transitions — both normative and non-normative events — strain the boundaries of existing behaviour and social definitions. A disorderly transition can require even more changes when it is coupled with other normative life-course transitions.

Women's responses to layoffs have been characterized in most economic models in terms of income replacement (the "added worker effect"), although the wife's income is usually not at the same level as the husband's lost income. Many of the demands on the wife's time and energies created by her husband's unemployment, however, occur within the household and within the marital relationship. Erickson (1993) advocates that "emotion work" be considered a component of family work. The term "emotion work" recognizes that provision of support requires skills and effort. This aspect of women's unpaid work may be expanded, given the range of feelings that husbands experience with unemployment. According to the findings of Conger and Elder (1994), economic pressure led to higher levels of depression, which then were, in turn, associated with increased hostility. Both of these factors affected wives' marital quality (the quality of their experience of the marriage) . However, wives' irritability lowered their husbands' marital quality more strongly than vice versa, an indication that wives may tolerate and attempt to mollify their husbands' emotions.

The Study

The Elliot Lake Spousal Project (ELSP) interviewed 525 women who were in marital or common-law relationships with participants in the Elliot Lake Tracking Study, a longitudinal study of former mine workers in Elliot Lake.

The 1995 ELSP database is the source for most of the analyses in this paper.[2] Information from focus groups and eight in-depth qualitative interviews have also been used to determine the different types of work included in the overall measure of the workload. The broadest definition of "work" has been used to cover all work, paid and unpaid, inside and outside the household for a seven-day period.

Women were asked to estimate the hours they give to a variety of activities and tasks both within and outside the household. In questions directed at obtaining time estimates on a monthly basis, the hours were divided by 4 to approximate a weekly schedule. The following components constitute the weekly workload that is examined here:

- household tasks, including childcare
- paid work, including commuting time
- providing care to elderly relatives or friends outside of the household
- babysitting for a relative or a friend without pay
- involvement in community-based organizations
- non-specific volunteering in the community,[3] and
- irregular work involving various types of unpaid economic exchanges.

Household tasks consisted of yardwork and gardening; house repair, renovation, and maintenance; car and appliance repair; sewing and mending; preserving food; cooking; cleaning up after meals; laundry; and vacuuming and house cleaning.[4] The childcare tasks were grouped into two categories: taking children places, and other childcare. The total amount of time spent in working with community organizations was the sum of hours per month given to religious, ethnic, union, political, charitable, women's, sports, service, or other types of organizations. In the context of a series of questions about irregular work, the women were asked about the amount of time they gave to volunteer work in the community.

The total workload ranged from 9 hours per week to 234, both of which seem implausible. The upper levels can be accounted for somewhat by the fact that many activities overlap, but they were measured and counted as if they were discrete. This tendency towards multi-tasking is especially true for childcare.[5] The lower limit may refer to a woman whose partner or someone else does much of the work because the woman is retired or incapacitated. Because of some imprecision in measurement when retrospective accounts of time use are reported, the workload totals were coded into four categories to constitute an ordinal-level variable.

The mid-point of the highest workload category, 137.1 hours, would allow for four hours of sleep per night. The workload hours were compared with the number of hours of sleep per night that each woman reported. The mean number of hours of sleep per night reported by the overall sample was 7.3 hours. Dividing the number of hours into two categories for those reporting above and below seven hours per night and comparing workload totals across these two categories did not show significant differences, although the trend was in the direction of less sleep per night for those with the highest workloads. About 30 percent of those with the highest workloads averaged less than seven hours per night compared with only 20 percent of those with the lowest levels of overall workload.

Table 1 shows that the higher levels of workload tended to be concentrated among women with preschool children. Women with only adult children were most likely to have workloads in the lowest range (9 to 51 hours). Women without children had workload hours falling into the intermediate categories. Cross-tabulations were run on the relationship between the life cycle categories and the likely covariates of these family life-cycle stages: the woman's birth cohort, the number of dependents living in the household, and the total number of children. As expected, all are significantly related to family life-cycle stage, so the

Table 1. Distribution of total workload hours across family life-cycle stages

	FAMILY LIFE-CYCLE STAGE				
TOTAL WORKLOAD HOURS	No children $n=18$ %	Preschool children $n=83$ %	School-age children $n=129$ %	Teenage children $n=126$ %	Adult children $n=129$ %
9.00–51.00	11.1	16.9	18.0	23.8	39.1
51.01–71.50	44.4	21.7	22.7	27.8	23.4
71.51–96.25	33.3	21.7	28.1	23.0	25.8
96.21–233.55	11.1	39.8	31.3	25.4	11.6

Chi square = 42.36, $p \leq .01$

effects of these variables were also reflected in the family life cycle categories. The women in the preschool and school-age children stage — those with the highest workloads — are almost exclusively from the baby-boom cohort. The mean age of these women was 43. Only 4 percent of the women were between 21 and 29 in 1995 and 5 percent were 60 or older. There was a tendency (significant at the .01 level in a chi square analysis) for more women without children to disagree (59 percent) or strongly disagree (35 percent) that wives should stay home and tend to the family while husbands engage in paid work outside the home. Women in the preschool children stage were the next highest group to reject this breadwinner ideology (62 percent of whom disagreed or strongly disagreed), while the group with only adult children were the least likely to reject this ideology (49 percent).

Husbands' employment status was classified across the 1990–96 time period. Husbands were classified as retired if they had retired any time within that six-year interval. The rest of the husbands were grouped according to whether they worked more or less continuously throughout this period, alternated between work and periods of unemployment, or were unemployed throughout the period (Mawhiney 1997). There were 21 cases in this last category, but very few of these workers met the criteria for work availability under the standard definition of unemployment since 81 percent of them were receiving or applying for disability compensation. Other data from the survey indicate that this categorization corresponds to the degree of economic difficulty experienced by each group. Of those women with husbands who had retired by 1996, 34 percent indicated in 1996 that they had "quite a bit" or "a great deal" of difficulty paying bills. In contrast, 73 percent of those with husbands who had remained unemployed and 47 percent of those with husbands who had intermittent unemployment said they were in that situation.

The analyses of wives' workload hours according to husbands' employment status since 1990 showed unemployment to be significantly related to heavier workloads for wives (see Table 2). Women with the lightest overall workload had husbands who retired between 1990 and 1996. The percentage of those whose husbands were continuously employed (26.2 percent) and the percentage of those whose husbands

Table 2. Distribution of workload hours by husbands' employment status

	HUSBANDS' EMPLOYMENT STATUS			
TOTAL WORKLOAD HOURS	Retired $n=68$ %	Continuously employed $n=165$ %	Unemployment spells $n=222$ %	Continuously unemployed $n=20$ %
9.00–51.00	42.6	25.6	19.5	15.0
51.01–71.50	23.5	23.2	26.2	25.0
71.51–96.25	23.5	25.0	26.2	25.0
96.26–233.55	10.3	26.2	28.1	35.0

Chi square = 19.8, df = 9, $p \leq .05$

were intermittently unemployed over the entire period (28.1 percent) were quite similar for the highest workload category. The highest percentage of those with the heaviest workload level fell to those women whose husbands were continuously unemployed (35 percent).

Both employment status and family life-cycle stage are associated with variations in the overall workload, and with each other. Not surprisingly, Table 3 shows that the retired group was heavily overrepresented among those with adult children. Women with teenage children were about as likely to have husbands who were employed intermittently (48.9 percent) as to have husbands continuously employed (43.5 percent). For those with preschool and school-age children, the balance was tipped towards having husbands with intermittent employment (63.3 percent and 51.1 percent respectively). Women without children were also disproportionately likely to have husbands with intermittent employment (55.6 percent).

Table 3. Husbands' employment status by family life-cycle stage

		FAMILY LIFE-CYCLE STAGE				
HUSBANDS' EMPLOYMENT STATUS		No children $n=18$	Preschool children $n=90$	School-age children $n=137$	Teenage children $n=131$	Adult children $n=139$
	n	%	%	%	%	%
Retired	74	5.6	5.6	5.6	2.3	41.0
Continuously employed	184	38.9	26.6	38.7	43.5	31.7
Unemployment spells	236	55.6	63.3	51.1	48.9	25.2
Continuously unemployed	21	0	5.6	4.4	5.3	2.2

Chi square $= 124.0$, $df = 12$, $p \leq .01$

In order to show the distribution of the workload components across husbands' employment status and family life cycle categories, the hours given to each major workload component were calculated as a percentage of the overall load. A table was produced for each workload component to determine whether certain components of the workload were more heavily distributed in one of the family life-cycle stages or one of the categories of the husbands' employment status. The results presented in Tables 4 and 5 are composed of data analysis results from the separate tables for each workload component. This composite table shows the percentages of women who fell into the fourth quartile of the distribution, that is, the upper 25 percent of the distribution for each of the workload components. The second column in each of Tables 4 and 5 shows the cutoff points for the upper end of the workload distribution indicating how much weight each component generally contributed to the overall workload. Percentages constitute a preliminary method for comparisons, which has the advantage of not altering the underlying distributions through pruning of outliers.

Table 4 shows that a greater percentage of women in the adult child stage (34.3 percent) fell into the top end of the distribution for household tasks. As expected, those with school-age and preschool children spent much more of their time in childcare than those in any other group. Although fewer women with pre-teen children fell into the high household workload category, their household work still adds up to an average of 78 hours per week for women with preschool children and 86 for those with school-age children. Another analysis (not shown) was performed, which separated the overall household work into childcare, traditional women's housework (cooking and cleaning), traditional men's housework (repairs), and housework oriented towards replacing market goods with home production (for example, canning). This further analysis showed that women with adult children were more heavily

Table 4. The top quartile of the distribution for each of the workload components by family life-cycle stages

		FAMILY LIFE-CYCLE STAGE				
% IN THE TOP 25% OF DISTRIBUTION	% of overall time	No children	Preschool children	School-age children	Teenage children	Adult children
		n†=18 %	n=83-87 %	n=129-132 %	n=125-132 %	n=129-139 %
Household work **	74.4	16.7	14.3	16.7	24.4	34.3
Childcare**	13.7	–	50.5	34.8	15.6	7.7
Extra-household						
Paid work**	47.0	66.7	14.3	20.3	25.2	24.5
Community organization	3.5	27.0	15.4	21.0	23.7	30.8
Community volunteering	1.0	16.7	17.6	33.3	24.4	21.0
Babysitting *	1.0	22.2	3.9	25.4	16.3	24.5
Elder care	.3	16.7	20.9	18.1	23.7	38.7
Irregular work††	.4	22.2	20.9	13.8	14.1	9.1

*Significant at p œ .05, ** Significant at p œ .01
†As this is a composite table, column n's will vary from one component to another because of missing values.
††Only 14.4 percent of the sample engaged in this activity, so 85.6 percent was the cut point.

represented in all areas of housework other than childcare, especially in the areas that have traditionally been women's work.

Of all work activities outside the household, paid work stands out as the most prevalent since it constituted almost half the workload for 25 percent of the sample. About 60 percent of the women were in paid employment in 1995; 54 percent of them were working on a part-time basis. Table 4 shows that a higher percentage of women who were childless (66.7 percent) were in paid employment and those with preschool children were the least active (14.3 percent). Those with no children worked 45 hours on average compared to 19 hours for those with preschool children.

All extra-household work in the community showed relatively lower levels of involvement than household work and paid employment. Only non-specified volunteer work showed significant differences across life-cycle stages. Women with school-age children were most heavily involved in this; 33 percent of them were in the upper 25 percent of the distribution. Other areas of extra-household work showed differences that can be interpreted, although the overall relationships in the table from which they came did not attain significance. For example, those with adult children were more likely to have somewhat higher percentages of their workloads dedicated to community organizations (30.8 percent) and to provision of elder care (28.7 percent). Those with preschool children (31.9 percent) were more heavily involved in providing childcare for others (babysitting).

When husbands' employment status was examined in relation to workload categories (see Table 5), the greatest concentration of higher percentages of housework hours was among women whose husbands retired (41.9 percent); these women were also more likely to have adult children. Those women with husbands unemployed across the entire six years did disproportionately higher shares of housework (28.6 percent) than those whose husbands were employed continuously (21.2 percent) or were intermittently unemployed (18.2 percent). Most notable in the area of childcare was the higher percentage of women with husbands intermittently employed whose childcare was over 14 percent of their workload.

Table 5 shows that the distribution of paid work among spouses was not found to be significantly related to husbands' employment status. Those with retired husbands or husbands continuously unemployed were somewhat less involved in the labour force. Those with retired husbands were more likely to be involved in work (unpaid) in various types of community-based organizations (35.1 percent). They were also more involved in providing elder care (33.8 percent). In contrast, those with husbands continuously unemployed were most active in unpaid work in non-specific volunteering activities in the community (38.1 percent), and a larger percentage of them provided babysitting informally for others (47.6 percent). Exchanges of services and other types of non-monetary activities were not significantly different across groups but were somewhat more predominant among those with continuously unemployed husbands (23.8 percent).

So far, the analyses show that both family life-cycle stage and husbands' employment status have effects on women's overall workload (Tables 1 and 2). Having at least one child of preschool age and a husband who was not continuously employed during the entire six-year period intensified the workload for each of the 57 women who were in this situation. The higher percentage of women with husbands intermittently unemployed who had heavier loads of childcare reflect their greater representation in the preschool stage of the family life cycle (Table 3).

Table 5. The top quartile of the distribution for each of the workload components by husbands' employment status

% IN THE TOP 25% OF DISTRIBUTION	% of overall time	HUSBANDS' EMPLOYMENT STATUS			
		Retired	Continuously employed	Unemployment spells	Continuously unemployed
		n†=68–73 %	n=165–175 %	n=221–229 %	n=20–21 %
Household work**	74.4	41.9	21.2	18.2	28.6
Childcare**	13.7	9.5	21.7	30.5	19.0
Extra-Household					
Paid work	47.0	17.6	22.3	25.8	19.0
Community organization	3.5	35.1	23.9	20.8	14.3
Community volunteering*	1.0	23.0	29.3	19.5	38.1
Babysitting*	1.0	21.6	20.7	25.0	47.6
Elder care	.3	33.8	19.0	21.6	23.8
Irregular work	.4	6.8	15.2	14.8	23.8

*Significant at p œ .05, **Significant at p œ .01
†As this is a composite table, column n's will vary from one component to another because of missing values.

To this backdrop of weekly work, we next add consideration of the additional burdens that come with unemployment. These variables were not measured in terms of time but on the basis of whether or not the women interviewed had performed the task. Emotion work tasks included understanding their husbands' moods, giving encouragement in looking for work, giving them help to feel good about themselves, and encouraging them to talk to others for support and work ideas. Each of these types of help was included if it had been given either intermittently or continuously after the layoff. Job-search tasks for either husbands or wives included reading ads, sending out résumés, talking to friends or relatives, speaking to previous employers or business acquaintances, and reading a book or article about getting a job.

Table 6 shows that the women with preschool children did more emotion work (17.6 percent), followed by those with teenage children (14.8 percent). Both women with preschool children and those with school-age children were involved in giving the most types of help to their husbands for job searching. Those with adult children were the least involved. The levels of involvement of women in their own job-search activities across family life-cycle categories roughly paralleled their involvement in the job-search tasks they performed for their husbands, except that more women in the preschool children stage were engaged in their own job search (15.4 percent) than they were in their husbands' job search (2.5 percent).

Table 6. Distribution of two or more types of additional work across family life-cycle stages

| ADDITIONAL WORK 2+Types | FAMILY LIFE-CYCLE STAGE | | | | |
	No children $n=18$ %	Preschool children $n=89-91$ %	School-age children $n=134-138$ %	Teenage children $n=134-135$ %	Adult children $n=139-143$ %
Emotion work*	–	17.6	8.0	14.8	7.0
Job search for husbands**	5.6	2.5	22.4	14.2	7.9
Job search for themselves**	5.6	15.4	25.5	17.2	5.0

*Significant at $p \le .05$, **Significant at $p \le .01$

The pattern of findings for the husbands' employment status in Table 7 shows that wives were most heavily engaged in emotion work when their husbands were unemployed, and least engaged in job search for their husbands or themselves when their husbands had been continuously unemployed or retired. Women whose husbands were intermittently employed showed relatively high levels of participation in emotion work coupled with the highest levels of engagement in job search for themselves and their husbands.

Table 7. Distribution of additional work with unemployment, by husbands' employment status

ADDITIONAL WORK 2+ Types	HUSBANDS' EMPLOYMENT STATUS			
	Retired $n=72-74$ %	Continuously employed $n=180-184$ %	Unemployment spells $n=232-236$ %	Continuously unemployed $n=21$ %
Emotion work**	4.1	7.6	15.3	19.0
Job search for husbands**	6.9	12.8	22.4	4.8
Job search for themselves**	4.1	14.8	20.9	4.8

**Significant at $p \leq .01$

The types of women's work associated with re-employment added to already very heavy loads. The bulk of emotion work fell to women with preschool children and aid in job searching to those with school-age children. Such heavy workloads carry a set of costs to women who absorbed them. In a tabular analyis (not shown here), 75 percent of women with preschool children and 77 percent of those with school-age children reported getting one hour or less of leisure time per day. This compares with only 50 percent of women without children and with adult children reporting only one hour or less of time available to themselves per day.

One theme that emerged in the qualitative analyses was the extent to which women's increased workload reduced their involvement with their social support groups.[6] One woman stated her concerns in the following way: "You get so overwhelmed with everything that you just have to stay focused all the time on something. But you lose your social skills, and I did, and I dropped my friends." Another participant in a focus group described the consequences of the heavy emotional and physical workload that she bore while her husband was commuting for weeks at a time to a job out of the community: "So that's all we focused on for so long — it was just having the family survive.... It was like we don't need anybody else; we've got to take care of our own, and we focused on family, that was it. You forgot everything else." Several wives indicated that their social support came from their job, rather than from friends and family, because they had no time to socialize with friends.

Stress and lack of sources of support can lead to both mental and physical problems (Gove and Geerken 1977). A comparison of the self-reported health status by overall workload shows that those with the higher workloads were significantly less likely to say that their health was adequate; only 59 percent of those with heaviest loads (96 hours and above) rated their health as adequate compared to 78 percent of those with the lightest overall loads. The rest of the women with the highest workload overall were almost evenly divided between those with the best level of health and those with the worst.

One further analysis sheds light on the extent to which the women's workload situation exacted costs. We have data on whether or not women would have liked to be involved in paid work, and this was compared with their work status at the time of the interview. The question asked women if they would want to have a job outside the home if they did not have to work for financial reasons. Those in the preschool children stage experienced the most congruence between their desires and actual work situation (50 percent), but congruence was much less for women in the school-age children family life-cycle stage (37 percent) and the teenage stage (40 percent). Women in the latter groups wanted to work but were not working (51 percent of the school-age child family life cycle group and 48 percent of the teenage children group). Comparing congruence with husbands' employment status shows that women with continuously employed husbands exhibited the greatest congruence (59 percent) and those with continuously unemployed husbands the least (39 percent). A higher percentage of women with continuously unemployed husbands (50 percent) wanted to work than either those with discontinuously employed husbands (44 percent) or those with husbands continuously employed (43 percent). Lack of congruence in either direction between the desire for and actual paid work situations can be interpreted as an indicator of stress and lack of empowerment as well as lowered opportunities for income generation.

Discussion and Conclusions

The principal objective of this study was to show the significance of all the paid and unpaid work that women perform, in order that we also understand the many valuable, but often unrecognized, contributions that women make to their families and their communities, particularly after an unanticipated event like a mass layoff. Although the measure of workload used in this study was more comprehensive than most (Mederer 1993),[7] there are many aspects of women's work that are still not captured. For example, one woman in the qualitative phase of the study mentioned that she worked at several part-time jobs in order to help finance a number of her husband's business ventures. Since he was unable to obtain a loan from banks in the community, she invested her income. Moreover, she indicated that she gave unpaid work time to her husband's latest business effort. Another example is the careful budgeting that many wives perform. Women also continued their education or took training courses in addition to their other responsibilities.[8]

The work that women do is not without its rewards, and women in the qualitative study acknowledged that they also received emotional support from their husbands. But it is still work in that it requires effort and contributes value to the well-being of others. It is of social concern when costs of supporting others' well-being is at the risk of the women's own well-being. Women with the heaviest workloads were least likely to report average levels of health; about equal proportions felt themselves to be either the healthiest or the least healthy.

The findings in this study confirm that parenting preschool children contributes to the heaviest burden of work among all categories of women analyzed. The analyses in Table 4 showed that the distribution in the proportions of women's paid and unpaid work corresponded to child-rearing demands. Those without children or with older children (teenage or adult family life-cycle stages) were more likely to be in the labour force, while those with preschool children had the heavier caregiving workload inside the household.

Women whose husbands were unemployed over the entire six-year period were somewhat less likely to be in paid employment, more likely to be involved in unspecified volunteer work in the community (not tied to organizations), and most involved in the emotional support of their husbands. They also helped out others by giving unpaid childcare. This profile indicates that the somewhat lower level of involvement of these women in the paid labour force is balanced by their unremunerated work. The time constraints resulting from all of this unpaid work might explain their comparatively lower level of involvement in their own or their husbands' job-search activities. Alternatively, if we were to hypothesize a causal relationship, we could say that a husband without his wife's assistance in his job-search activities is less likely to be successful in finding a job. Women in these circumstances were doubly vulnerable to the negative effects of their husbands' continued unemployment both because they lost their husbands' income and because they had no access to income of their own despite the contributions that they made to others through caregiving work. They carried the heaviest overall burden of work and had husbands who were physically incapacitated and perhaps more in need of care themselves than they were in a position to lessen their wives' workload.

Women whose husbands were not continuously employed throughout the period had, understandably, the heaviest workload in the area of job-search assistance for their husbands. They also tended to be involved in raising preschool children or to have no children at all. The workload profile of those with husbands intermittently employed is likely a reflection of their placement into two family life-cycle groupings. It may be that the higher percentage of women who are working are those with no children, while the greater proportion of those who are offering childcare to others have preschool children. The policy implications would then be twofold for this group. It is likely that women without children who are as heavily involved in their own job search as they are in the job search of their husbands need greater access to well-paying jobs. Women with preschool children require access to daycare and respite care to reduce their overall workload and make paid work a possibility. Since this group of women is already involved in providing childcare to others (as is the group with continuously unemployed husbands), they would benefit from childcare subsidies that would allow them to be paid by the parents of the children for whom they provide care (Eichler 1997).

The results of this study have implications for the health of the community as well as for individual and family functioning. Community organizational work was done most heavily by those with no children and those with adult children. Women whose husbands were continuously unemployed gave the least amount of time to volunteer organizations of all groupings based on husbands' employment status. Women with continuously unemployed husbands appear to have been more involved in community volunteer work that was not attached to organizations. Given their involvement in childcare activities, they may have been helping with school and recreational activities that were not captured in the survey questions.

It is in the intersect between the differential demands of the family life cycle and unemployment that the consequences of workload weights for community involvement are made visible. For women whose husbands were not employed steadily throughout the time period, it may have been the combination of the husbands' intermittent employment and having preschool children that reduced the involvement of these women in community organizations. Somewhat higher levels of organizational community involvement were found for women whose husbands were continuously employed than for those whose husbands were unemployed (either long term or intermittently), and the latter group had a somewhat higher percentage of families in the child-rearing family life-cycle stages. While some of these community activities may also represent time associated with children's activities on the part of those women with continuously employed husbands, they could also represent greater involvement in the organizational structure of the community. If women with unemployed husbands do, in fact, participate less in the organizational life of the community, this could mean that the voices of those most needing to be heard are the most silent. Their workload profiles show that they need supportive services such as childcare to enable them to participate in both paid and unpaid community work and that they could benefit from recognition in the form of some financial remuneration for the community and kinship-based contributions they already make on an informal basis.

Notes

[1] The data used in this study are part of a larger longitudinal study, the Elliot Lake Tracking and Adjustment Study, funded by Human Resources Development Canada. The members of the research team and administrative staff have contributed in innumerable ways to the construction of the database used in this report. I wish to acknowledge the work of Monica Neitzert and Anne-Marie Mawhiney, the helpful comments of Derek Wilkinson and Anne-Marie Mawhiney, and the support of Marge Reitsma-Street for this project. Special thanks are due to the hardworking women who did the work reported in this study and used their scarce time to respond to our questions.

[2] The only exception is the emotion work variable that was computed based on the 1996 data. The rest of the data analyzed were from the 1995 study, in order to keep constant the time frame. There might be misspecification of categories of husbands' employment status owing to differences in time periods for calculation. Some of the husbands classified as continuously employed might have been laid off in the 1996 layoff with the closing of Stanleigh Mine, but they had been employed for the bulk of the six previous years.

[3] There may be some overlap in the hours reported for non-specific volunteer work in the community and the hours counted across organizations. However, the organizational types mentioned did not cover school-related activities or activities for children. In order not to bias either measure of community-based work but to capture all the time that might be involved, the two community volunteer work measures are kept separate.

[4] The overall time spent on housework does not here include shopping because this was not measured in the 1995 survey. According to Harvey, Marshall, and Frederick (1991), Canadian women over the age of 15 in 1986 devoted an average of seven hours per week to shopping and service

activities (including travel time). Inclusion of these activities would only add to an already long work week.

[6] It is also difficult to assess what constitutes childcare hours when the question asks for total hours because much of childcare involves indirect supervision and some of our respondents gave a standard reply of 14 hours per day, all their children's waking hours.

[6] Quantitative data on this aspect are under construction.

[7] The one exception is the exclusion of shopping.

[8] This variable has not been fully cleaned and prepared for data analysis at the time of this writing.

References

Baines, Carol T., Patricia M. Evans, and Sheila M. Neysmith. (1991). *Women's Caring.* Toronto: McClelland and Stewart.

Bronfenbrenner, Urie. (1979). *The Ecology of Human Development: Experiments by Nature and Design.* Cambridge, MA: Harvard University Press.

Brubaker, T. (1990). "Families in later life: a burgeoning research area," *Journal of Marriage and the Family* 52: 959–81.

Conger, Rand, and Glen Elder Jr. (1994). *Families in Troubled Times: Adapting to Change in Rural America.* New York: Aldine de Gruyter.

Eichler, Margrit. (1997). *Family Shifts: Families, Policies and Gender Equality.* Toronto: Oxford University Press.

Erickson, R. (1993). "Reconceptualizing family work: the effect of emotion work on perceptions of marital quality," *Journal of Marriage and the Family* 55: 888–900.

Folbre, N. (1994). *Who Pays for the Kids? Gender and the Structures of Constraint.* New York: Routledge.

Gove, W. S. and M. Geerken. (1977). "The effects of children and employment on the mental health of men and women," *Social Forces* 51: 34–44.

Harvey, A.S., K. Marshall, and Judith Frederick. (1991). *Where Does Time Go?* General Social Survey Analysis Series. Ottawa: Statistics Canada.

Mawhiney, Anne-Marie. (1997). *Report on the Social Consequences of Mass Layoffs: Miners and Their Families Seeking Help in Elliot Lake.* ELTAS Report Series #1R2. Sudbury, ON: INORD, Laurentian University.

Mederer, H. (1993). "Division of labor in two-earner homes: task accomplishment versus household management as critical variables in perceptions about family work," *Journal of Marriage and the Family* 55: 133–45.

Rindfuss, R., C. Swicegood, and F. Rosenfeld. (1987). "Disorder in the life course: how common and does it matter?" *American Sociological Review* 52: 785–801.

Chapter 8
Where Are the Miners Going?
Occupational Mobility in Elliot Lake[1]
David Robinson and Derek Wilkinson

Permanent layoffs are a feature of today's Canadian labour market. Because of the enormous diversity in workers and jobs, there is a need for industry-specific and region-specific studies of the adjustment process. This chapter presents descriptive data on the short-run occupational and geographical mobility of a set of workers displaced from Elliot Lake, a single-industry mining town in Northern Ontario. Occupational mobility is examined in a framework provided by the 1991 National Occupational Classification (NOC).

Although the population we examine originates in a narrow occupational and geographic niche, the experiences of this group can shed some light on a number of intersecting issues of interest to other situations, as well. Prominent among them are the decline of single-industry towns, the exit from declining primary industries, and the prospects of prime age workers in declining regions and industries. Although only 5 percent of the workforce was female, our data provides interesting evidence on the degree of gender integration achieved in this part of the mining industry, and on whether women's gains are maintained when production declines.

Workers displaced in mining are affected by a number of major trends. Primary sector jobs and traditional production jobs in general make up a decreasing part of the economy. Employment in Canadian metal mines declined from 58,591 in 1961 to 48,284 in 1990, when our study began, and an estimated 6,000 additional jobs in metal mining disappeared between 1990 and 1992. Studies from the U.S. show that about half of all displaced workers do not return to the same broad industry and occupational group (Horvath 1987). For an industry shedding workers the percentage should be considerably higher. Educational requirements are rising in these sectors, as in others, and since substantial numbers of workers in these industries are relatively uneducated, both re-entry and entry to occupations offering comparable income may be difficult.

Shifts in the composition of the labour force may also work to decrease the re-employment prospects of the group we are studying. Rising participation rates have pushed up unemployment even as total employment has risen, and rising expectations about educational attainment has increased competition. As a result, displaced workers in the group we are considering are at risk of slipping into long-duration unemployment or chronic underemployment.

Furthermore, the problems for job seekers are intensified when mass layoffs occur in a single-industry town. The local job markets may be swamped by the layoffs, and displaced workers may face increased pressure to change their occupation or to move. The Elliot Lake Tracking Study, begun in 1990, was intended to throw light on labour adjustment in a specific corner of the market. We begin with a brief description of the project. We then describe the National Occupation Classification (NOC) before proceeding to present a detailed description of occupational movement among workers displaced in Elliot Lake.

Methods

Sample. In 1990, Rio Algom Mines and Denison Mines announced they would lay off about half of their total workforce of uranium workers in Elliot Lake. It had a population in 1986 of 17,984. The town was built during the 1950s to house workers producing uranium. Although the uranium mining workforce had been shrinking from a peak of over 4,500 in the mid-1980s, the announcement represented a significant increase in the rate of decline. In late 1994, only 570 were still employed by the two companies in Elliot Lake.

In September 1990, as the first layoffs took effect, four researchers at Laurentian University began a longitudinal study of the population eligible for layoffs, with subsequent rounds of interviews conducted in the spring of 1992, 1994, 1995, 1996, and 1998. The interviews were designed to capture information similar to that in the U.S. Displaced Worker Survey and Statistics Canada's Labour Force Survey as well as a great deal of additional demographic information on family structure, education, and attitudes. The interviews were conducted in person and took about an hour each to administer. Of 2,700 on the lists provided by the companies and unions, we interviewed 1,182 in 1990. Of these we have retained 1,007 in the final round. While the number of women in the sample is small (44 in 1990), as can be expected in mining, the women in this sample are of considerable interest.

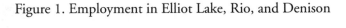

Figure 1. Employment in Elliot Lake, Rio, and Denison

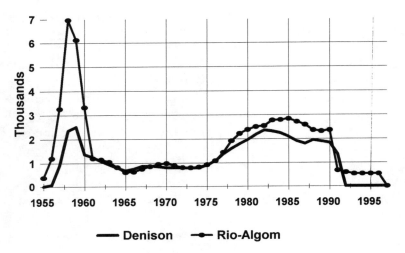

The National Occupational Classification. We have classified occupations in our sample using the National Occupational Classification (NOC), a systematic taxonomy of occupations in the Canadian Labour market. It is intended to replace Canada's previous occupational classification systems, the 1971 Canadian Classification and Dictionary of Occupations (CCDO) and the closely related Standard Occupational Classification (SOC) of Statistics Canada.

The NOC was developed by Employment and Immigration Canada in collaboration with Statistics Canada in part to facilitate the study of occupational mobility. An objective in the development process was to develop groupings for which the potential for mobility or substitution of workers is greater within groups than across groups. The NOC provides a four-digit classification based on skill level and skill type.

Ten broad "skill types" (see Table 1) are defined based on the type of work performed. Factors incorporated are the educational field of study required for entry and the industry of employment. Although the NOC skill type resembles an industrial classification, the difference is important for our purposes. First-aid attendants in a mine, for example, are in the mining industry, despite the fact that the occupation is classified as a "health occupation" (skill type 3). In a previous paper (Robinson and Wilkinson 1994) we found the NOC a useful tool for studying the structure of occupations and post-layoff occupational mobility. Our current sample is concentrated in "occupations unique to primary industry" (skill type 8).

Table 1. Skill types of the National Occupational Classification

First digit	Skill type category
0	Management
1	Business, finance, and administration occupations
2	Natural and applied sciences and related occupations
3	Health occupations
4	Occupations in social science, education, government service, religion
5	Occupations in art, culture, recreation, and sport
6	Sales and service occupations
7	Trades, transport, and equipment operators and related occupations
8	Occupations unique to primary industry
9	Occupations unique to processing, manufacturing, and utilities

"Skill level" refers to the level of training or experience required to enter the occupation. There are five levels (see Table 2).

Table 2. Skill levels of the National Occupational Classification

Second digit	Skill level name
0	Management
1	Professional
2 or 3	Technical
4 or 5	Intermediate
6	Labouring

Skill levels in the NOC are intended to reflect actual occupational entry requirements. For example, "technical" (skill level 2), where the bulk of our sample originates, is described as requiring: two to three years of postsecondary education at a community college, institute of technology, or CEGEP; or two to four years of apprenticeship training; or three to four years of secondary school and more than two years of on-the-job training, training courses, or specific work experience.
Except for management occupations, the first two digits of the NOC represent skill type and skill level respectively. Together the first two digits identify 26 "major groups." Our analysis is based on the major groups (see Table 3).

Table 3. National Occupational Classification major group structure

00	Senior management occupations
01–09	Middle and other management occupations
11	Professional occupations in business and finance
12	Skilled administrative and business occupations
14	Clerical occupations
21	Professional occupations in natural and applied sciences
22	Technical occupations related to natural and applied sciences
31	Professional occupations in health
32	Technical and skilled occupations in health
34	Assisting occupations in support of health services
41	Professional occupations in social science, education, government services and religion
42	Paraprofessional occupations in law, social services, education and religion
51	Professional occupations in art and culture
52	Technical and skilled occupations in art, culture, recreation and sport
62	Skilled sales and service occupations
64	Intermediate sales and service occupations
66	Elemental sales and service occupations
72–73	Trades and skilled transport and equipment operators
74	Intermediate occupations in transport, equipment operation, installation and maintenance
76	Trades helpers, construction labourers and related occupations
82	Skilled occupations in primary industry
84	Intermediate occupations in primary industry
86	Labourers in primary industry
92	Processing, manufacturing and utilities supervisors and skilled operators
94–95	Processing and manufacturing machine operators and assemblers
96	Labourers in processing, manufacturing and utilities

Results

The initial distribution of occupations. The NOC is conveniently presented in the form of a matrix. The vertical dimension of the matrix is the skill rating, while the horizontal dimension represents skill types. Moving downward in the table to a job at a lower skill level may represent "de-skilling,"[2] while upward movement is associated with career advancement for individuals and rising skill levels for the workforce as a whole. Not all cells of the matrix are filled — very low educational levels do not appear in the scientific and technical occupations, for example, and there are no "occupations unique to the primary industries" that require postgraduate education.

Table 4 shows the original distribution in the NOC framework of occupations of 1,044 workers. Of the 26 major groups, 19 were occupied. (The management level is a single major group.) Notably under-represented or absent were mid-level technical occupations and mid- and lower-level occupations in health professions, education, the social sciences, and the arts (32, 34, 42, and 52). The largest major groups in 1990 were underground miners and related occupations (408,

Table 4. Distribution of occupations, 1990

Skill level	Skill type									Totals for levels
	1	2	3	4	5	6	7	8	9	
0	2					1		4		7
1	3	28	1	2	1					35
2–3	17	54	7			2	266	408	13	767
4–5	69					1	20	196	48	334
6						22	2		13	37
Totals	91	82	8	2	1	26	288	608	74	1180

Occupations are defined only for shaded cells.
One upper management worker is not included.

major group 82), "trades and skilled transport and equipment operators" (266, major group 72–73) and mine service workers (196, major group 84). These were followed by "technical occupations in the natural and applied sciences" (54, major group 22), "clerical occupations" (69, major group 14), and "processing and manufacturing machine operators and assemblers" (48, major group 94).

Figure 2 gives us a snapshot of the skill inputs for mining in Elliot Lake. While the bulk of the workers were in three major groups involved directly in removing ore from the ground, 5.8 percent of our sample were engaged in clerical occupations, and 7 percent were in scientific or technical occupations. It is likely that administrative and managerial occupations were under-represented in our sample. However, many supervisory functions are incorporated into "trades, skilled transport and equipment operators" (major group 72) or "skilled occupations in primary industry (major group 82).

Most of the workers in the Elliot Lake Tracking Study were skilled production workers. Industry sources inform us that Elliot Lake miners were experienced and well trained. They are concentrated in occupations at skill level 2, demanding two years of college or two or more years of on-the-job training, and in a group of occupations (skill type 8) unique to the primary industries. The skills are generally industry-specific and to a large extent learned on the job. There is also a large group of workers classed as trades, transport, and equipment operators (skill type 7).

Figure 2. Occupations 1990, full sample

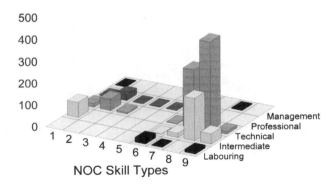

Employment in 1996. The simplest way of assessing the impact of the layoffs is to look at employment status in 1996. This classification ignores the distinction between voluntary and involuntary non-employment. Table 5 shows the percentages of workers that were still employed, re-employed, or not employed in 1996. The differences between men and women were not statistically significant in our sample.

Table 5. Employment status in 1996

Employment status	Men %	Women %
Still employed	15.0	15.2
Not employed	44.8	37.0
Re-employed	40.1	44.8

At work in one of Denison's mines.
City of Elliot Lake

Leaving work at Denison Mines.

City of Elliot Lake

Not all of those who were not employed in 1996 were available for work. Table 6 presents the percentage of each employment status that reported themselves on disability, awaiting arbitration, or retired or both in 1996. A large majority were retired, receiving disability payment, or both. Of those not employed, less than 30 percent reported neither disability nor retirement. Of those with new jobs, 45 reported being on disability, one being retired, and one being both retired and on disability. Nonetheless, most of the laid-off who were active in the labour market in 1996 were in fact re-employed, and we can for most purposes restrict our attention to them.

Table 6. Availability for work in 1996

Employment status	Neither disabled nor retired %	Disabled %	Retired %	Both disabled and retired %	Total %
Still employed	90.4	9.6	0	0	100
Not employed	29.4	25.1	24.4	21.1	100
Re-employed	91.1	8.6	0.2	0.2	100

Occupational mobility can be looked at in several ways. We might look at the last reported occupation for every member of the sample, focusing on the amount of occupational movement of the whole sample. However, since 15 percent of the sample remained employed with Rio Algom until after the last round of the survey, this approach would include people who were not yet laid off. It would therefore obscure our view of the mobility of displaced workers. It would also include people currently not employed. Anyone currently not employed is represented by their most recent job, even when it was the job held in 1990.

For all of the reasons stated above, we restrict attention in Figures 3 and 4 to those who were re-employed in 1996. Comparing Figure 2 with Figure 4, we see that the original occupational distribution for those with new jobs in 1996 is not noticeably different from that of the whole sample before the layoffs. The 1996 NOC distribution for the re-employed provides the best available description of the pattern of mobility. We therefore focus on occupational changes for this group.

Figure 3. 1990 Occupations for re-employed

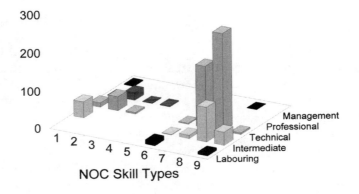

Figure 4. Last reported occupations for re-employed

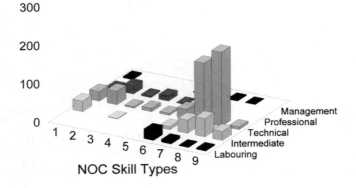

We found two striking features. First, a large number were re-employed in core mining occupations. Second, workers who left the core occupations appear to have spread quite uniformly across the occupational map. There have been gains in mid-level administrative occupations, management, the social service sector, sales and service, and lower level trades, transport, and equipment operation. The differences between the heights of the bars for each major group for the two years represent job losses or gains. The overall difference in mass represents unemployment and retirement.

"Professional occupations in health" (major group 31) and "professional occupations in social science, education, government services, and religion" (major group 41) have increased. These increases represent a move to social service occupations. The increase may be an artifact of public funding of adjustment services. The increase in "management occupations" (major group 00) and "upper-level administrative work" (major group 12) includes some people who developed small businesses. Eighteen people reported themselves owners, owner-managers, or proprietors of businesses after 1990. Six reported management jobs in the public sector and three in the non-profit sector.

Mobility from specific major groups. The pattern of occupational destinations varied according to occupational origins. Since occupations with higher skill levels have by definition greater human capital requirements, workers in these occupations should collect rents on their human capital. We expected workers to be less inclined to change occupation, since they would then forgo the rents. We confirmed this hypothesis for "skilled occupations in primary industry" (major group 82) and "intermediate occupations in primary industry" (major group 84).

The largest occupation of origin was "skilled occupations in primary industry" (major group 82), which includes underground miners as well as supervisors. Of 408 initially in major group 82, 83 percent remained in our sample to 1996. Of the 283 who got new jobs, 64 percent remained in major group 82. An additional 24 percent moved to adjacent major groups, primarily trades, transport, and equipment operation (major group 72–73). Twelve point eight percent moved down a single skill level, and 4.3 percent dropped by two skill levels. Despite the fact that the entire primary base of the remote community of origin has disappeared since 1990, there is little movement out of major group 82 for those with the highest level of skill and the most industry-specific skills. Furthermore, the workers in this major group exhibited this surprising occupational persistence although the entire mining industry continued to shrink until the last half of 1994.

Of the 340 workers originally in a major group for which we have constructed a participation measure, 75.1 were working in 1996, 5.4 percent were looking for work, and 19.5 percent were out of the labour force, in the sense that they had not searched for work in the four weeks preceding the interview. In 1996, 23.3 percent reported they were receiving disability payments[3] or awaiting arbitration. For "intermediate occupations in primary industry" (major group 84), 48.5 percent were employed in 1996, only 7.25 percent were actively searching, and 43.3 percent had not searched in the preceding four weeks. In addition, 15 percent described themselves as retired, and 37 percent were receiving disability payments or awaiting arbitration.[4]

The high levels of disability are features of the mining industry. Workers injured in the more physically demanding jobs nearest the mining face (primarily major group 82) frequently move to less demanding jobs on the surface and in the warehouses. As a result, disabilities are more common among those farther from the face. When they are moved to less demanding jobs, they may not go on compensation or receive disability payments. Some of the cases awaiting arbitration are injured workers who were still active in the mines. Major group 74, which includes materials handlers, loader operators, and various trades at lower skill levels, is of special interest. Of these workers, 44 percent were out of the labour force by 1996, and 47 percent of those for whom we have data were receiving disability payments or awaiting arbitration. These extremely high levels reflect the normal movement of miners to less onerous work. Loss of the opportunity to move into such jobs is one of the hidden costs of layoffs, since it represents a normal career path that is only available with long-term employment.

The strong attachment for workers in major group 82 contrasts with the much higher mobility of the workers in "intermediate occupations in primary industry" (major group 84). Only 20 percent remained in the major group. Interestingly, 40 percent moved to occupations at higher skill levels. Clerical workers in major group 14 showed similar upward mobility. On the other hand, downward mobility (13 percent) was no stronger among these less-skilled workers. There was proportionately more movement to other skill types, such as the social sector (skill type 4) and technical occupations (skill type 2).

We conclude that in the core occupations, human capital is conserved and that occupational mobility is concentrated in the less-skilled workers. This result complements results reported by Picot and

Pyper (1994) and Picot, Lin, and Pyper (1996), who found permanent layoffs concentrated among younger and less-skilled workers.

It is of considerable interest that more than half of those in core mining occupations have remained in mining through a period of significant contraction and extremely weak local labour markets. A colleague working with our data reports that over half of those who remained in Elliot Lake and who are currently employed are commuting to other communities to work, which suggests that the adjustment is not yet complete and that there may be substantial hidden costs of adjustment. When we examined the occupations of those originally in major group 82 using 1994 data (Robinson and Wilkinson 1994), we found rather higher rates of movement out of the industry. Workers with high stocks of human capital have apparently been returning to the industry due to an increase in hiring. It appears that highly skilled workers had been "parking" their human capital until demand picked up.

"Professional" and "technical workers in occupations related to natural and applied sciences" (major groups 21 and 22) exhibited similar immobility. The relative immobility may reflect human capital considerations similar to those discussed above. Clerical workers from major group 14 (not shown) exhibited slightly more mobility.

Lateral movement was more frequent at the lower skill levels. This is consistent with increasing levels of occupation-specific human capital and with segmented labour market models.

Women. Mining is traditionally men's work. The uranium mines at Elliot Lake reflected traditional roles. Very few women worked for the mining companies, and only a small fraction of those women worked in core mining occupations. In this section we attempt to throw some light on the circumstances of women in this male-dominated industry and on their adjustment to the layoffs that began in 1990.

Figure 5. Women's occupations, 1990

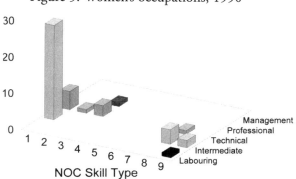

The distribution of women's occupations in Figure 5 shows a very different pattern. It is clear that the women in the sample are predominantly in clerical occupations with relatively low entry requirements. The pattern of occupations for the women in the production end is particularly interesting. The largest single group of male workers was in the two-digit class 82, highly skilled workers in occupations unique to the primary industries. It is striking that while a group of women were in occupations that cluster around class 82, there were very few that were actually in the most central mining occupations. The gender division of occupations in the workforce is clear from the figures. It appears that the women were disproportionately in office jobs and rarely in the core mining occupations.

Figure 6. Women with new jobs in 1996

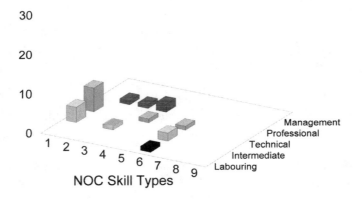

The evidence on occupational mobility of women in mining after layoffs is contained in Figure 6. Three points stand out. The core mining occupations vanish: the few women who were in core mining occupations in 1990 did not maintain their attachment to this sector. They tended to have less seniority and would have been subject to earlier layoff, as well as being less likely to be hired elsewhere. They may have been less mobile and therefore less able to take a core mining job elsewhere than the men. They were also concentrated at lower skill levels to begin with, and lower skill levels generally showed weaker occupational attachment.

Second, the women leaving the lower "clerical occupations" (major group 14) tended to move upward in the NOC table. Accumulated experience may account for the tendency to move into occupations with a higher skill requirement. Finally, there is, as with the men, a tendency to spread across the rest of the NOC fairly uniformly. Women appear to move to higher skill levels in the occupations requiring literacy, while, by way of comparison, the men who leave their original categories are more likely to move to lower skill levels in the occupational types that require less literacy.

An alternative classification confirms the presence of occupational segregation. Occupations involved in mining uranium can be roughly classified in terms of "distance from the face" by combining the codes for occupation type with information on whether the work was underground or above.[5] As in many industries, the degree of specialization varies. In mining there is generally increasing pay, increasing danger, and increasing amounts of industry-specific capital as people approach the "face." Because possession of industry-specific human capital increases the likelihood of re-employment in mining at high wages, we created a variable that orders occupations on the basis of their normal proximity to the face. We expect this variable to be associated with higher re-employment wages as well.

Some of the women in our sample did work underground, but they did not work in the most physically demanding and dangerous jobs. They also did not work in the most highly paid jobs. In Table 7, workers were classified according to the location of their work.

Table 7. Distance from the face

Worksite	Men %	Women %
Mining, at the face	38.0	4.3
Underground support	34.0	23.9
Mill	18.7	10.9
Office	9.3	60.9

If our sample is representative of the division of labour for the rest of the mining industry, women's work in 1990 was still in the office, and work at the face was still men's work. While there are signs that gender-based division of labour has been breaking down, very few women have reached the core occupations in the industry.

Table 8 shows the changes in the numbers of women in each occupational category since 1990.

Table 8. Change in women's occupational distribution, 1990–1996

Skill level	Skill type									Totals for levels
	1	2	3	4	5	6	7	8	9	
0										0
1		1		2						3
2-3	3	-1	-2	1	1	1		-1		2
4-5	-18		1			2		-4	-2	-21
6						1			-1	0
Totals	-15	0	-1	3	1	4	0	-5	-3	-16

Half the percentage of women (7 out of 44, or 15.9 percent) compared with men (332 out of 1,123, or 29.6 percent) reported having trades certification in 1990. None of the women reported having inter-provincial trades certification, while 12 percent of men did, suggesting a lower average level of trade training for women. Also, only 19 percent of women, compared to 62 percent of men, had common core (an industry skills certification to facilitate labour mobility), providing further evidence that women's occupations and occupational paths were less likely to be in the core mining occupations. No women reported having higher than module three, but 26 percent of men did.

Discussion

Our results show that the NOC is useful for analyzing occupational change, at least in the group of workers we have analyzed. It classifies as contiguous those occupations between which we observe larger movements. This was particularly true for men in major groups 82 and 84, which form the core mining occupations. These destinations are connected in having relatively higher manual components and lower reliance on literacy, especially for the lower levels.

The same was true, with one exception, for the women who were clerical workers and were likely to move to occupations of skill types 3 and 4. The exception was the large movement into the retail sector, at skill type 6. It would seem that skill type 6 is an intermediate industry type that lies between two type clusters.

Our finding that women left the resource sector as a result of layoffs may confirm views that minimal gender integration has occurred to date in this industry. There was in 1990 only a small contingent of women insecurely attached to jobs previously reserved for men. By 1990, layoffs eliminated these jobs and the women moved to other occupations.

An important and reassuring result is that much less movement out of high-skill occupations occurred than out of related lower-skill occupations. This is not to say that no highly skilled mining workers were lost to the industry; only that despite an extremely difficult labour market, 64 percent of those in the major group with the highest level of industry-specific human capital remained in the same occupational group. There were individuals who moved to occupations with lower entrance requirements, but there were compensating numbers of individuals who moved to occupations with higher entry requirements. Our study therefore provides no support for the view that workers in this industry are undergoing systematic de-skilling. An unexpected result was that a number of individuals managed to move into management positions. Nevertheless the majority of people who became employed stayed at the same general skill level.

The occupational mobility we observed may have been accompanied by serious transitional difficulties. Elsewhere we have reported lower wages in new jobs (Wilkinson, Suschnigg, Robinson, and Leadbeater 1993), long average spells of non-employment, and relatively high levels of unemployment (Wilkinson and Robinson 1996). There is no precise connection between the NOC and monetary income, and even those who moved to higher NOC skill levels have in some cases suffered substantial income reductions. Additional work on these issues is under way. The geographical story may also be an important one. Our earlier work has shown that surprisingly few people left Elliot Lake prior to 1995. The most recent data show much higher out-migration, raising the possibility of delayed adjustment, and concern that even our six-year study will miss essential features of the adjustment process.

Although other measures of success in responding to layoffs must be considered, we found no indication of systematic decline in occupational requirements (de-skilling) for the workers we have observed. Human capital is generally conserved in core mining occupations, but there may be some loss of industry-specific human capital as workers move to unrelated occupations. Both men and women mining employees tended to move to contiguous NOC locations. The women from this study have, however, completely lost their foothold in underground mining.

Notes

[1] Data collection for this paper was supported by Human Resources Development Canada, the Ontario Ministry of Northern Development and

Mines, and the Institute of Northern Ontario Research and Development (INORD) at Laurentian University. The contents are entirely the responsibility of the authors. The authors thank David Leadbeater and Peter Suschnigg for their part in initiating the project, in instrument design, and in data collection. The arduous task of coding occupations was performed by George Schaut. Interpretation, and especially misinterpretations, are entirely the responsibility of the authors and not of the Elliot Lake project team.

[2] The classic development of the hypothesis that the skill levels of workers are being systematically reduced is Braverman (1974).

[3] Four in major group 82 did not answer the question on disability, reducing the base to 336; 408 responded to the question on retirement.

[4] We have labour force participation for 166 in major group 82, retirement information for 196, and disability information for 164.

[5] This classification was suggested by Suzanne Dansereau.

References

Braverman, Harry. (1974). *Labor and Monopoly Capital: The Degradation of Work in the Twentieth Century.* New York: Monthly Review Press.

Employment and Immigration Canada. (1993). *National Occupational Classification: Occupational Descriptions.* Cat # MP5325/–1993E.

Horvath, F.W. (1987). "The pulse of economic change: displaced workers of 1981–1985," *Monthly Labour Review* 3, 21: 3–12.

Picot, Garnet, Zhengxi Lin, and Wendy Pyper. (1996). "Permanent layoffs in Canada: overview and longitudinal analysis." Mimeo, Business and Labour Market Analysis Group, Statistics Canada, May 1996.

Picot, Garnet and Wendy Pyper. (1994). "Worker displacement within the context of a dynamic labour market." Paper presented at the Canadian Employment Research Forum Workshop on Displaced Workers and Public Policy, Montreal, December 2.

Robinson, David and Derek Wilkinson. (1994). "Occupational and geographical mobility of displaced miners: preliminary results from Elliot Lake." Presented at the Canadian Employment Research Forum Workshop on Displaced Workers and Public Policy, Montreal, 2 December 2 1994.

Wilkinson, Derek and David Robinson. (1996). *Durations of Non-Employment Spells of Displaced Miners.* ELTAS Analysis Series #2A16. Sudbury, ON: INORD, Laurentian University. Presented at the Annual Meetings of the Canadian Sociology and Anthropology Association, St Catharines, ON, June 1996.

Wilkinson, Derek, Peter Suschnigg, David Robinson, and David Leadbeater. 1993. *Elliot Lake Tracking Study Phase Two: Interim Community Report.* Sudbury, ON: INORD, Laurentian University.

Chapter 9
Transitions of Rio Algom Employees at Stanleigh Mine[1]
Barry Ferguson

The permanent closure of Stanleigh Mine in June 1996 brought to an end several decades of uranium mining in Elliot Lake. In this chapter, I will discuss the process and measures that were implemented to help Stanleigh employees cope with the transition to either retirement or new employment. I believe that the adjustment model that we adopted for Stanleigh employees was successful. Why? First, we took a proactive approach; and second, we had the support of all partners — employees, unions, government agencies, and the company. The community and the employees had known since 1991 of the plan to close Stanleigh Mine in 1996.

The decision was made to provide employee transition services through an in-house team called the Stanleigh Mine Employee Adjustment Committee (EAC). This committee had representation from all employee groups, with each representative backed up by an alternate. Representatives on the committee were appointed by their respective union locals or, in the case of the non-union employees' representative, selected by the non-union employees themselves. The committee then selected an independent chair from qualified candidates in the local community. The initial chair was Roger Taylor, and following his untimely passing, these duties have been ably discharged by Harold Kenny. Committee members include: Dave Lea, representing non-union employees; Kevin Seabrook, representing members of United Steelworkers of America (USWA) Local 5417; Murray Warner, representing members of USWA Local 5980; and myself, representing Rio Algom Limited.

123

The responsibilities and objectives of the committee are: to research and assess, and to plan and recommend a private program of adjustment for staff and unionized employees of Rio Algom Limited, Stanleigh Mine, Elliot Lake; to recommend to the employer and the employees joint private courses of action the committee considers essential to the development of an effective adjustment program; and to use appropriately and effectively all applicable public programs and services.

The EAC became active on a part-time basis on October 20, 1994, and has been engaged full-time since August 1, 1995. We anticipated that the EAC would continue to operate until March 31, 1997; however, it was subsequently extended until June 30, 1997. To facilitate access to the EAC, a separate office with secretarial support was established at the mine site. When the mine and mill clean-up was complete, the EAC office was transferred to an off-site location in town in September 1996.

The administration of the EAC is covered by an Adjustment Incentive Agreement, formerly called an Industrial Adjustment Service Agreement, in which all parties (federal and provincial governments, all unions, non-union employees, and the company) are signatories. Both levels of government and the company share the costs of the EAC based on a specific formula. We found the assistance and advice provided by federal and provincial representatives very helpful. Initially, the cost-sharing formula was fairly evenly balanced between the parties. However, during the last year of the agreement the company's contribution increased significantly in response to decreases in contributions from both levels of government, due to cutbacks. The EAC administration budget covered by these agreements is $455,000; however, this represents only a portion of the total cost of providing transition services to Stanleigh employees. One important support that was funded by government programs during the 1990 layoffs was relocation assistance. Despite strong appeals by the EAC, however, relocation assistance was not provided by government programs for the 1996 employee transitions.

With the formation of the EAC in 1994, the representatives and alternates initially attended a number of training seminars to plan and prepare an Employee Adjustment Program. Early in 1995, meetings were held with all employees for the purpose of introducing EAC members and presenting its proposed plans and activities. Although the EAC had a good idea as to the types of services that employees would require, employee input and buy-in was essential. In March 1995, a detailed, personalized needs assessment questionnaire was provided to each employee. The response rate of 47 percent for the survey was considered good, and confirmed the services that employees considered important.

A now-retired welder at the entrance to Rio Algom's Quirke I mine, 1987.

United Steelworkers of America, Local 5417

Celebrating twenty and twenty-five years of service in the uranium mining industry in Elliot Lake by many employees of Denison Mines Limited.

City of Elliot Lake

Based on the responses to the questionnaire, an action plan was developed. Of particular importance was the request of employees for financial and retirement advice. To avoid any potential conflict of interest, the committee elected not to use any commercial investment organization to provide financial or retirement advice. The EAC engaged a financial educator, Financial Knowledge, Inc., to deliver one-day financial and two-day retirement seminars to interested employees. Based on employee feedback and favourable comments of the local financial institutions, the seminars were successful.

During 1994, the company and unions recognized the importance of providing for an orderly Stanleigh closure in 1996 and negotiated a Closure Agreement which would supersede the respective collective bargaining agreements at designated dates or activities. The significant items addressed included expanding eligibility for unreduced pension, improving severance pay, and providing a mechanism to permit employees to elect voluntary early departure. Identical enhanced pension eligibility and early departure provisions were also extended to non-union employees.

The pension plans were enhanced to permit employees with 25 years of service or whose combined age and service totalled 75 to retire with an unreduced pension. A total of 193 employees had elected retirement as of December 31, 1996, and included in this group were 147 employees who became eligible for retirement through the enhanced pension provision.

The voluntary early departure program was introduced effective July 1, 1995, and benefited both employees and the company. It permitted a restricted number of employees to terminate their employment with Rio Algom voluntarily in order to secure alternative employment and still receive severance pay or to retire earlier than the actual closure date. Throughout the program, the company was able to maintain minimum staffing levels necessary to achieve production requirements and all early departure requests were granted. A total of 142 employees participated in the program.

The EAC provides many of the standard services for employees involved in job-search campaigns, such as telephone, fax, job-posting bulletin board, and a drop-in centre that assisted in providing client contact and support. One innovative job-search technique initiated by the Stanleigh Mine EAC has been the Disk Service. A list of available candidates, with résumés and job descriptions attached, was put onto a computer diskette and mailed out to potential employers across Canada. We focused on mines, paper mills, and industries that would employ people with skills similar to those held by Stanleigh employees. The Disk Service is continually updated and has been mailed out three times to up to 204 different companies.

By June 1997, the EAC had operated for a 33-month period preparing employees for retirement or relocation to new employment. This in-house team provided continuity of transition services to employees and has been instrumental in maintaining high employee morale under very difficult circumstances. From the start, the EAC maintained one overall goal and objective: *to fully meet and satisfy needs and expectations of our clients.* A critical element in the success of any project is engaging the right people. I believe that the best possible group of people was put together for this very challenging and important project. The team members worked effectively with one another, demonstrated empathy for their clients and, most importantly, had the trust of the employees.

Table 1. EAC services used by employees to December 31, 1996

Employees requesting covering letters		498
Résumés completed		441
Interview skills workshop		167
Career counselling		30
Adult education upgrading to grade 12		30
a) basic mathematics	16	
b) essential employability skills	15	
c) choices program	11	
d) basic communications	9	
e) Pathways (HRDC)	13	
f) Individual retraining plan (IRP)	17	
Financial planning		122
Mock general aptitude testing battery (GATB)		102
Gas fitter II course		27
Retirement counselling		106
Small business seminar		77
Peer helping seminar		10
Programmable logic controls (PLC) course		14
CPP presentation		44
Transitions presentations		90
Stress seminar		10
HRDC presentation		312
Rigging safety course		20
CFC (refrigeration) course		21
CWB Class "S" welders test		15

The EAC asserted their advocacy role through several meetings and with volumes of correspondence with Mayor George Farkouh, MPP Mike Brown, MP Brent St. Denis, provincial and federal ministers, and a host of government bureaucrats. This advocacy was successful in opening many doors that led to additional funding, access to programs, and re-employment of Stanleigh people.

Table 1 shows the number of people who have used the various services offered by EAC up to December 31, 1996.

Due to continued demand for adjustment services, the operation of the EAC was extended to June 30, 1997. These services are being provided through one counsellor and one secretary, who have been relocated to the Human Resources Development Canada office in Elliot Lake. This partnership between Rio Algom and HRDC is advantageous because it maintains company contact with former Rio Algom employees while providing clients with easier access to the full range of government services.

Of the 553 employees laid off or retired, almost 400 had been successful with their adjustment programs by April 30, 1997: 238 had secured employment, 25 had started their own business, 11 were participating in training or educational upgrading, and 123 had retired from active employment.

The success of the Stanleigh Mine Employee Adjustment Committee can be attributed to two key factors: the commitment of a dedicated in-house adjustment team and the proactive implementation of adjustment measures over a period of 33 months.

Note

[1] I wish to acknowledge personally the excellent effort and dedication exhibited by Harold Kenny, Dave Lea, Murray Warner, and Kevin Seabrook in leading the Stanleigh Mine employee transition process. In particular, I wish to acknowledge also the office support provided by Shelley Sabourin. She kept the paper flowing, was well organized, and maintained a very positive and professional image of the EAC in its interaction with management, unions, employees, and government officials.

Part Two

Refusing to Become Another Ghost Town

In this part of the book we look at the ways in which the community itself worked to revive its local economy. Because communities are made up of people, it is difficult to talk about the community of Elliot Lake without talking also of the people who have built it and the people who have recently come to live there.

As Shawn Heard pointed out in the historical overview at the beginning of the book, the community of Elliot Lake was working on ways to diversify the local economy even before the layoffs were announced in 1990, to reduce its dependence on uranium mining as its main economic activity. This meant that the community had a head start in its response to the announcements. The development of the

Families enjoying the field day sponsored by the United Steelworkers of America at the time of the closure of Rio Algom's Quirke mine in 1990.
United Steelworkers of America, Local 5417

Retirement Living Program, the establishment of a local research field station for researchers, and the creation of a private arts program were all hailed as successful strategies. Some observers, however, feel that these successes mask aspects of the community's collapse that are less visible in the publicity that surrounds the Elliot Lake story. What has happened to the mining families who have remained in Elliot Lake? In what ways have they been included in the revival of the community?

Chapter 10, by Carrie Chenier, provides a different viewpoint from the one that concluded the first part of the book. Written from a union perspective, this report examines the difficult labour adjustment process experienced by local mining families and questions its success for some. The next two chapters, written by ELTAS researchers, tell of the consequences of the layoffs for many of the mining families remaining in Elliot Lake. David Leadbeater's chapter looks at the community's increased dependency on government transfer payments (employment insurance, public assistance, and government pensions), and compares it with Elliot Lake before the layoffs, and with other regions of Canada. Anne-Marie Mawhiney and Jan Lewis highlight some perceptions about the social effects of the layoffs for the community.

The remaining chapters in this section describe the transformation of the community from a uranium-mining community to a retirement community. Mayor George Farkouh provides an overview of the seven years since the layoffs were announced. Journalist Mick Lowe describes his positive impressions of the advent of retirees in Elliot Lake. The next chapter, by Raymond W. Pong, Alan Salmoni, and Shawn Heard, shows the shifts in population base since 1990, demonstrating the changes in demographics as older people come into the community. David Robinson of ELTAS collaborated with Merlyn Bishop, treasurer for the City of Elliot Lake, to show the positive economic benefits to the municipal finances of the decision to rent and sell local housing to retired people who relocate to Elliot Lake. Alex Berthelot, Jr., a local business owner, gives his perspective on the revival of the business community in the last few years. A chapter by health researchers (Pong, Salmoni, and Heard) points out the ongoing need to monitor the availability of health services for the elderly population of Elliot Lake. In order to maintain the momentum of the retirement community, local access to specialized health services is needed. The final chapter in this section is written by a community-based researcher-manager, Deborah Berthelot, who discusses the ways in which a partnership between a university and a local research centre can be instrumental in developing a clearer understanding of the revival of the community after an economic collapse and can at the same time contribute to local job creation.

Chapter 10
Community Roots or the Lack Thereof
Carrie Chenier

I have been asked to speak as a woman, a worker, and a longtime resident of this community. As examples will demonstrate, workers seldom if ever get to tell their own stories, or talk about their hurts or their fears. Their successes are usually claimed by others.

The word *union* instantly places persons in political and corporate power in a defensive mode. Yet we are all members of a union — be it a church denomination, a service organization, or the very root of all unions, the human race. Historically it has been the trade unions that have been the social conscience of countries and corporations, and it is the

Grievance chairman Carrie Chenier in her Steelworkers office in 1986. The last employed Steelworker in Elliot Lake when the local closed in October 1997, she was then its senior compensation officer.

United Steelworkers of America, Local 5417

women who have borne the final brunt of all social and class struggles. It is also women who are the custodians of our emotional history.

In this community, the founding people came from other mining camps, gave up their mobile homes and packsacks, and put down roots. The corporate bodies that made their billions of dollars in this camp are rooted on Bay Street; there are no permanent residences here for them. When these people saw the profit margin narrowing in Elliot Lake, they made a corporate decision to dump the project. There wasn't then, nor will there ever be, any reasonable, impartial body that was accountable for that decision in human terms. So many changes were made in such a short time — with money at the root of them all. There was little if any consultation with those affected the most — us, the workers. A picture often presented by the media, and in my opinion, a false one, is that we, as workers in Elliot Lake, are over that terrible bump in our life's path and are quite satisfied with our fate. We are resigned maybe, but never satisfied.

If this were true, would we be able to see, on any given day, countless numbers of 50-year-olds aimlessly wandering through the streets and the mall of this town? Forced early retirement, contrary to what others try to tell us by repeated programming propaganda, is not a newfound freedom, but exactly what the words say — forced early retirement. This mine closure has taken 15 years from our lives' net earnings and watered down our pensions. Will there be a specialized community set up for us when we reach the age of 65, when we hit that financial wall that the government keeps eroding? Obviously not. We, as older workers, are already being told to be thankful, almost made to feel guilty because we have a small pension. These pensions are deferred wages: it is our money exchanged for our labour. In an age where politics drives the reporting of history, will the true cost of these early idled hands and minds ever be tallied? How can you put a price tag on self-worth?

Somewhere, sometime, somebody must admit that the influx of persons with no roots elsewhere has made a great impact and has brought about unnatural changes in every element of life in this small town. Ideally, a community should consist of the three areas of life: the roots (our past and stability, from which we get the nourishment), the trunk (our present and the reality), and the leaves and buds (our young and the dreamers). In Elliot Lake's case, by design, the politicians and companies have altered forever the face not only of this town, but also that of every community in which the Retirement Living Pied Piper van stopped. The elders and the history were stolen from these communities. We are told time and time again that if we do not learn from history, we are doomed to repeat it. Who will speak of this to the young in these villages? There will be no Thunder Woman in the sweat lodges to instruct the young in the way of Mother Earth and its dignity. By making the elderly our main business, and allowing our young to fly to other places, we have no one to hear the old of Elliot Lake speak. Elders knew someone who knew someone who knew someone who really knew a different world. We wouldn't be here if our ancestors had not passed on life to us. Linking back puts the future in perspective.

What does this imbalance do to the tree of life in Elliot Lake? Is it morally right or responsible to create a geriatric ghetto? What will history decide? This is tampering with the very roots of our existence, the substance of life. And that tampering is now playing havoc with groups in this community, the women and the volunteers who are the unpaid workers. The Auxiliaries in Elliot Lake, as in other small communities, are dependent on one another's goodwill, and they had an unwritten "ladies' agreement" when it came to social fund-raising events. The Legion did the Hallowe'en tea, the Anglican church the pancake breakfast, and the Catholic Women's League, of course, did up St. Paddy's Day. These revenues helped pay their taxes, but most of the profits were returned to community charities. With the development of the Renaissance Centre, all agreements were off, and mutual respect for others' endeavours was thrown out with the dishwater. Instead of integrating with groups already here, these new arrivals, with withered and worn hands of their own, have been encouraged to segregate and optimize the benefits for themselves in their own walled city. Little, if any, moneys are recycled for the benefit of the community as a whole. I am not judging; but I know that when one makes the rounds of the annual teas, etc., all one sees are the pioneer faces. The old saying holds true: "When the watering hole shrinks, the fight gets tougher at the trough." Unfortunately, we have already seen, as a direct result, the closing of one respected seniors' organization: and others will follow.

Workers by definition know only work. Unions were and still are the only channel that the workers had through which to collectively demand respect, and to ensure honesty, fairness, and accountability in the corporate decisions that controlled every aspect of their lives. As an advocate, I have found it interesting to watch those who were company clones and cling-ons scrambling to find other political arenas or rising stars to attach themselves to — their particular talents are still very much alive in this town. The tentacles of a mining master spread far and wide, and those who dared to question policy or the fairness of a decision now find themselves blacklisted in hiring. "A union steward, you say?"

United Steelworkers of America leaders at the opening of the new Steelworkers Union Hall, March 1987: Leo Gerard, district director; Murray Quittendon, president of local 8950; Dan Hutchinson, president of local 5417; Steve Bonifero, president of local 5980; Ivan Cherier, president of local 5982; Brian Bushey, president of local 8515; and Dave Mellor, staff representative for all locals.
United Steelworkers of America, Local 5417

Unions are far from being perfect, but certainly they were the reality. Their members were the trunk of the tree, and they contributed greatly to this community. The Women's Crisis Centre, the Men's Support Centre, the Family Life Centre, Detoxification Services, and hospital equipment were all initiated and financed by United Steelworkers of America. Yet do we see plaques proclaiming our virtues?

There does exist in Elliot Lake, at a specific site chosen by CEOs and politicians, the foundation of a museum that ostensibly salutes the miners. Yet there has been no input in its planning from workers or miners. There are those who will be quick to deny that statement, and give you the name of a paper-pusher who through some unclear sense of self-importance claims to represent the local that had the miners as members. But as a worker, and the advocate of those men, I say to you, "Shame!" Show me one person on that board who knows what it's like to have his hands freeze in one to five seconds at minus 10 degrees, or who is familiar with the smell of the oilers, or who wears a hearing aid due to the deafening roar of the drill, or a woman widowed early due to industrial disease, and I will take back my words. It is only the singer who knows the song! By pretending to speak for us, you insult our intelligence and demean our dignity.

The retirees' clubs were formed in our union halls. Union money furnished the rooms and supplied the gaming tables, yet now they are run by retired management personnel under the guise of incorporations. You must buy a membership. Have the workers not already paid their dues for this club? Yet some express wonder that the workers feel uncomfortable there. And surprise! we have no female retirees.

In my role as compensation advocate, I endeavour to seek rightful compensation for the sick and the lame, the human tailings unwanted and discarded by the industry. One of my duties is also to seek justice for the widows of those miners who have succumbed to the elements, while corporations prosper.

Last month I went to yet another funeral for an ex-employee, who had given 27 years of work to this employer. Ten years ago, the first two pews would have been filled with the "who's who" of the management type: his shifter, the captain, the mine superintendent, etc., but on this day, though the church was full, there was not one person from among those whom he had supported with the fruits of his labours. Jerry was the same guy he had been ten years ago, so what had changed? Priorities and image, of course. But the roots held true — the workers honoured this worker.

What of our middle age, the trunk of the tree? Well, now they must travel outside their community for work — but they're lucky to have a job, right? How many families are learning to be without Dad for the 12 shifts in? Is this the natural way of life? Is it what we want as Northerners? Is this the kinder face and the more educated way of raising the balanced children, our shoots on the tree of life for the next millennium? I think not. When I divorced, single-parent families were the shame of society, and we all knew that children raised by one parent were doomed to go straight to hell. Now, apparently, we are encouraging it. Where will the mental and physical relief come from for the female who is the trinity in the household for days on end? There are no easy answers I admit, but if we care — and we must — then as a community we have to accept this challenge and the responsibility for this human cost. Women cannot always bear these burdens; that trunk of the tree will snap.

Life has not always been easy for Carrie the worker, or Carrie the woman. My destiny has been to march to a different drummer, but I am proud of my route march. Fate has given me a third eye that allows me insight into far too many situations and dramas. As a woman growing older, I now pay less attention to what men say, electing instead to watch what they do. This is a lesson we, as women, should teach our younger sisters from the time they leave the cradle.

In closing, I would ask you to take a fresh look at this community, please, putting aside for a moment the economic agenda. Political energies and a fraction of the money spent on changing the direction of this town could well have been spent in retraining the laid-off workers for new opportunities or relocation. The funds that are coming out of town coffers now were put there by workers, not new retirees. How much effort was really put into saving even a minute number of jobs? Furthermore, there are no concrete signs of any tangible benefits to the older workers who are forced to remain out of work. There are some of us who know full well the extent of the betrayal and who the players are.

I do not apologize for my defence of the original community. I do not entirely welcome the newer element in this town. For 31 years this was my playground — and it still is. It amazes me that the politicians in this community adopt a patronizing attitude, telling me again and again and again how everything about their agenda is good for me. If others want to play in my sandbox, then I want these persons to meet two criteria: first, they must respect the rules; second, they must bring more sand to the box, not dump out all the existing sand. The powers that be showed the greatest disdain for Elliot Lake when they gave away that which was not theirs to give.

I would like to close with a small poem that puts things in perspective, I believe.[1] Nothing is inconsequential, and we have choices about what and who we make important.

> The wounds you have inflicted
> May scar me all of my years
> I am fearful of the future
> Like so many of my peers
> But I have a new awareness
> That will overcome my fears
> And I'm choosing my side wisely
> As the day of reckoning nears.

Note

[1] These lines are excerpted from a poem entitled "If I Knew Then," by June Wilson, p. 23 in *Down — But Not Out*, which she published herself in British Columbia in 1985.

Chapter 11
Increased Transfer Dependency in the Elliot Lake and North Shore Communities[1]
David Leadbeater

> Everyone has the right to work, to free choice of employment, to just and favourable conditions of work and to protection against unemployment.... Everyone has the right to a standard of living adequate for the health and well-being of himself [sic] and of his family, including food, clothing, housing and medical care and necessary social services, and the right to security in the event of unemployment, sickness, disability, widowhood, old age or other lack of livelihood in circumstances beyond his control.
> **The United Nations Universal Declaration of Human Rights (1948)**

For over three decades, from the mid-1950s to the 1980s, Elliot Lake was the largest uranium mining centre in Canada and probably the world. In 1990, only months after Elliot Lake incorporated itself as a city, the two mining corporations in the area, Denison Mines Limited and Rio Algom Limited, began to shut down their operations and lay off hundreds of employees. In the course of six years, until the last mine closed in June 1996, Elliot Lake lost over 4,000 mining jobs.[2]

Given that the mining industry accounted for about 40 percent of the labour force in Elliot Lake, the impact of these mass layoffs on the local economy was devastating. The population of Elliot Lake had been declining even before the 1990 layoffs, and by the June 1991 census, it had dropped to 14,089. Statistics Canada reported this was a fall of 21.7 percent since the 1986 census, the largest decline for any small municipality in Canada.[3] The 1996 census has recently reported a further, though much smaller decline, to 13,588 people.

Elliot Lake is the largest community in the area, and the one most directly affected by the layoffs, but the impact was felt throughout the North Shore region of Lake Huron, particularly in the main communities of Algoma Mills, Blind River, Iron Bridge, Massey, Serpent River, Spanish, Spragge, and Walford (see map on p. 4). The Elliot Lake Tracking and Adjustment Study has taken the commutershed of Elliot Lake to be along the Trans-Canada highway from Massey to Iron Bridge. Table 1 contains a list of the main commutershed communities, their populations, and distances from Elliot Lake. Elliot Lake itself is located 26 kilometres north of the Trans-Canada highway, while the other communities affected are along the highway as it passes through the North Shore area between the cities of Sudbury and Sault Ste. Marie.

Table 1. Main communities within or near the commutershed for Elliot Lake, by distance and population, 1994[1]

Community[2]	Population[3]	km from Elliot Lake[4]	
Elliot Lake[5]			
—City of Elliot Lake	12,387	0	
Within commutershed:			
Serpent River [P0P 1V0]		26	
Serpent River First Nation	295		
—Cutler [P0P 1B0]		33	
Spragge [P0R 1K0]		33	
Spanish [P0P 2A0]		44	
—Township of Shedden	809		
Algoma Mills [P0R 1A0]		45	
—Township of the North Shore	665		
Walford (Station) [P0P 2E0]		54	
Blind River [P0R 1B0]		56	
—Town of Blind River	3,911		
—Township of Thompson	105		
Mississagi River First Nation [P0R 1B0]	328	61	
Massey [P0P 1P0]		66	
—Town of Massey	1,063		
—Township of the Spanish River	1,476		
Sagamok First Nation [P0P 1P0]	NA	73	
Iron Bridge [P0R 1H0]		82	
—Village of Iron Bridge			
East of commutershed:			
Webbwood [P0P 2G0]		83	
-Town of Webbwood	554		
McKerrow [P0P 1M0]		93	
-Township of Baldwin	646		
Espanola[6]		96	
-Town of Espanola	5,144		
West of commutershed:			
Thessalon First Nation [P0R 1L0]	NA		92
Thessalon [P0R 1L0]		108	
-Town of Thessalon	1,371		
-Township of Thessalon	973		
-Townships of Day and Bright Additional	255		

Notes to Table 1:

[1] The Elliot Lake Tracking and Adjustment Study has taken as the primary area of the study Elliot Lake and the North Shore communities along the Trans-Canada highway from Massey to Iron Bridge. This can also be treated as the commutershed for Elliot Lake.

[2] The first place name indicates the postal code area used for the economic dependency (taxfiler) data. Where there is a village, town, township, or city centred in that postal code area, these are indicated beneath together with populations.

[3] The municipal population figures, which are taken from the 1996 *Ontario Municipal Directory*, are based on the 1994 enumerations. According to the directory, these population figures include residents of institutions, such as homes for the aged, but not cottagers, residents of jails, or those on short stay at general hospitals. Neither do they include Indian Reserves. Some municipalities may have updated their 1994 population figures. For First Nations, the population figures (if available) are as of May 1996, based on the 1996 *Census of Canada* (Statistics Canada catalogue number 93–357–XPB).

[4] The distances are based on those indicated in the Ontario Ministry of Transportation Map Series Map 3, Manitoulin Island–Sudbury Area (1992). Acknowledgement is due also to Léo Larivière, technologist cartographer of the Department of Geography of Laurentian University, for his suggestions and the maps he has produced for the ELTAS project.

[5] The economic dependency data for Elliot Lake are from the postal code areas beginning with "P5A," including P5A 2S9. Some of the latter "suburban services" may be outside the city limits.

[6] The economic dependency data for Espanola cover the postal code areas of P0P 1C0 and those beginning with P5E.

This paper focuses on the massive increase in economic dependency, particularly transfer-program dependency, that occurred in Elliot Lake and the surrounding North Shore communities following the layoffs that began in 1990. The economic dependency emerging in Elliot Lake and the surrounding North Shore communities has had two main sources. First, increased economic dependency was generated primarily *within* the region, through such direct effects of the layoffs as increased unemployment, poverty, and early retirements, as well as through the ageing of the pre-1990 Elliot Lake population. Second, Elliot Lake also had a migration of economically dependent persons into the region, in large part to take advantage of the lower cost of housing that resulted from the collapse of housing prices and rents following 1990.[4]

Increased economic dependency in Canada's regions is a serious economic problem and policy issue, particularly in the current context of major cuts to social program standards. If a community loses a highly productive sector or a high proportion of its population in productive employment, living standards (or average consumption levels) will fall — *unless* there is some means of redistribution or inter-regional equalization. The main means of inter-regional equalization in Canada today is still the social transfer system, particularly through Unemployment Insurance, Social Assistance, Workers' Compensation, and public pensions. However, the social transfer system is under attack and is being replaced gradually by policies generally more regressive in their distributional implications, both socially and regionally. Smaller communities in Canada's hinterland regions, particularly those suffering mass layoffs or other economic setbacks, will be among those areas hardest hit by reductions in or elimination of social transfer programs. It is important therefore to study the actual pattern of economic dependency in a hinterland area hit by mass layoffs.

The Meaning of Economic Dependency

The basic idea underlying the concept of economic dependency is that every society can be divided into two groups, the *dependent* (N) and the *non-dependent* (N). Everyone is either a dependent or a non-dependent, so the two groups together make up the entire population ($D + N = P$).

The non-dependent group is viewed as the producing or supporting part of the population, while the dependent group is viewed as being supported by the economic activity of the producing part of the population for all or at least a part of their consumption. For the dependent population to be supported wholly or partially, there must be a *transfer* from the non-dependent population. Of course, the non-dependent population also consumes, and the dependent population often conducts some production. In more precise terms, the non-dependent are viewed as net producers or at least as self-supporting, while the dependent are viewed as net consumers.

Given a distinction between the dependent (D) and the non-dependent (N), it is possible to give a measure of the relationship between the two with the *economic dependency ratio* (EDR): EDR = $D/N \times 100$.

The economic dependency ratio has been measured in two basic ways: in terms of people, that is, the number of dependent persons (by whatever definition) over the number of non-dependent persons; or in terms of dollars (or other monetary or material units) indicating the amount of transfer (or non-producer) income over the amount of employment (or producer) income. All other things being equal, a higher economic dependency ratio suggests a higher economic burden of dependency, while a lower ratio suggests a lower burden.

The key problem — and much controversy — in applying the concept of economic dependency arises with how to define "dependent" and "non-dependent." It goes beyond the limits of this paper to discuss the many, sometimes complex, issues involved in developing precise, operational definitions of economic dependency, but it is important to note that different political-economic approaches have given rise to different definitions and, in turn, to different types of economic dependency ratios.[5] These include demographic dependency ratios, labour-force dependency ratios, social-program dependency ratios, and net-consumption dependency ratios.

Historically, the basic concept of dependency has commonly been linked directly or by analogy to the family. Typically, children, the aged, and even married women have been deemed to be dependents while adult providers, especially male breadwinners, have been deemed to be non-dependents. Issues of who is or is not dependent then turn on such things as what ages define childhood or being aged (for instance, under 15 or over 64) or how to define marital status. Disability and long-term illness or being in an institution have also figured into definitions of dependency. Here the issues defining dependency become the particular level of disability or illness or types of institutions (whether prisons, sanatoria, rehabilitation centres, etc.) and the duration of stay.

The rise of industrial capitalism and the ideology of laissez-faire liberalism deeply affected political views about state programs of public relief or social assistance for those suffering unemployment, disability, or age-related incapacity. The concept of dependency was also affected. A major emphasis was placed on *paid* employment, as distinct from age, marital, or institutional status in determining non-dependence. Thus, those who are recipients of social assistance or other social programs are deemed dependent in contrast to those with paid employment, who are deemed non-dependent. However, this raises issues about the economic and social importance of paid work versus unpaid work, particularly the household work of women. Further, within the cash economy there are issues about whether those on private pensions or in receipt of dividends, interest, other non-employment incomes, or even those in receipt of certain types of paid employment (such as "makework projects" or certain types of government or non-commercial jobs) can be considered as economic dependents.

Thus, various elements — age, marital status, gender, employment and class status, institutional status, in receipt of public relief or not, within or outside the cash or the market economy, type of economic sector or job — have all played a role in defining economic dependency and the variety of approaches that currently exist.

The present paper discusses economic dependency of the transfer program type or, simply, *transfer dependency*. This is because transfer dependency ratios and, to a lesser extent, demographic dependency ratios dominate the official statistics and discourse on economic dependency produced by the Canadian government through such important institutions as Statistics Canada.

The current official concern with economic dependency understood as transfer dependency is driven largely by the pressures for deficit reduction or fiscal austerity and, more broadly, by the neoliberal political-economic ideology currently gripping the federal and most provincial governments. In this context, the definition of economic dependency as transfer dependency is narrowed to mean primarily the use of one or more of the several social or public programs involving a regular cash benefit or payout to individuals, from the Canada and Quebec Pension Plans to Unemployment Insurance to Social Assistance to Workers' Compensation to the Child Tax Benefit.

Transfer dependency measures can give a misleading picture of the dependency effects of some government policies to remove people from certain social programs such as social assistance by tightening eligibility. By definition, any resulting reduction in transfer payments, even where the persons removed from support are not able to re-enter cash employment, leads to a decline in measured transfer dependency. The cash dependency measure would not pick up, for instance, the fact that such a privatization of economic dependency from the public to household spheres often intensifies household dependency, whose burden is borne disproportionately by women. Thus, the cash measures of transfer dependency used here must be interpreted with caution, as they can underestimate the burden in terms of household dependency and, more generally, within the non-cash and non-government spheres.

Despite its limitations, the official approach to economic dependency offers some insights into the development of economic dependency, especially in a regional context. Further, as has been shown elsewhere, despite their marked differences in approach to economic dependency, most types of dependency ratios show a similar direction in the movement of economic dependency — increasing economic dependency in Canada since the 1980s or earlier.[6] This trend is not primarily the result of an inevitable aging of the Canadian population, but of a historic slowing of job and output growth coupled with certain government distributional policies. However, rather than deal here with such larger issues, this paper discusses the particular regional crisis of increasing economic dependency in the Elliot Lake and North Shore area.

An Official Measure of Economic Dependency

Statistics Canada produces economic dependency ratios that indicate a type of transfer dependency. Statistics Canada's economic dependency ratio simply takes the ratio between total transfer incomes received and total employment incomes received in a given geographical area:

$$\text{EDR} = \frac{\text{transfer income (\$)}}{\text{employment income (\$)}} \times 100$$

The official measure uses annual data as reported in Canadian personal income tax returns, which, because they cover close to all the Canadian adult population, permit the measure of economic dependency ratios for large as well as small geographical areas down to the level of a town, township, or village.[7]

Employment income includes both wage and salary income, as well as self-employment income.[8] For Canada as a whole in 1994, this was approximately 85 percent of all market-based (or non-transfer) income.[9] The rest of market-based income includes interest, dividends, and other investment income; it could be considered property income, or income derived from ownership of financial or business assets, as opposed to employment or labour income. Transfer income includes most cash transfer programs provided by the federal and provincial governments. According to national accounts data for Canada in 1994, government transfers to individuals were an amount equivalent to about 21 percent of employment income.

To illustrate the official measure of economic dependency, Table 2 displays the total employment income and the main forms of social program transfers as reported for Elliot Lake for the year 1994. The economic dependency ratio (transfer dependency ratio) is shown for the total transfers as well as for individual social programs.

Table 2. Officially measured economic dependency at Elliot Lake, 1994

		All	Females	Males
Elliot Lake				
Employment income	(1) $	122,592,000	43,169,000	79,424,000
	(2) no. of persons	5,580	2,500	3,080
	(3) $/person	21,970	17,268	25,787
Transfer income	(4) $	84,889,000	30,374,000	54,515,000
	(5) no. of recipients	7,880	3,910	3,970
	(6) $/recipients	10,773	7,768	13,732
Economic dependency ratio (EDR) [(4):(1)]		69.25	70.36	68.64
Transfers by type				
Employment	—$	20,746,000	4,309,000	16,437,000
pensions (non-public)	—recipients	1890	600	1290
	—EDR	16.92	9.98	20.70
CPP/QPP	—$	17,747,000	5,762,000	11,984,000
	—recipients	3,010	1,250	1,760
	—EDR	14.48	13.35	15.09
Social Assistance	—$	12,222,000	7,253,000	4,970,000
	—recipients	1,640	830	820
	—EDR	9.97	16.80	6.26
Workers'	—$	10,485,000	1,937,000	8,548,000
Compensation	—recipients	900	180	730
	—EDR	8.55	4.49	10.76
OAS/Net Supplements	—$	10,078,000	4,866,000	5,212,000
	—recipients	1,900	890	1,020
	—EDR	8.22	11.27	6.56
UI	—$	8,312,000	2,473,000	5,839,000
	—recipients	1,590	660	920
	—EDR	6.78	5.73	7.35
Child Tax Benefit	—$	2,473,000	2,391,000	82,000
	—recipients	1,680	1,590	80
	—EDR	2.02	5.54	0.10
GST Credit	—$	1,482,000	779,000	703,000
	—recipients	4,490	2,200	2,290
	—EDR	1.21	1.80	0.89
Provincial Refundable	—$	1,343,000	603,000	740,000
Tax Credits/QFA	—recipients	3,620	1,610	2,010
	—EDR	1.10	1.40	0.93
Public transfers only	—$	64,142,000	26,064,000	38,078,000
- federal	—$	40,092,000	16,271,000	23,820,000
- provincial	—$	24,050,000	9,793,000	14,258,000
Pensions	—$	48,571,000	14,937,000	33,633,000
- public	—$	27,825,000	10,628,000	17,196,000
- non-public	—$	20,746,000	4,309,000	16,437,000

The economic dependency ratio for Elliot Lake for all persons was 69.25, which can be interpreted as saying that for every $100 in employment income earned by people residing in Elliot Lake, $69.25 was received in transfers.[10] The economic dependency ratio was slightly higher for females (70.36) than for males (68.64).

The largest single transfer overall and the largest for men, $20.7 million, came from employment pensions. This refers to pensions outside the public pension system (Canada/Quebec Pension Plan and Old Age Security), from employment in either the private or the public sector. Strictly speaking, the official statistics should not treat private employment pensions as (public) transfers; for private-sector pensions in particular, ownership, control, terms, and operation are determined largely outside the state, though they are subject to government regulation. If one includes such essentially private transfers, then why not include other private transfers as well, such as dividend and interest payments? For purposes of the present paper, however, I have used the data on employment pensions, though most often separately identified, in order to keep the discussion largely consistent with and internal to the official approach.

The second largest transfer was the Canadian government's main public pension program, the Canada Pension Plan/Quebec Pension Plan ($17.7 million). Third in overall importance, but the largest single transfer to women, was the Ontario government's Social Assistance transfers ($12.2 million). Workers' Compensation benefits were very important in Elliot Lake, amounting to nearly $10.5 million. The other two large programs were the Canadian government's Old Age Security pension ($10.1 million) and Unemployment Insurance ($8.3 million). The remaining programs were relatively small in impact and tied directly to the income tax system: the federal Child Tax Benefit ($2.5 million), the federal Goods and Services Tax Credit ($1.5 million), and Ontario's Provincial Refundable Tax Credits ($1.3 million).[11]

What Do Changes in the Economic Dependency Ratios Mean?

Generally, economic dependency ratios are taken to indicate a level of economic burden: an increasing ratio suggests an increasing burden, while a decreasing ratio suggests a decreasing burden. This burden is usually treated in terms of its effect on living standards. All else being equal, an increasing economic dependency ratio leads to a problem of decreasing living standards or average consumption. This problem has a long history of discussion and debate.

At least one major stream in economic thought (including Adam Smith and Karl Marx) would argue that the material wealth — and average consumption — of any given society is dependent on two fundamental factors: the proportion of the population in productive employment (N/P), and the level of output per person productively employed (output/N). The first is a form of the economic dependency ratio, while the second is simply labour productivity. A decrease in the economic dependency ratio and/or an increase in productivity will increase the wealth — "the pie" — available to society for consumption and, hence, average consumption. However, an increase in the economic dependency ratio, particularly one uncompensated for by an increase in productivity, will reduce wealth and average consumption. A region, too, that loses productive employment will also face a decline in average living standards — unless there are transfers from outside the region.

This reasoning is based again on the assumption that every member of the society (who consumes any of the social output) is either a dependent or non-dependent. However, there is an important difference in the case of transfer dependency ratios. Take the case where a government reduces transfer payments by, for example, cutting people off social assistance or unemployment insurance benefits. All other things being equal, this may reduce total transfer incomes and hence the transfer dependency ratio. But this does not necessarily reduce economic dependency defined more broadly. The government action might simply redistribute dependency away from the state to individual families and intensify household poverty. Only if the dependent person is able to move to productive employment (and into the denominator of the ratio) is the social output — the pie — increased and the economic dependency ratio shifted downwards.

Increases (or decreases) in transfer dependency can take place in different ways. In principle, every economic dependency ratio is decomposable into the following for any given period:

$$\text{Economic dependency ratio} = \frac{\text{transfer income}}{\text{employment income}} \times 100$$

$$= \frac{\text{number of recipients} \times \text{rate of benefits}}{\text{number of earners} \times \text{rate of earnings}} \times 100$$

An increase in the economic dependency ratio over time across geographical areas can take place through any one of the four components by itself or in combination:

• an increase in the number of transfer recipients, such as occurred when the numbers using UI increased following the mine layoffs at Elliot Lake;
• an increase in the average benefits per recipient per year, either through a higher category of benefit and/or through a longer duration of the benefit during the year;

• a decrease in the number of employment-income earners, such as occurred in Elliot Lake with the massive loss of mine jobs;
• a decrease in the average earnings, such as also occurred through reduced wage rates and numbers of weeks worked in a year.

In the context of the Elliot Lake and North Shore communities two broad trends affected the transfer situation during the period. First, the federal and provincial governments were generally reducing transfer program *standards*.[12] The reduction of standards does not mean that, in the short term, total transfer incomes necessarily fall, particularly in conditions of mass unemployment; but, over a longer period, the reduction in eligibility (fewer people receive what previously they would have received) or the lowering of benefits rates (those eligible receive less per year than previously) will usually reduce transfer flows. Second, and more evident, there was a definite decline in labour market conditions. Many secure, better-paid unionized jobs were eliminated, unemployment expanded, and average wages declined. Both of these trends could be expected to constrain the growth of transfers if not to reduce them absolutely.

Economic Dependency in Elliot Lake in 1994

Four years after the first main wave of mine layoffs, the level and structure of transfers in Elliot Lake had started to stabilize. Table 3 shows the relative importance of particular social transfers to Elliot Lake in 1994, the latest year for which data are available at the time of writing. The programs are displayed according to which level of government has primary responsibility, federal or provincial, with the essentially private employment pensions last.

Table 3. The structure of social program transfers at Elliot Lake, 1994

		All	Females	Males	Females as % of all
Transfer income— $		84,889,000	30,374,000	54,515,000	35.8
Transfer program—% of total:		100	100	100	
Federal:					
CPP/QPP	—% of $	20.9	19.0	22.0	32.5
OAS/GIS	—% of $	11.9	16.0	9.6	48.3
UI	—% of $	9.8	8.1	10.7	29.8
Child Tax Benefit	—% of $	2.9	7.9	0.2	96.7
GST Credit	—% of $	1.7	2.6	1.3	52.6
Provincial:					
Social Assistance	—% of $	14.4	23.9	9.1	59.3
Workers' Compensation	—% of $	12.4	6.4	15.7	18.5
Provincial Tax Credits	—% of $	1.6	2.0	1.4	44.9
Private & public sectors:					
Employment pensions	—% of $	24.4	14.2	30.2	20.8
Public transfers only	—% of $	75.6	85.8	69.8	40.6
—federal	—% of public	62.5	62.4	62.6	40.6
—provincial	—% of public	37.5	37.6	37.4	40.7
Pensions	—% of $	57.2	49.2	61.7	30.8
—public	—% of pensions	57.3	71.2	51.1	38.2
—non-public	—% of pensions	42.7	28.8	48.9	20.8

Pensions were the single largest source of transfers, at about 57.2 percent of all transfers. While employment pensions were the single largest transfer, and the largest transfer for men, federal public pensions provided well over half of all pension income — 57.3 percent. For women, federal public pension income was even more important — 71.2 percent of all pension income, compared to 51.1 percent for men. Women received only 20.8 percent of employment pension benefits.

In terms of the provincial government, and for women, the single largest transfer at Elliot Lake was Social Assistance. This was followed closely by Workers' Compensation benefits, which, after pensions, was the largest transfer received by men. Unemployment Insurance provided a large transfer (about 10 percent of the total), though less than has sometimes been popularly believed. The federal Child Tax Benefit in Elliot Lake was relatively small in terms of total transfer income, but for women it was substantial, nearly as large as Unemployment Insurance transfers.

Public programs were about three-quarters (75.6 percent) of officially measured transfers. The federal government was by far the single largest source of transfer income, followed by the provincial government, then by private and public sector employment pension transfers. However, for men in 1994, employment pension transfers were somewhat larger than provincial transfers. Public transfers were relatively more important for women than for men as a percentage of total transfers (85.8 percent compared to 69.8 percent) though (as Table 2 has indicated) men received more dollars in total through the federal government.

Social programs were widely used in Elliot Lake. Table 4 shows the percentage of all transfer recipients using particular programs. Note that the percentages using the individual transfer programs do not add up to 100. This is because some persons use more than one transfer program in any given year (such as a combination of unemployment insurance and social assistance). In terms of the number of persons making use of transfers, the importance of pensions is again evident. No less that than 38.2 percent of transfer recipients made use of the Canada/Quebec Pension Plans, the highest level of use of the major transfer programs. Nearly one in four drew either Old Age Security or employment pensions (or both). Nearly one in five received Unemployment Insurance benefits or Social Assistance or the Child Tax Credit.

Table 4. Transfer program use at Elliot Lake, 1994

		All	Females	Males	Females as % of all
Transfer income	—$	84,889,000	30,374,000	54,515,000	35.8
	—recipients	7,880	3,910	3,970	49.6
Percent of recipients using:		100	100	100	
Federal:					
CPP/QPP	—% recipients	38.2	32.0	44.3	41.5
OAS/GIS	— recipients	24.1	22.8	25.7	46.8
UI	—% recipients	20.2	16.9	23.2	41.5
Child Tax Benefit	—% recipients	21.3	40.7	2.0	94.6
GST Credit	—% recipients	57.0	56.3	57.7	49.0
Provincial:					
Social Assistance	—% recipients	20.8	21.2	20.7	50.6
Workers' Compensation	—% recipients	11.4	4.6	18.4	20.0
Provincial Tax Credits	—% recipients	45.9	41.2	50.6	44.5
Private & public sectors:					
Employment pensions	—% recipients	24.0	15.3	32.5	31.7

In terms of the official measures, overall transfer program use was almost evenly divided between women and men. By contrast, the most gender-related programs were the Child Tax Benefit for women (94.6 percent of recipients) and Workers' Compensation for men (80.0 percent of recipients). Almost as many men as women used Social Assistance; the fact that Social Assistance was the single largest transfer to women reflects the higher average level of need women faced, particularly with their generally greater responsibility for care of children. As a whole, there is a larger gender gap in transfer amounts than in the incidence of transfer use. In 1994, women were 49.6 percent of all transfer recipients, but received 35.2 percent of all measured transfers (40.6 percent of public transfers and 20.8 percent of employment pensions).

Elliot Lake Compared to Ontario and Canada

Economic dependency in Elliot Lake in 1994 was much higher than the average for Canada. As indicated in Table 5, the economic dependency ratio for Elliot Lake was over two and a half times that for Ontario and for Canada: 69.25 percent compared to 25.89 and 26.85 percent, respectively.

Table 5. Structure of social transfers, Elliot Lake, Ontario, and Canada, 1994

		Elliot Lake	Ontario	Canada
Employment income	(1) $	122.6	150,076.3	367,925.2
	(2) no. of persons	5,580	5,306,800	14,195,310
	(3) $/person	21,971	28,280	25,919
Transfer income	(4) $	84.9	38,856.0	98,790.9
	(5) no. of recipients	7,880	5,272,740	14,821,620
	(6) $/recipients	10,774	7,369	6,665
Economic dependency ratio (EDR) [(4):(1)]		69.25	25.89	26.85
Transfer program—% of total:		100	100	100
Federal:				
CPP/QPP	—% of $	20.9	18.8	18.0
OAS/GIS	—% of $	11.9	16.1	17.7
UI	—% of $	9.8	10.4	14.5
Child Tax Benefit	—% of $	2.9	4.6	5.3
GST Credit	—% of $	1.7	2.5	2.8
Provincial:				
Social Assistance	—% of $	14.4	14.4	12.1
Workers' Compensation	—% of $	12.3	4.2	3.6
Provincial Tax Credits	—% of $	1.6	2.2	1.7
Private & public sectors:				
Employment pensions	—% of $	24.4	26.7	24.3
Public transfers only	—% of $	75.6	73.3	75.7
—federal	—% of public	62.5	71.5	77.1
—provincial	—% of public	37.5	28.5	22.9
Pensions	—% of $	57.2	61.6	60.0
—public	—% of pensions	57.3	56.6	59.5
—non-public	—% of pensions	42.7	43.4	40.5

In terms of the structure of social transfers, there are several notable similarities between the pattern at Elliot Lake and that for Ontario and for Canada. Contrary to some popular beliefs, Unemployment Insurance transfers were somewhat less important in Elliot Lake than in Ontario or Canada as a whole. Social Assistance transfers were at about the level for Ontario and only a little more than the average for Canada. Also, employment pensions were comparable in relative importance to the level in Canada and a little below that for Ontario; and CPP/QPP was only a little above the levels for Ontario and for Canada.

However, two major differences did appear. The first is the striking importance of Workers' Compensation at Elliot Lake compared to Ontario and to Canada. The second is the much lower relative weight of Old Age Security income at Elliot Lake. These two differences also help to account for why provincial government transfers play a larger role at Elliot Lake than the average for Ontario or for Canada.

Given the relatively few differences in the overall structure of transfers compared to the average for Ontario and for Canada, how can the much higher level of economic dependency at Elliot Lake be explained? It is possible to break down the economic dependency ratios into the factors accounting for the differences.

Take particularly the economic dependency ratio for Elliot Lake compared to that for Canada. The Elliot Lake economic dependency ratio is 2.58 times higher than the ratio for Canada (69.25 compared to 25.89). The differences in the ratios can be broken down into differences in the ratios of transfer recipients to employment-income earners and in the ratios of rates of transfer benefits to rates of earnings. For these two factors, the ratio of recipients to earners at Elliot Lake is 1.35 times higher than for Canada, while the ratio of transfer rates to earnings rates is 1.91 times higher.[13] Further, breaking down the rates of transfers relative to the rates of earnings, the rates of transfers at Elliot Lake were 1.61 times higher than the average for Canada, while the average earnings rate for Canada were 1.18 times the average for Elliot Lake.[14]

In essence, Elliot Lake had a higher ratio of transfer recipients to earners *as well as* both lower per person employment incomes and higher per person transfers. Between the recipients-to-earners ratio and the transfers-to-earnings-rates ratio, the rates had a larger effect on the economic dependency ratio. Between the differences in rates for transfers and rates for earnings, the higher transfer rates per recipient at Elliot Lake had a larger effect than the lower earnings rates per earner.

This is the picture for transfers and employment incomes as a whole. In terms of individual programs, Elliot Lake had a higher incidence of use for the major transfer programs than Ontario and Canada. In 1994, all types of pensions were more heavily used than the average for Ontario or for Canada. This was especially the case with the Canada/Quebec Pension Plan, which was received by no less than 44 percent of male transfer program users and 32 percent of female transfer program users compared to 27 percent and 22 percent, respectively, for Canada. Old Age Security was also more heavily used in Elliot Lake, especially by men.

Elliot Lake had over twice the use of Workers' Compensation than the average for Ontario or Canada. This reflects the history of the uranium-mining industry in Elliot Lake, as well as the in-migration of some newcomers on compensation from injuries or disabilities suffered elsewhere. Social Assistance also had a higher percentage of users than the average for Ontario and for Canada, and male use relative to female use was somewhat higher than for Ontario and for Canada as a whole.

It is important to note that, contrary to some popular beliefs, by 1994 the use of Unemployment Insurance at Elliot Lake was only a little above the average for Canada, and only four percentage points higher than for Ontario. The use of Unemployment Insurance by women in Elliot Lake was actually lower than the average for Canada.

Table 6 displays the transfer income per recipient for individual transfer programs. The overall situation, for both females and males, is that employment incomes were lower and transfer incomes higher at Elliot Lake than for Ontario or for Canada, although the picture varies substantially for individual programs.

The particular configuration of employment earnings history and need at Elliot Lake is complicated by the fact, noted earlier, that data distinguishing within-region and newcomer dependents are not available. In general, however, for programs based more on need than on employment earnings history, the transfer levels per recipient are somewhat higher in Elliot Lake than for Ontario or for Canada.

In the case of employment pensions, the average employment pension per recipient was lower than for Ontario or for Canada. By contrast, for Social Assistance, Elliot Lake levels were much higher for females than the average for both Ontario and for Canada, though for males it was in between, lower than the average for Ontario but higher than the average for Canada. The latter has to do with the fact that women tended more to be on longer-term, higher-benefit Family Benefits than men, who tended more to be on shorter-term, lower-benefit General Welfare Assistance.

For Workers' Compensation, average benefits received in 1994 were substantially higher than for Ontario and for Canada. Again, this reflects both the high level of industrial injury, disability, and death in uranium mining and the above-average wage levels in mining.

Average Unemployment Insurance benefits were higher overall at Elliot Lake than for Ontario and for Canada. This does not appear surprising, given that both males and females at Elliot Lake had higher rates of unemployment than existed for Ontario and for Canada. However, closer inspection shows that the average benefits for males were higher than for Ontario and for Canada, while female rates were lower than the average, because the mass layoffs in mining directly affected

Table 6. Transfer income per recipient, Elliot Lake, Ontario, and Canada, 1994

		All	Females	Males	Female as % of male
Employment income ($/employed person):					
	Elliot Lake	21,971	17,268	25,787	67.0
	Ontario	28,280	21,648	34,109	63.5
	Canada	25,919	19,721	31,184	63.2
Total transfer income ($/recipient):					
	Elliot Lake	10,774	7,768	13,732	56.6
	Ontario	7,369	6,178	8,901	69.4
	Canada	6,665	5,696	7,837	72.7
Transfer income by program ($/recipient):					
Federal:					
CPP/QPP	Elliot Lake	5,896	4,610	6,809	67.7
	Ontario	5,216	4,483	5,987	74.9
	Canada	4,966	4,272	5,669	75.4
OAS/GIS	Elliot Lake	5,304	5,467	5,110	107.0
	Ontario	5,427	5,692	5,091	111.8
	Canada	5,727	6,021	5,360	112.3
UI	Elliot Lake	5,228	3,747	6,347	59.0
	Ontario	4,738	4,230	5,255	80.5
	Canada	4,909	4,130	5,618	73.5
Child Tax Benefit	Elliot Lake	1,472	1,504	1,025	146.7
	Ontario	1,478	1,486	1,238	120.0
	Canada	1,521	1,531	1,219	125.6
GST Credit	Elliot Lake	330	354	307	115.3
	Ontario	315	331	296	111.8
	Canada	316	331	300	110.3
Provincial:					
Social Assistance	Elliot Lake	7,452	8,739	6,061	144.2
	Ontario	7,281	8,063	6,343	127.1
	Canada	6,234	6,931	5,419	127.9
Workers' Comp.	Elliot Lake	11,650	10,761	11,710	91.9
	Ontario	6,022	5,429	6,270	86.6
	Canada	5,173	4,611	5,410	85.2
Provincial Tax Credits	Elliot Lake	371	375	368	101.9
	Ontario	367	373	360	103.6
	Canada	370	396	343	115.5
Private and public sectors—Employment pensions:					
	Elliot Lake	10,977	7,128	12,742	55.9
	Ontario	11,824	8,010	14,741	54.3
	Canada	11,355	7,864	13,915	56.5

more men than women, and though average earnings at Elliot Lake had already fallen below the Ontario and Canadian averages, the duration of unemployment was longer, especially for males. As will be seen, total female employment income actually increased over the period, while that for men fell sharply.

If the Canada/Quebec Pension Plans reflected exclusively the employment earnings history of recipients, it might, like employment pensions, be at or near the average for Ontario and for Canada. However, the program contains a disability component; it also contains provisions for the exclusion of periods of zero or low earnings due to caring for children under seven and for credit-splitting between spouses in the event of marriage breakdown. These need-related provisions help account for the generally higher CPP/QPP levels in Elliot Lake compared to those for employment pensions, including the lower gender gap for CPP/QPP relative to employment pensions (67.7 percent compared to 55.9 percent).

The situation with Old Age Security — where the average benefit at Elliot Lake is a little lower — is somewhat more complex, especially given the inadequacies of existing data on income distribution and various combinations of transfers. Old Age Security data for June 1994[15] suggest that although Elliot Lake had a higher proportion of OAS users than Ontario and Canada, these seniors were in younger age cohorts, which generally have lower levels of income inadequacy than higher age cohorts. Compared to Canada, a lower proportion of seniors at Elliot Lake received the income-tested Guaranteed Income Supplement; while compared to Ontario, a higher proportion received the Supplement (though fewer of these received the maximum supplement). The relatively high incidence among male seniors of Guaranteed Income Supplement use in Elliot Lake compared to Ontario (despite overall younger ages) helps explain the higher average male benefit compared to Ontario.

Changes in Economic Dependency Since 1989

It is well known in the Elliot Lake area that employment incomes have fallen and transfer incomes have risen since the first wave of mine layoffs began in 1990. But increased transfers fell far short of the income losses suffered.

Table 7 covers the period 1989 to 1990. The base year, 1989, is the full year before the first wave of mass layoffs hit Elliot Lake. Unfortunately, the official taxfiler data prior to 1993 excludes data for the Guaranteed Income Supplement and Spousal Allowance programs within the Old Age Security system. Also, totals on provincial government transfers are not broken down by program prior to 1994, and provincial data as a whole are excluded prior to 1990. To obtain greater year-to-year consistency, the transfer data in Table 7 include both federal public transfers and employment pensions, but they exclude provincial transfers.

To begin, there was a massive increase in economic dependency over the period. The economic dependency ratios for federal transfers and employment pensions shifted upwards from 10.24 to 49.63, nearly fivefold. We will see in a moment that the ratio for 1989 was well below the ratio for Ontario and even more so for Canada. One year later, in 1990, Elliot Lake had moved above the Ontario and Canadian levels.

Table 7. Economic dependency at Elliot Lake, pensions and federal transfers, 1989–1994

	1989	1990	1991	1992	1993	1994	1989–94 change ($000)	(%)
Employment income ($000)								
—all	220,234	176,437	141,598	134,959	120,415	122,592	-97,042	-44.3
—females	42,713	40,024	41,537	43,752	43,311	43,169	456	1.1
—males	177,521	136,413	100,060	91,207	77,104	79,424	-98,097	-55.3
Employed persons (no.)								
—all					5,410	5,580		
—females					2,480	2,500		
—males					2,930	3,080		
Income/employed person ($)								
—all					22,258	21,970		
—females					17,464	17,268		
—males					26,315	25,787		
Pensions, federal transfers ($000)								
—all	22,545	28,735	43,126	50,188	59,187	60,839	38,294	169.9
—females	8,504	9,827	12,394	14,964	18,001	20,581	12,077	142.0
—males	14,041	18,908	30,732	35,225	41,186	40,257	26,216	186.7
Recipients (no.)								
—all	6,350	6,580	6,920	7,350	7,610	7,880	1,530	24.1
—females	2,770	2,900	3,040	3,250	3,680	3,910	1,140	41.2
—males	3,570	3,690	3,890	4,100	3,930	3,970	400	11.2
Income/recipient ($)								
—all	3,550	4,367	6,232	6,828	7,778	7,721	4,170	117.5
—females	3,070	3,389	4,077	4,604	4,892	5,264	2,194	71.3
—males	3,933	5,124	7,900	8,591	10,480	10,140	6,207	157.8
Employment pensions ($ 000)								
—all	6,550	8,600	12,448	15,079	18,263	20,746	14,196	216.7
—females	1,573	1,809	2,121	2,723	3,549	4,309	2,736	173.9
—males	4,977	6,791	10,327	12,356	14,714	16,437	11,460	230.3
Recipients (no.)								
—all	860	1,120	1,270	1,530	1,730	1,890	1,030	119.8
—females	310	360	390	470	540	600	290	93.5
—males	550	760	890	1,070	1,190	1,290	740	134.5
$ /recipient								
—all	7,616	7,679	9,802	9,856	10,557	10,977	3,360	44.1
—females	5,074	5,025	5,438	5,794	6,572	7,182	2,107	41.5
—males	9,049	8,936	11,603	11,548	12,365	12,742	3,693	40.8
Federal transfers ($ 000)								
—all	15,995	20,135	30,678	35,109	40,924	40,093	24,098	150.7
—females	6,931	8,018	10,273	12,241	14,452	16,272	9,341	134.8
—males	9,064	12,117	20,405	22,869	26,472	23,820	14,756	162.8
Recipients (no.)								
—all	6,350	6,580	6,920	7,350	7,610	7,880	1,530	24.1
—females	2,770	2,900	3,040	3,250	3,680	3,910	1,140	41.2
—males	3,570	3,690	3,890	4,100	3,930	3,970	400	11.2
Income/recipient ($)								
—all	2,519	3,060	4,433	4,777	5,378	5,088	2,569	102.0
—females	2,502	2,765	3,379	3,766	3,927	4,162	1,659	66.3
—males	2,539	3,284	5,246	5,578	6,736	6,000	3,461	136.3
Economic Dependency Ratios								
Employment pensions + federal transfers								
-all	10.24	16.29	30.46	37.19	49.15	49.63		
—females	19.91	24.55	29.84	34.20	41.56	47.68		
—males	7.91	13.86	30.71	38.62	53.42	50.69		
Employment pensions								
—all	2.97	4.87	8.79	11.17	15.17	16.92		
—females	3.68	4.52	5.11	6.22	8.19	9.98		
—males	2.80	4.98	10.32	13.55	19.08	20.70		
Federal transfers								
—all	7.26	11.41	21.67	26.01	33.99	32.70		
—females	16.23	20.03	24.73	27.98	33.37	37.69		
—males	5.11	8.88	20.39	25.07	34.33	29.99		

Thus, from being below the average for economic dependency in 1989, Elliot Lake rose to a level among the most highly transfer-dependent communities in Canada. This shift needs to be looked at in terms of its two main components: the decline in employment income and the rise in transfer payments.

From 1989 to 1994, Elliot Lake suffered a major collapse in employment income — by nearly $100 million over five years — to about $123 million per year or 55 percent of its 1989 level. Cumulatively, this was an enormous loss — over $405 million for the years 1990 to 1994.[16] This loss was mostly in the employment incomes of men; apart from 1990 and 1991, women's total employment income actually grew a little over the period.

During the same period, federal transfer income increased from $16.0 to $40.1 million, or about 151 percent, while employment pension income increased from $6.6 to $20.7 million or about 217 percent. Cumulatively, for federal transfers alone, this was an increase of about $87 million. Cumulatively, for both federal transfers and employment pensions, this was an increase of about $129 million.

The total increase in transfers amounted to about 46 percent of the total loss of employment income, or a net revenue loss of about $220 million as of 1994. These figures cover only cash transfers to individuals and cannot be taken to be a full accounting of the social costs of the changes in Elliot Lake following 1990. For instance, they do not include increases or decreases in transfers to corporations, or to municipalities, such as provincial transfers to the municipality for debt reduction or other programs.

The changes in transfer income differed by type of transfer. The percentage increase in total employment-pension income was greater than for federal transfers, but the absolute amount of the federal transfer was much larger. The increase in employment-pension income was more the result of an increase in the number of recipients, especially male recipients, than in an increase in the per-recipient value of the pensions, though the latter did increase. By contrast, the increase in federal transfers was more the result of an increase in the per-recipient value of transfers — an approximate doubling, from $2,519 to $5,088 — than it was in the number of recipients, which grew by 24.1 percent.[17]

In terms of individual transfer programs, there were increased levels of transfers to Elliot Lake for all federal transfer programs except benefits directed to children. The decline in these latter benefits occurred because the universal Family Allowance was eliminated by the Mulroney Conservative government in 1992, and the full loss was not made up by the increases in the Child Tax Benefit program. Of the total $24.1 million increase per year in federal transfers to Elliot Lake, the increases, in order of size, came through the Canada/Quebec Pension Plans (47.4 percent), Old Age Security (28.4 percent), Unemployment Insurance (20.7 percent), the Federal Sales/GST Tax Credits (5.3 percent) and, negatively, benefits to children (-1.8 percent).

It is important to note, however, that a peak in total federal transfers may have been reached in 1993, as a result of a 42.3 percent decline in Unemployment Insurance transfers between 1993 and 1994. It remains to be seen whether the 1993 peak in federal transfers was a short-term or long-term phenomenon, although without a major increase in employment or a mass exodus of the non-employed population, it is unlikely that the economic dependency situation will soon return to pre-1990 conditions. What seems clear now is that there has been a sharp fall in the number of those receiving Unemployment Insurance benefits in Elliot Lake, from a peak of 2,150 in 1991 to 1,590 in 1994. As well, the rate of benefits for both women and men was also declining, from $7,554 per recipient in 1993 to $5,228 in 1994. That said, the cumulative total on Unemployment Insurance benefits received within Elliot Lake above the 1989 level was about $35 million and still rising, even if more slowly.

Changes in Elliot Lake Compared to Ontario and Canada

How did the growing transfer dependence in Elliot Lake compare to what was happening in Ontario and in Canada?

The Canadian economy was undergoing major changes between 1990 and 1994, both structurally, with free trade, the GST, and continuing technological change, as well as cyclically, with a "recession" (or depression) beginning in 1990. Thus, it is useful to consider whether the general movement of economic dependency in Ontario and Canada could alter the picture for Elliot Lake. Table 8 shows that there was a major increase in economic dependency for both Ontario and Canada during these years. In fact, the economic dependency ratio for Ontario more than doubled between 1989 and 1994, from 12.57 to 26.85, shifting Ontario from below the Canadian average (15.28) to slightly above it (25.89).

The increase in economic dependency in Elliot Lake was not only large in its own terms but it also increased relative to the Ontario and Canadian levels, at least until 1993. The upward shift in the dependency ratio differed between women and men. Comparing the Elliot Lake situation in 1989 with Canada, women were already above the Canadian

Table 8. Economic dependency ratios for selected communities
in the North Shore Region, 1989–1994*

	1989	1990	1991	1992	1993	1994
Canada	15.28	17.77	23.47	25.80	26.92	25.89
Ontario	12.57	20.38	21.48	24.31	25.89	26.85
Algoma Mills	14.53	24.80	38.81	36.84	43.46	40.12
Blind River	14.91	27.28	34.54	40.83	48.27	47.18
Elliot Lake	**10.24**	**21.39**	**40.24**	**51.58**	**69.70**	**69.25**
Espanola	14.45	21.21	24.27	26.81	30.45	29.63
Iron Bridge	24.68	41.41	51.17	53.48	64.32	59.72
Massey	23.51	36.83	48.03	54.54	61.16	54.12
McKerrow	21.95	38.34	37.27	38.43	45.87	41.49
Serpent River	13.55	29.86	54.08	73.38	96.71	77.13
Spanish	19.80	31.17	49.70	67.47	78.53	74.96
Spragge	14.74	25.67	47.93	63.42	67.52	68.45
Thessalon	24.72	39.21	42.70	47.32	49.93	52.99
Walford Station	23.75	41.03	69.12	82.25	101.82	98.12
Webbwood	21.91	33.87	43.20	54.21	52.62	43.24
Average (unweighted)	*18.7*	*31.7*	*44.7*	*53.1*	*62.3*	*58.2*

* 1989 excludes provincial transfers, and 1989 to 1993 excludes the GIS and SPA.

average, then rose further above the average; Elliot Lake men were below the Canadian average in 1989 and 1990, then in 1991 jumped above not only the Canadian average but also the level for women in Elliot Lake. The increase in the overall economic dependency ratios from 1990, the first year of the mass layoffs, to 1994 was more strongly affected by the massive increase for men compared to women (a jump of 4.2 times compared to 1.8 times).

To examine some of these changes at the level of individual programs, Table 9 shows the changes in transfers between 1989 and 1994 in three major areas, employment pensions, the Canada/Quebec Pension Plans, and Unemployment Insurance. The table reinforces the observation that Elliot Lake shifted in economic dependency from being below to much above the average for Canada. For all three areas, the percentage increases in numbers of recipients and amounts per recipient were much higher than for Canada.

Table 9 also shows that, between 1989 and 1994, the benefit rate per recipient for employment pensions was below the Canadian average in 1989 and remained below it in 1994, though less so. By contrast, the rate of Canada/Quebec Pension Plan benefits was above the average in Canada in both years and increasing slightly relative to the average. The increase in the benefit per recipient was more dramatic with Unemployment Insurance. From being well below the Canadian average in 1989, the Unemployment Insurance benefit per recipient moved to be above the average. These upward increases are consistent with the general pattern, and for both women and men. In 1989, the average benefits of women and men for federal and employment pension benefits at Elliot

Table 9. Economic dependency, selected transfer programs,
Elliot Lake and Canada, 1989 and 1994

	1989	1994	% change
Employment pensions:			
Amount ($000) Elliot Lake	6,550	20,746	216.7
—recipients (no.)	860	1,890	119.8
—per recipient ($)	7,616	10,977	44.1
Amount ($000) Canada	14,378,205	24,013,695	67.0
—recipients (no.)	1,696,440	2,114,840	24.7
—per recipient ($)	8,476	11,355	34.0
Per recip: Elliot Lake/Canada	89.9	96.7	
EDR Elliot Lake	2.97	16.92	469.7
EDR Canada	4.43	6.53	47.4
EDR: Elliot Lake/Canada	67.0	259.1	
Canada/Quebec Pension Plan:			
Amount ($000) Elliot Lake	6,328	17,747	180.5
—recipients (no.)	1,350	3,010	123.0
—per recipient ($)	4,687	5,896	25.8
Amount ($000) Canada	10,627,862	17,811,510	67.6
—recipients (no.)	2,667,710	3,586,670	34.4
—per recipient ($)	3,984	4,966	24.7
Per recip: Elliot Lake/Canada	117.7	118.7	
EDR Elliot Lake	2.82	14.48	413.5
EDR Canada	3.28	4.84	47.6
EDR: Elliot Lake/Canada	86.0	299.2	
Unemployment Insurance Benefits:			
Amount ($000) Elliot Lake	3,325	8,312	150.0
—recipients (no.)	1,160	1,590	37.1
—per recipient ($)	2,866	5,228	82.4
Amount ($000) Canada	10,660,440	14,357,913	34.7
—recipients (no.)	2,818,600	2,925,010	3.8
—per recipient ($)	3,782	4,909	29.8
Per recip: Elliot Lake/Canada	75.8	106.5	
EDR Elliot Lake	1.51	6.78	349.0
EDR Canada	3.29	3.90	18.5
EDR: Elliot Lake/Canada	45.9	173.8	

Lake were below that for Canada, but over the period these averages increased to above the average for Canada.[18]

The North Shore Communities and Elliot Lake

The sharply increased level of economic dependency that occurred in Elliot Lake extended into the adjacent North Shore communities (see Table 1, and map on p. ?). Many people who were laid off in mining or who experienced related layoffs in Elliot Lake resided in these communities. As well, businesses and employment inside these communities were affected by the major contraction in aggregate demand in the region.

Table 8 also shows changes in the economic dependency ratios for the main North Shore communities as well as for Elliot Lake itself. The table includes some communities that might be deemed as bordering or just outside the North Shore commutershed for Elliot Lake: Espanola, McKerrow, Thessalon, and Webbwood. The dependency ratios in 1989 are lower than actual because the transfers exclude provincial transfers; this exclusion exaggerates the increase from 1989 to 1990. However, including the year 1989 does permit an initial comparison of the situation of the various communities in the North Shore area before the first of the mass layoffs in 1990.

In 1989, Elliot Lake had the lowest level of economic dependency and was the only community below the averages for Ontario and for Canada, although Algoma Mills, Blind River, Espanola, Serpent River, and Spragge were still below the average for Canada. That soon changed. In 1990, every community was above the average for both Ontario and Canada, a situation that continued until at least 1994. A nearly parallel upward shift in economic dependency occurred throughout the Elliot Lake commutershed. Only Espanola, which still has a major forestry-related industry and is outside the commutershed, had an economic dependency ratio even close to that of the Ontario or Canadian averages.

In those communities to which Elliot Lake was closest, Serpent River, Spanish, and Spragge, the levels of economic dependency surpassed those of Elliot Lake itself. The previously high-dependency communities of Iron Bridge, Massey, Thessalon, and Walford faced even higher levels of economic dependency. In 1993, for example, the small community of Walford was receiving an amount in transfers about equal to its residents' employment incomes.

The unweighted average for the communities suggests that economic dependency reached a peak in 1993. Again, it remains to be seen whether this was a short- or long-term phenomenon, but average economic dependency did decline a little in 1994; in general, it declined more outside Elliot Lake than in the city itself. Spragge and Thessalon were exceptions; economic dependency there continued to increase in 1994.

What accounts for the differences among the North Shore communities? Each community has a variety of features (size, location, economic structure, social composition, etc.) that are reflected in differences in employment incomes and in the structure of transfers. Take the two rather different North Shore communities of Blind River and Spragge (which are presented later in Table 11): Blind River has a lower economic dependency ratio than Elliot Lake, mainly because it has a lower ratio of recipients to earners and because it has both a lower rate of benefits per recipient and a slightly higher rate of employment income per earner. On the other hand, Spragge has a very similar economic dependency ratio to Elliot Lake, even though it has a lower ratio of recipients to earners. This is because it had both a lower rate of benefits and an even lower rate of employment income per earner. Further, Blind River and Spragge are different from Elliot Lake in terms of the structure of transfer programs. In particular, both depend less on employment pensions but more on public transfers, particularly Social Assistance, UI, and, for Spragge, CPP/QPP and Workers' Compensation.

Economic Dependency in Other Hinterland Regions

The situation at Elliot Lake and the North Shore communities is not unique to Canada. Many other hinterland communities have suffered mass layoffs, and relative and absolute regional decline. It is useful, then, to view Elliot Lake in relation to some other selected hinterland areas. Table 10 displays the level of economic dependency in 1994 in selected mining/resource hinterland areas.

The levels of economic dependency at Elliot Lake (and the North Shore generally) appear to be as high as, if not higher than, most of the selected hinterland areas. These include areas which often are stereotyped as chronically dependent, like parts of Nova Scotia and Newfoundland.

Some of the areas shown in Table 10 have gone through a period of decline for many years, such as the decline in mining in Buchans, Cape Breton, Schefferville, or Rabbit Lake. There the level of transfer dependency remains high, though in some cases not even as high as at Elliot Lake. By contrast, in some fairly active mining areas, like Elkford, Sparwood, and Tumbler Ridge in British Columbia or Thompson in Manitoba, the dependency ratios were much lower for both females and males and below the provincial averages.

To give one last brief comparison of the situation at Elliot Lake and the North Shore relative to an area widely viewed as chronically dependent, Table 11 displays the structure of economic dependency for Elliot Lake, Blind River, and Spragge alongside that for the Cape Breton region and Sydney in Nova Scotia, as well as for Canada as a whole.

The Elliot Lake–North Shore region and the Cape Breton region share the common features of virtually all highly transfer-dependent areas: they have higher than average transfers and lower than average employment incomes.

At the same time, there are some differences in the dependency ratios. In particular, Cape Breton has a lower economic dependency ratio than Elliot Lake even though the two have similar ratios of recipients to earners. The key difference is that Cape Breton's rate of benefit per

Table 10. Economic dependency ratios for selected areas of Canada, 1994

	All	Females	Males
Canada	**26.85**	**35.92**	**21.98**
Ontario	**25.89**	**34.10**	**21.31**
Atikokan	32.36	44.22	27.14
Elliot Lake	69.25	70.36	68.64
Kapuskasing	34.09	40.02	31.31
Kirkland Lake	46.96	61.77	38.26
North Bay	38.18	48.34	32.17
Sault Ste Marie	41.56	51.23	36.40
Sudbury	33.90	41.19	30.20
Thunder Bay	30.83	39.39	26.36
Timmins	28.22	42.82	21.62
Newfoundland	**42.06**	**55.37**	**35.69**
Baie Verte	39.40	42.03	37.97
Buchans	78.97	82.85	77.06
Nova Scotia	**37.56**	**49.44**	**31.55**
Cape Breton County	60.77	82.20	50.06
Glace Bay	70.18	103.50	55.19
New Glasgow	39.20	58.84	30.35
Pictou County	45.53	64.13	36.92
Sydney	48.39	64.93	39.43
Québec	**29.42**	**39.48**	**24.05**
L'Amiante	38.59	53.81	31.57
Rouyn-Noranda	27.44	38.87	22.25
Schefferville	51.54	75.80	39.44
Sept-Rivières-Caniapiscou	22.49	36.06	17.56
Thetford Mines	37.96	51.67	31.00
Manitoba	**29.64**	**40.30**	**23.68**
Thompson	12.53	21.21	8.79
Saskatchewan	**30.24**	**42.49**	**23.69**
Rabbit Lake	55.10	63.02	50.08
Alberta	**18.67**	**27.30**	**14.50**
Cache Creek	34.11	46.68	29.27
British Columbia	**24.86**	**32.77**	**20.63**
Alberni-Clayoquot	32.19	47.63	26.33
Campbell River	23.10	35.77	18.13
Central Kootenay	36.63	45.83	32.10
Elkford	8.22	22.29	5.10
Kimberley	36.00	49.98	30.21
Port Hardy	14.60	29.52	9.28
Sparwood	24.12	47.30	17.77
Trail	44.44	59.49	37.59
Tumbler Ridge	5.38	16.39	2.83
Yukon	**15.65**	**16.53**	**15.01**
Faro	27.78	32.76	25.80

Table 11. Structure of social transfers, Elliot Lake
and selected areas, 1994

	Elliot Lake	Blind River	Spragge	Cape Breton	Sydney	Canada
Employment income						
(1) $m	122.6	48.9	1.6	967.3	418.5	367,925.2
(2) persons (no.)	5,580	2,190	100	49,820	19,470	14,195,310
(3) $/person	21,971	22,340	16,100	19,415	21,495	25,919
Transfer income						
(4) $m	84.9	23.1	1.1	587.8	202.5	98,790.9
(5) recipients (no.)	7,880	2,690	130	71,670	25,420	14,821,620
(6) $/recipient	10,774	8,580	8,477	8,201	7,967	6,665
Economic dependency ratio [(4):(1)]						
	69.25	47.18	68.45	60.77	48.39	26.85
Transfer program–% of total:	100	100	100	100	100	100
Federal:						
CPP/QPP –% of $	20.9	17.1	23.7	19.8	20.6	18.0
OAS/GIS –% of $	11.9	12.8	10.1	15.4	17.7	17.7
UI –% of $	9.8	12.3	12.4	22.1	18.4	14.5
Child Tax Benefit –% of $	2.9	4.9	2.7	4.4	4.1	5.3
GST Credit –% of $	1.7	2.4	2.5	2.6	2.6	2.8
Provincial:						
Social Assistance –% of $	14.4	20.8	16.2	11.5	11.0	12.1
Workers' Comp. –% of $	12.3	9.8	17.8	5.2	2.8	3.6
Prov. Tax Credits –% of $	1.6	1.8	1.5	0.0	0.0	1.7
Private & public sectors:						
Employment pensions						
–% of $	24.4	18.0	13.2	19.0	22.6	24.3
Public transfers only–% of $	75.6	82.0	86.9	81.0	77.3	75.7
—federal –% fed.	62.5	60.4	59.2	79.5	82.1	77.1
—provincial –% prov.	37.5	39.6	40.8	20.5	17.9	22.9
Pensions –% of $	57.2	47.9	47.0	54.2	60.9	60.0
—public –% public	57.3	62.4	71.8	65.0	62.9	59.5
—non-public –% priv.	42.7	37.6	28.2	35.0	37.1	40.5

recipient and rate of employment income per earner were not only absolutely lower than those of Elliot Lake (but not lower than those of Spragge), but also the benefits rate was even lower relative to the employment-income rate. For Sydney, the ratio of dependents to earners was actually lower than the level for Elliot Lake (and about the level of Spragge). On the other hand, the rate of employment income was close to that of Elliot Lake while the benefits rate was much lower.

In terms of the structure of transfers in these hinterland areas, pension income as a whole had a relatively smaller share of all transfers than the average for Canada. Among types of pension income, employment pensions were larger at Elliot Lake than in the other areas, where public pensions played a bigger role. By contrast, Unemployment Insurance was more important in the Cape Breton area than in the Elliot Lake–North Shore area and compared to the Canadian average, while

Social Assistance was more important in the Elliot Lake-North Shore area and compared to the Canadian average. Workers' Compensation played a much bigger role in the Elliot Lake–North Shore area compared to the Cape Breton area, though it was still more important in Cape Breton as a whole than the average for Canada.

In all these areas, federal transfers were larger than provincial transfers, but federal transfers were even more important in the Cape Breton region. In the Elliot Lake–North Shore region, provincial transfers, especially Workers' Compensation and Social Assistance, played a larger role; indeed, the federal share of public transfers was below the average for Canada while the provincial share was above it.[19]

Conclusion

This paper has examined some of the increase in economic dependency, particularly transfer dependency, that occurred in the Elliot Lake and North Shore communities over the years from 1989 to 1994. These were crisis years for the region, caused mainly by the mine closures and mass layoffs at Elliot Lake between 1990 and 1996.

Economic dependency increased in the Elliot Lake and North Shore communities much beyond the Ontario and Canadian averages to a level in the range of other hinterland communities that have gone through mine closures and other resource-industry decline.

The causes of the dramatic shift in Elliot Lake's economic dependency ratios are clear — lower incomes and higher transfers. These in turn were made up of increases in the ratio of transfer recipients to earners and in the ratio of average benefit rates to average income rates. The increase in the number of transfer recipients relative to the number of persons with employment earnings reflected the massive job loss and unemployment in the area. In terms of official transfer dependency measures, however, increases in rates of benefits and decreases in the rates of income had a bigger impact on the economic dependency ratios. Elliot Lake had higher than average benefits in several types of transfers, particularly in programs geared more to need than to employment-earnings history or to a mixture of the two, such as Social Assistance or Workers' Compensation. Although employment pensions were the single largest transfer and the largest for men, the average value of employment pensions at Elliot Lake was below the average for Ontario and for Canada.

What does this discussion of transfer-type economic dependency suggest for the short- to medium-term future of Elliot Lake and the

North Shore communities? Social program transfers are directly affected by declining labour market conditions and by the current trend of the federal and provincial governments to cut program standards. For example, Unemployment Insurance transfers, already declining in Elliot Lake, will likely decline further, not only in the average amounts of benefits but also in the number of eligible recipients, as the number and quality of jobs declines and ineligible self-employment or informal economic activity increases. At the present time, the major cuts of the Chrétien Liberal government to Unemployment Insurance (renamed and introduced as Employment Insurance as of July 1, 1996) are now beginning to be felt.

Pension transfers will continue to be a major source of transfer income. But these, too, are affected by declining labour market conditions in the region. Over time, pension incomes will decline as local workers with lower or no employment income reach retirement. Newcomer pensioners may compensate to some degree for this. A major problem, however, could come from corporate pressures on the federal government to further reduce the role of the public pension system in Canada, which would have major adverse effects on the region.

The loss of the mining industry in Elliot Lake means that the region will have much less of the high levels of industrial injury, disability, and death associated with mining. But it also means that, over time, there will be a decline in Workers' Compensation transfers, which have been exceptionally important to the region.

Social Assistance is the program most directly driven by absolute need and the "residual" program most directly burdened by cuts to other social programs such as to Unemployment Insurance. It is likely to face pressure for increased transfers. The cuts of the provincial Harris Conservative government to Social Assistance (which began under the Rae NDP government) may have caused a reduction in caseloads, but it is doubtful, barring a major increase in employment or exodus of population, whether such caseload reductions can go further or even be sustained, given the current economic situation of regional decline. Perhaps, more than any program, Social Assistance is likely to remain a major factor in the transfer structure of the region.

It is an important fact about the Canadian taxation and transfer system that cuts to transfer spending tend to have more regressive distributive effects than cuts to taxes. Whatever the particular federal or provincial government, a continued policy direction of cuts to transfer programs is likely to have disproportionately adverse effects on low-income, high-transfer regions like Elliot Lake and the North Shore. This policy direction will also add to persisting pressures for an exodus of the population, particularly younger people, that could compound the difficulties of economic development in the region.

At this point, no government appears willing to address the underlying problem of economic dependency and declining living standards in the Elliot Lake-North Shore region or, for that matter, in other hinterland areas of Canada. For many of us, this will remain an unacceptable status quo. Without a major improvement in the quantity and quality of jobs available in the region, transfer dependency is likely to remain high by average standards for Ontario and for Canada. This transfer dependency will deeply affect economic and social life in the region not only for the "old-timers" who built the communities but also for the coming generation.

Notes

[1] A longer version of this paper (ELTAS Analysis Series #1A6) is available from INORD at Laurentian University. This paper has been produced as part of the Elliot Lake Tracking and Adjustment Study (ELTAS) sponsored by Laurentian University and sustained by the continued support and participation of many people in Elliot Lake and the North Shore. ELTAS has been funded largely by a grant from the Innovations Branch of Human Resources Development Canada, but the contents of this paper are the responsibility of the author and do not necessarily reflect the views of Human Resources Development Canada. I would like to acknowledge the work of colleagues and staff in and around the ELTAS project, including Jane Pitblado of INORD, and last but not least, the personal support of Mary, Kate, and Jane.

[2] At the end of August 1990, Rio ended production at two of its three mines in the area, Panel Mine and Quirke Mine; Stanleigh Mine, the third mine and the last producing uranium mine in Ontario, was closed in June 1996. Denison partially cut its workforce at the end of July 1990, but its mine was closed and the bulk of its mine workforce laid off at the end of April 1992.

[3] Statistics Canada, *The Daily*, 28 April 1992. Small municipalities were defined as having populations from 5,000 to 24,999. The labour force percentage is from the *1986 Census* (Statistics Canada, catalogue no. 94–112, 6).

[4] A major portion of this in-migration came as a result of Elliot Lake's Retirement Living program, which promoted Elliot Lake as a low-cost, amenity-rich community for outside retirees to move to. The Retirement Living program and its related in-migration is widely viewed as being the main factor responsible for a stabilization of the declining population of Elliot Lake during the years considered here. While it would be useful to know the relative portion of within-region versus newcomer dependency, we unfortunately do not yet have the data needed. At the time of writing, a key

source of this type of data, the 1996 census, has not yet been released.

[5] A deeper discussion of some of these and related issues is available in: David Leadbeater, "'Economic dependency' in the decline of the Welfare State: problems of meaning, measurement, and policy," unpublished paper, 1997; and David Foot and David Leadbeater, "What is measured by dependency ratios," paper presented to a joint meeting of the Canadian Economics Association and the Canadian Population Society, University of Prince Edward Island, Charlottetown, June 5, 1992.

[6] Foot and Leadbeater, "What is measured by dependency ratios."

[7] The data and details of definitions and sources for the tables presented in this paper are contained in the special-order tabulations for "Economic dependency profiles" of the Small Area and Administrative Data Division of Statistics Canada.

[8] Included together with wage and salary income are "commissions from employment, training allowances, tips and gratuities." Self-employment income is defined as "net income from business, profession, farming and commissions." Quoted from "Economic dependency profiles" of the Small Area and Administrative Data Division of Statistics Canada.

[9] Canada, Department of Finance, *Economic reference tables.* Catalogue no. F1–26. (Ottawa: Canada Department of Supply and Services, 1996), 23. Employment income was about 70 percent of all personal income (market-based income plus transfers). These and the personal income data in this paragraph are derived not from taxfiler data but from Statistics Canada's national accounting data. Government transfers to individuals accounted for about 18 percent of all personal income.

[10] For the overall economic dependency ratio, the amount for total transfers for Elliot Lake (row 4) is compared to the amount for total employment income (row 1) for all persons who reported employment or transfer income. The result of division can be multiplied by 100 and used in the form of a percentage (69.25) as is done here, but it could also be left as a fraction (0.6925 to 1).

[11] A few points about the data in Table 2 and later tables need to be noted. First, based as they are on taxfiler data, the amounts for both employment and transfer income are subject to some limited under-reporting. The actual number of persons reporting is quite high. In 1994, taxfiler data covered 68.3 percent of the Canadian population of all ages, or about 85.7 percent of the population 15 and over. Most children do not file, nor do some seniors nor a relatively small number of others, because they have little or no income. The percentage of the population reporting has been rising somewhat during the 1990s possibly in part because filing became necessary to obtain the GST credit and Child Tax benefits.

Second, in terms of the amounts reported, it is difficult to know precisely whether there has been more or less reporting error in employment incomes relative to transfer incomes, though this problem is reduced somewhat by using the dependency ratios. For instance, a 4-percent level of underreporting of employment income and a 3- or 4-percent level of transfer income will mean no change or much less than a 3- or 4-percent change to the economic dependency ratio. As well, the level of coverage for transfer payments is known to be relatively high, for instance, 91 percent for Canada/Quebec Pension Plan benefits, 90 percent for UI benefits; the lowest level of coverage, for Social Assistance, was still at 78 percent. The level of coverage refers to the amount reported by taxfilers relative to the amount known to have been spent through administrative data. For 1994, the reported coverage for other programs was 100 percent for Child Tax benefits, 85 percent for Old Age Security benefits, and 95 percent for Workers' Compensation. If there is a limited reporting bias in the taxfiler data for the years covered here, it would probably be towards a somewhat lower percentage of error in the reporting of transfer income and a somewhat higher percentage of error in the reporting of employment income (the latter due mainly to the decline in the importance of formal wage-earner jobs with deduction at source). This would mean that the increases in economic dependency ratios after 1989 could be slightly overstated, though not to any extent large enough to alter the basic picture of sharply increased economic dependency that emerged in the Elliot Lake and North Shore communities.

[12] The standard-reduction trend in federal policy is documented in Ken Battle and Sherri Torjman, *Federal Social Programs: Setting the Record Straight* (Ottawa: Caledon Institute for Social Policy, 1993). A temporary exception was probably Unemployment Insurance standards related to training access, in which there was somewhat increased support in the early 1990s.

[13] The ratio of recipients to earners (person units) for Elliot Lake is 7,880/5,580 = 1.412, while for Canada it is 14,821,620/14,195,310 = 1.044; these in turn give an Elliot Lake to Canada ratio of 1.352 (1.412/1.044). The ratio of transfer rates to earnings rates (dollar units) for Elliot Lake is 10,773/21,970 = 0.4904, while for Canada it is 6,665/25,919 = 0.2571; these in turn give an Elliot Lake to Canada ratio of 1.907. These Elliot Lake to Canada ratios can account for the 2.58 times higher economic dependency ratio for Elliot Lake than for Canada (1.35 x 1.91). This said, the absolute difference in rates of transfers ($4,108 per recipient) was similar to the absolute difference in the rates of earnings ($3,949 per earner).

[14]
$$\frac{RT_{EL}/RE_{EL}}{RT_C/RE_C} = \frac{RT_{EL}}{RT_C} \cdot \frac{RE_C}{RE_{EL}} = 1.907$$

The ratio of Elliot Lake to Canada transfer rates (in dollar units) is 10,773/6,665 = 1.616. The ratio of Canada to Elliot Lake earnings rates is 25,919/21,970 = 1.180. These factors can account for the 1.91 times higher transfer to earnings rates ratio for Elliot Lake than for Canada (1.62 x 1.18).

[15] These observations are based on Old Age Security data provided by the Social Program Information and Analysis Division of Human Resources

Development Canada. I would like to acknowledge the work of research assistant Victoria Nadalin in helping to prepare tables using these Old Age Security data.

[16] These and the following calculations are neither discounted nor deflated. They simply assume the 1989 income or transfer flow had continued unchanged in current dollars. The losses would be somewhat less if later net losses were discounted relative to earlier net losses.

[17] Between 1989 and 1994, total transfer income increased from $16.0 million to $40.1 million or by $24.1 million. Assuming the 1994 numbers of recipients but 1989 amount per recipient would give $19.9 million; while assuming the 1989 numbers of recipients but 1994 amount per recipient would give $32.3 million. The increase in numbers of recipients, then, accounts for $3.9 million or 16.0 percent of the $24.1 million change; while the increase in amounts per recipient accounts for $16.3 million or 67.7 percent. The remaining $3.9 million or 16.3 percent is their joint effect.

[18] In 1989, the average amount for recipients of federal transfers and employment pensions at Elliot Lake was $3,550 compared to $4,125 for Canada. For women, it was $3,070 compared to $3,445 and, for men, $3,933 compared to $4,779. In 1994, the average for women was $5,264 for Elliot Lake compared to $4,606 for Canada, and for men, $10,140 compared to $6,607. (Table 7 for Elliot Lake numbers; the Canada numbers are from the unpublished "Economic dependency profiles" data cited earlier.)

[19] Though not reported here, the federal share was also below the Ontario provincial average (71.5 percent), while the provincial share was above it (28.5 percent).

Chapter 12
Local Service Providers' Perceptions of the Effects of Mass Layoffs[1]
Anne-Marie Mawhiney and Jan Lewis

In this chapter, we look at the impact of the layoffs on the community of Elliot Lake through the eyes of health, legal, and social service providers. Our intent is to estimate the wider, and perhaps more hidden, social consequences of the layoffs by learning about the more general effects of the layoffs on the community. We describe the results of the first stage of the Social and Institutional Costs Sub-Project of the Elliot Lake Tracking and Adjustment Study funded by Human Resources Development Canada. This paper is based on the *Inventory of Perceived Effects of Layoffs in Elliot Lake, Ontario* (Mawhiney and Lewis 1996).

Our Framework

It is important to place the question of "adjustment" in a broad context that looks at the effects of mass layoffs and plant closures not only on individuals but also on families, neighbourhoods, and the community as a whole. An ecological framework provides a way of thinking about the question of the effects of the layoffs on the community. This framework has been used in other studies on labour market and employment status (Liem and Rayman 1982, Moore and Laramore 1990). In social work, this framework considers the transactive nature of people and the environments in which they are living. According to the ecological framework, people's well-being is optimized when supported socially, economically, and politically by a nurturing and equitable environment. This support is realized through personal networks from the family (extended and nuclear), the neighbourhood in which they are living,

170

their colleagues in their workplace or classroom, informal and formal group activities, and the formalized structures and services of the community itself. This nurturing environment is effective in supporting all family members, whether adults or children. The community, or the immediate environment in which people live, is also highly influenced by social, economic, and political structures that are its parts. A community-wide crisis, whether a natural disaster or one created by people, has a negative impact on the community as well as on all the people — breadwinners, partners, children, retired people, politicians, spiritual leaders — who are part of it.

The ecological framework, however, is limited in its application, unless we also consider the reality that people are not equitably supported and nurtured within their environments; the starting place for those laid off differs from one situation to another. Material conditions, gender, race, class, family structure, quality of family relationships, individual capacities and skills of each family member, and the extent to which the environment is supportive and sustainable are all factors that create diversity from one family situation to another. It is here that ecofeminism broadens the ecological framework to consider also the concepts of domination and hierarchy (Plumwood 1986, 124) and the ways that these limit the day-to-day realities and ways of living of people who are subordinate to those with power.

The model that emerges from this framework suggests that those people who have experienced an economic crisis, such as permanent layoff, will immediately rely on their own network for support: their immediate and extended family members, close friends and neighbours, other social supports such as church groups and recreational groups, and work-related associations such as unions. Those who do not have these supports, or those whose networks are not supportive, may turn to the formalized services offered within the community: spiritual leaders, doctors, lawyers, and social service providers. This model is suggested by Linn and McGranahan (1980, 87). Our assumption here is that social networks mitigate the negative effects of the layoffs so that people's capacities remain at a level that maintains their well-being, and that an erosion in social support results in a deterioration of capacities. Of course, there are also other reasons why those laid off may seek help from formalized services. For example, those who were experiencing interpersonal or personal difficulties prior to the economic crisis and those for whom the permanent layoff results in serious emotional or family problems will also seek this kind of help regardless of their support network.

Linn and McGranahan's model is limited in helping us understand the broader dynamics of mass layoffs and permanent closure of the main industry in single-resource communities such as Elliot Lake. The model's focus on the worker means that we fail to consider the impact of the layoffs on other family members and on the community. What is also missing from the model is consideration of the serious erosion of networks when neighbourhoods undergo complete transformations: when large numbers of families move to other communities for employment or further education; when large numbers of primary breadwinners commute outside the community for extended periods for employment or further education leaving behind essentially single-parented households; and when parents move to other communities for employment, and adolescent children are left in the community to complete their education. Transformations also occur when many of the social activities in the community, formerly organized and funded by the company and union, are no longer available. The model also does not consider the erosion in supportive networks for those families who have moved to other communities and no longer have the needed support to help them through the transition from one place to another. What happens to a community when the social networks are eroded to the extent that the natural supports are no longer in place? What happens to those people who were isolated prior to the crisis, and to those whose social networks are no longer in place? These questions lead to a more general one: What are the effects of mass layoffs on the community?

Literature

It is important to understand the consequences of mass layoffs and high rates of unemployment on communities. Little research has been undertaken that looks at the effects of plant shutdowns and mass layoffs on *communities*, although what literature does exist supports the significance of research in this area. As Liem and Rayman point out, "unemployment does not simply happen to individuals. The vast structured and less formal interdependencies that describe present-day social relations are the channels through which families, extended kin networks, and whole communities are potentially affected by the joblessness of individuals" (1982, 119). It is becoming increasingly important to understand the community dynamics associated with economic disruptions as industries in other communities go through restructuring processes similar to those occurring in Elliot Lake at the present time. Some of these effects are also described in the literature. For instance, Dail (1988) suggests that high rates of unemployment are related to "rising crime rates, drug abuse, and family violence." Scapegoating and conflict across social groups may also become evident in communities with high levels of unemployment (Social Planning Council of Metropolitan Toronto 1986). In their study of the effects of job loss on workers, Cobb and Kasl (1977) found that much of the sense of "community" in urban settings is derived from the work setting itself. When the workplace is closed, this sense of community ceased, along with the supportive networks that were part of the workplace. In rural settings, the workplace was less important, and the community itself more important in maintaining social support and an identity as being part of a community (174). Large-scale layoffs show their impact first in the business community and then the region. Loss of taxes can affect revenues for schools and cause a reduction in social services at the time when they are most needed (Fedrau 1984, 87). Unemployed people tend to spend more time with their families and lose contact with the wider community, as well as with their former co-workers (Gallagher, Ohri, and Roberts 1983, 194; Binns and Mars 1989, 668 and 677). There is little reliance on social service agencies, since pride causes people to delay seeking help until an emergency occurs, or to rely on family and friends (Biegal et al. 1989, 404; Rayman 1982, 328).

Naturally, since communities are made up of people living within them, it is difficult to separate effects of layoffs on the community from personal and family effects. In this study we have used an integrated approach in order to capture the effects on the community as well as those effects experienced by individuals and families living within the community.

There is a well-established literature showing a connection between economic factors and the ways that people cope in their day-to-day lives (Brennan and Stolen 1976; Dooley and Catalano 1980; Catalano and Dooley 1983; Catalano, Dooley, and Jackson 1981; Albee 1982; Starrin and Larsson 1987; Barling and Handal 1980; Frank 1981; Redburn and Buss 1982). However, much of this earlier literature on labour adjustment examined only the effects of labour disruptions on the (usually male) workers, themselves. Marshall critiques this literature, pointing out that "there are good sociological reasons why the reactions to job loss among women may be different from those of men" (Marshall 1984, 234). For instance, as Marshall points out, married women who work for pay usually carry the dual role of paid worker as well as unpaid homemaker. The constraints and additional burdens placed on women because of these combined roles may have further implications when women become unemployed (Marshall 1984, 239). In fact, studies since

1984 have shown differences among the ways in which women react to their own unemployment. For example, Starrin and Larsson (1987) in their interviews with 36 women found that the women's reactions to unemployment varied depending on their "relation to wage labour" and their "relation to alternative activities" (163). Four groupings of women emerged: the "giver-uppers," the "clenchers," the "refocusers," and the "ambivalents" (165). Some of these women reacted in ways similar to unemployed men; others, however, who had a partner with a full-time paid job, adjusted to not having paid work by refocusing their energies into more creative pursuits. Similarly, Swaim and Podgursky's study (1994) also shows a split-model of labour force participation by unemployed women: some search for jobs while others withdraw from the labour market (640). The authors conclude that "labour force withdrawal plays an important role in explaining the wide variation in post-displacement jobless spells and that single-population models — which do not accommodate labour force withdrawal — provide an incomplete and potentially misleading tool for analyzing post-displacement jobless spells" (654).

In addition to understanding the effects of labour disruption on unemployed women, we need also to understand the effects of mass layoffs on women whose partners have been laid off. Similarly, we need to consider the ways in which mass layoffs affect other family members, including children and adolescents. A parent's unemployment has an impact on children's physical health, apparently because the financial difficulties mean that children are denied adequate clothing, food, housing (Brennan and Stolen 1976, 682). There are too many factors that affect a child's reaction to unemployment to be able to describe a specific one as typical, although children seem to worry more the longer the unemployment lasts (Pautler, Lewko, and Baker 1987, 237). Also, the more worried parents are about their situation, the more problems the child will have in school and with relationships (Perrucci 1994, 88). According to Flanagan (1990, 173), adolescents in families where a parent has just experienced a demotion or a layoff experience more conflict than other adolescents. In his study, Flanagan found that boys externalize their conflict and anxiety by challenging their fathers' authority, becoming delinquent, and using drugs (248). Girls, on the other hand, internalize their conflict and anxiety by becoming depressed, isolated, by being pessimistic about the future, and feeling inadequate (174). In general, unemployment increases the amount of family stress (Dail 1988, 32), which in turn affects the children in the family.

The ecological framework helps us to consider how the layoffs affect the workers, their family members, and the community itself. By broadening this framework to include concepts of hierarchy and power, we can also understand more comprehensively the hidden costs associated with mass layoffs. This, in turn, can influence the ways in which policies are developed in response to the present economic shifts occurring in various communities throughout Canada.

Both the literature and present adjustment policies of the provincial and federal governments underscore the need for programs that are intended to support individuals who have been laid off. Employment Insurance, Health Insurance, Family Benefits and General Welfare, and Retraining Programs may offer certain support to laid-off miners in Elliot Lake, at least in the short term. However, it is also important to consider ways in which policies can be formulated that support needs that are wider than those of the worker. Ignoring the wider and perhaps longer-term costs associated with mass layoffs as these are experienced by workers, their spouses, their children, and the community means that there is a huge gap between the actual realities experienced by those affected by the layoffs and the support that is offered to them. For instance, if we assume that a worker has "successfully adjusted" because he has found work in another community, we fail to take into account the costs that might be associated: the spouse's loss of income; social isolation and alienation; the social and economic costs of family separation when the worker is commuting; and the displacement costs of children and adolescents who have to choose between staying in their home community without family support or moving to another community, making new friends, and starting in a new school.

The framework we are using here suggests some additional policy areas to consider; some of these are also discussed in the literature and raise important policy questions. For example, to what extent are new policies needed that would support women in retraining and education programs? Women who have been laid off may have different training needs than their male colleagues. Women who have been working in the home, without pay, might benefit themselves and the rest of their family if specific retraining programs were available to facilitate their transition into, or back into, the paid workforce. Another possible question is: What policies and programs can support children and adolescents through the stresses associated with mass layoffs? These stresses can include those related to family breakup, changes in family role, changes in material conditions, social isolation, deterioration in physical and emotional health, and moves to other communities. A third question is:

What are the wider effects of mass layoffs on the community in which they occur? And finally, a fourth question: Who is most at risk for problems in adjustment and what policies can mitigate these problems?

These are important policy questions that would be missed in any study that is based on standard views of labour adjustment and that are being examined in the various projects of the Elliot Lake Tracking and Adjustment Study.

Method and Research Question

Research workshop method. The research workshop method, using a nominal group approach, was selected to address the question: "What are the effects of the layoffs on the community of Elliot Lake?"

This method was used for several reasons. First, it encouraged face-to-face participation of agency representatives and engaged them in the process of understanding the effects of the layoffs. As well, it satisfies our need to collect aggregate data to support or refute various perceptions about the effects of the layoffs. A third reason this method was selected was that we believed in the importance of community-based involvement in all stages of the project. This method was seen as the most effective way of initiating this involvement, while respecting the heavy workloads of the workers involved by minimizing the amount of time that they would need to spend in this preliminary phase of the project. Fourth, it would provide an opportunity for service providers across work settings to brainstorm together, so that new ways of thinking and working together could emerge as commonalities across disciplines and work settings became evident. This secondary benefit was consistent with the rationale used by Callahan and Attridge (1990) for the same method. The design considerations of Callahan and Attridge were also applicable to our own situation, namely:

> the need to stimulate participants to think beyond their personal experience ... to stimulate creative thinking ... the need to obtain individual as well as group perspectives ... the need to generate data from participants which would be usable and uncontaminated by the views of the researchers of resource people ... the need to provide a workshop experience that would benefit participants as well as meet researcher goals (Callahan and Attridge 1990, 11).

In this study, we distinguish among impressions, observations, personal experience, and those effects that can actually be measured quantitatively.

Impressions are framed from the person's own subjective standpoint, and may be shaped by personal values and intuition. For example, there may be an impression that more women are looking for paid work outside the home. Impressions of one person may contradict or support impressions of others. Some people in Elliot Lake have the impression that suicide attempts increased after the mine closures were announced, but others have the impression that the number of suicide attempts stayed the same. For this reason, while impressions are a useful starting place for collecting effects, further verification is needed to validate impressions. Such validation may occur in two different ways. First, we can validate an impression by the number of times it is mentioned by a variety of people and by asking others if they share the impression. Second, we can verify impressions using data from other sources. These sources may include the Elliot Lake Tracking Study (ELTS), the Elliot Lake Spousal Project (ELSP), and aggregate data from various institutional settings. [See "Introduction" to Part 2 for a description of these projects.] So, for instance, we could verify whether more women are looking for paid work by analyzing data from employment centres, by asking women in the ELSP if they have been looking for paid work, or by verifying this impression with local economic development officers. Likewise, we could verify whether or not suicide attempts increased by analyzing data from the local hospital and police.

Observations of effects are those that a person has seen herself or himself. For instance, an observation may be made that six families have moved out of the neighbourhood in the last eight months. The observation is more precise than an impression and is based on a more objective assessment of what is happening within the sphere of observation of the respondent. When an effect is observed by several people it emerges as one that may warrant closer examination.

Personal experiences are those effects felt by the respondent herself or himself. As is the case with observations, the more frequently different people describe having the same experience, the more important it is that we look at this effect in more detail.

Impressions, observations, and personal experiences are subjective indicators of possible effects of the layoffs in the community. By themselves, they provide a wide range of possible anticipated and unanticipated effects of mass layoffs and mine closures. They also help point us to possible effects that should be verified by other studies, either with the Elliot Lake Spousal Project, other ELTAS sub-projects, including the Social and Community Costs Sub-Project, or new projects in Elliot Lake or in comparable communities.

Initial contacts. Individual interviews with key agency informants were held before and after the workshops. The initial contact interviews were to orient agency directors about the project. The initial contact process turned out to be a lengthy one. It took approximately 16 weeks to identify, obtain, and organize information on the agencies to be included in this study. An organized and comprehensive community services directory has never been developed in the area, and access to information was complicated by the multi-layered structure of most area agencies, which are sub-groups of larger agencies/institutions located elsewhere (particularly in Sault Ste. Marie and Sudbury). Initial contact information was gathered from numerous telephone calls, face-to-face meetings, agency brochures and pamphlets, and 16 fragmented, pre-existing lists of agencies and institutions. All contacts were recorded onto Contact Sheets developed for each agency. In order to add to the list of effects, individual interviews were held after the workshops with key informants who did not attend the workshops.

Time constraints precluded realization of the original intent to include all agencies and institutions within commuting distance of Elliot Lake. Legal, social, and health services not included in other ELTAS sub-projects and located primarily within the boundaries of the community of Elliot Lake became the focal point of the research activities in this study. During this initial phase, information was gathered on 120 agencies. The agencies were classified according to the main kind of services provided, and compiled into a master list. Information from the master list was then used to prepare information sheets describing each agency/institution included in the project. In the end, 95 agencies were selected, coded, and grouped according to sector, to participate in varying degrees in specific stages of the study.

The form was mailed out to 81 of these agencies. We received responses from 35, with 27 indicating plans to attend the workshops. Actual attendance was 25 representatives from 23 agencies. The workshop for francophone services was cancelled because only one person registered. She joined one of the other workshops.

The workshops. Each workshop began with introductory remarks describing the overall purpose of the workshops, hoped-for outcomes and products to result from the workshop, and a brief overview of the day's proceedings.

A workbook, based on guidelines developed by Algoma Steel's Problem Solving and Cost Savings Workshop was prepared prior to the workshops and distributed to all participants. It provided an ordered and consistent framework for each workshop, gave us a permanent record of the individual ideas of each participant, and guided each participant through a structured set of stages (Macpherson 1983, Davis 1986).

In the first stage — silent generation of ideas — participants were asked to write a list of effects that they had observed. They spent ten minutes answering the central question: "What are the effects of the layoffs on the community, based on what you have seen at work, and with neighbours, family, and friends who had been laid off?"

During the second stage — pooling of ideas — small groups were asked to share their lists and to develop a composite list. Each small group was then asked to select the ten effects mentioned most frequently in their group and report their list to the rest of the participants. This stage was intended to assist the group members in a process of clarifying and explaining individual ideas.

In the final stage — consolidation — a master list was generated by the workshop recorder. The effects were recorded by large group recorders and a composite list of the most frequently noted effects (and the number of times each effect was noted) was compiled.

We found that the nominal group technique stimulated creative thinking and provided a rich interplay between individual and group participation. Participants appreciated having the opportunity to grapple with the effects of the layoffs in a group setting. They spent a considerable amount of time developing consensus on the most frequently noticed and the most significant effects of the layoffs. Participants were impressed to see that "even coming from different backgrounds, the needs and effects are the same." They noted the "good teamwork" and liked the fact that the final list was achieved "without compromises" to positions that individuals believed to be important. The workshop was described as "an interesting and worthwhile endeavour."

Findings on the Effects of the Layoffs

We grouped the effects into sub-themes and separated out direct and indirect effects. The first were those effects experienced by individuals, families, and the community directly because of the layoffs. The second were those experienced as a result of new directions taken by the community to offset the layoffs. Indirect effects were chiefly those related to the local economic development strategy of making Elliot Lake into a retirement centre for seniors. Themes mentioned most frequently were those for which there was a shared impression from one person to another, and which by virtue of being shared by several people might be either more objective than those suggested by only one person or else more pervasive than other effects. In either case, it was important to verify by way of further examination some of these as well as the effects mentioned by individuals.

We counted the number of times each effect was mentioned, not to "quantify" the qualitative information that we obtained but rather to show a level of complexity to particular themes.[2] So, for instance, participants in the workshops and in the individual interviews could sum up the commercial or business effects of the layoffs in five different ways. These effects can be discussed easily and seem straightforward and easy to conceptualize. In contrast, the effects of the newcomers on the community were summed up in 12 different ways, and on agencies in 28 ways, suggesting that this is a more complex issue to discuss. In addition, the emphasis that has been placed on the effects of the newcomers to the community means that in the second stage of this project we will need to examine data carefully to separate out the direct costs of the layoffs on the workers, their families, and the community and the indirect costs associated with the community's decision to become a retirement community as a way of maintaining an economic base in Elliot Lake (see Mawhiney with Kauppi 1997). The former costs are of interest for policies intended to mitigate effects in other communities where mass layoffs and plant closures occur, whereas the costs associated with the newcomers are not as directly related to the purpose of this project.

The most frequently mentioned effects are listed below, in order of frequency. The sub- themes mentioned most often were negative:

- division of the family unit (male works elsewhere) causes stress and problems;
- increase in substance abuse;
- more separation and divorce;
- youth in crisis: increased crime, substance abuse, violence, dropouts, and pregnancies;
- changing roles within family (father out of town, mother working, and father at home) have a huge impact on family functioning;
- increased social dependency and lower standard of living;
- teens living alone after family moves away, children supported less;

- teens suffering most from stress of families separating;
- increased family violence;
- loss of friends and networks as families move away;
- high levels of stress throughout the community; and
- increase in depression, anxiety, and psychological problems.

Some of the sub-themes were positive, with those reporting them seeing opportunities that have emerged from the layoffs. These included:

- women have been empowered in terms of education and employment;
- layoffs have permitted miners to find rewarding careers and pursue other dreams;
- some families have pulled together and become stronger; and
- some men are seeking help and learning new ways of relating.

Indirect effects included:

- people moving into Elliot Lake are multi-serviced families that have chronic problems, are lonely, or handicapped;
- there is increased demand on local agencies, the hospital, and police services;
- demographic shifts have occurred: in some instances the community cannot respond to needs in others, shifts in resources have occurred;
- there is an influx of low-income families; and
- the community is divided into two separated groups: newcomers and old-timers.

The most frequently mentioned effect, discussed in a variety of ways, relates to the change in family structure that has occurred because of the mass layoffs, and the stresses that this change has engendered. One change in family structure occurs because of increases in divorce and separation, meaning that the number of single-parent households and blended families has increased. In the case of divorce or separation in Canada, it is the mother who typically becomes the custodial parent.

Another change in family structure in Elliot Lake is that some laid-off workers have not been able to find paying work and their spouses have become the primary breadwinners. The stresses associated with these changes, sometimes seen as positive and empowering and sometimes creating resentment and conflict, also need further study. The extent to which the division of household labour has changed as the result of the layoffs will also be studied by the ELSP group (see Porter, Chapter 7 in this volume). In addition, it is important to understand the impact of these changes on children and youth.

A third way that family structure has changed is the result of a different way of organizing the forms of work that are available: the mining industry has developed sites to which workers commute for extended periods of time. Because there are few work opportunities in Elliot Lake, many of the men have found work on these sites and are away for long periods of time, returning to Elliot Lake on a weekly, monthly, or longer basis. In essence, women become single parents in terms of the day-to-day operations within the home and see their husbands on their regular but infrequent visits home. When these women are also working for pay outside the home, their children may not have the same level of parental support that they had previously when both parents were at home. This can have the positive effect of fostering more independence, or the negative effect of providing more opportunity for acting out. Some community service providers report that many women have returned to school to further their education and others have returned to the paid workplace.

Some daughters, in particular, are apparently more motivated to stay in school as they now have the positive modelling of their mothers. Other daughters and sons, however, are choosing other ways of adjusting to the new family circumstances — by living on their own, isolating themselves from peers and family members, drinking, and taking drugs. Teen pregnancies seem to have increased since the layoffs, although this needs to be clarified further and compared with other communities. In some cases where both parents move to another community for work, adolescent children are staying in Elliot Lake on their own, some without family supervision. Some may be supported financially by their family, but others may be supported through general welfare or foster care. Further examination of this effect is needed before policies can be developed to address concerns related to this change in family structure. The adjustments associated with changing forms of family structure can be both positive and negative, and some of these adjustments will be examined further in the ELSP.

Finally, we have learned that a number of adolescents have chosen to remain in Elliot Lake on their own in order to complete secondary school with their friends, rather than move with the rest of the family to another community. That there are costs associated with this form of family structure seems evident. Along with some of the focus groups on coping strategies, the ELSP is looking into these costs, but the long-term costs are likely to remain unknown for some time.

Symptoms of community stress in Elliot Lake are found among a variety of social and economic indicators to which the literature points. Increases in crime, family violence, community violence, suicides and suicide attempts, teen pregnancies, substance abuse, and dependency on social agencies are all ways to measure the hidden costs of adjustment after a mass layoff. So far in this project, we have gathered only impressions and observations, which we now need to verify with more objective data. However, should these impressions and observations be supported by the data, then we would be in a position to consider the hidden costs of mass layoffs — costs that cannot be calculated merely on the basis of whether or not the person laid off has found another job.

Another effect that was mentioned frequently related to the negative impact of loss of friends, support networks, and separation of family members. Friends have been lost because they have moved away, because there is a feeling of alienation between those laid off and those still working, because there are fewer opportunities for community activities, and because many of the previous activities were planned through the work setting. The effects of this loss of friendship are felt by the workers, their spouses, and their children. The loss of support networks is closely related to loss of friends and separation of family members.

The community is also under stress from decisions that were made to buffer the effects of the layoffs by developing a retirement community within Elliot Lake. The results of this experiment are being followed by the Elliot Lake Retirement Living Program. However, it is suggested by our participants that among the indirect effects of the layoffs are additional stresses on community agencies, increased resentment and polarization between longtime and new citizens and, perhaps, community-based scapegoating of the seniors.

Local service providers also report that much of their additional workload is related to the influx of these newcomers, who bring with them a wide variety of service needs. It is the impression of many of the service providers that the laid-off workers and their families have not increased demand in service, but that the newcomers have. The extent to which these impressions are accurate, namely that most of the service workload in the last five years has been because of newcomers, warrants further analysis in the next stage of this project.

What emerges from these findings is a community that is under tremendous stress. Large numbers of the community's inhabitants have moved to other communities, an influx of newcomers has placed additional strains on community resources, and many of the families that have chosen to remain in the community have had to make substantial changes in family structures and ways of functioning. These shifts in family structure and functioning are pervasive and have an impact on the wider community. Services for youth and seniors have increased at times, apparently straining resources. There are also increased levels of social dependency, a lack of job openings, and a shrinking tax base, which create tensions among those who are still working and those who are not employed, and between newcomers and old-timers. Businesses and community agencies are opening and closing, lending an air of constant flux and insecurity in the kinds of support and services that community members rely on. Children and youth are exhibiting signs of the wider strain being experienced in the community, with impressions among service providers that there are increases in school dropouts and truancy, teen pregnancies, crime among youth, use of drugs and alcohol, social isolation, and foster care.

Some of the impressions about the effects of the layoffs on community services are contradictory and need to be considered in relation to data that we gather from the appropriate agency settings. Some of the contradictions include:

> • The Children's Aid Society reports that their workload has decreased, but that the number of children in foster care has increased. One other agency reports an increase in the number of referrals to Children's Aid because of child abuse.
> • Some report that there is an increase in teen violence; others report that teen violence was higher fifteen years ago.
> • Some report an increase in crime, while others say that crime has stayed pretty much the same as before.
> • Some report an increase in family violence and domestic charges; others say there is a decrease in the number of calls for domestic violence.
> • Some say there has been an increase in suicide attempts; others say there has been a decrease.

These are examples of impressions that need further verification through analysis of data kept by various agencies. This is the purpose of the second stage of this project.

Conclusions

In this paper we summarize the results of a series of workshops and interviews that were conducted in the fall of 1995 with service providers in Elliot Lake, Ontario. We have found that the effects of the layoffs from Denison and Rio Algom were far-reaching and touched virtually all aspects of personal, family, and community life. In addition, we have found some interesting contradictions in impressions from one person to another and from one group of service providers to another. We will be looking at these contradictions more closely in the second phase of this study (Mawhiney with Kauppi 1997). We are not surprised that impressions and observations would vary from one person to another. Liem and Rayman point out that unemployment "is not a uniform experience. Different scenarios of economic, social and personal dynamics can give job loss different meanings" (1982, 1121).

Notes

[1] The authors would like to acknowledge the important contributions of all the service providers who participated in this study. Their names, along with the names of their organizations, are listed in Mawhiney and Lewis (1996). Stephanie Bassis and Sharon Gow provided important assistance throughout this study, and Jane Pitblado and Judy Lynn Malloy assisted in the final preparation of the manuscript. The authors are part of a wider study, the Elliot Lake Tracking and Adjustment Study, funded by Human Resources Development Canada.
[2] The authors thank Dr Suzanne Dansereau, research associate with ELTAS, who guided this way of thinking about the effects.

References

Albee, George. (1982). "Preventing psychopathology and promoting human potential," *American Psychologist* 37, 9: 1043–50.

Barling, Phillip and Paul. J. Handal. (1980). "Incidence of utilization of public health facilities as a function of short-term economic decline," *American Journal of Community Psychology* 8, 9: 31–39.

Biegal, David, James Cunningham, Hide Yamatani, and Pamela Martz. (1989). "Self-reliance and blue-collar unemployment in steel town," *Social Work* 34, 5: 399–406.

Binns, David and Gerald Mars. (1984). "Family, community and unemployment: a study in change," *The Sociological Review* 32, 4: 663–95.

Brennan, Mary and Bryan Stolen. (1976). "Children, poverty and illness," *New Society* 36, 716: 681–82.

Callahan, Marilyn and C. Attridge. (1990). *Women in Women's Work*, Research Monograph #3, University of Victoria.

Catalano, Ralph and David Dooley. (1983, March). "Health effects of economic instability: a test of economic stress hypothesis," *Journal of Health and Social Behavior* 24: 46–60.

Catalano, Ralph, David Dooley, and Robert Jackson. (1981). "Economic predictors of admissions to mental health facilities in a nonmetropolitan community," *Journal of Health and Social Behavior* 22 (September): 284–97.

Cobb, Sidney and Stanislav Kasl. (1977). *Termination: The Consequences of Job Loss.* Cincinnati, OH: U.S. Department of Health, Education and Welfare.

Dail, P.W. (1988). "Unemployment and family stress," *Public Welfare* (Winter): 30–35.

Davis, Liane. (1986). "A feminist approach to social work research," *Affilia* 1, 1: 32–47.

Dooley, David and Ralph Catalano. (1980). "Economic change as a cause of behavior," *Psychological Bulletin* 87, 3: 450–68.

Dorin, Casey. (1994). "The Psycho-social effects of unemployment," *Le Travailleur Social/ The Social Worker* 62, 1: 9–12.

Fedrau, Ruth. (1984). "Responses to plant closures and major reductions in force: private sectors and community-based models," *The Annals of the American Academy of Political and Social Science* 475: 80–95.

Flanagan, Constance A. (1990). "Changes in family work status: effects on parent-adolescent decision making," *Child Development* 61, 1: 163–77.

Frank, Jeanine A. (1981). "Economic change and mental health in an uncontaminated setting," *American Journal of Community Psychology* 9, 4: 395–410.

Gallagher, Jim, Ashok Ohri, and Les Roberts. (1983). "Unemployment and community action," *Community Development Journal* 18, 1: 3–9.

Liem, Ramsay and Paula Rayman. (1982). "Health and social costs of unemployment," *American Psychologist* 37, 10: 1116–23.

Linn, J. Gary and David McGranahan. (1980). "Personal disruptions, social integration, subjective well-being and predisposition toward the use of counseling services," *American Journal of Community Psychology* 8, 9: 87–100.

Macpherson, K.I. (1983). "Feminist methods: a new paradigm for nursing research," *Advances in Nursing Science* (January): 17–25.

Marshall, Gordon. (1984). "On the sociology of women's unemployment, its neglect and significance," *The Sociological Review* 32, 1: 234–59.

Mawhiney, Anne-Marie with Carol Kauppi. (1997). *Report on the Social Consequences of Mass Layoffs: Miners and Their Families Seeking Help in Elliot Lake.* ELTAS Report Series #1R2. Sudbury, ON: INORD, Laurentian University.

Mawhiney, Anne-Marie and Jan Lewis. (1996). *Inventory of Perceived Effects of Layoffs in Elliot Lake.* ELTAS Report Series # 1R1. Sudbury, ON: INORD, Laurentian University.

Moore, Thomas S. and Aaron Laramore. (1990). "Industrial change and urban joblessness: an assessment of the mismatch hypothesis," *Urban Affairs Quarterly* 25, 4: 640–58.

Pautler, Katherine, John Lewko, and David Baker. (1987). "Children's reactions to a community economic crisis: an exploratory analysis," *Sociological Studies of Child Development* 2: 225–42.

Perrucci, Carolyn. (1994). "Economic strain, family structure and problems with children among displaced workers," *Journal of Sociology and Social Welfare* 21, 3: 79–91.

Plumwood, Val. (1986). "Ecofeminism: an overview and discussion of positions and arguments," *Australasian Journal of Philosophy* Supplement to Volume 64 (June): 120–30.

Redburn, F. Steven and T.F. Buss, eds. (1982). *Public Policies for Distressed Communities.* Lexington, MA: D.C. Heath and Company.

Rayman, Paula. (1982). "The world of not working: an evaluation of urban social service response to unemployment," *Journal of Health and Human Resources Administration* 37, 10: 319–33.

Starrin, Bengt and Gerry Larsson. (1987). "Coping with unemployment — a contribution to the understanding of women's unemployment," *Social Science Medicine* 25, 2: 163–71.

Social Planning Council of Metropolitan Toronto. (1986). *Brief to the Commission of Inquiry on Unemployment Insurance.* Toronto: The Social Planning Council of Metropolitan Toronto.

Swaim, Paul and Michael Podgursky. (1994). "Female supply following displacement: a split-population model of labor force participation and job search," *Journal of Labor Economics* 12, 1: 640–56.

Chapter 13
"Never Say Die": Seven Years Later, Elliot Lake Enjoys New Business and Renewed Optimism[1]
Mayor George Farkouh

For the young mining community of Elliot Lake, situated halfway between Sault Ste. Marie and Sudbury, 1990 was a really bad year. The writing was on the wall for its primary industry, as far cheaper and better-quality uranium ore was becoming available to Elliot Lake's main customer, Ontario Hydro. In 1990 the city's two mining companies, Rio Algom Limited and Denison Mines Limited, announced the closure of three mine sites, resulting in the layoff of over 2,000 mine workers in that year. In 1992, Denison shut down its entire operation, throwing the lives of yet another 1,100 employees and their families into chaos. The remaining 553 employees of Rio Algom lost their jobs in June 1996.

Homecoming banner, for celebrations from November 1997 to summer 1998, hangs in the Economic Development Office of the City of Elliot Lake.

Jane Pitblado

Prior to 1990, Elliot Lake's economy was 100 percent dependent upon the revenues of its mining companies. The population in 1986, for example, stood at 17,984, of which 4,858 were directly employed by the mines. Another 3,962 members of the labour force were employed by a combination of local businesses and essential municipal, educational, health and social service agencies, all providing products and services to the mines and their employees.

In 1990, the news of devastating losses in employment signalled a death knell for the community and a worst-case scenario was projected (see Figure 1). By 1997, Elliot Lake was expected to become a "ghost town" with no more than 160 jobs. In reality, by the close of 1994 the population had stabilized at 14,300, and estimates for 1997 are showing a population of 14,500 and a stable employment level of approximately 2,500 (see Figure 2).

Figure 1. City of Elliot Lake
Estimated impact of mine closures on population and jobs
(assuming no economic diversification)

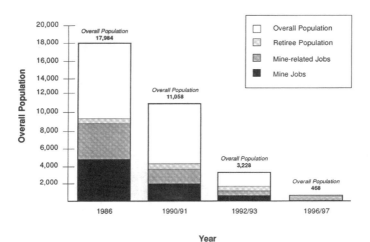

	1986	1990/91	1992/93	1996/97
Overall Population	17,984	11,058	3,228	468
Retiree Population	530	600	500	200
Mine-related Jobs	3,972	1,686	526	131
Mine Jobs	4,858	2,000	550	25

Figure 2. City of Elliot Lake
New targets based on economic diversification

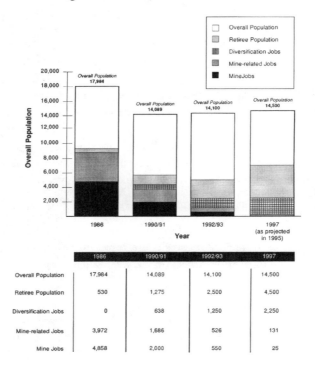

	1986	1990/91	1992/93	1997
Overall Population	17,984	14,089	14,100	14,500
Retiree Population	530	1,275	2,500	4,500
Diversification Jobs	0	638	1,250	2,250
Mine-related Jobs	3,972	1,686	526	131
Mine Jobs	4,858	2,000	550	25

Early Preparation Heads Off Disaster

In 1990, faced with limited time, money, and expertise, the residents of Elliot Lake began the monumental task of restructuring the economic base of a community that had always been single-industry dependent. Fortunately, there were a number of local individuals who had seen the need for economic diversification a few years earlier, before it became an issue of survival.

In 1987, these individuals created an Economic Development Committee, through which a strategy was developed and adopted by the municipality in 1990. Several short-term objectives were established based on the principle of building upon existing local resources, together with government partnerships, to create new opportunities for investment and growth. The most positive economic impact in Elliot Lake from 1990 to 1997 has been felt from three of these initiatives: retirement living, tourism, and small business diversification.

Retirement Living

Community objective: to create new opportunities for business development by increasing the number of retirees and their level of expenditure in Elliot Lake

As early as 1987, a group of community leaders, under the chairmanship of Claire Dimock, a local councillor and a senior executive at Denison Mines, came up with the idea of marketing the mines' vacant housing stock to retirees. The retirees would bring their own guaranteed annual incomes and would stabilize the local economy with their expenditures. The program was under way by the end of 1987, attracting 25 people that year. By the start of 1991, an independent not-for-profit organization, Elliot Lake Retirement Living, was formed to acquire many of the homes (thanks to a provincial grant), to manage the properties, and to continue the successful marketing program in Ontario. In 1993, the news of this program attracted a real estate development firm from southern Ontario, Active Living, to buy up more housing from the mining companies and to offer it to retirees for sale. Advertising house prices as low as $19,900, the company could barely keep up with market demand. Today, a number of other private developers are involved in apartment-to-condominium conversions and a couple of assisted-living housing projects.

Up to 1997, over 3,600 retirees have moved to Elliot Lake. Another 3,000 visit the community each year to check out the opportunities. Retirement Living is one of the largest organizations in the province catering to retirees, with 1,520 housing units.

The impact of the retirement program has translated not only into a

Early advertisement for housing through the Retirement Living Program.
City of Elliot Lake

more secure municipal tax base (see Robinson and Bishop, Chapter 16 in this volume), but also into big business for local renovators, new customers for local retailers, particularly those selling hardware and furniture, and diversified product lines for fashion and drug stores (see Berthelot, Chapter 17 in this volume). The efforts of Elliot Lake Retirement Living and other private developers have ensured that more than $30 million is injected into the local economy on an annual basis.

Tourism

Community objective: to create new opportunities for business development by increasing the number of tourists and their level of expenditure in Elliot Lake

Located within a glorious wilderness area north of Lake Huron's North Channel, Elliot Lake lies on the age-old Pre-Cambrian Shield and enjoys a dramatic landscape accented by ancient forests, rivers, and over 4,000 lakes. Perfect for fishing, hunting, hiking, canoeing, boating, snowmobiling, cross-country skiing, and a host of other year-round recreational pursuits, the area has excellent tourism potential, which was largely ignored until 1990. A small hospitality industry made up of motels and lodges, fishing and hunting outposts, a few hiking and snowmobiling trails, a ski hill, golf course, and other municipal recreational facilities had been established for the enjoyment of the locals and visiting mining executives.

Under the direction of the city's Economic Development Office, the city obtained provincial government grants and federal job creation programs in 1991 to enhance the tourism infrastructure. Initiatives included the development of a 120-kilometre scenic driving route called the Deer Trail; the Trailhead Visitors' Information Centre; the hilltop Fire Tower Lookout Station with panoramic views; new boardwalks, boat ramps, and docking facilities on nearby lakes; and new hiking and snowmobile trails.

With the help of a public relations campaign aimed at "soft adventure" travellers in southern Ontario, Ohio, Wisconsin, and Michigan, the area has started to attract visitors to its recreational and sporting events and for short vacations. Between 1993 and 1997, it is estimated that over 47,000 people have visited the tourist attractions in the Elliot Lake area.

Thanks to a three-year promotional commitment from Wayne and Bob Izumi, best known for their "Real Fishing" television and radio shows, the numbers continue to increase. The Izumi brothers fell in love with the area when they came up to tape one of their regular fishing

Ice fishing on one of the many lakes in the Elliot Lake area.

City of Elliot Lake

shows in 1993 and, recognizing the tourism potential of the region, decided to help promote Elliot Lake on all their shows. At the same time, they saw the real estate opportunities and went on to market 170 four-season recreational properties that attracted buyers and renters from as far away as Germany and England.

A number of other businesses have either re-organized, expanded, or started up from scratch to serve the new tourist market coming to Elliot Lake. Three of the most established inns and lodges (Inn on the Lake, Roadhouse Inn, and Wilderness Lodge) have changed ownership, with a management style now geared to external marketing. Another beautiful property, Laurentian Lodge, has expanded its facilities in order to operate year-round, adding a bar, restaurant, and hot tub. Elliot Lake Retirement Living has expanded its services to provide two-day orientation tours of the area for interested retirees, and a handful of other brand new companies are now up and running. For example, a number

Elliot Lakers enjoy nearby ski hill.

City of Elliot Lake

of exciting outdoor adventure tours are now available in the Elliot Lake area, offering everything from cultural and historical tours to fishing, hiking, canoeing, rock climbing, camping, snowmobiling, and even dog sledding. Other local businesses have also set up shop to rent and service recreational equipment, canoes, boats, motors and other vehicles, and one has recently received provincial accreditation for its outstanding program of wilderness guide training (one of only three in Ontario).

Small Business

Community objective: to retain and develop business enterprise in Elliot Lake

In 1990, most of the manufacturing operations in Elliot Lake were dependent on the mining companies and, to a lesser extent, on other local markets for the sale of their products and services. As circumstances changed, an Economic Development Committee and more than 200 committed volunteers set out to retain, develop, and attract new businesses.

The community's economic diversification strategy recognized that local manufacturers had already invested in Elliot Lake and were employing local people. It made sense, therefore, to assist these manufacturing companies in developing alternative products and markets, and to help them through the tough times by setting up programs to reduce their operating costs and improve their access to professional expertise and non-traditional financing. Local manufacturers were encouraged to work together and, with assistance from the Economic Development Office, they formed the Elliot Lake Mine Manufacturers' Association.

Three local programs were formulated to help reduce operating costs: the Short Term Job Creation initiative, the Regional Energy Efficiency Retrofit Program, and the municipality's own tax abatement program.

In addition to existing government funding programs designed to help businesses in Northern Ontario — such as FedNor and the Northern Ontario Heritage Fund Corporation (NOHFC) — the Economic Development Committee recognized the need to provide business planning and management expertise, as well as to finance programs that were tailored to the unique circumstances of Elliot Lake. A $2-million Elliot Lake Emergency Fund was set up to provide immediate assistance to existing businesses and the $23-million Elliot Lake and North Shore Corporation for Business Development (ELNOS) was created in 1994 to take a longer-term approach to investment in new and existing businesses. Serving the City of Elliot Lake, the Town of

Blind River, the Townships of the North Shore and Shedden, and the Serpent River First Nation, ELNOS is funded from a $250-million settlement from Ontario Hydro.

Thanks to the determination of the local business people themselves — and the support provided by these programs — many local manufacturing and service companies have survived the past seven years through product or market diversification, and several new companies have been established during the same period. In fact, during the year ending June 1997, the Economic Development Office reported the opening of 30 new businesses in the city, bringing the total number of employers in Elliot Lake to 421.

Just the Beginning

In the past seven years, Elliot Lake has clearly "refused to roll over and die," as one newspaper headline predicted in 1991. The population has not dwindled to less than 500, as was once anticipated — it has even started to climb, from about 14,000 at the end of 1990 to an estimated 14,300 today. The municipal infrastructure is intact, the influx of active retirees is bringing fresh faces and renewed optimism, and the city's businesses are providing employment. City officials are confident that the worst is over and that economic stability has been achieved.

The potential effect of ELNOS in particular on new business stimulation in Elliot Lake is starting to be realized. During the fiscal year ending July 1997, the organization made investment commitments totalling $3.5 million to new and existing businesses in the region. In January 1998, ELNOS launched its new Telecommunications Centre by introducing its first major tenant — StellarCom. Within the first two months, the new call centre hired 32 people. And, in keeping with the trend to recycle vacant buildings, the new centre is expected to contribute to the revitalization of the city centre over the next two years. The ELNOS Telecommunications Centre is expected to house a second call centre, bringing the total of new employment opportunities to 250. This is just one of ten ELNOS-supported projects in the City of Elliot Lake.

The success of Elliot Lake's diversification program over the past seven years is partly due to the funding programs, but, most importantly, it results from the substantial investment of time and money by the local community in directing and managing its own future. The creative energy contributed by existing businesses in finding alternative means of survival, and of former mine employees in making their business dreams viable sources of profit, cannot be underestimated. Their success stands as an inspiration to others in the community and as a challenge to other new or expanding businesses in Canada.

Note

¹ The material presented in this chapter was prepared with the assistance of Dianna Bratina, Director of Economic Development at the Economic Development Office of Elliot Lake, and is the basis of the presentation made by Mayor Farkouh at the 1997 INORD conference. Ms. Bratina also compiled the data for the figures and made the projections for 1997.

A new sign graces the entrance to what was formerly the Steelworkers' Union Hall.

Jane Pitblado

Chapter 14
Elliot Lake: Where Wildcat Strikes Have Given Way to Line Dancing[1]
Mick Lowe

In the 1970s, the Steelworkers' Union Hall in Elliot Lake, Ontario, was a lively, occasionally raucous place, the venue for turbulent meetings that determined the fate of some 4,000 hardrock miners in the self-styled "Uranium Capital of the World." And so it is with considerable curiosity and a little trepidation that I return to Elliot Lake after a dozen-year absence and enter the old union hall, now renamed the Renaissance Seniors' Centre.

As I descend the stairs to the main meeting room, memories come flooding back. They were a tough lot, the men who moiled for uranium, but then they needed to be. Canada's nuclear industry liked to boast that not a single life was lost in a Chernobyl-style reactor disaster, but the claim conveniently overlooked what was happening inside the mines where the industry's raw fuel was produced. Between 1957 and 1995, 108 men were killed in mining accidents in Elliot Lake, and over 1,000 have died to date from a host of industrial diseases directly linked to uranium mining.

The uranium miners of Elliot Lake became famous for their wildcat strikes, illegal actions that filled the main hall with angry, sweating, swearing miners screaming at their angry, sweaty, swearing union bosses who urged their charges, unsuccessfully as often as not, to return to work. One such wildcat strike in the early 1970s, over deplorable health and safety conditions underground, led directly to a Royal Commission on mine safety that eventually reformed health and safety legislation for all Ontario workers. The reforms continue to save lives to this day.

For an old newsman, then, the union hall is storied, even hallowed

197

Steelworkers' training school in the newly opened Union Hall, March 1987. The Elliot Lake Steelworkers were proud of the high quality of their training programs.

United Steelworkers of America, Local 5417

Seniors line dancing at the Renaissance Centre.

City of Elliot Lake

ground, and as I turn the corner to enter the dingy meeting room I stop, transfixed. The air, which was once blue with cigarette smoke and invective, is filled with the sound of Billy Ray Cyrus singing "Achy-Breaky Heart." The room is now clean, well-lit, and smoke-free. The floor is filled with sixtyish women in slacks, moving intently but demurely to the voice of Nashville's latest hunky heartthrob. They are *line dancing! Line dancing matrons have replaced the hardrock miners of Elliot Lake in their own union hall!*

It is the first of many shocks I will receive over the next two days. The Uranium Capital of the World has been transformed into the Retirement Capital of Ontario. Welcome to the new Elliot Lake. Welcome to the future of — us all?

Who Would Move Here?

"Even my colleagues at work asked me, 'What have you been smoking?'" Claire Dimock's husky, smoke-roughened voice on the other end of the phone rings with rich, self-deprecating laughter at the memory of the hunch that launched Elliot Lake's transformation. Now 65, Dimock is one of a handful of Elliot Lakers who have seen it all. Saw the first boom in 1958, when a major influx of people moved in to mine uranium, living in tents and trailers connected by planks that crossed "streets" knee-deep in mud. The population rose to close to 25,000. Then came the first bust a few years later, when the uranium prices collapsed. Houses were boarded up and sold for a dollar. Saw a second boom in the late '70s when the population climbed from a low of about 6,600 to around 18,000. A decade later, cheaper, richer ore from northern Saskatchewan threatened to turn Elliot Lake into a near ghost town once again.

Dimock survived it all. She rose steadily through the ranks of Denison Mines Limited. Eventually she became Denison's vice president of community relations and housing, an Elliot Lake town councillor, and a legend in her own right. By 1987, Denison and their cross-town counterpart, Rio Algom Limited, were saddled with whole subdivisions of detached homes, semi-d's, townhouses — many only 10 years old — some of which had never even been occupied.

There must be somebody, somewhere who could be lured by the prospect of cheap, affordable housing, Dimock reasoned. They would have to be financially independent and able to move — and then it came to her. "How many people back in Toronto retire on a Friday night and have no place to go but back to their third-floor walkup apartment with no yard and no garden, people who look in the mirror after a lifetime of hard work and say, 'Is that all there is?'"

Dimock placed a modest ad in the *Toronto Star,* and to her surprise it produced a trickle of queries that she wasn't sure how to answer. In the first six months of 1987, 38 retirees actually moved to Elliot Lake, while hundreds of miners and their families moved out. Over the next year, the trickle of inquiries became a steady stream.

Even so, Elliot Lake's vacancy rates were still rising when, in the summer of 1990, the town was hit with the most devastating news in its rollercoaster 35-year history: Ontario Hydro was cancelling its long-term uranium contracts with Rio and Denison in favour of Saskatchewan ore. Both mining companies were closing their operations in Elliot Lake. "The Uranium Capital of the World" was losing its sole *raison d'être* — forever.

The closing of Elliot Lake mines was every bit as devastating as the closure of the Newfoundland cod fishery, though admittedly on a smaller scale. Some 15,000 people still resided in Elliot Lake in the summer of 1990. About 3,000 of them were employed in high-paying industrial jobs in the uranium mines and mills. In Newfoundland, there is the faint hope that some day the fish will return. But in Elliot Lake, the mines will be allowed to fill with water, and the headframes and mills and administrative offices will be razed. A whole culture and a way of life will disappear.

The blow was softened somewhat by the creation of a $250-million adjustment fund by Ontario Hydro. More than half the money, $160 million, would go to keeping Rio Algom open until June 1996. The remaining $90 million was pledged to retire the municipal debt and somehow ease the transition into a post-industrial economy for whoever was left in Elliot Lake.

Retirement Living

The first systematic attempt to turn a Canadian mining town into a retirement mecca began in February 1991 with the incorporation of Elliot Lake Retirement Living Inc., a non-profit corporation funded with $7 million from the Hydro transition fund. Retirement Living assumed the title to hundreds of virtually worthless mining company housing units. The housing stock was upgraded; expensive electric furnaces were converted to natural gas, exteriors were painted and re-clad, and the largest installation of ground-source heat pumps in Canada was completed. Retirement Living's mandate was to act strictly as a rental, as opposed to sales, agency. It offered retirees excellent housing at unbeatable rents, such as $298 a month for a one-bedroom or $493 a month for a three-bedroom detached home.

The non-profit company advertised its cheap rents in newspapers, radio and television in southern Ontario and took its sales pitch on the road. The Retirement Living Caravan, a white motor home, began making the rounds in southern Ontario. Retirement Living personnel offered free room and board for a weekend to any retiree who made his or her way to Elliot Lake. Sceptical observers, including, it must be admitted, this one, had a field day recalling the old put-down: "First prize, a weekend for one in beautiful ELLIOT LAKE! Second prize, a weekend for two...." But Ontario seniors living on fixed incomes weren't laughing. In 1991 alone, 3,000 of them took advantage of Retirement Living tours.

By the spring of 1995, Retirement Living had become a $6-million-a-year business with 17 full-time employees and an additional 25 to 35 seasonal workers. The non-profit company now owns a total of 1,413 rental units with an occupancy rate of 90 percent. "Two-bedroom units are already tight, and we're hoping for 100 percent occupancy by the end of the year," concludes John Wilson, controller of Retirement Living.

But even with the success of Retirement Living, hundreds of units still remained vacant in 1993, representing $400,000 per year in unpaid municipal property taxes and another $1 million annually in maintenance and utility bills. Whole streets of empty, modern houses stood as a ghastly and expensive reminder of what might have been. The mining companies and municipal authorities began to contemplate simply bulldozing them into the ground.

But an enterprising developer/entrepreneur from southern Ontario, Derek Tennant, wondered whether the private sector couldn't replicate the success of Retirement Living without the aid of a government start-up subsidy. In December 1992, he incorporated Active Living in Elliot Lake.

After months of tortuous negotiations, the key players in Elliot Lake finally agreed to sell vacant units to Active Living for $9,000 per home, provided Tennant agreed to sell (not rent) them, and provided he wouldn't promote them to Elliot Lake residents. Tennant took possession of his first batch, 262 units from Denison Mines, in June 1993. He invested a further $8,000 per unit in overhead and renovations, and placed ads in 32 publications, and the Toronto dailies.

"I could see that it had to be dramatic, so we focused our effort on seniors and set a price point of $19,900. We sold 100 units right off the bat. They'd never seen anything like this in the registry office in Sault Ste. Marie," Tennant recalls with a grin.

Over the next two years, Active Living would buy a total of 613 housing units in Elliot Lake, and by the fall of 1995 only a handful remained unsold.

The final and most bizarre players on the Elliot Lake housing scene entered the picture in December 1993. With some 2,000 lakes within a 200-mile radius, the town had long been an angler's paradise, a fact well known to Malcolm "Red" Briffett, a transplanted Newfoundlander and proprietor of Elliot Lake's Little Hooker Bait and Tackle Shop. For months back in 1993, Briffett had been pursuing Bob and Wayne Izumi, the star and producer respectively of the syndicated TV show "Real Fishing with Bob Izumi," to come and shoot a segment on the fish-laden waters around his adopted home town.

Just before Christmas 1993, Wayne Izumi arrived in Elliot Lake, and Briffett showed him a group of empty townhouses that were slated for demolition by Rio Algom. "Well, Red, I can sell those houses," Izumi told Briffett. Six months later, the Izumi brothers had taken possession of 170 Elliot Lake townhouses, which they proceeded to flog to viewers of "Real Fishing," which is syndicated in 30 countries around the world.

Red and the Izumi brothers enlisted the aid of long-time Elliot Lake realtor John Shamess to spearhead their efforts, and the results were phenomenal. By April 1995, only 45 units were left. "My personal goal is to sell the rest of them by the end of May," pronounces Shamess. Thanks to the Izumis, Shamess has had a number of inquiries from outside the country, especially Germany. "When we mention the price in Germany, people call John and ask, 'Do these places have doors on them?'" Red chortles.

Shamess nods. "We had a banker from Frankfurt who refused to loan one of our customers money because, he said, 'There's no place in the world you can buy a house for that money.'" Both men are still dining out on the story of one German client who came to visit and liked the town and the fishing, and bought a unit on the spot with his credit card. "The Elliot Lake area reminds 'em of the Black Forest," Red confides.

Like everyone else I talk to, Shamess and Briffett see the 4,000 seniors who have taken up residence in Elliot Lake as the salvation of their town, and their businesses. "We're getting a maturity and depth here we've never had before," says Dimock.

Epilogue

The town is basking under a hot August sun when I return, and the horizon on the hills surrounding Elliot Lake is a sea of soothing green.

The lawns of the Retirement Living housing units are rich and verdant and manicured, giving the place the spotless, spruced-up appearance of an army base or a private golf course. Flowers in full bloom hang from baskets on *faux* Victorian wrought-iron lighting standards downtown. Only the Stanleigh headframe, visible across the lake, betrays that this was once a gritty hardrock mining town.

I head straight for the "Ren Centre" as the place is commonly known. The line dancing ladies have been replaced by a co-ed group of seniors contentedly playing darts and chatting over coffee.

The clacking of billiard balls leads me to John and Agnes Morrall. He is 70 and a retired accountant. She is 68, and a retired secretary. They fairly radiate happiness, contentment, and good health. They moved from Toronto three years ago. They have temporarily abandoned their cottage in Muskoka for the pleasure of Elliot Lake in the summer. Like many long-time married couples, John and Agnes tend to complete one another's sentences.

"Do you know we lived in the same apartment in Toronto for 40 years?" John asks, lining up a red ball.

"And we didn't even know our neighbours," Agnes beams as John scratches.

"Here we get back from the cottage, and we no sooner get out of the car than four or five people are waving and saying, 'Hi John, Hi, Agnes.'" Agnes sinks her shot with authority.

"Living here you can do the other things you want to because the price is right," John scratches again but is unperturbed. "Now when we go back to Toronto and get to the Holland Marsh and see that yellow haze in the sky, we say, 'Hey, we did the right thing.'"

Welcome to the new Elliot Lake — and the future of us all? We should be so lucky.

Note

[1] This article first appeared in the November/December 1995 issue of *HighGrader Magazine*, 11–14. It is used in this volume with the permission of the author.

Chapter 15

Aging in a Hurry: Changing Population Profile in Elliot Lake[1]

Raymond W. Pong, Alan Salmoni, and Shawn Heard

When Rio Algom Limited and Denison Mines Limited announced their intention in 1990 to shut down uranium mining in Elliot Lake, an economic catastrophe began for this single-industry community in northeastern Ontario. Within a couple of years, more than 2,500 mine workers, representing about 70 percent of the mining workforce, were laid off. The few remaining mining jobs disappeared in 1996 when the last mine was closed for good.

The end of uranium mining in Elliot Lake could have meant the demise of this community if no viable economic alternatives were found. Like Uranium City in Saskatchewan,[2] Elliot Lake could have become another ghost town. But it refused to be just a footnote in a historical geography textbook. Instead, it vigorously lobbied the provincial and federal governments for assistance and launched a number of economic diversification initiatives, including the retention and attraction of small businesses and government offices, the development of training facilities in the community, and a major expansion of the Retirement Living Program (Farkouh 1992). It is this last initiative that has attracted most attention and has had the greatest impact on the community thus far. Originally designed to absorb the excess housing stock held by the mining companies, the Retirement Living Program was quickly expanded and energetically marketed in other parts of the country. A consultant's study commissioned by the city administration detailed a strategy to attract eventually up to 3,000 retirees, with a view to injecting tens of millions of dollars into the local economy.

The Retirement Living Program has been a success to date. Within several years, a large number of older persons moved to Elliot Lake to take advantage of cheap housing and other benefits. At the same time, many original residents of Elliot Lake left the community in search of employment elsewhere. According to the Elliot Lake Tracking and Adjustment Study, conducted by Laurentian University social scientists, the out-migration of mine workers was lower than expected, possibly due to relatively high unemployment across the country at that time. Still, close to 30 percent of the laid-off miners left Elliot Lake by 1994 (Wilkinson and Robinson 1995). Many people with mining-related jobs and in the service sector also left, even though the exact numbers are not known. Thus, in-migrating retirees replaced out-migrating miners. It is highly symbolic that the new Renaissance Centre, a social and recreational facility for seniors, occupies the building that was once the Steelworkers' Hall. Since most of the in-migrants were older persons and many of the out-migrants were relatively young mine workers, the demographic profile of Elliot Lake changed dramatically within a few short years (see Chenier, Chapter 10 in this volume).

The Elliot Lake Wood Carvers now meet weekly in the room that was formerly the reception area in the Steelworkers' Union Hall.

Jane Pitblado

The rapid growth or sudden demise of single-industry towns is nothing new. But Elliot Lake is a special case. Instead of becoming a ghost town when its natural-resource-based economic fortune came to a sudden end, it converted itself quickly into a retirement community. The transformation is demographic as well as economic. This rather unique experience deserves some attention, as it has implications for human service provision, long-term planning, and gerontological research. The primary purpose of this descriptive study is to document the demographic changes. A related objective is to examine the characteristics of the older persons who have chosen Elliot Lake as the place in which to spend their retirement years.

Data Sources

The community hardly had time to prepare for the onslaught of retirees. But realizing that it could not just invite retirees to settle in Elliot Lake without providing adequate support services, the city administration commissioned a team of researchers at Laurentian University to conduct a large-scale needs assessment, with a view to finding out the characteristics of the older population and then strengthening health care and other community services.

The Elliot Lake Seniors' Needs Assessment was officially launched at the end of 1994. The data-gathering phase consisted of two surveys. The first was a telephone survey of all residents aged 50 and over, the purpose of which was to construct a database that contained baseline information on as many older persons residing in Elliot Lake as possible. Research staff called every telephone number in Elliot Lake to determine if qualified individuals lived at that residence. If an initial call was not answered, two more attempts to establish contact were made. In order not to miss any eligible person, the researchers conducted a publicity campaign. Eligible persons who had not been surveyed were encouraged to contact the research office. More than 14,000 calls were made between December 1994 and July 1995, with 3,448 completed telephone interviews lasting from 15 to 30 minutes each. An estimated 10 percent of the eligible population was missed because some people could not be reached and a small number of residents refused to take part in the study.

The second component was a mail survey conducted in the summer of 1995. While the telephone survey gathered basic information on a broad range of topics from most older persons, more in-depth information was needed to support short- and long-term planning. The mail survey asked for considerably more detailed information. A random sample of those who had been surveyed by telephone was selected to take part in the mail survey. Slightly more than 500 completed questionnaires were returned, of which about 480 were found to be useful. Data from the two surveys were eventually merged. In this chapter we rely primarily on data obtained from the telephone survey, since it covered most of the older residents in Elliot Lake.

Another source of population data is the Canadian censuses. Both census data and data from the telephone survey are used in the following sections. These two sources of data complement each other: while census data are particularly useful for studying long-term population trends, the survey data allow us to examine in greater detail the characteristics of the older population.

The Changing Population Profile

First of all, as shown in Figures 1 to 3, the population in Elliot Lake fluctuated widely from one census to another, most likely reflecting the upswings and downturns of the uranium-mining industry. The demographic profile of the community changed abruptly in the early 1990s following the mine closure announcements. The age pyramids of the Elliot Lake population for 1976 and 1981 are shown, respectively, in Figures 1 and 2. The population in each of these two years was characterized by a large proportion of younger and working-age persons and a very small proportion of people in the older age categories.

Figure 1. Age and sex composition: Elliot Lake, 1976

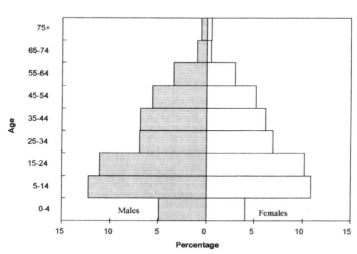

Source: 1976 Census, Statistics Canada   Total Population: 8,850

Figure 2. Age and sex composition: Elliot Lake, 1981

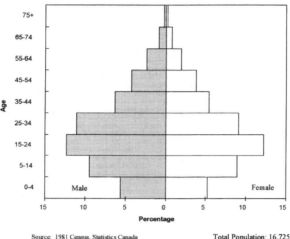

Source: 1981 Census, Statistics Canada   Total Population: 16,725

The age-sex compositions of the population for 1986 and 1991 are shown in Figure 3. In this diagram, one age pyramid is superimposed on the other in order to highlight the dramatic changes in the age structure. There was a sizeable reduction in the percentage of people aged 15 to 34. On the other hand, the proportion of people belonging to the older age categories increased considerably. Since 1991 was only one year after the mine-closure announcements, the age pyramid for that year reflects the initial impact of the mine closures and the Retirement Living Program.

Another way of looking at the demographic shift in Elliot Lake between 1986 and 1991 is to compare the age dependency ratios[3] for these two years. The ratio changed from 48.4 in 1986 to 51.3 in 1991. However, the slight increase in age dependency masks some profound changes in the age structure of the population. While the number of children under 15 dropped sharply from 5,385 in 1986 to 3,500 in 1991, the number of persons 65 years of age and older increased substantially from 475 in 1986 to 1,275 in 1991.

Unfortunately, because the detailed results of the 1996 census were not available at the time when this study was prepared, it was not possible to have a comparable age pyramid and an age dependency ratio for 1996. But Figure 4 shows the number of people 55 years of age and over in 1986 and 1995. Whereas the 1986 population figure was from the census, the 1995 figure was obtained from the telephone survey of the Seniors' Needs Assessment.

Figure 3. Age and sex composition: Elliot Lake, 1986 and 1991

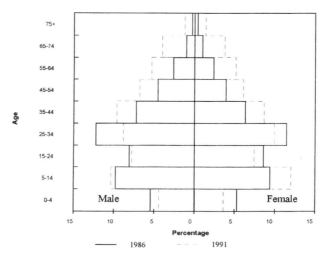

Source: 1986 Census & 1991 Census, Statistics Canada

1986 Total Population: 17,975
1991 Total Population: 14,080

Figure 4. Number of Elliot Lake residents aged 55 and over
and 65 and over, 1986 and 1995

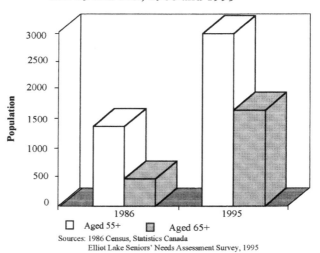

Sources: 1986 Census, Statistics Canada
Elliot Lake Seniors' Needs Assessment Survey, 1995

The number of people 65 years of age and over in Elliot Lake grew from 475 in 1986 to more than 1,657 in 1995, an increase of at least 250 percent in less than 10 years. It is worth repeating that most of that increase took place after 1990 as a result of the expansion of the Retirement Living Program and that the figure of 1,657 represents an underestimate because the telephone survey missed about 10 percent of the target population. It should also be noted that the influx of retirees is continuing, albeit at a steadier pace. In other words, the number and proportion of older persons in Elliot Lake are probably larger today than in 1995 when the research was conducted.

Old-Timers and Newcomers

Besides knowing that the Elliot Lake population has aged considerably as a result of the out-migration of younger workers and a substantial in-migration of retirees, it is important from a planning perspective to find out if the recent in-migrants are different from the older persons who have been residing in the community for some time. In other words, is the demographic transformation limited to the increase in the number of older persons or have the characteristics of the older population also changed?

To answer this question, we compared older persons who had resided in Elliot Lake for some time with those who had recently relocated to Elliot Lake, using a number of demographic and socioeconomic measures. The length of time in Elliot Lake was used as the criterion to differentiate the two groups of older residents. Persons aged 50 and over who had been living in Elliot Lake five years or more at the time of the survey were classified as "old-timers." Those 50 years of age and over who had been in the community less than five years were classified as "newcomers." Because the latter took up residence after the 1990 mine-closure announcements, it is safe to assume that most of them moved to Elliot Lake as a result of the expansion of the Retirement Living Program.

Figure 5 shows the differences between the old-timers and newcomers with respect to age. The newcomers were considerably older. Whereas only 6 percent of them were in the 50–54 age category, 18 percent of the old-timers were in this age group. Conversely, 28 percent of the newcomers were in the 65–69 age category, compared with 16 percent of the old-timers.

As can be seen in Figure 6, the two groups were virtually identical with respect to marital status. A great majority (77 percent) of both the old-timers and newcomers were married or in a common-law relationship.

Figure 5. Age distribution of Elliot Lake residents aged 50 and over

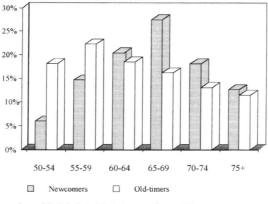

Source: Elliot Lake Seniors' Needs Assessment Survey, 1995

Figure 6. Marital status of Elliot Lake residents aged 50 and over

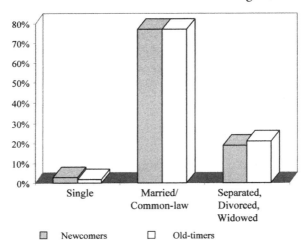

Source: Elliot Lake Seniors' Needs Assessment Survey, 1995

Figures 7 and 8 provide some insight into the extent of social relatedness. Not surprisingly, the old-timers had more relatives living in the community or were sharing a household with others. In contrast, the newcomers were likely to be on their own in their newly adopted community. Figure 7 shows that 16 percent of the old-timers, compared with only 7 percent of the newcomers, were living in households with three or more persons. Furthermore, 69 percent of the newcomers had no family members living in the community. Only 38 percent of the old-timers did not have family members in Elliot Lake. It should be pointed out that not having other people living in the same household or family members in the same community does not necessarily imply social isolation, since there are formal support systems and informal networks of friends and neighbours that can be just as important. Nonetheless, it appears that the old-timers had more closely related people nearby to whom they could turn if company or assistance was needed.

Figure 7. Number of people living in households of Elliot Lake residents aged 50 and over

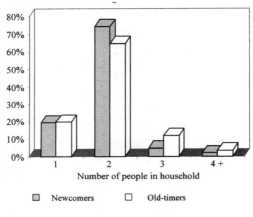

Source: Elliot Lake Seniors' Needs Assessment Survey, 1995

Figure 8. Proportion of residents aged 50 and over with family members living in Elliot Lake

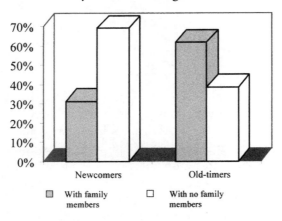

Source: Elliot Lake Seniors' Needs Assessment Survey, 1995

Figure 9. Educational attainment of Elliot Lake residents aged 50 and over

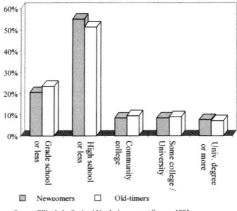

Source: Elliot Lake Seniors' Needs Assessment Survey, 1995

Levels of educational attainment are displayed in Figure 9. The old-timers and newcomers were very similar. Likewise, as shown in Figure 10, the two groups were comparable in occupational backgrounds. Occupational background refers to the occupations of the subjects at the time of the survey or their most recent occupations prior to their retirement or becoming unemployed. While the newcomers were somewhat more likely to be found in white-collar employment and the old-timers in blue-collar work, the differences between the two groups were relatively small. Together, these two sets of data suggest that the

Figure 10. Occupational background of Elliot Lake residents
aged 50 and over

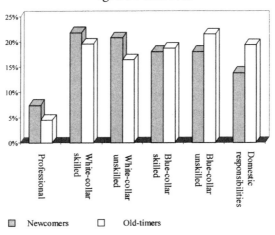

Source: Elliot Lake Seniors' Needs Assessment Survey, 1995

Retirement Living Program did not attract to Elliot Lake older persons with substantially divergent backgrounds. It is not known if this was the result of a deliberate recruitment policy of the program or if retirees chose Elliot Lake for reasons of affinity and compatibility.

Figure 11 shows the labour force status of the two groups of older persons. While 94 percent of the newcomers were no longer in the labour force, only 69 percent of the old-timers were retired. Conversely, 26 percent of the old-timers, compared to only 5 percent of the newcomers, were employed. This is not surprising in view of the objective of the Retirement Living Program to attract retirees to the community. Also, this could be due to the fact that the newcomers were considerably more advanced in age than the old-timers. It is also obvious from Figure 12 that the old-timers had a much higher annual household income than the newcomers. Slightly over three-quarters of the latter had a household income of less than $30,000 per year, while only 58 percent of the former were in this category. On the other hand, 23 percent of the old-timers had a household income of $45,000 or more, compared with only 6 percent of the newcomers. The differences in household income between the two groups could be due to the fact that very few of the newcomers were still in the labour force, and the majority of them probably relied on a combination of savings, pensions, and various income maintenance programs.

Figure 11. Labour force status of Elliot Lake residents aged 50 and over

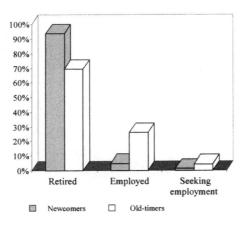

Source: Elliot Lake Seniors' Needs Assessment Survey, 1995

Figure 12. Household income of Elliot Lake residents aged 50 and over

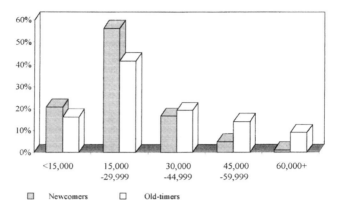

Source: Elliot Lake Seniors' Needs Assessment Survey, 1995

Summary and Discussion

Elliot Lake has experienced some dramatic changes in its population due to the shutdown of uranium mining and the subsequent shift from natural resource extraction to retirement living as the economic mainstay of the community. The ensuing demographic transformation has four salient aspects. First, there was a decline in the total population in Elliot Lake from 17,984 in 1986 to 14,089 in 1991, a drop of just over 20 percent. The 1996 census shows a further slight decline in the city's population to 13,588. Second, there was a significant population "exchange" in the sense that while there was an exodus of younger mine workers and their families, an influx of older retirees into the community took place, resulting in a substantial aging of the population. Third, the aging of the population in Elliot Lake happened rapidly, mainly after the mine-closure announcements in 1990. Population aging — a demographic process that usually takes decades, if not generations, to eventuate — transpired in a few short years in this community. Fourth, while not totally different from the older persons who had been in Elliot Lake for some time, the in-migrating retirees altered the characteristics of the older population in some ways. The two groups of older persons were very similar in terms of marital status, educational attainment, and occupational background. But compared with the old-timers, the recently arrived retirees had fewer closely related persons living nearby, were more likely to be on their own in the community, were much less likely to be economically active, and had a considerably lower annual household income.

All this has important implications for Elliot Lake. Most urgent and important of all is the provision and planning of services for the elderly. Until very recently, Elliot Lake was a community with a relatively young population. Services for older persons were generally not a high priority. The Retirement Living Program has changed all that. The influx of a large number of older persons has forced the city administration to turn its attention to issues that it did not have to deal with in the past. Older and younger persons often have different needs, interests, and concerns. It is known that senior citizens engage in different recreational activities, use a disproportionate amount of health care, need different types of municipal services, have dissimilar shopping and consumption patterns, and so on. Therefore, it is important for the success of the Retirement Living Program that these emerging needs be recognized and met. The long-term impact on the provision of human services is especially critical. As Longino and Biggar (1981) have pointed out in their study of retirement migration in the U.S., while older migrants initially contribute to the economic welfare of the retirement communities, they will likely increase the local demand for health care, public welfare, and other services as they age into their later years.

There are indications that Elliot Lake is well aware of these implications and has started a much-needed realignment of priorities and long-term planning processes. The commissioning of the Seniors' Needs Assessment is one step in this new direction. The data of the surveys are meant to be used for medium- and long-term planning, particularly in health care and other human services. A few studies have already been completed, using the survey data for needs-assessment and service-planning purposes (see Pong, Salmoni, and Heard, Chapter 18 in this volume; Salmoni et al. 1996).

It is not merely the expansion of services for older persons that is needed. Equally important is the design of services that meet the needs of an older population with special characteristics and needs. For instance, as the above analysis has shown, the retirees who have recently relocated to Elliot Lake are different in some respects from the longtime residents. It is possible that health and support services that rely heavily on informal caregivers may be less suitable for the newcomers than for the old-timers because the former tend not to have relatives living nearby and are less likely to share households with other people.[4] This does not mean that home care and informal caregivers should not be used for this group of older persons. What may be needed are special programs to help them develop and strengthen social networks and informal support systems.

There are other important issues that need to be addressed. Are the older residents satisfied with the community? Do they plan to stay in Elliot Lake on a permanent or long-term basis? How can generational conflicts be prevented in the wake of such rapid and profound demographic changes? Can retirement living provide an adequate economic base for Elliot Lake in the long term? What types of services will be needed 10 or 15 years from now as the population ages further? The Seniors' Needs Assessment has provided some useful data to begin the needs assessment and planning processes. But the situation in Elliot Lake is still fluid and more changes are likely. In order to address long-term issues in an effective manner, it is necessary to monitor changing circumstances on a regular basis and to have up-to-date data to support policy decisions and program planning.

From a research perspective, Elliot Lake provides a rare opportunity to study population aging while it is happening. Studies of the consequences of population aging tend to be speculative in nature, since the process is generally lengthy and slow. Also, few societies have actually experienced population aging on a large scale. In the case of Canada, the real aging crunch will not begin for at least another 15 years (McDaniel 1987). Examining what has taken place in Elliot Lake is like getting a glimpse of the future by pushing the "fast forward" button. In this sense, it is a unique and valuable case study in social gerontology.

Notes

[1] The authors gratefully acknowledge the assistance of Dave A. Pearson of the Centre for Rural and Northern Health Research, Laurentian University, in preparing the diagrams.

[2] Uranium City in Saskatchewan, another community that depended solely on uranium mining, almost disappeared when mining activities came to an end in the early 1980s. Its population plummeted from 2,748 in 1981 to 173 in 1986, according to the Saskatchewan Bureau of Statistics.

[3] The age dependency ratio typically refers to the ratio of the combined child population (persons under 15) and elderly population (persons aged 65 and over) to the population of intermediate age (persons aged 15 to 64).

[4] The research by Joseph and Cloutier (1991) on the elderly has provided some support for this view. Comparing the types of health services used by non-migrant, short-distance-migrant, and long-distance-migrant retirees in Grey County, Ontario, the authors found that older persons who had retired to this area from far away, those who were thus less likely to have family members and friends living close by, were potentially more reliant on the formal support system than the others.

References

Farkouh, George. (1992). "Elliot Lake," in *At the End of the Shift: Mines and Single-Industry Towns in Northern Ontario,* ed. Matt Bray and Ashley Thomson. Toronto: Dundurn Press.

Joseph, Alun E. and D.S. Cloutier. (1991). "Elderly migration and its implications for service provision in rural communities: an Ontario perspective," *Journal of Rural Studies* 7, 4: 433–44.

Longino, Charles F., Jr. and J.C. Biggar. (1981). "The impact of retirement migration on the South," *The Gerontologist* 21, 3: 283–90.

McDaniel, Susan. (1987). "Demographic aging as paradigm in Canada's welfare state," *Canadian Public Policy* 13, 3: 330–36.

Salmoni, A., V. Sahai, S. Heard, R. Pong, and J. Lewko. (1996). "Predicting future long-term care needs in a community," *Canadian Journal of Public Health* 87, 6: 418–21.

Wilkinson, Derek and D. Robinson. (1995). *Three Questions about the Mobility of Laid-off Mine Workers from Elliot Lake, 1990–1994.* ELTAS Analysis Series #2A14. Sudbury, ON: INORD, Laurentian University. Paper presented at the annual meeting of the Canadian Sociology and Anthropology Association in Montreal, June 4, 1995.

Chapter 16
Layoffs and Municipal Finance: The Case of Elliot Lake
David Robinson and Merlyn Bishop

In 1976 the Department of Regional Economic Expansion reported that 25 percent of Canadians living outside metropolitan areas lived in single-industry towns. These communities have been a vital part of our experience of Canada and make a disproportionate contribution to Canada's export trade. They are also subject to boom-and-bust cycles as world prices change or resources are exhausted. This paper deals with an issue neglected in the literature on local government and taxation and in writings on the life cycles of single-industry towns. We look at the effect of the collapse of the principal industry on the municipal revenues and expenditures for a particular single-industry town in Ontario, Elliot Lake. We look for lessons that may be of use to other municipalities, and we consider what the experience of Elliot Lake can tell us as we move into a period of reform of the municipal system.

The Fair Tax Commission pointed out that "one of the major problems with the various reform exercises ... is that they have been based on the assumption that there is a 'typical' local government.... Nothing could be farther from the truth."[1] Another assumption, still less obvious, is that local governments are reasonably stable entities. The case of Elliot Lake shows both that local government finance can undergo rapid and unexpected shifts and that specific features of local government finance can have an important effect on how successfully a community responds to mass layoffs.

It is important to put the role of local government in context. In 1988, our reference year, all governments together controlled 44 percent of the gross domestic product (GDP). Of that, the local government

219

share was 17 percent.[2] If we make the important distinction between exhaustive expenditure, which uses up resources that would otherwise be available to the public sector, and transfers, which simply shift income from one sector to another,[3] we find that 48.3 percent of total government expenditure was on goods and services and capital formation. The rest went to transfers and payments on the debt. In contrast, 88.7 percent of local government expenditure went to goods, services, and capital formation. In total, local governments spent 33.8 billion on goods and services, while provincial governments spent 37.68 billion. Of the three levels of government, it is local governments that are most heavily concentrated on delivering services.[4] If we include primary and secondary education and health,[5] most of the services enjoyed by Canadians are delivered by local governments.[6] Whether it is social services, schooling, sewage, streets, or protection for persons and property, local governments provide the day-to-day necessities for business and life.[7]

Local governments are increasingly dependent on the province for funding. From 1960 to 1990, own-tax revenue of local governments in Ontario declined from 68 percent to 30 percent of total revenues. Taking a longer perspective between 1926 and 1988, government expenditure rose from 15 percent of GDP to 44 percent, and the provincial share of total government expenditure rose from 20 to 33.4 percent. Over the same period, the municipal share fell from 44 percent to 17 percent. These changes reflect a significant shift in fiscal power away from the local level to the province. The shift is less advanced in Ontario than in Canada as a whole, however. In 1987, Ontario provincial expenditures per capita were only 81 percent as high as the Canadian average, while local and hospital expenditures per capita were 25 percent above the national average.[8]

Despite their importance in so many aspects of citizens' lives and their quasi-constitutional status as a third level of government, local governments have extremely limited autonomy, as recent events in Ontario have dramatically demonstrated. The province has the constitutional right to tax and responsibility for all the services provided by the municipalities. The province assigns specific duties to the municipality and it provides money in the form of transfers or tax space to carry out those duties. Legally, local governments are mere creatures of their provincial governments. In addition, the allocation of responsibilities is complex and variable. According to the Ontario Fair Tax Commission, "the system of local government is so complex and arcane that it is incomprehensible to most Ontario residents."

Furthermore, "those few who know the system well accept as a given that virtually every component of Ontario's system of local government finance is in a state of crisis or near crisis."[9] The system is widely held to be confusing and unfair.

It is in the context of a rapidly evolving fiscal situation that we discuss the dramatic changes in local finance in Elliot Lake. The paper is organized as follows. First, we describe briefly the community and history of Elliot Lake and provide a few details on mining towns in general. Next, we provide a short course on municipal finance in Ontario, using the figures from Elliot Lake prior to the layoffs. There follows a description of the changes in revenue and expenditure for the period 1987 to 1993. Finally, we draw some conclusions from the Elliot Lake experience.

The Community

Elliot Lake developed in order to serve the mining of uranium. It was a planned community, intended from the beginning to be a full-service residential community. After massive expansion in the late 1950s, however, the community shrank when the U.S. defence industry switched to domestic sources of uranium. A second boom began in the mid-1970s, and raised the population to around 18,000 in 1983. By the late 1980s, however, Elliot Lake faced competition from much lower-cost producers, and Ontario Hydro terminated its contracts. Employment at both mining companies in Elliot Lake (Rio Algom and Denison) declined rapidly, and ended with the closure of the Stanleigh Mine in 1996. With that closure, primary-sector employment vanished.

Theory and experience predict that a rapid decline in population should follow the layoffs. Each primary-sector job supports some secondary and tertiary employment. So if the primary-sector job is lost, others typically follow. In Elliot Lake, secondary employment was limited, but there were some firms supplying the mining industry and a significant tertiary, or service, sector.

Figure 1 shows that the population declined sharply when employment fell in the early 1960s. The population also declined when the mine workforce began to fall in the late 1980s. But the population figures for Elliot Lake hold a surprise for the theorist. Population dropped sharply after 1989, as expected, but then recovered significantly. It is now projected to return to 1990 levels by the turn of the century. The impact of the layoffs on city finances has been and will be muffled by this surprising turnaround. There are two general reasons for the pattern that actually occurred. The first is that there was slower out-migration than expected, and the second is that the city found a replacement population. Each of these deserves further explanation, and each has influenced the city's finances.

Slow out-migration may be explained in part as a result of the strong attachment that Elliot Lakers feel for their community. Other factors may, however, be more important. It is convenient to discuss migration in terms of "push" and "pull" factors. Both were weak in Elliot Lake in the early 1990s. Push factors are those that cause people to leave. There were workers near retirement who had no need to move for new employment.

Figure 1. Primary employment and population, Elliot Lake, 1955–1996

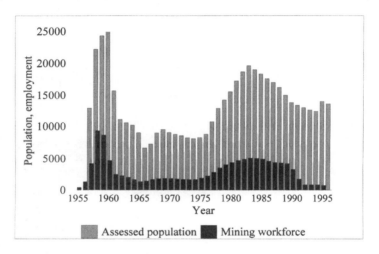

Households with second earners were less likely to move, and were likely to move more slowly than single-earner families, slowing the overall population response. Home ownership was high among the company employees, and that meant that it was relatively cheap to stay in Elliot Lake and required a strong "pull" to draw them away. Furthermore, severance packages, unemployment insurance, and a variety of job-creation programs temporarily reduced for many the pressure to move. More important still, the early 1990s saw a serious recession. It takes jobs to pull people away from their homes. Mining employment, in particular, fell across Canada, and normally mobile mining workers had fewer opportunities elsewhere. Overall, the impact of the massive change in the local labour market was muffled.

The community also found a way to attract a new class of residents. The story of how Elliot Lake successfully marketed itself as a retirement community and attracted a replacement population has become a classic of Canadian community development. That success rested in part on maintaining the city's infrastructure and service level, and on keeping property taxes as low as possible—which of course brings us back to issues in municipal finance.

In addition to a change in gross population, we expect a drop in family incomes as high-paid jobs disappear. In 1986, incomes in Elliot Lake were 29 percent above the national average at $16,452 per capita. With an average family size of 3.3, mean annual household income was over $54,000. In 1986, the growth rate of the community was reported to be 126.7 percent per decade.[10] Not only did high-wage jobs disappear, but the replacement population was largely on fixed and relatively low incomes. This shift in the income profile also has a negative effect on the service sector, on property values, and eventually on city revenues.

Declining population and declining incomes ultimately present reduced city revenues. The pathway is not as direct as it might seem, however, as we discuss in the next section.

The "new subdivision" at Horn Lake. Many of the new retirees in Elliot Lake live here.

City of Elliot Lake

Before the Flood: The 1988 Budget

We begin with a brief description of the municipal budget for 1988. We have selected 1988 because it precedes the layoffs. Figure 1, which shows primary employment and population for the city, reveals that by 1988 there had already been a substantial decline in the city's population.

On one level, municipal finance is fairly simple. Revenue is equal to expenditure. This is less a result of virtue than legislation. Under the Municipal Act, a local government is allowed to run neither deficit nor surplus. The municipal council decides how much to spend. From this amount, the treasurer subtracts the transfer revenues and projected program revenues. Council must fund from tax revenues whatever is left. The tax rate is set to cover the level of expenditure that the municipality projects.

There are in fact exceptions to this. The municipality may take on long-term debt to finance capital works, although it requires Ontario Municipal Board approval for borrowing in excess of a certain amount. The municipality may also maintain a number of reserves — any surplus is simply transferred to a reserve fund. Capital works are pre-financed out of capital funds. There are working funds, and equipment replacement funds, as well as specific reserve funds to cover expenditures on sick leave, infrastructure development, and other specified purposes. These totalled in 1988 over $3.5 million for Elliot Lake. By 1994, reserves had grown to over $10 million, including almost $3 million in a "mill rate stabilization fund" created to buffer the expected collapse of the assessment base and to finance capital items that would impact on the mill rate. For the purposes of this chapter, we will ignore changes in the reserve funds and debt.[11]

In 1988 Elliot Lake had two main sources of revenue and two much smaller ones. Program revenue, at $2.8 million, is an increasingly important component of municipal budgets in Ontario, and across Canada, as councils turn to user fees for revenue. In 1988, for example, water billing brought the City of Elliot Lake $634,127. Subsidies and grants supply a significant proportion of municipal funds. Grants are generally formula-based. The size has depended not on population but on residential units. Because of the formula, transfers from the province respond only slowly to changes in population. This tends to have a stabilizing effect on local budgets.

Tax revenue for the municipality comes primarily from real property taxes, with significantly smaller amounts arising from local taxes on businesses and from special assessments. Boadway and Kitchen reported that in 1981, 85 percent of municipal tax revenue in Canada was derived

Figure 2. Sources of revenue, Elliot Lake, 1988 budget
(in millions of dollars)

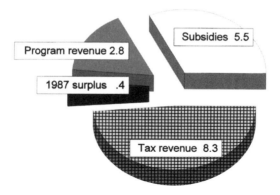

from real property taxes.[12] Tax revenue comes from three sources: residential, commercial, and business. Figure 3 shows the assessed values of the three types of properties for Elliot Lake. Note that the revenue value of the residential properties is overstated because they are taxed at 85 percent of assessed value. Residential property taxes have provided a decreasing proportion of municipal operating revenue in Ontario since 1970. Provincial operating transfers have been increasing, as have business occupancy taxes.[13]

Figure 3. Shifting structure of tax assessment base, Elliot Lake

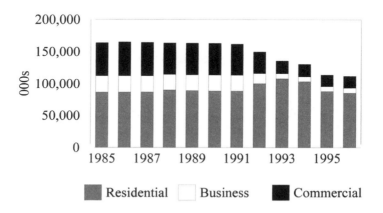

Elliot Lake, like some other resource-based communities, enjoyed a relatively large commercial tax base, mainly consisting of properties owned by the mining companies. Furthermore, because the companies cannot move to other communities and continue their business, the tax base was insensitive to the mill rate. As a result, the town was able to raise mill rates and keep user charges low relative to most other communities. In effect, the budget was set to shift costs to the companies. Furthermore, since the two major mining companies owned 50 percent of the housing stock, financing services through the mill rate may have shifted even more of the cost of services to the companies.

Changes

In 1993, the city reported a 20-percent reduction in assessments between 1990 and 1994. It projected a further decline of 36 percent by the end of 1996, when the Stanleigh Mine was scheduled to close and decommissioning was expected to be completed.[14] The decline was not uniform, however. Business and commercial assessments declined, while residential assessments remained fairly constant. Figure 3 shows the decline in non-residential assessments. The rise in residential assessments between 1991 and 1995 is an artifact of the treatment of non-operating commercial properties. When a commercial property is inactive, it is redefined as residential because residential properties are assessed at a reduced rate.

Changes in assessments do not directly affect the municipal revenues because mill rates must be set to balance the budget. What they do affect quite directly is the distribution of the tax levy across different property types. When the mines closed down, the revenue that they had contributed had to come from other sources. It might seem that costs would decline proportionately, but in fact the mines received very little in the way of services. They maintained their own fire services and other functions.

In 1990, then, at a point when population was falling and the community was beginning to focus on attracting new businesses and new residents, Elliot Lake was also faced with the prospect of rising property taxes and rising user fees.

At this point there was real danger that a vicious fiscal circle would set in. Even without a decline in population, taxes were threatening to rise. Rising taxes could discourage people from moving to the community. As population declines, the cost of servicing the community falls, but more slowly than the population. The snow in front of empty houses still has to be ploughed, for example. As a larger residential tax bill is spread over a smaller number of taxable units, tax bills rise more. Rising tax bills discourage still more potential in-migrants and may start to drive away existing residents, especially when earnings have fallen.

The resulting collapse of local housing prices has important distributional consequences. For workers, housing is an important investment, a form of alternative employment, and a form of insurance. Mortgage payments are a way to enforce savings. During layoffs and temporary periods of unemployment, workers can invest time in home improvements, making efficient use of their time and skills. Finally, they can sell a house and live on the returns. In single-industry towns, however, unexpected closures wipe out the value of the housing for both the workers involved and for other members of the community. Savings vanish and the alternative job is no longer productive. In single-industry towns, housing is an insurance policy that is cancelled when it is needed. Actions at the municipal or provincial level that stabilize housing prices help workers maintain both savings and job-market mobility. They can go some distance towards reducing the negative impact of plant closings in small towns.

By 1993, the structure of municipal revenues in Elliot Lake had changed significantly, as Figure 4 shows. There had been an increase in subsidies that helped to deal with the decline in commercial and business assessments. The new subsidies came from money paid by Ontario Hydro and distributed under Regulation 296–91 of the Power Corporation Act. These transfers, combined with reserve funds that the city had been building since 1988, allowed the City of Elliot Lake to delay mill rate increases until a system of user fees could be expanded. Figure 5 shows a major shift in revenue sources. Program revenue rose from 16.78 to 27.7 percent of the operating expenses budget. The transfers were used to pay down debts and fund capital expenditures.

By 1996 the City of Elliot Lake appeared to have made a surprisingly successful transition from mining town to retirement town. Realistically, the transition is not over. As the labour market improves, some laid-off workers who stayed will find work in other communities. The initial demographic impact of the layoffs was softened by external economic conditions, unemployment insurance, and job creation. Furthermore, the decline in household incomes has not yet depressed residential assessments. It is not clear yet whether the city has achieved a sustainable level of services, given its tax capacity. Finally, initial calculations suggest that provincial downloading will have an impact on municipal finances comparable to that of the layoffs. The impact is expected to be larger for communities with high social

Figure 4. Sources of revenue, Elliot Lake, 1993 budget
(in millions of dollars)

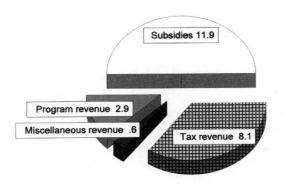

Figure 5. Sources of revenue, Elliot Lake, 1996 budget
(in millions of dollars)

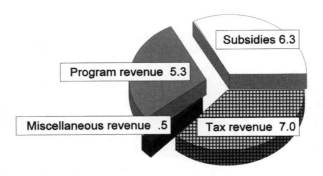

assistance populations, and Elliot Lake may pass from being a low-assistance to a high-assistance community as the demographic transformation proceeds. There is a real possibility that the provincial government will break the camel's back just as it is climbing to its feet.

Conclusions

Elliot Lake provides some clues as to how local public finance influences the ability of single-industry communities to survive the collapse of their core industries. Communities will do better if:

- they have large reserves;
- they have experienced and skilful municipal management;
- they have high-quality, well-maintained infrastructure;
- they have access to subsidies to smooth the impact on mill rates;
- they have a pool of potential new residents;
- there are barriers to mobility, as survival may be more likely during a recession, when workers don't move away to jobs.

There are three parties involved in the kind of crisis Elliot Lake went through: the people of the city; the municipality as an entity, led by municipal staff and council; and the provincial government. It takes all three to deal with the kinds of problems the city faced. Citizens brought a level of creativity and energy that produced successful, long-term responses and they provided the political weight needed to access provincial financial resources. The contribution of the federal government was minimal. Its most important function lay in maintaining federal employment longer than strictly necessary.

In the case of Elliot Lake, it was the municipality that provided leadership, in one notable case actually writing the funding criteria for distributing funds controlled by the province. Without municipal initiatives, the damage to the city's fiscal position might have been quite severe.

The crucial role of the province lay in providing bridging subsidies. These subsidies assisted the municipality to deal with the immediate shortfalls that arose when major taxpayers disappeared. The main job-creation programs that helped to stabilize population also came out of provincial funds. Provincial responses were not quick, and it is clear that the province does not have any systematic approach to dealing with fiscal changes beyond the capacity of municipalities.

Jobs and people are mobile. Mobility may or may not be necessary for the efficient working of the labour market, but there is no reason why the structure of municipal finance in Ontario should burden those who neither want nor need to move to follow jobs.

A number of policy conclusions can be drawn on the basis of the experience in Elliot Lake, some for town councils and some for the province. Councils in single-industry towns should build up reserves to deal with fluctuations in revenue. If councils are loading the mill rate to make the major industry carry the tax burden, they should begin as early as possible to shift to a user-pay formula, and transfer surplus generated to savings in the form of reserve funds. Quality infrastructure contributes to economic development. Using reserves to maintain or improve infrastructure may be more effective than reducing mill rates directly.

The design of the municipal finance system presents councils and provincial government with difficult incentive systems. If the province moves to withhold subsidies from communities with high reserves, it will effectively penalize any move by the community to prepare for revenue declines. If it stands ready to bail out municipalities, the province risks encouraging loose practices. There is a role for the province as a kind of insurance agency, if the moral hazard problem can be solved. Moral hazard refers to the temptation to take less care when an insurance policy is in force. Foresight has its dangers for municipal councils in the current situation as well. Any move by the provincial government in the direction of downloading fiscal responsibility will reduce the capacity of threatened communities to respond effectively. Similarly, if the province requires municipalities to pay the social service costs and then to bill the province for its 50 percent, the province would gain working capital at the expense of tying up municipal working reserves.

The province should have a coherent policy on aiding communities in transition. The province must maintain the fiscal capacity to assist municipalities that encounter unexpected declines in revenue. By preventing fiscal collapse, it can maintain sustainable communities and reduce long-term costs. The province should allow municipalities to retain reserves so they can respond to large fiscal fluctuations. The province should structure the municipal revenue base for stability and to track the expenditure requirements. Increasing local fiscal responsibility for family benefits and welfare goes counter to this principle.

Notes

[1] *Fair Taxation in a Changing World: Report of the Ontario Fair Tax Commission* (Toronto: University of Toronto Press, 1993), 663.
[2] Statistics Canada, *National Income and Expenditure Accounts* (13-001). Canada, Department of Finance, *Quarterly Economic Review: Annual Reference Tables*, Fourth Quarter 1988 (Ottawa: Department of Finance,

September 1994). See tables 7 and 53.

³ Irene Ip, "Overview of Provincial Government Finances," in *Provincial Public Finances: Plaudits, Vol. 1: Problems, and Prospects*, ed. Melville McMillan, Canadian Tax Paper #91 (Toronto: Canadian Tax Foundation, 1991), 27-86. See page 34.

⁴ Canada, Department of Finance, *Reference Tables*. See tables 55, 57, 59.

⁵ Sixty-three percent of the 19.3 percent provincial budgets spent on education and 62 percent of the 25 percent of provincial budgets spent on health are essentially local expenditures.

⁶ Although almost three-quarters of the combined expenditures by provincial government, municipal government, and school boards in Ontario were made by the Government of Ontario in 1991–92, for example, most of the health care expenditures were payments on behalf of citizens and transfers to local hospital authorities. Most of the educational expenditure took the form of transfers to local school authorities, and a substantial part of the rest took the form of transfers to municipal governments. See *Fair Taxation in a Changing World*, 139.

⁷ The best sources for this are Statistics Canada, *Public Finance Historical Data, 1965/66-1991/92*, Cat. 68–512 (Ottawa: Statistics Canada, 1992), and Statistics Canada, *Provincial Economic Accounts, Annual Estimates*, Cat. 13–213 (Ottawa: Statistics Canada, 1991).

⁸ Harry Kitchen, "Ontario: Provincial Public Finances," in *Provincial Public Finances: Plaudits, Vol. 2: Provincial Surveys*, ed. Melville McMillan, Canadian Tax Paper #91 Toronto: Canadian Tax Foundation, 1991), 160–183.

⁹ *Fair Taxation in a Changing World*, 599.

¹⁰ Financial Post Information Services, *Canadian Markets 1986* (Toronto: Maclean Hunter Ltd., 1986), 302.

¹¹ There is some fear among municipal officers that in the current restructuring, the provincial government will find a way to use these municipal funds to reduce provincial debt.

¹² Robin W. Boadway, and Harry M. Kitchen, *Canadian Tax Policy*, 2nd edition, Canadian Tax Paper #76 (Toronto: Canadian Tax Foundation, 1984).

¹³ *Fair Taxation in a Changing World*, 13. Fair Tax Commission calculations are based on Ontario Ministry of Municipal Affairs database.

¹⁴ City of Elliot Lake, *Request for Funding under Section 7 of the Ontario Unconditional Grants Act* (September 1994).

Chapter 17
Bringing the Business Community Through Transition
Alex Berthelot, Jr.

To appreciate properly the plight and reactions of the business sector after the announcement of the mine closures, it is important to understand how sudden and massive those closures were. Most people here had believed that the future of the mines was assured until at least the year 2020 under terms of contracts signed by Rio Algom Limited and Denison Mines Limited to supply Ontario Hydro. The general public and business community alike felt secure in this knowledge, since both mining companies in their recruiting efforts cited the long-term nature of the contracts with Ontario Hydro, indicating that the stability of the community was assured well into the future.

As the actual contracts were never public information, however, most people were unaware that they contained a clause that would allow Ontario Hydro to opt out under certain conditions. There had been massive investment in Elliot Lake in the previous 15 years, and only a few months before the announcements, many small businesses were still investing new money in their enterprises. For a number of years Elliot Lakers had enjoyed the highest disposable income per capita of any community in the country. It was a good place to be in business.

Although there had been warnings raised about the cost of production at these mines, it is safe to say that to most people the announcement of mine closures hit like a lightning bolt. Even those who had considered the possibility of some mines closing were dumbfounded to learn that the entire industry would be completely shut down.

It was the suddenness and severity of these events that marked one of the significant differences between what happened in Elliot Lake and what has happened in other single-industry towns, where the main industry typically deteriorates over a number of years until the final closure. There was no gradual emigration in Elliot Lake of people and businesses through a series of downsizings. The collapse was immediate and massive. We were *all* still here and all in a crisis situation together. In retrospect, it is interesting to consider that the suddenness of the collapse may have worked in the community's favour in the long run. There had been very little "leakage" of the local talent pool, and the massive layoffs were worthy of national attention.

The reaction of the business community was almost as swift as the announcements themselves. It was immediately clear that all local businesses fell into two broad categories: 1) direct suppliers of goods and services to the mines, and 2) everybody else. For the direct suppliers the impact was immediate. The fact that many of these businesses had the local mines as their main and often only market made their situation desperate. Other businesses would have somewhat more time to consider their options and try to adapt. Some of the closures would be staggered. Unemployment insurance and retraining benefits would flow into the community for some time. Also, there would still be significant work to be had in mine decommissioning.

In almost all cases, there was a very rapid rationalization of local businesses. Most operations were cut to bare bones. Owners became more directly involved in the day-to-day operation of their businesses. Almost everyone cut and tried to stabilize, while they considered their options and watched events unfolding. Many of the most marginal businesses closed very quickly. Several large companies lost confidence in the community and were quick to close local branch operations: The Co-Operators insurance company, Woolco and Zellers, for example. Bell Canada cut back on capital expenditures and Ontario Hydro itself closed its offices. The Royal Bank moved its regional office from Elliot Lake to Blind River, and all banks lost confidence and curtailed activity.

The upper levels of government also reacted very quickly. The Atomic Energy Control Board (AECB) — which owed its birth to the resources of Elliot Lake — closed its offices almost immediately, leaving not a single job in Elliot Lake. This despite the fact that the community was left with the largest uranium mine tailings in the world, in terms of both surface area and volume, and it is the AECB's responsibility to assure the proper decommissioning of the mines and management of the tailings. The RCMP offices were closed, the offices of the OPP were closed, and funding to the airport was cut. The CANMET labs in Elliot Lake are scheduled to close in by the summer of 1998.

For many good reasons, the local business community became the most committed and highly motivated group in the restructuring of the local economy. First, there are not many social support services for failed business owners: no severance pay, no unemployment insurance benefits, no relocation grants, no offers to buy back their homes, and no retraining programs from Employment Canada. For these people, the success of their business is essential for their survival. The option of moving on and starting over somewhere else is less attractive to this group than to any other affected group.

Secondly, many business people have very deep roots in the community. In most cases, a very significant portion of their family wealth is invested here. It is essential for them that the region prosper in order to protect assets that they have accumulated over more than one generation.

Thirdly, although Elliot Lake is a very young community, many enterprises are already second- and third-generation family businesses. So in addition to financial roots, family roots in Elliot Lake are very deep for this group.

Finally, most of the community's citizens are anxious to see the local business sector survive, both because those who are staying require the goods and services they provide, and because for many of those displaced by the mine closures, self-employment and employment in local businesses are the most viable and attractive alternatives.

All of this makes for a very committed core group to participate in restructuring. It is interesting that the same level of commitment was not as evident in franchise operations, where very often the parent company either withdrew support or offered to assist in relocating and re-establishing the owners or managers elsewhere. With the growing trend of franchise-type operations supplanting locally owned, financed, and operated businesses, one has to wonder who will lead the charge to restructure the economies of single-industry towns in the future.

This is a very important consideration, because the business group should represent a very valuable asset in the community's efforts to restructure. This group should possess many of the traits and skills necessary for the transformation of the economic base. They have accumulated much related experience and knowledge. They tend to be action-oriented, adaptable, creative, independent by nature, and generally capable. Many have other business connections that may be useful. Many also have political connections and well-developed lobbying skills.

The importance of organizing and focusing this pool of talent to deal with restructuring the local economic base cannot be overstated. The municipal and provincial governments, along with the local Chamber of Commerce, did an excellent job of helping the business community to reorganize and develop new strategies and vision for the future. This led to the formation of many interesting strategic alliances and many business people came forward to offer their skills and services in the restructuring efforts.

The first of these collaborations was the joint submission made to the province by the municipalities of the region, the United Steelworkers, and the local business community. This led directly to the $250-million settlement the region received as compensation for the early cancellation of the contracts with Ontario Hydro. The five local municipal governments, the then president of the Elliot Lake and District Chamber of Commerce, Andy Mitchell, and Leo Gerard of the United Steelworkers were instrumental in negotiating this settlement that would help stabilize the community and begin the process of restoring confidence.

Of this package, $160 million was earmarked to keep Stanleigh Mine operating for a further period of five years. Municipal and school-board debts were retired and, among other things, a $23-million venture capital fund was established to assist and attract business. This provided some breathing room. But more importantly, it was the first tangible sign that if we maximized our skills and made the required effort, there was a chance we could be successful in rebuilding.

Buoyed by this and the burgeoning success of the Retirement Living Program, local business people flocked to information and planning sessions organized by the municipal and provincial governments. Leaders from every sector of society began the task of devising a stabilization and recovery strategy. The importance of developing a plausible, realistic recovery plan was paramount. It had a calming, reassuring effect and allowed for organized, focused action.

Confidence began to grow and with it a tremendous enthusiasm. At one time, there were over 200 volunteers working on various committees

The new logo encouraging economic development in Elliot Lake.

City of Elliot Lake

to implement the developed strategies. They showed boundless energy, interesting innovation, and tremendous dedication. With every little success came a little bit more confidence and more new initiatives.

The principle of strategic alliances flourished. For the direct mine suppliers, the Mining Manufacturers' Association was initiated by Lembi Buchanan with the direction, assistance, and support of the local Economic Development Office. These manufacturers organized themselves to get training and to search for new markets. They negotiated a pool of emergency funding to allow for a transition period. Some of the mine suppliers, like the Nelson Brothers of Ram Hydraulics, showed themselves to be very innovative and successful at developing new products and markets. The Economic Development Office, capably directed by Dianna Bratina, was instrumental in organizing and supporting many strategic alliances and initiatives of this nature.

As impressive as all these efforts were, none of this would have been possible without the remarkable success of Elliot Lake's Retirement Living Program. The success of this program attracted other new investors, notably Active Living, Inc., and Izumi Outdoors, who purchased and marketed hundreds of housing units in Elliot Lake. This helped to stabilize the tax base and the economic base of the community, but there were also a number of other important side benefits.

The establishment of enterprises like Retirement Living and the Elliot Lake and North Shore Corporation for Business Development (ELNOS), and the subsequent attraction of businesses like Active Living and Izumi Outdoors dramatically expanded the local business talent pool and increased the number of capable stakeholders vitally interested in the economic health of the region. Retirement Living was very conscious of its role not only in filling housing units but in providing leadership and helping the local business community adapt to the new realities of an economy based on the needs of the new population of seniors.

Another of the important and interesting side benefits of the Retirement Living Program is the fact that they were adding significantly to the local talent pool by attracting many retirees who had a wide range of skills and experience. Many of these retirees were thrilled at being able to make a contribution to the successful future of their new community. Many of them felt more empowered to affect their quality of life than ever before, and they made significant contributions by participating actively in the restructuring efforts.

With the success of Retirement Living and a number of other projects like the Laurentian University Field Research Station, the Oaks Treatment Centre, Collège Boréal, the White Mountain Academy of the

Arts, and the new Civic Centre to name a few, confidence in the community's future continued to grow. We began to see a mini-explosion of small and micro businesses. When the mines were operating, most of the tradespeople were employed there. Many of these tradespeople found niches in contracting work where the community had previously been severely under-serviced. With the influx of new residents buying or renting homes here over the past few years, the market for building supplies and contracting services has been robust. A host of small businesses have sprung up to service the building maintenance needs of Retirement Living and to supply goods and services to the new population of seniors.

The Oaks Treatment Centre. Gerry Morin, photographer.
City of Elliot Lake

ELNOS, the $23-million business development corporation referred to earlier, has been a valuable tool in helping stabilize the local economy and will no doubt continue to play a significant role in redeveloping the economic base of the region. ELNOS has a broad mandate to provide a range of support services to existing businesses, to provide venture capital for viable business opportunities, to assist financially and with expertise in "special projects" deemed important to the overall health of the region's economy, and to attract new businesses to the region.

ELNOS represents a very significant innovation in dealing with the needs of a community in economic crisis. For the first time ever, a business development and assistance corporation was designed by the people of the affected region to meet their own specific needs. Furthermore, for the first time ever, the investment decisions and management of the funds are being undertaken entirely at the local level. This has led to a unique hybrid where the lines between business needs and societal responsibilities are sometimes blurred. This can lead to some very difficult situations, since the views of the role of the corporation tend to vary fairly dramatically from one interest group to the next. It is further complicated by the sense of entitlement many people in the region have about access to the funds. There are some groups who feel that the funds were provided for the benefit of the community and that they should be able to access them for whatever they see fit.

I firmly believe that the approach of a locally designed and managed fund of this nature is an important and valuable innovation. ELNOS has already made a significant contribution to the stabilization and redevelopment of the local economy and there is no doubt it will have a major role to play in the years ahead.

I would not like to leave the impression that all of this has happened without pain and difficulties. This region, and the City of Elliot Lake in particular, operated in a highly charged crisis mode for several years. We had many successes, but we also had our fair share of failures. People worked long hours and with a tremendous sense of urgency; emotions ran very high, and the strain was often evidenced by heated arguments and disagreements. In the end, however, I believe most people recognize the importance of getting by those disagreements and keeping the strategic alliance of business, labour, and municipal and provincial government strong.

The businesses that have survived and prospered have shown their strength and an ability to adapt to shifting paradigms. As a result, I believe the community has been left with a core business community to build around that is strong, capable, self-confident, and vital.

The experience of this region is an important one. Elliot Lake was not the first single-industry town to face the closure of its main employer. Yet when our particular crisis struck, there was precious little in the way of documentation of the experiences of other single-industry towns in crisis and of their efforts to redesign themselves. It has always been my contention that the efforts of single-industry towns to redesign their economic base should be well documented. The structures put in place — the successes and failures — should be analyzed and evaluated to provide a starting point for other single-industry towns in crisis. The work done through the Laurentian University Field Research Station and the Elliot Lake Tracking and Adjustment Study makes a good start in this direction. It is our hope that some day a comprehensive document can be developed about the experience of Elliot Lake that will be of use to other communities like ours in the future.

There have been many players and many factors in the amazing recovery of the Elliot Lake region. We are not yet "out of the woods" by any measure, and we will forever have to be aggressive in business development. But at the heart of Elliot Lake's success, I believe, is a very dedicated citizenry with an indomitable pioneer spirit, determination, vision, and tenacity. We're open for business and happy to be here!

Chapter 18
Physician Visits by Older Persons in Elliot Lake: Issues and Challenges[1]
Raymond W. Pong, Alan Salmoni, and Shawn Heard

Emergence of a Retirement Community

The transformation of Elliot Lake from a uranium-mining town into a retirement community was as dramatic as it was daring. The bottom fell out of Elliot Lake in 1990, when Denison Mines Limited and Rio Algom Limited announced the imminent shutdown of their uranium mining operations. Refusing to become another ghost town, Elliot Lake vigorously lobbied the provincial and federal governments for assistance and launched several major economic diversification initiatives, one of which was the Retirement Living Program (Dixon 1996, Farkouh 1992).

Realizing that the vacant houses left behind by the mining companies could be used to attract retirees from other places, the community leaders quickly expanded the Retirement Living Program and conducted an aggressive marketing campaign to attract retirees to settle in Elliot Lake. The strategy worked. Within a few short years, thousands of older persons moved to Elliot Lake to take advantage of cheap housing and other benefits that the Retirement Living Program had to offer. Thus, in-migrating retirees replaced out-migrating younger miners. The demographic profile of Elliot Lake changed rapidly from the relatively young population of a typical mining town to the much older population of an emerging retirement community (see Pong, Salmoni, and Heard, Chapter 15 in this volume).

Population aging is a concern to many sociologists, demographers, economists, health care planners, pension fund administrators, and so on, because it could have a major impact on many social institutions. The aging of the Elliot Lake population at such a breakneck speed presents a special challenge. One of the main concerns is the provision of health care, which is the focus of this analysis. In particular, this is an exploratory study of access to physicians' services by older persons residing in Elliot Lake.

Research Focus

The relationship between population aging and health service utilization has attracted considerable research attention. Studies have consistently shown that older persons use more health services and see physicians more often than younger people do (see, for example, Black et al. 1995, Denton and Spencer 1980, and Haas and Crandall 1988). While some writers believe that this is due to the growing number of senior citizens and their poorer health status as a result of advancing age, others (for example, Barer et al. 1995 and Black et al. 1995) attribute it to increased service intensity. Regardless of the reasons, a critical issue facing the health care system is its ability to cope with growing health care demands by the elderly at a time when public-sector spending is being curtailed.

A related issue is the maldistribution of physicians, which is seen by many as a major challenge in health care provision in this country. Slightly over 30 percent of Canadians lived in rural areas in 1991, if communities with less than 10,000 population are considered rural, but only about 11 percent of physicians practised in these rural areas (Rourke 1997). Most informed observers believe that Ontario has an adequate supply of physicians. But, as in other provinces, physicians in Ontario tend to concentrate in major urban centres. There are chronic shortages of physicians in northern and rural areas, despite efforts by the provincial

St. Joseph's General Hospital in Elliot Lake.

City of Elliot Lake

government to encourage a more even distribution of physicians. The situation is particularly critical in smaller and more remote communities. Physician specialists are rarely available in such places, and family physicians usually have large caseloads and have to be on call frequently. Physician recruitment difficulties, burnout, and high turnover are common predicaments.

The fact that Elliot Lake is a small city located in a region with chronic physician shortages, combined with the fact that it is experiencing rapid population aging, has made access to medical care a critical concern. The in-migration of so many retirees in so short a time could overburden a service system that was developed over time to serve a mining community with a relatively young population. The impact of elderly migration on retiree-receiving communities, particularly their ability to provide adequate health care and other human services, is an important issue. Various writers (for example, Bryant and El-Attar 1984, Lee 1980, Longino and Biggar 1981, Longino and Biggar 1982, and Patrick 1980) have studied elderly migration to popular retirement destinations and other communities in the United States. They generally agree that unless retirees are moving to areas where there are already abundant services, expansion of resources and enhancement of services are needed. In this country, Joseph and Cloutier (1991) have examined the effects of elderly migration on service provision in Grey County, Ontario. The authors believe that in rural communities with a significantly aging population, "even more daunting is the prospect that migration-induced stress will overlay and exacerbate long-standing problems of providing services to scattered communities within the context of finite budgets" (443).

The challenge facing Elliot Lake is not just the extent of change, but also the speed at which changes are occurring. There are urgent needs to reshape the service system and to plan for the future. To this end, Elliot Lake commissioned a group of researchers at Laurentian University to conduct a large-scale needs assessment with a view to gathering baseline data to help formulate service provision strategies and monitor changes in service needs. The purpose of this study is to use some of the data collected to examine one aspect of health service provision in this emerging retirement community, namely, physician visits by older residents (that is, persons aged 50 and over). The study has several aspects: (1) analyzing the frequency of visits to physicians, (2) estimating the total number of visits to physicians in a year, (3) determining the extent to which older residents had to seek medical care outside Elliot Lake, and (4) identifying problems experienced by those who had to leave the community for medical consultation. In addition, the implications of the findings are discussed in the final section.

Data Sources

Officially launched at the end of 1994, the Elliot Lake Seniors' Needs Assessment comprised two surveys: a telephone survey and a mail survey. The details of the survey methodology are described in Pong, Salmoni, and Heard (Chapter 15 in this volume). This study used data from both surveys. The telephone survey allows us to estimate the total number of older persons in Elliot Lake and the numbers of people in different age groups. The mail survey, on the other hand, provides more detailed information on physician visits.

Another source of data used in this study was the Ontario Health Survey (OHS), which was conducted in 1990 by Statistics Canada on behalf of the Ontario Ministry of Health and the Premier's Council on Health, Well-Being and Social Justice. Close to 46,600 individuals (weighted to an effective population of about 7,774,500 Ontario residents) aged 15 years and over participated in the survey. The OHS covers a broad range of health topics including the frequency of contacts with physicians and other practitioners (see Ontario Ministry of Health s.d.). The OHS data are used in this study primarily for comparison purposes.

Findings
The findings of the surveys are reported under four headings.

Physician visits. The mail survey asked the respondents to indicate the number of times they had seen a family physician (or general practitioner) and/or a physician specialist in or outside Elliot Lake in the 12-month period prior to the survey. The information provided was used to estimate the total number of physician visits made by older residents. Since the questions asked in the Elliot Lake survey were almost identical to those used in the OHS, it is possible to compare the findings from the two surveys. The OHS data represent a provincial norm against which the Elliot Lake findings can be gauged. The mean numbers of visits to family physicians and specialists by older residents in various age categories are shown in Table 1, which also contains comparable data from the OHS.

Table 1. Mean number of visits to family physicians and specialists,
Elliot Lake Needs Assessment Survey (1995), and
Ontario Health Survey (1990)

Age group	Elliot Lake Survey		Ontario Health Survey	
	Mean number of visits to family physician	Mean number of visits to specialists	Mean number of visits to family physician	Mean number of visits to specialists
50–54	6.41	2.14	4.11	1.21
55–59	5.67	1.14	4.06	1.20
60–64	4.22	0.69	4.63	1.31
65–69	5.91	1.22	5.16	1.82
70–74	7.36	1.45	5.55	1.88
75–79	5.66*	1.46*	5.98	1.54
80+			6.73	1.56

* figures for age 75+
Sources: Elliot Lake Seniors' Needs Assessment: Mail Survey (1995)
Ontario Health Survey (1990)

Two aspects are worth noting. First, with a few minor exceptions, the OHS data show that as people got older, they saw physicians more often. For instance, subjects in the 55–59 age group visited family physicians 4.1 times a year on the average. The mean number of visits to family physicians increased to 6.7 times for those in the 80-and-above age group. In other words, frequency of physician contacts (for both family physicians and specialists) tends to increase with age. However, a similar positive relationship between frequency of physician contacts and age was not found among the Elliot Lake survey respondents. It is possible that random variations and outlier effects were not evened out due to the much smaller sample size (about 480 subjects) in the Elliot Lake mail survey.

Second, with a few exceptions, the Elliot Lake respondents saw family physicians more often than the OHS subjects. Conversely, the OHS subjects were more likely than the Elliot Lake respondents to have specialist consultations. This is not surprising in view of the fact that since specialists are few and far between in smaller communities in the north, patients are more prone to rely on family physicians. It is known that in such areas, family physicians often have to deal with medical problems that would typically be handled by specialists in an urban setting.

Estimated numbers of physician visits. The estimated numbers of visits to family physicians and to specialists by older residents are shown in Tables 2 and 3, respectively. The estimates were obtained by multiplying the mean number of visits for each age group by the number of respondents in that age group, based on data obtained from the telephone survey. Since, as noted earlier, the telephone survey might have missed about 10 percent of eligible residents, an adjustment was made by adding 10 percent to the "estimated number of physician visits." Thus, it was estimated that Elliot Lake residents aged 50 and over made 21,831 visits to family physicians and 4,851 specialist visits in the 12-month period prior to the survey.

Table 2. Mean and estimated number of visits to family physicians by older persons in Elliot Lake, 1994/95

Age group	Mean number of physician visits	Number of survey respondents	Estimated number of physician visits	Adjusted number of physician visits*
50–54	6.41	452	2,897	3,187
55–59	5.67	655	3,714	4,085
60–64	4.22	660	2,785	3,064
65–69	5.91	721	4,261	4,687
70–74	7.36	524	3,857	4,242
75+	5.66	412	2,332	2,565
Total	**5.85**	**3,424**	**19,846**	**21,831**

*10% adjustment for non-response
Source: Elliot Lake Seniors' Needs Assessment: Telephone and Mail Surveys

Table 3. Mean and estimated number of visits to specialists by older persons in Elliot Lake, 1994/95

Age group	Mean number of physician visits	Number of survey respondents	Estimated number of physician visits	Adjusted number of physician visits*
50–54	2.14	452	967	1,064
55–59	1.14	655	747	821
60–64	0.69	660	455	501
65–69	1.22	721	880	968
70–74	1.45	524	760	836
75+	1.46	412	602	662
Total	**1.26**	**3,424**	**4,410**	**4,851**

*10% adjustment for non-response
Source: Elliot Lake Seniors' Needs Assessment: Telephone and Mail Surveys

While these are crude estimates, they provide a rough idea of medical manpower requirements. If a typical family physician works 230 days a year and sees about 30 older patients per day,[2] slightly more than three family physicians would have to devote their entire practice to older patients in order to look after the primary care needs of this segment of the Elliot Lake population in 1994/95.

Physician visits in and outside Elliot Lake. To determine the extent to which older residents had to seek medical care outside Elliot Lake, the mail survey asked the subjects to indicate if they had to leave the city to see a doctor. Of those who answered the questions, 46 percent had to leave Elliot Lake at least once in 1994/95 for medical appointments. The other 54 percent did not have to leave the community to see a physician. Table 4 shows the proportions of physician visits in and outside Elliot Lake in 1994/95. Over 95 percent of the visits to family physicians took place in the city. On the basis of this information, it seems that there were enough family physicians to meet the primary care needs of the older residents in 1994/95. On the other hand, two-thirds of the specialist visits took place outside Elliot Lake. This suggests that there were insufficient specialist services in the city, resulting in the need for many older persons to travel long distances to see a specialist.

Table 4. Proportions of family physician and specialist visits in and outside Elliot Lake

	In Elliot Lake %	Outside Elliot Lake %
Family physician visits	96.2	3.8
Specialist visits	33.7	66.3

Source: Elliot Lake Seniors' Needs Assessment: Mail Survey

Out-of-town medical appointments. Several questions in the mail survey pertained to the experiences of seeking medical care outside Elliot Lake. As can be seen in Figure 1, the great majority of the people who had to see a physician in another community travelled by car. They either drove or were driven by their family members or friends to medical appointments. Relatively few people used buses or planes. This could be due to inconvenient schedules, high costs of public transportation, personal preferences, or some combination of these.

Figure 1. Modes of transportation to medical appointments outside
Elliot Lake

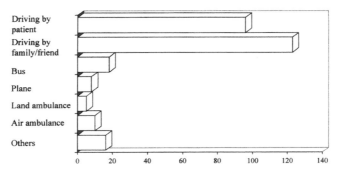

Source: Elliot Lake Seniors' Needs Assessment: Mail Survey

Figure 2. Problems encountered in relation to out-of-town
medical appointments

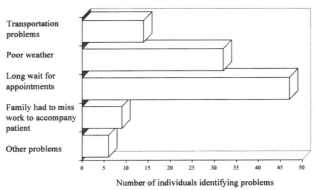

Source: Elliot Lake Seniors' Needs Assessment: Mail Survey

Figure 2 lists the problems encountered by people who had to travel long distances for medical appointments. The problem mentioned by the largest number of respondents was "long wait for appointments." "Poor weather" was the second most frequently mentioned problem. It is interesting to note that these two most-often-identified problems are generally beyond the control of the patients. On the other hand, things over which patients have a certain degree of control, such as arranging transportation, were seen by fewer people as problematic.

Discussion

It is important to begin the discussion by pointing out the limitations of this study. Unlike the OHS, the Elliot Lake Seniors' Needs Assessment did not focus exclusively on health issues. Instead, it covered a broad range of human and community services. Thus, the limited amount of data on medical care utilization precludes a comprehensive and in-depth analysis. Because of this, the estimated numbers of visits to physicians should not be construed as an assessment of the adequacy of physician supply in Elliot Lake. As a matter of fact, we did not have information on the number of resident and non-resident physicians practising in Elliot Lake in 1994/95. Besides, the surveys did not include persons under age 50 and had little or no information about the health status of the population, the health care needs of the community, physician practice patterns, or how health and related services are organized and delivered in the city. It is also important to bear in mind that having access to medical care does not necessarily mean that the care is adequate or effective. Again, the surveys did not ask for such information.

These limitations notwithstanding, this study provides some initial information that could be useful for health service planning in Elliot Lake. According to our analysis, accessing primary care in the city by older persons did not seem to be a problem. In order to corroborate this conclusion, we reviewed the lists of communities designated as underserved with respect to family physicians by the Underserviced Area Program of the Ontario Ministry of Health.[3] Elliot Lake was not one of the communities designated as underserved in 1994 and 1995. In other words, either the city did not apply for physician-recruitment assistance or, insofar as the ministry was concerned, Elliot Lake did not have a critical shortage of family physicians. Thus, the two sources of information are consistent.

It appears that, with respect to the provision of primary care, the focus of long-term planning should be on ensuring or improving the quality of care, like encouraging family physicians to be current on geriatrics and gerontological issues. In their study of the impact of retirement migration on rural medical practice in two southern states, Haas and Crandall (1988) have found that the growing retiree population has changed the types of diseases treated by physicians and has shifted their perspective from the curing of illnesses to the management of chronic conditions. Physicians in Elliot Lake may have experienced similar changes in their practice, which could have considerable implications for continuing medical education or retraining.

Although access to primary care in 1994/95 did not appear to be problematic, this should not be used as an excuse for not closely monitoring the physician supply situation in Elliot Lake. If the number of retirees continues to increase, and as the existing population becomes more advanced in age, the demands for medical care will almost certainly be greater. In smaller communities such as Elliot Lake, the loss of one or two physicians could mean major disruptions to service delivery. It is also important to realize that there is more to health care for the elderly than physician consultations. Medical manpower requirements must be considered in the broader context of human service provision and organization. While it is crucial to have a sufficient number of physicians, the effective coordination of physician services, home support, informal care, and other community programs is equally important.

Specialist consultations were an entirely different matter. Two-thirds of the visits to specialists took place outside Elliot Lake. In other words, most older persons had to travel long distances to see a specialist. In addition, many of them had to wait a long time for appointments. It is also possible that a considerable amount of the specialist care obtainable in Elliot Lake was not provided by resident specialists. According to informed sources, some specialists who saw patients in Elliot Lake did not reside in the community. Instead, they were itinerant doctors who travelled to Elliot Lake on a periodic basis, possibly with financial support provided by the Ontario Ministry of Health under the Travelling Physician Specialist Program.

A review of the lists of communities designated by the Underserviced Area Program of the Ontario Ministry of Health as underserved in relation to specialists shows that Elliot Lake was not on the list in 1994 and was designated in 1995 as requiring one general surgeon. This did not necessarily mean that Elliot Lake had sufficient specialists. More likely than not, the fact that Elliot Lake was not designated (with the exception of one general surgeon in 1995) meant that the city did not have a large enough population to support more resident specialists.

In this situation, several strategies may be considered. The first is to make the best use of family physicians. As noted earlier, many family physicians in rural areas have to deal with clinical problems that would typically be referred to specialists by their urban counterparts. To this end, upgrading the training of family physicians and increasing continuing medical education opportunities may be necessary. Also, closer collaboration between specialists and family physicians would enable the latter to expand their scope of practice with adequate backup.

Second, since it is highly unlikely that all specialist care can be provided by resident physicians, Elliot Lake should make the best use of such enabling programs as the Travelling Physician Specialist Program in order to bring itinerant specialists to the community on a regular basis. Participation in other outreach programs like the chemotherapy outreach clinics of the Northeastern Ontario Regional Cancer Centre should also be considered.

Third, although some out-of-town travelling for medical purposes is inevitable, the amount of travel can be minimized by making use of technologies like telemedicine where feasible and appropriate. Broadly defined, telemedicine is the use of telecommunications technologies, such as teleradiology and videoconferencing, to provide or support health care when geographic distance separates the practitioner from the patient or from other practitioners.

Finally, the city administration and voluntary bodies may wish to look into improving public transportation between Elliot Lake and other cities, coordinating carpooling and encouraging volunteers to drive elderly patients to medical appointments.

The present study has explored the tip of the medical-care iceberg. To have an adequate assessment of physician service utilization by older persons and medical manpower requirements in Elliot Lake, we need to know a lot more about the morbidity patterns of the older residents, their utilization of other health services, how medical care and ancillary services are delivered, and the practice profiles of resident and non-resident physicians. Both the situation in Elliot Lake and provincial health-care policies are changing rapidly. What the Seniors' Needs Assessment discovered in 1995 may no longer hold true today, even though the surveys provided useful data for addressing some immediate concerns in the wake of the large influx of retirees. It is important, therefore, to have periodically updated data for monitoring, planning, and evaluation purposes.

The success or failure by Elliot Lake to meet the health-care needs of its fast-growing older population and the strategies it uses will undoubtedly be watched closely by other rural or northern communities. Elliot Lake could play a vanguard role in addressing emerging health-care issues in relation to population aging.

Notes

[1] The authors thank Roger Pitblado, Department of Geography, Laurentian University, for analyzing the Ontario Health Survey data and Dave A. Pearson, Northern Health Human Resources Research Unit, Laurentian University, for preparing the tables and diagrams.

[2] Family physicians in rural areas typically see more than 30 patients a day.

However, consultations involving older patients tend to take more time. As well, women physicians tend to see fewer patients than their male counterparts, and an increasing proportion of younger physicians are female (Pong 1997). Thus, we use 30 consultations per day in this estimate.

³ "Lists of areas designated as underserviced for general/family practitioners" in 1994 and 1995.

References

Barer, Morris L., R.G. Evans, and C. Hertzman. (1995). "Avalanche or glacier? Health care and the demographic rhetoric," *Canadian Journal on Aging* 14: 193–224.

Black, Charlyn, N.P. Roos, B. Havens, and L. MacWilliams. (1995). "Rising use of physician services by the elderly: the contribution of morbidity," *Canadian Journal on Aging* 14: 225–44.

Bryant, Ellen S. and M. El-Attar. (1984). "Migration and redistribution of the elderly: a challenge to community services," *The Gerontologist* 24, 6: 634–40.

Denton, F. and B. Spencer (1980). "Health care costs when the population changes," in *Aging in Canada: Social Perspectives*, ed. V.W. Marshall. Don Mills, ON: Fitzhenry and Whiteside Ltd.

Dixon, Catharine. (1996). *The Power and the Promise: The Elliot Lake Story.* Elliot Lake, ON: Gillidix Publishing Inc.

Haas, William H., III, and L.A. Crandall. (1988). "Physicians' views of retirement migrants' impact on rural medical practice," *The Gerontologist* 28, 5: 663–66.

Joseph, Alun E. and D.S. Cloutier. (1991). "Elderly migration and its implications for service provision in rural communities: an Ontario perspective," *Journal of Rural Studies* 7, 4: 433–44.

Lee, Anne S. (1980). "Aged migration: impact on service delivery," *Research on Aging* 2, 2: 243–53.

Longino, Charles F., Jr. and J.C. Biggar. (1981). "The impact of retirement migration on the south," *The Gerontologist* 21, 3: 283–90.

Longino, Charles F., Jr. and J.C. Biggar. (1982). "The impact of population redistribution on service delivery," *The Gerontologist* 22, 2: 153–59.

Ontario Ministry of Health. (s.d.). *The 1990 Ontario Health Survey: Documentation.* Toronto: Ministry of Health.

Patrick, Clifford H. (1980). "Health and migration of the elderly," *Research on Aging* 2, 2: 233–41.

Pong, Raymond W. (1997). "Changing sex composition in the Canadian physician workforce: implications for health care." Poster presented at the Canadian Population Society annual meeting in St. John's, Newfoundland, June 9–11, 1997.

Rourke, James. (1997). "In search of a definition of 'rural,'" *Canadian Journal of Rural Medicine* 2, 3: 113–15.

Chapter 19
The Regional University as a Participant in Community Economic Diversification and Stablilization
Deborah Berthelot

The Elliot Lake Research Field Station (ELRFS) of Laurentian University was established in 1991 through a $3-million grant from the Northern Ontario Heritage Fund Corporation (NOHFC). The grant was part of a $15-million provincial economic diversification and stabilization program in Elliot Lake, Ontario, at the time of the uranium mine closures.

The field station was to draw on the expertise and resources of the regional university, Laurentian University, to assist the City of Elliot Lake in achieving one of its goals: "to establish Elliot Lake as an international centre for Research and Development related to mine decommissioning and waste management."[1] The original objective of the field station was to provide employment in Elliot Lake by way of research projects that would aid in the environmentally acceptable closure and reclamation of mining and other similar industrial projects.

The original contract with NOHFC differed from most research grants in that Laurentian University was also mandated to undertake "active pursuit of funds from other sources for additional studies or projects with a view to operating the field station beyond September 30, 1994." This mandate, in combination with the allocated resources and university affiliation, provided much of the environment required for ELRFS to evolve from 100-percent grant-funded to 100-percent self-sufficient in a five-year period. Another key factor was the support offered by the city, government, and local industry to this community-based organization.

The original NOHFC contract funded six research projects (Table 1) and related administrative and facility operating costs. In order to accommodate facility and project development requirements, a three-year contract was given to deliver the six two-year projects.

Table 1. Original NOHFC research projects

Project	Amount
Environmental radioactivity	$1,193,000
Water quality monitoring—aquatic/terrestrial linkages	385,000
Detection and monitoring of acid mine drainage by remote sensing	221,000
Expert systems for environmental data analysis	147,000
Brittle rock failure processes	214,000
Ultrasonic hardrock fragmentation	324,000
Field station administration	401,000
Field station renovations	115,000
TOTAL	$3,000,000

From the beginning, the field station was able to use its position as a community-based, university-led research facility to lever additional development opportunities and form strong working relationships with local industry and governments. Examples of early support and co-operation include partnering with the City of Elliot Lake to acquire the physical plant for the field station at 75 Dieppe Avenue and to undertake the required renovations. The field station had support from local mining companies (Rio Algom Limited and Denison Mines Limited) in the form of laboratory equipment and infrastructure, and support from both local mining companies and government agencies in the form of analytical service and training contracts.

The success of these early initiatives influenced heavily the direction of the field station in that they clearly demonstrated the importance of community support and the opportunities for niche service markets.

The major achievement of the field station is that it has evolved from a two-year grant-funded project into a self-sustaining research, training, and technical services organization with high potential for maintaining a long-term presence in the community of Elliot Lake. Over the five years of operation, the original $3-million grant has been used to attract an additional $4.25 million in contracts and grants.

Technically, the field station has provided support to 11 Master of Science students, and the research undertaken under the auspices of the field station has resulted in over 40 publications, with 20 more submitted or under development. Staff and researchers affiliated with

Working in a laboratory at the Elliot Lake Research Field
Station. Gerry Morin, photographer.

City of Elliot Lake

Michael Courtin in the mapping laboratory at the Elliot Lake
Research Field Station. At INORD's January 1997 conference
in Elliot Lake, Courtin gave a computer demonstration of the
use of GIS (geographic information systems) to map various
aspects of the Serpent River Watershed. Gerry Morin,
photographer.

City of Elliot Lake

Figure 1. Elliot Lake Research Field Station employment history (person-years)

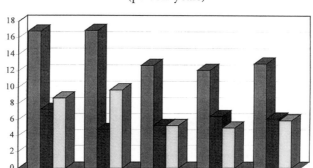

Figure 2. Elliot Lake Research Field Station employment history (funding source)

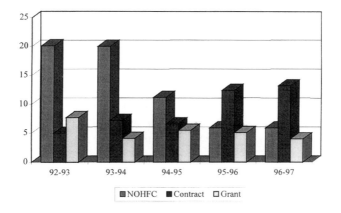

the field station have secured an additional 16 research, 25 service, and 15 training projects.

The field station has had a direct economic impact on the community. Over 136 person-years of employment have been created involving over 200 individuals. Research, training, and service contract activities at the field station have created an annual employment equivalent to 25 person-years generating over $600,000 in salaries (Figure 1). In any given year, just over half of the employment is in full-time positions (12 to 13 in recent years), and the remainder is almost equally divided between part-time positions and students. On an annual basis, the field station employs between 20 and 30 students, making it one of the largest student employers in the City of Elliot Lake. Local annual expenditures exceed $750,000.

The declining NOHFC employment and increasing contract employment (Figure 2) is consistent with trends observed in revenue sources (Figure 3).

Figure 3. Elliot Lake Research Field Station revenue history

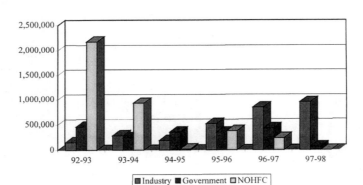

Growth in industrial revenues has been largely the result of retaining services that otherwise would have been contracted outside the community (analytical services), providing technical services not previously available in Elliot Lake (data management), and undertaking environmental rehabilitation research.

In addition to the direct economic impact, the Elliot Lake Research Field Station has provided indirect economic benefits to the City of Elliot Lake by providing applied technical training, improving the pool of available expertise, enhancing the city's external image, and identifying and developing economic diversification initiatives.

In its five years of operation, the field station has provided applied technical training to 119 students and 14 adult learners. All training programs have been designed to enhance the scientific, literacy, and employment skills of the participants. In addition, the field station participates in the education sector of Elliot Lake by making facilities and expertise available to other educational institutions and interest groups in the community.

The field station also provides cost-effective expertise for community projects. The results of the City Quality of Services Assessment, one of the station's projects, and of the Seniors' Needs Assessment are being used to assess resource allocation and to support the budgetary decisions of the City of Elliot Lake, Huron Lodge, and St. Joseph's Hospital.

Small conference and tour spin-off contributions to the hospitality industry have averaged $15,000 to $20,000 per year. The field station also contributes to the community's external image of successful transition in academic and technical circles through participation in conferences, lectures, meetings with professional associations, and committees.

Potentially the largest indirect economic impact of the field station to the community of Elliot Lake will be the identification and development of new businesses to serve external niche markets identified through the Elliot Lake decommissioning experience. For example, delivery of data management and analytical and environmental research programs have placed the field station in the leadership role for the development of a new mine rehabilitation services company with projected revenues of $2.8 million per year employing an additional 25 people.[2]

One of the key elements of the success of the field station has been the sharing of common objectives by the City of Elliot Lake and Laurentian University. Both organizations have recognized mining-related environmental technologies and economic development as key components of their respective development plans. Furthermore, participation in the Elliot Lake project has demonstrated the university's commitment to the northeastern Ontario regional mandate of their strategic plan.

The field station has also benefited from the political climate in the province. At the time the field station was established, the provincial government strongly supported public participation and funding of economic development projects. The change in government and resulting funding cutbacks have pushed the field station to pursue more non-traditional revenue sources like service contracts.

The development strategy of the field station has been to identify niche markets that are complementary to and provide cost-sharing opportunities with the research that is being conducted. In this manner, a reliable revenue stream has been developed to help maintain the equipment, expertise, and other infrastructure required to undertake research. In those cases where the university resources are not fully sufficient to capitalize on identified commercial opportunities that present themselves, the field station has identified and recruited strategic partners for the final development and implementation of the initiative. The intent is to reinvest any profits from these joint ventures into university research projects.

During implementation of the development strategies, the field station has benefited tremendously from the support of key clients including the local mining companies, the City of Elliot Lake, and the provincial and federal governments. Both NOHFC as the funding agency and the university as the contract delivery agent have demonstrated flexibility and innovative approaches to facilitate a successful implementation and transition. Another key element of success has been the active and direct participation of university professors working in close relationship with Elliot Lake-based research associates. In all cases, significant growth in research activities has been directly related to the success of these working relationships.

The future of this cooperation between Laurentian University and the community of Elliot Lake is promising. The university is committed to continuing its research, training, and technology transfer role in the City of Elliot Lake. Research, training, service and investment revenues, assets, and resources are being directed towards supporting a long-term presence in the community, and all parties look forward to continued co-operative efforts to improve the economy of Elliot Lake.

Note

1 Dianna Bratina, *Report of the Director of Economic Development for Consideration of Mayor and Council*, Report DED 93–4 dated 16 February 1993 (Elliot Lake: City of Elliot Lake, 1993).
2 In early 1998, Mine Waste Management Inc. was formed to provide care and maintenance services for dormant mine sites. A comprehensive contract to operate Rio Algom Limited's Elliot Lake sites was implemented 1 March 1998.

Part 3

Reclaiming the Land

With its vast tracts of uninhabited land, its forests and lakes, Northern Ontario provides an attractive and — to those living in other parts of the country — an almost mythical environment, where nature offers recreational opportunities in all four seasons. However, resource industries throughout Northern Ontario have inevitably had negative long-term ecological consequences. Natural scientists have been studying these effects and trying to find ways of helping Mother Nature by "speeding up" the natural recovery process. The uranium tailings in the Elliot Lake area have presented unique opportunities to experiment with this recovery process.

The tailings ponds of the Rio Algom Limited's Quirke Mine Waste Management Area, fall 1996.
Rio Algom Limited

Chapters 20 and 21 (by Mark Prystupa et al. and Donald W. Hine et al.) present results of social scientific studies that examine the perceptions of residents of Elliot Lake and potential newcomers to Elliot Lake to determine the extent to which they perceive the presence of the tailings as a risk to their day-to-day well-being. The following two chapters (by Peter Beckett et al. and Bryan Tisch et al.) describe reclamation activities by natural scientists who have been experimenting with ways to improve the local environment by transplanting wetland vegetation to stabilize acid-generating tailings. The final paper, by Sharon Gow, a local environmental activist, suggests ways in which members of the community can work together to ensure that the perpetual care of the local eco-system is carefully planned and implemented.

The top photo, taken in May 1992, shows the Denison mill complex and two tailings management areas at mine closure. Below, the same area is shown in October 1997 after rehabilitation.

Denison Mines Limited

Chapter 20
Stakeholder Perceptions of Risks Related to Elliot Lake Area Mine Tailings[1]

Mark Prystupa, Donald W. Hine, John Lewko, and Craig Summers

In recent years, people have become more concerned about possible environmental risks associated with living in their communities. While experts have attempted to calculate accurately the amount of risk an individual may face, critics have pointed out that the complexity of environmental systems and the differing values that people possess make quantifying the exact risks a person may find acceptable virtually impossible (Dwyer 1990). Consequently, people's beliefs and perceptions will often be at the forefront of discussions about what risks exist and how significant they are. The purpose of the present study is to identify some of the factors that affect why certain groups of people often have quite different risk perceptions. Specifically, the example of the risk perceptions associated with the decommissioning of uranium mine tailings in the midst of an environmental assessment review in the Elliot Lake area is used to investigate this issue. The study's results will be of general interest to the residents of Elliot Lake in that they highlight the differences of opinion that do exist in the region and, therefore, may facilitate future discussion of how ongoing management of the tailings should be conducted. Other mining companies might also find this research useful as they plan their tailings management programs, as it could help them understand where potential conflicts might arise, and point to ways to resolve them before costly delays and uncertainty resulted.

Figure 1. Uranium mines in the Elliot Lake area

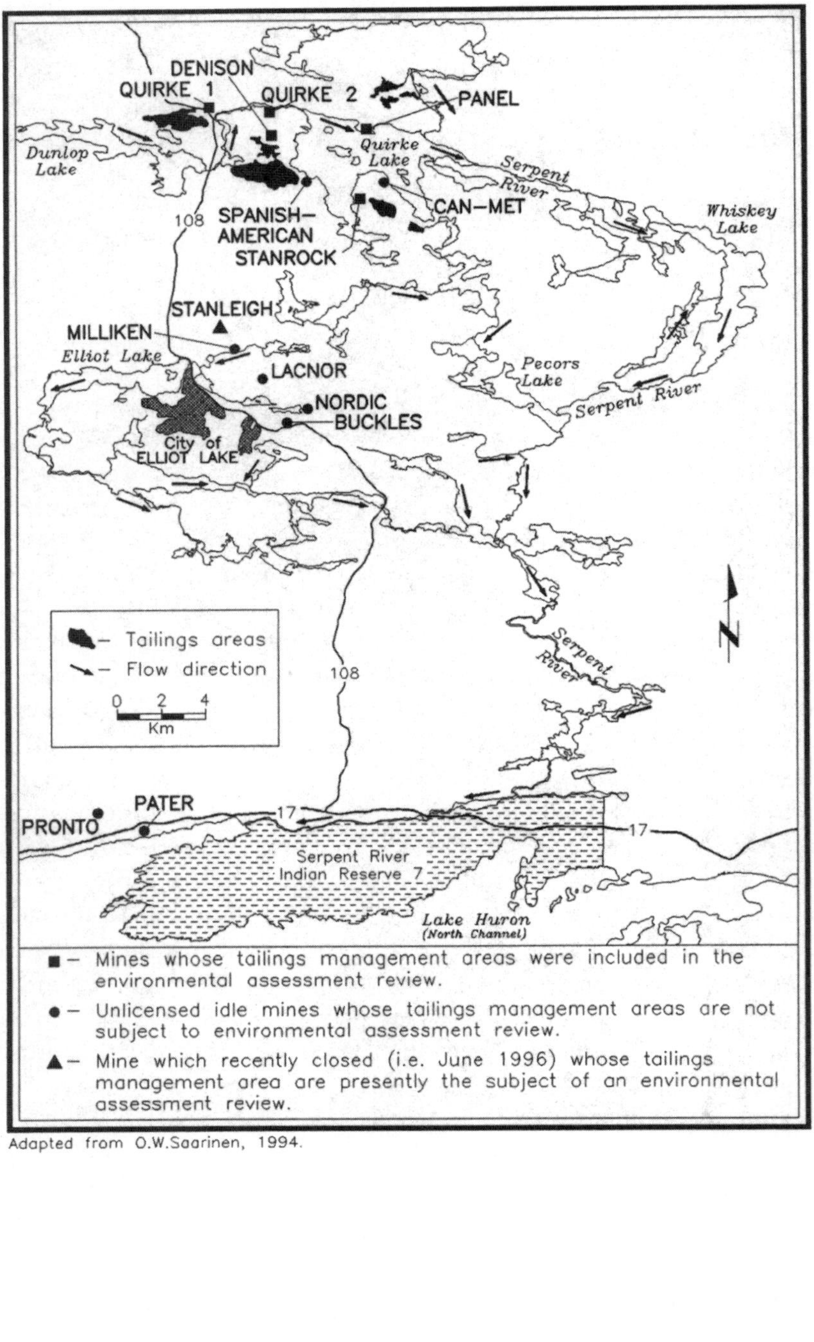
DENISON
QUIRKE 1
QUIRKE 2
PANEL
Dunlop Lake
Quirke Lake
Serpent River
SPANISH-AMERICAN
STANROCK
CAN-MET
Whiskey Lake
108
STANLEIGH
MILLIKEN
Elliot Lake
LACNOR
Pecors Lake
Serpent River
NORDIC
BUCKLES
City of ELLIOT LAKE
Serpent River
Tailings areas
Flow direction
0 2 4
Km
108
PATER
PRONTO
17
17
Serpent River Indian Reserve 7
Lake Huron (North Channel)
■ – Mines whose tailings management areas were included in the environmental assessment review.
● – Unlicensed idle mines whose tailings management areas are not subject to environmental assessment review.
▲ – Mine which recently closed (i.e. June 1996) whose tailings management area are presently the subject of an environmental assessment review.

Adapted from O.W.Saarinen, 1994.

Background

Staking for uranium began in the Elliot Lake area in the summer of 1953. Between 1955 and 1958, 12 mines were established in the region (see Figure 1), primarily to satisfy the demand created by the American nuclear weapons program during the Cold War (Rio Algom Limited 1995, Dixon 1996). Most of these mines went bankrupt, or suspended operations in the 1960s, when the American Atomic Energy Commission cancelled many of its contracts and decided to meet its requirements through domestic producers instead (Rio Algom Limited 1995). However, a resurgence in demand for uranium developed with the first OPEC oil price shock in 1974 and the increasing use of nuclear power, primarily in Western Europe, Japan, and the United States (Dixon 1996). To ensure that the expansion of the uranium mine industry in Elliot Lake proceeded in a rational manner the provincial government held a public assessment of this industry. The review lasted three years and at the conclusion of this extensive process it was decided that the proposed reopening of the Panel and Stanrock mines, as well as the expansion of the Quirke and Denison mines, could proceed (Rio Algom Limited 1995). As a result of this expansion of mineral production, licences with new regulatory requirements were given to these facilities by the federal Atomic Energy Control Board (AECB). By the 1980s, however, higher-grade uranium was available elsewhere, resulting in the closure in the 1990s of all remaining operational mines in the Elliot Lake area (Dixon 1996).

In 1992, Rio Algom Limited and Denison Mines Limited sought regulatory approval from the AECB for the decommissioning of the tailings and waste management areas of the Quirke, Panel, Denison, and Stanrock mines. (Rio Algom owns the Quirke and Panel mines, while Denison owns Denison and Stanrock.) In February 1993, the AECB concluded that there were potentially significant environmental impacts associated with the decommissioning activities, and recommended that the Minister of the Environment establish an Environmental Assessment Panel to conduct an environmental review (Canadian Environmental Assessment Agency [CEAA] 1996). A three-member panel was then established through the Environmental Assessment and Review Process Guidelines Order (which was replaced in January 1995 by its successor legislation, the Canadian Environmental Assessment Act). The mandate of the panel included an examination of the environmental and social effects of the decommissioning proposals made by the proponents. After public meetings in late 1993 to identify issues and concerns, the panel's terms of reference were expanded to include the contribution of the four mines under review to the cumulative environmental impact arising from seven additional "idle" mines (that is, those mines that were closed before new regulatory requirements came into effect in the mid-1970s and that were therefore not required to undergo environmental screening). Rio Algom, which owns all of these idle mines, has subsequently voluntarily applied for new licences from the AECB, thereby bringing them under the new regulatory requirements.

Scoping meetings were held in December 1993 to identify issues to be addressed in the review process. In response to the panel's information requirements, the mining companies released environmental-impact statements in May 1995. Public hearings were held in late 1995 and early 1996 to provide opportunities for citizens, interested groups, and government agencies to present information that would assist the panel in formulating its final report (CEAA 1996), released in June 1996. The federal government accepted the majority of the recommendations of the panel, including those that were in basic agreement with the mining companies' proposals for the decommissioning process — which included the flooding of three tailings areas and a vegetated soil cover for the other.

What We Did

For the most part, key informants for each stakeholder group were selected because they were recognized to be knowledgeable about the decommissioning of the Elliot Lake mines, and had been active in the community with respect to this issue. The one exception was the retiree group, which included a mix of established residents and individuals who had recently relocated to Elliot Lake. The Elliot Lake Research Field Station helped identify potential respondents. In total, 31 interviews were conducted: nine with business owners, five with environmentalists, 10 with First Nations people, and seven with retirees (including both long-term residents of Elliot Lake and recently arrived retirees). Seven of the 10 First Nations people were members of the Serpent River First Nation. Ages ranged from 28 to 71; 19 respondents were men and 12 were women.

The interviews were conducted in the summer of 1995, either in the respondents' homes or at another location of their choice. The interview procedure, which we refer to as "mental models interviewing," was based on the Johnson-Laird (1983) theory of mental models, and Kiss's (1972) work on recursive interviewing. The approach was designed to maximize disclosure while minimizing the imposition of the interviewer's perspective on respondents' conceptualizations. After being told the purpose of the study (that is, to better understand people's opinions about the mine tailings stored near Elliot Lake and possible risks associated with them), respondents were asked to list all the thoughts and images that came to mind in response to the cue words "mine tailings." After a full listing had been elicited, the interviewer reviewed the concept list and asked the respondent to elaborate on each concept. If new concepts were identified during the elaboration phase, they were added to the list. This process continued until the list was exhausted and no new concepts were forthcoming.

We taped, transcribed, and then coded all interviews for prominent themes related to mine decommissioning and tailings. We read each of the transcripts and created category labels that described the essence of text segments. Then we reread the coded segments and made notes about the frequency and meaning of the coding categories. We compared coding results across groups to identify similarities and differences. After identifying central themes for each group and describing them in memos, we read the transcripts again for data that either supported or refuted the memos. In writing the results, we used representative statements from the respondents to illustrate the themes. Then we systematically compared these categories to each other to identify the core category and relate the other categories to it.

What We Found

Five primary themes were identified in the interviews: trust, potentially adverse health effects, public risk perceptions, contamination of the watershed, and long-term monitoring of the tailing sites. Each stakeholder group emphasized different themes and had different perspectives on them. A characterization of the themes for each group follows.

Environmentalists. Environmentalists, as one might expect, expressed great concern about the potential for adverse environmental effects from the mine tailings. A lack of trust appeared to be at the root of this concern. As one respondent stated, "It's a matter of trust, and we don't know if we can." Environmentalists questioned the ability of scientists to predict impacts accurately, and the ability of government agencies and mining companies to regulate and control potential hazards effectively. For example, one respondent questioned whether regulators could manage the tailings at Elliot Lake, given their poor past performance in preventing acid mine drainage in other locations. Another questioned whether government could be trusted to look after the best interests of environment and local residents, stating, "I wouldn't even trust Atomic

Energy. I never would trust the government agencies themselves." In addition to distrusting scientists and government regulators, several environmentalists doubted the commitment of the mining companies to fulfilling their pledge to ensure that environmental impacts were minimized. As one exasperated respondent stated,

> In [the mining companies'] environmental impact statements, they indicate they're going to take care of [the tailings].... We've heard promises before and I think that's one area where they're lacking.

In terms of specific impacts, the issue that attracted the greatest attention from environmentalists was the possibility of contaminants from the tailings ponds being released into the Serpent River Watershed. All five respondents in this group indicated that seepage and leaching from the tailings ponds were serious concerns.

> They have internal dykes. They have outside berms. They're all supposed to contain seepage, runoff. I don't buy it. I don't buy it at all.

> You can dam all you want but there's going to be leaching and spilloff.

Several environmentalists feared that tailings in the watershed would have potentially devastating effects on biodiversity and the ability of the ecosystem to heal itself. Others also expressed concern that mobilization of heavy metals associated with acid mine drainage could contaminate the food chain and drinking water, producing a serious health threat for both animals and humans.

> The Serpent River system has had serious degradation for the last 40 years because of the uranium mine tailings.

> Water goes wherever it wants to go. It has a mind of its own. So people think about seeping water problems and leaching-into-groundwater problems. There have been problems with spills and accidents into water systems in our area. The results were pretty horrific if you were a fish or a small creature in that water system.

Several environmentalists also stressed that provisions for ongoing monitoring and maintenance of the tailings sites were needed, and noted that the threat of contamination was not a short-term problem. As one informant stated:

> We're talking a long time. We're not talking 10 to 15 years. We're talking hundreds of years.

Three others complained that even monitoring of the sites covered by environmental review would not completely solve the problem, because there are many other potentially dangerous sites in the Elliot Lake region that fall largely outside the assessment panel's terms of reference. One pointed out that there are

> orphan mines that aren't being talked about in this environmental assessment. They're scattered. We have them right in our backyard.... It's only the licensed properties. This is, to me, a farce.

Another concern of the environmentalists was that the general public was not being given the "full story" about potential hazards associated with the tailings, and as a consequence were exhibiting less concern about the tailings than they should have.

> I don't think they're really being kept informed as to what's happened. They're taking tours and seeing how it's being done and whatever, but that's all. That's all cosmetic. They show you that there was a mine that's no longer there and they're doing this with the tailings, but I don't think people have a real grasp. I don't think they have a real understanding. Sure, they're concerned, but if they really knew the effect of runoff and leaching, I think they would be a bit more concerned.

This perspective contrasts dramatically with that of Elliot Lake business owners who, as we shall discuss next, tended to argue that people needed more information so that they would be less, not more, concerned about potential risks associated with the tailings.

Business owners. The predominant issue for Elliot Lake business was counteracting the perception "that we glow in the dark." Eight of the nine respondents in this group indicated that they believed that widespread misperceptions about the danger of the tailings prevented potential residents and businesses from moving to Elliot Lake. Several business owners blamed the media for the community's tarnished public image.

> Given that we are in a pristine trout lake area, one has to always be sensitive to the fact that somebody out there could easily write an article and say, "You're entering a zone that is contaminated." That has the complete opposite effect of the positive pristineness of the area.

> It's very damaging any time those articles are written.... If people want to do harm to us, they can easily do that. We're very vulnerable.

> This city constantly has to defend itself to the outside world against all the myths and misinformation.

Concern was also expressed that the public hearings associated with FEARO would further stigmatize the community.

> One of my concerns ... is that if the environmental groups start to come in here and unfold all of the real negative side of it, it's going to have a real impact.

> The negative image is there, and I think that when the environmental hearings start, it may even become more negative.

To overcome fears and negative perceptions, business owners believed the community needed to initiate a risk communication strategy to counteract the negative messages conveyed by the media. This strategy would be directed at prospective residents and businesses and would involve addressing common misperceptions about Elliot Lake and providing scientifically credible information about the true risks associated with the tailings.

> We have a communications problem.... We're trying to do economic development here. We don't even know how many people have been touched before we get to touch them. The fact of the matter is that ignorance will influence their decision before we get a chance to try.

> Once people can be given the proper information about what

risks there may be and how the risks are being dealt with, I think the natural beauty of the area and everything else overrides an awful lot of that kind of basic fear.

As may be surmised from the above comments, most business owners (there was one exception) did not believe that the tailings posed a serious threat. Thus, relative to the environmentalists, business owners tended to place much less emphasis on the potentially adverse environmental and health effects of the tailings. This should not be misconstrued as suggesting that the business owners were willing to trade off the public's safety for potential economic benefits. In fact, several business owners emphasized public safety and the importance of dealing with the tailings in a responsible manner. Compared to the environmentalists, the business owners were more trusting of scientists and government regulators to manage the tailings in a responsible and effective manner.

I'm quite content to allow somebody with technical expertise to make those decisions.

Three business owners viewed the decommissioning process as a potential business opportunity. They believed that it might be possible to market Elliot Lake's experience to other countries, making it an internationally recognized centre of expertise for tailings management. They noted that this would help the community diversify its economy while producing an extremely useful exportable service.

View towards Elliot Lake from the Scenic Look-Out Tower, officially opened in 1992.

City of Elliot Lake

So both the environmentalists and business owners indicated that they felt the general public were not adequately informed about the risks associated with the tailings. Where the environmentalists believed that providing the public with better information would increase their concern about the tailings, the business owners believed that this would decrease their concern.

Retirees. Interviews with the retirees revealed that most of this group actively sought out information about the tailings, and what they found comforted them.

> We were assured that it was safe. We haven't had any problems and we've been here five years.

> I mean the chemists, scientists and all that…. Those people that are analyzing and checking the water system wouldn't gamble or second-guess or give us false information, because it's affecting their own families.

> We didn't hesitate to make inquiries and talk to people. So not having any real threat revealed to us, I assume there probably is no real threat around.

> I have no concerns about the mine tailings. I believe the mines are doing exactly what they said they would do. I've been out there and I've seen it.

Most retirees indicated that they obtained their information from displays by Rio Algom in the Algo Mall, from tours conducted by the mining companies, or from the Retirement Living Program, a local company that markets Elliot Lake as an attractive, inexpensive retirement community. One could argue that all of these sources might be less inclined to present negative information about the risks associated with the tailings, and therefore, might not have exposed the respondents to all sides of the issues.

Like the business owners, retirees expressed only limited concern over potential health problems stemming from the uranium mine tailings. In fact, over half indicated that they believed that living in Elliot Lake would be healthier than living in a big city such as Toronto.

> I went to see my doctor when I came to Elliot Lake. He told me

that a person coming to live in Elliot Lake is going to extend their life by two or three years at least. [They'll have] clean air and water and everything, and most of all they'll get rid of the stress of the big-town living — the traffic, the pollution, and stuff like that.
We worry about tailings here. What about Toronto with all the pollution in the air, and all the smog, and all the diseases going around? I think they worry more than we do down in southern Ontario. If they don't, they should.

I think our risk of being environmentally affected by the tailings in Elliot Lake is far less than the risk of somebody walking down Yonge Street in Toronto breathing that smog at 90%F, with all the smoke from the exhaust from those cars. I would think that our risk in Elliot Lake is a lot less than that.

Other retirees took comfort from the fact that they knew of many people who had lived in Elliot Lake for many years and had not developed any health problems:

There are people who have been living here for 35 years. I don't think the death rate due to cancer is any higher than anywhere else.

I worked underground at Rio Algom for 25 years. If there was any exposure that I was going to get from uranium, I think I'd have it. The amount that I'm going to get from a leached byproduct is not going to affect me healthwise.

I've been here 39 years and it hasn't affected me yet. I've been drinking the water for all those years, well before we had that most modern system that we have now with our water treatment plant. As years go by, things become more modernized and more efficient. I never worried then, so why should I worry now?

One person who recently moved to Elliot Lake thought that there would be health problems from long-term exposure to the tailings, but was not concerned because of their own older age. They reasoned that they would die of old age before the tailings-related health problem would have much of an effect upon them. This informant was more worried about people who had lived in the Elliot Lake area for a long period of time.
As a group, retirees perceived few significant risks associated with

living in Elliot Lake. For the most part, they believed the information that was provided to them — that the tailings posed no risk to them or to the environment — and they trusted the government and mining companies to minimize the hazards associated with decommissioning.

First Nations people. In general, Native respondents were very sceptical about claims that tailings do not pose a significant risk to the environment or people's health. This is consistent with the results of a previous study that found that Natives from the Serpent River First Nation had a much stronger risk perception associated with the uranium tailings than did non-Natives from Elliot Lake and the Township of the North Shore (Prystupa, Hine, Summers, and Lewko 1997). This apprehension was rooted in the problems of the 1950s and 1960s when there were few controls on what was allowed in the tailings or on where water flowing past the tailings went (McCrea, Philips, and Isacsson 1990). Since the Serpent River First Nation is downstream from the tailings areas (Figure 1) and relied on the river for drinking water and for fish, its residents bore the brunt of the adverse impacts.

> A lot of the waterways were severely polluted in the past, and we were told by the government that the water was polluted and unsafe to drink because of the radiation factors.

> Studies prior to that show that the quality of the river had deteriorated from its natural state to the point where they were recommending that we don't eat the fish. If you listen to some of our own people, they'll say there are no fish to eat ... [anyway] ... because of the effects of tailings on the river.

> The area itself I don't believe will be restored to its natural state because of the damage that's been done.... So I look at it as a loss of water, a loss of wildlife, a loss of fish population.

This environmental damage, as cited by six of the interviewees in this group, led to the abandonment of traditional areas for traditional hunting, fishing, trapping, and the collection of medicines because people were fearful of the health effects associated with eating what they believed to be contaminated.

The Serpent River Basin used to be part of the traditional

hunting territory and it was the main route for canoeing and trapping and everything else associated with fishing, gathering berries, that kind of thing.... That's changed over the years. Since the mines have situated there and the operation has continued over the years, people have a tendency to stay away from the area for ... traditional activities, and go to other places.

We used to be able to hunt and fish and that, but I don't think that the animals, that you can eat them really. They tell us not to eat the heart and the liver and what else is there.

Seeing what this stuff [uranium mine tailings] can do, I would feel leery about eating anything that is around the tailings area.

While the Serpent River Watershed has shown some signs of improvement (Halber et al. 1995) with stricter environmental regulations, Natives did not believe the situation would improve enough to allow them to pursue fully their traditional activities in abandoned areas. Some of the respondents stated that the situation would not improve, because the federal and provincial governments did not look after their interests in the past. They felt, therefore, that the governments would not look after them in the decommissioning process either. Most of the distrust was, however, levelled at the mining companies, because they were viewed as trying to maintain profit margins rather than develop an effective means of handling the tailings.

We can't just go by what they [the mining companies] say because they'd be looking for a cheap and economical way of disposing of these tailings.

I don't think that just because an option is the cheapest option that it makes it the best alternative. It might be the best alternative for you if you are a corporation and you're intent on saving money, but as locals it's not acceptable.

It [the preferred decommissioning option] was developed by the mining companies who have a vested interest in saving money.

Lack of trust among Natives led them to express strong concerns about the tailings' effects on wildlife and people's health. This finding is consistent with the results of a study conducted by Hine et al. (1997, in press) that found Natives' distrust of regulators led them to perceive higher costs associated with a proposed nuclear waste repository.

Whereas several retirees pointed to people who had lived in the region for many years without ill effects, many Natives cited examples of health problems in their own people that they attributed directly to the tailings. For instance, one person noted that several people were dying of cancer at early ages in their community and attributed it to radioactivity from the tailings. Another informant commented that the people who worked in the mines and with tailings suffered a higher percentage of health effects than those who did not.

Well, a lot of people that are having it [cancer] are in their sixties, forties. I'd say that's pretty young.

The people who worked at the mines and their families have a larger percentage of health defects than those who didn't. We can't help but associate the cause and effect of that.

Nine of the ten aboriginal informants commented that since they will continue to live in the area long after others have moved away, they are adamant about the necessity to ensure the tailings are dealt with in a way that will be safe for them and will not be a burden on their future generations.

You may not be here, but certainly we will be here. So it's not a case of what we do in terms of tailings management for 10 years, or 20 years, or 30 years, but what are we talking about in terms of 100 years, 200 years.

As I mentioned before, we're here to stay. We're not going to go away. So the way those tailings get dealt with will have an impact on our people for a long time to come. So we want to be sure that it's done properly.

So we put them in some kind of containment device and leave the material there for future generations to worry about.... I'm just not sure it's a just solution to let our future generations worry about it.

For this reason Natives, like the environmentalists, attached a great deal of importance to proper monitoring. Five Natives also demanded greater participation in the management of the tailings.

Conclusion

Trust, potential adverse health effects, public risk perceptions, contamination of the watershed, and long-term monitoring of the tailing sites were identified as primary themes in the coding of the transcripts. Trust emerged as the central factor in affecting how the stakeholder groups perceived mine tailings in the Elliot Lake area. Business owners and retirees had trust in scientists, government agencies, and the mining companies to have the capacity and willingness to look after the tailings in an appropriate manner, while Natives and environmentalists did not.

Business owners and retirees exhibited trust because they believed that the people who were looking after the tailings were trained and educated and, therefore, had the necessary skills and knowledge to deal effectively with the tailings. Conversely, Native distrust was rooted in the adverse impacts they have suffered as a result of being downstream from the tailings areas and in their loss of use of lands for traditional purposes. They had no faith in the mining companies involved in the environmental review to adopt an acceptable decommissioning plan; nor did they trust the government to protect aboriginal interests. Like the Natives, environmentalists did not believe that the mining companies would put together an acceptable plan for handling the tailings. But unlike the Natives, they did not distrust government agencies because of past impacts. Rather, environmentalists lacked faith in the federal and provincial governments because they had not included several other unlicensed mine tailings areas in the environmental review. As well, environmentalists expressed greater scepticism about the ability of science to predict impacts accurately and to find ways to avoid them.

Because of the differences in trust between the groups, there was a large split of opinion between them on the hazards associated with the tailings. Environmentalists and Natives perceived many and significant impacts, while business owners and retirees perceived few and insignificant impacts. Both environmentalists and Natives were particularly concerned about tailings getting into the watershed as a result of seepage from a control dam or its failure, which would lead to the release of radioactive substances and acid mine drainage. Both groups identified impacts to the environment and health, with Natives also stressing the greater impact on traditional pursuits. Retirees believed that from a health standpoint they were safer living in Elliot Lake, with its slow pace of life and plenty of outdoor activities, than in the hustle and bustle of the big city. Business owners were the most concerned that people outside Elliot Lake might think that the area was unsafe to live in,

276 Boom Town Blues

and that the perception would discourage new residents and businesses from moving into the area. Business owners believed that if people knew more about the tailings they would be less concerned, while environmentalists believed that if people knew more about the issues they would be more concerned.

It is clear that there are significant differences of opinion among residents in the Elliot Lake area about how the uranium mine tailings should be managed in the future. The controversy is not likely to end soon. The environmental assessment review will have to deal with ongoing management decisions for the tailings and regulatory and assessment processes for the "idle" mines and tailings will have to be instituted as these sites become licensed. We hope that some sort of forum for these discussions (as recommended by the Environmental Assessment Panel, but not accepted by the federal cabinet because of its lack of authority on the matter) will be developed by the mining companies, so that there can be open debate about these issues, debate that leads to joint problem-solving and consensus.

Note

1 We are grateful to all the informants who were willing to be interviewed for this study. The map was prepared by Léo Larivière, technologist for the Department of Geography at Laurentian University. Funding was provided by the Centre for Resource Studies at Queen's University.

References

Canadian Environmental Assessment Agency. (1996). *Decommissioning of Uranium Mine Tailings Management Areas in the Elliot Lake Area.* Report of the Environmental Assessment Panel (June 1996) of the Canadian Environmental Assessment Agency of Environment Canada.

Dixon, Catharine. (1996). *The Power and the Promise: The Elliot Lake Story*, Elliot Lake: Gillidix Publishing.

Dwyer, J.P. (1990). "Limits of environmental risk assessment," *Journal of Energy Engineering* 166, 3: 231–45.

FEARO. (1994). *Decommissioning of Uranium Mine Tailings Management Areas in Elliot Lake: Revised Terms of Reference*, Press Release, August 4, 1994, Ottawa, FEARO.

Halber, B.E., P. Arthurs, C.T. Hoggarth, S. Januszewski, and A. Vivyurka. (1995). "Evaluation of the aquatic environment in the Serpent River Watershed," in *Conference Proceedings, Sudbury '95: Mining and the Environment, May 28-June 1, 1995*, 745–54.

Hine, D., C. Summers, M. Prystupa, and A. McKenzie-Richer. (1997, in press). "Cultural and economic effects on public support for a proposed nuclear waste repository in Canada: a path analysis," *Risk Analysis*.

Kiss, G.R. (1972). *Recursive Concept Analysis.* Unpublished manuscript. Edinburgh, Scotland: MRC Speech and Communication Unit, University of Edinburgh.

Johnson-Laird, P.N. (1983). *Mental Models.* Cambridge, UK: Cambridge University Press.

Prystupa, M., D. Hine, C. Summers, and J. Lewko. (1997, in press). "The representativeness of Elliot Lake uranium mine decommissioning public hearings under the Environmental Assessment and Review Process," in *Canadian Environmental Assessment in Transition,* ed. J. Sinclair. University of Waterloo, Department of Geography, Publication Series.

McCrea, G., D. Philips and M. Isacsson. (1990). *Uranium* [Film]. (Available from the National Film Board of Canada, 3155 Côte-de-Liesse Road, St. Laurent, Québec, H4N 2N4).

Rio Algom Limited. (1995). *Summary of the Environmental Impact Statement with Respect to Rio Algom's Application to the AECB to License the Decommissioning of the Quirke and Panel Waste Management Areas.*

Strauss, A.L. and J. Corbin. (1990). *Basics of Qualitative Research: Grounded Theory Procedures and Techniques,* Newbury Park, CA: Sage.

Chapter 21

Risk Perceptions and Relocation Decisions of Prospective Residents of Elliot Lake: A Mental Models Study[1]

Donald W. Hine, Mark Prystupa, John Lewko, and Craig Summers

Many communities, willingly or unwillingly, serve as hosts to industries that pose potential risks to the health of residents and the local environment. Sometimes the perceived risks associated with such industries far outweigh the actual risks. Other times they do not. Regardless of their accuracy, public perceptions of risk have the potential to exert a huge influence on the economic viability of communities as tourist and retirement destinations and as business centres (Slovic et al. 1991). In this chapter, we present the community of Elliot Lake as a case study that explores retirees' relocation decisions from a risk-perception perspective.

At present, all of the uranium mines in the Elliot Lake area (see map in Chapter 20 of this volume) are closed and federally mediated decommissioning hearings have been held to develop a procedure for ensuring the long-term safety of the mine sites.

Prior to the mine closures, uranium tailings were stored after milling, using the following process. In the mill, uranium ore is crushed and treated with chemicals to remove the uranium. For each tonne of ore that is processed, one tonne of solid waste and two tonnes of process liquid are produced. The solid wastes, the bulk of which resembles coarse sand, are referred to as tailings. The tailings contain radioactive decay products of uranium. Of these, thorium-230 has the longest half-life: 76,000 years. Thorium decays into radium-226 which is similar to calcium and, if ingested, can concentrate in the bones, teeth, and breast milk of mammals, posing a potential cancer risk. When radium decays, radon gas and radon progeny are released, both of which are known carcinogens (Halpern and Warner 1994, U.S. National Research Council 1988).

According to the mining companies and independent experts, the probability of a significant release of radiation, radon, or tailings waste water into the environment is extremely small (Brummer and Chegini 1995, Denison Mines Limited 1995, Rio Algom Limited 1995), assuming proper storage measures are employed (for example, providing a water cover for the tailings). However, past spills and leaks in the region have led several groups to question the accuracy and good faith of these estimates (for example, Hutchinson 1995, Lloyd 1995). While acknowledging problems with past practices, the mining companies argue that significant technical improvements have been made in recent years, and that past failure rates are not indicative of present risks (Nightingale and Payne 1995).

With the loss of its two main employers, Denison Mines Limited and Rio Algom Limited, Elliot Lake is faced with the difficult task of restructuring its economy. Several new initiatives have been introduced to attract new residents and businesses to the community, the largest of which is a nation-wide marketing campaign promoting Elliot Lake as an affordable retirement locale. One potential obstacle to the success of these initiatives is the fear among prospective residents and business owners that there may be unacceptable health risks associated with living in Elliot Lake, due to the radioactive mine tailings stored near the community (see Gow, Chapter 24 in this volume). Although the environmental-impact statements produced by the mining companies indicate that the tailings, if managed properly, do not pose a significant health threat (Denison Mines Limited 1995, Rio Algom Limited 1995), the community is concerned that the perceived risks may be strong enough to prevent prospective residents and businesses from relocating to the region. This concern is consistent with past findings that suggest laypersons' estimates of radiation-related risks often dramatically exceed risk estimates offered by scientific experts (Cohen 1983, Slovic 1987). It should also be pointed out that the potential negative impact of risk perceptions and stigmatization on economic development is not a problem that is unique to Elliot Lake. For example, in a study assessing the potential impact of building a repository for high-level nuclear waste in Nevada, Slovic et al. (1991, 694) concluded:

> In sum, our analysis indicates that the development of the Yucca Mountain Repository will, in effect, force Nevadans to gamble with their future economy. The nature of the gamble cannot be

specified precisely, but it appears to include credible possibilities (with unknown probabilities) of substantial losses to the visitor economy, the migrant economy, and the business economy.

Indeed, it seems that the issues raised in this paper would be relevant to many communities with so-called "hazardous" industries forming their economic base.

If prospective residents are choosing not to relocate to Elliot Lake because of incomplete knowledge and/or misconceptions about the magnitude and nature of the actual risks posed by the tailings, it would be useful for the community to document these gaps and misconceptions and develop a risk communication program to help counteract their effects. Bostrom, Fischhoff, and Morgan (1992) propose a methodology for mapping out risk-related knowledge and beliefs using influence diagrams (Howard 1989). An influence diagram is like a causal map containing a collection of nodes (concepts) connected to one another by arrows (see Figure 1). The approach of Bostrom et al. (1992) consists of four main steps: creating an expert influence diagram that adequately summarizes expert knowledge associated with a given hazard; eliciting laypersons' knowledge and beliefs regarding the hazard using an open-ended interview format, and contrasting those beliefs with the concepts in the expert influence diagram; identifying knowledge gaps and misconceptions in laypersons' understanding of the hazard; and specifying the implications for risk communication. The advantages of this type of approach over more structured methods for measuring knowledge (for example, true-false and multiple-choice tests) have been documented elsewhere (for example, Bostrom et al. 1992, Maharik and Fischhoff 1993, Pidgeon et al. 1992).

Expert influence diagram for tailings risks. The expert influence diagram (see Figure 1) was developed from interviews with mining experts at the Geomechanics Research Centre at Laurentian University and the Elliot Lake Research Field Station, and from several technical reports on tailings storage at Elliot Lake (Denison Mines Limited 1993 and 1995, Rio Algom Limited 1993 and 1995, SENES Consultants 1993). The diagram describes the main paths through which individuals could be exposed to radiation or other pollutants from the tailings, assuming current storage methods. We believed it was unreasonable to expect lay persons to be familiar with all of the concepts included in the expert influence diagram. Therefore, in conjunction with the experts, we selected 16 that we thought were most critical to a sound understanding of the hazards posed by the tailings. In accordance with the terminology used by Bostrom et al. (1992), we refer to these as "basic" hazard concepts. In Figure 1, these basic concepts are presented in bold font.

Figure 1. Expert influence diagram for mine tailings risk in Elliot Lake

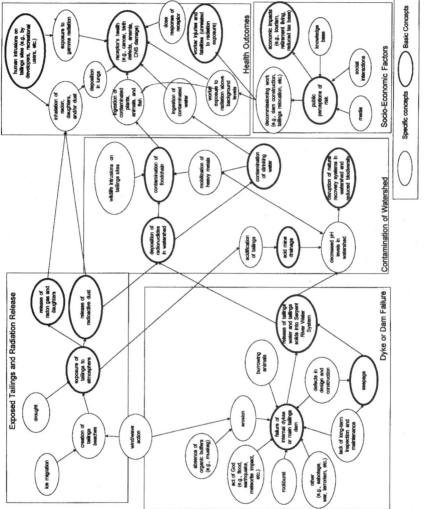

Method

Respondents. Twenty interviews were conducted in the Sudbury region by two interviewers, the first author, and a research assistant with previous interview experience. Potential respondents were randomly selected from a list of 201 Sudbury residents who had taken a community-sponsored tour of Elliot Lake during the past three years, but had not moved to the community. The tour, operated by the Retirement Living Program, introduces interested parties to Elliot Lake and highlights the advantages of Elliot Lake as a retirement community. Respondents were contacted by telephone and were asked to participate in a study of retirees' lifestyle choices. Of those contacted, 80 percent agreed to participate. The sample consisted of 13 men and 7 women. Ages ranged from 49 to 75 years old, with an average age of 65.6. Of the respondents, 85 percent were retired or semi-retired. The remaining 15 percent indicated that they were contemplating retirement.

Procedure. Respondents were interviewed in a quiet setting, either at the university or in their own home. Prior to the interview, they were told that the study was concerned with retirees' lifestyle choices, and in particular, with how retirees make decisions about where to "settle down" when they retire. The interview itself consisted of two phases and was similar, but not identical, to that used by Bostrom et al. (1992). During the initial, non-directive, phase of the interview, respondents were simply asked to list everything that came to mind when they thought about "Elliot Lake." After an initial list of concepts had been elicited, the interviewer reviewed the list, and asked the respondent to elaborate on each concept that had been listed. If new concepts were generated during the elaboration phase, these were added to the list and were subject to further elaboration. This process continued until no new concepts were forthcoming.

The second phase of the interview was more directive and involved specific questions related to risks associated with living in Elliot Lake. Respondents were asked whether they believed there were any hazards associated with living in Elliot Lake, how people might be exposed to the hazards, what consequences might occur if people were exposed to the hazards, and how the hazards could best be managed to minimize the risk to the general public. As in the initial phase of the interview, respondents were prompted to elaborate on their responses.

Following the interview, the interviewer collected demographic information from the respondents and debriefed them about the purpose of the study. The interviews ranged from 20 minutes to over 90 minutes in length.

Coding and analysis. All interviews were taped, transcribed, and coded into the concepts in the expert influence diagram. Concepts that could not be coded into the diagram were classified into two main categories: hazard-related misconceptions (incorrect knowledge), and non-hazard-related concepts associated with relocation decisions. Preliminary coding revealed six common themes in the non-hazard concepts: affordable housing, scenic beauty, outdoor activities, lack of facilities, isolation from family and friends, and leaving one's present medical caregiver. Two independent coders coded five randomly selected interviews. Inter-coder agreement was very high: 94 percent for the expert influence diagram, 89 percent for misconceptions, and 89 percent for the non-hazard concepts. Given these high levels of agreement, a single coder coded the remaining 15 transcripts.

Results

Descriptive statistics. A breakdown of responses by interview phase (non-directive and directive) and concept type (exposure concepts and effects concepts) is presented in Table 1. On average, respondents produced only 2.35 (that is, approximately 12 percent) of the basic concepts present in the expert influence diagram. However, there was considerable variability within the sample, with five respondents producing no expert concepts and two producing more than eight.

Table 1. Breakdown of concept types by interview phase

Measures	Non-directive phase			Directive phase		
	All concepts	Exposure concepts	Effects concepts	All concepts	Exposure concepts	Effects concepts
Average [a]	.90	.60	.30	1.35	.70	.65
Proportion [b]	.20	.20	.20	.70	.45	.65

[a] Mean number of expert concepts generated by respondents
[b] Proportion of respondents who generated concepts in the expert influence diagram.

As one might expect, the proportion of respondents who produced one or more expert concepts was significantly higher for the directive phase of the interview (.70) than for the non-directive phase (.20, chi square = 12.07, $p < .01$). Respondents also generated slightly more expert concepts in the directive phase (m = 1.35) than in the non-directive phase (m = .90), although this difference was not statistically reliable [t (19) = .71, ns].

Misconceptions were rare, occurring in only one instance. A respondent indicated that it would be impossible to be exposed to uranium-related pollution in Elliot Lake given that mines were no longer operating. This statement is incorrect on two counts. First, when the interviews were conducted, not all of the mines had been completely shut down. Second, even if the mines had been shut down, there are still risks associated with the tailings stored in the area.

In summary, our sample of retirees appeared to have little knowledge about the potential risks associated with the mine tailings stored near Elliot Lake. However, the small amount of information that they possessed was accurate.

Knowledge of specific tailings hazards. Table 2 summarizes the frequency with which each basic expert concept was mentioned by the respondents. Most of the expert concepts were mentioned by only a few of the respondents, and several were not mentioned at all. The presence of tailings wastes in the watershed was the most common exposure concept, mentioned by 25 percent of the respondents. Fifteen percent of respondents indicated that tailings might enter the watershed by seeping through the tailings pools, but no one mentioned the possibility that an internal dam or dyke might fail. Several respondents (15 percent) mentioned that the presence of radon gas and/or radon progeny in the air posed a potential hazard, but none explained the process by which radon entered the air, even with prompting. Interestingly, very few respondents mentioned the possibility of radiation and other contaminants entering the food chain (10 percent) or water supply (5 percent). This is important given that knowledge of this type would likely have an impact on decisions about what not to eat and drink. Another notable finding was that no one mentioned the possibility of human intrusion into the tailings sites (for example, by a hunter or hiker), another piece of knowledge relevant to safe lifestyle choices.

In terms of effects concepts, 65 percent of the sample indicated that they believed the mine tailings stored near Elliot Lake posed a potential health hazard. However, most of these responses came during the directive phase of the interview when respondents were specifically asked about potential hazards, suggesting that tailings-related fears were not at the forefront of their consciousness. Few respondents mentioned potential economic impacts (for example, not being able to sell products manufactured in the community due to contamination fears) or environmental impacts (for example, reduced biodiversity in the Serpent River watershed) during either phase of the interview.

Although the majority of respondents believed there were health hazards associated with living in Elliot Lake, only one respondent indicated that these hazards would influence his decision about whether

Table 2. Number of respondents mentioning expert concepts

Concepts	Non-directive phase	Directive phase	Proportion[a]
Exposure			
Dam failure	0	0	0
Seepage	0	3	.15
Tailings in watershed	3	2	.25
Tailings exposed to air	1	0	.05
Radon gas	1	2	.15
Radioactive dust	1	1	.10
Human intrusions on tailings site	0	0	0
Radionuclides in watershed	0	0	0
Acid mine drainage	0	0	0
Contamination of food chain	1	1	.10
Contamination of water supply	1	0	.05
Public perceptions	1	1	.10
Effects			
Disruption of natural recovery	1	0	.05
Reduced biodiversity	1	0	.05
Health risks	2	13	.65
Worker injuries and fatalities	0	0	0
Economic impacts	2	0	.10

[a] Proportion of respondents who mentioned concept at least once

to move to the community. Most indicated they were unconcerned about the possible risks. Typical responses included:

> There's always the question of radioactivity, but it's not something that we're terribly concerned about. I don't worry too much about that type of thing.

> That sort of thing [radon gas] doesn't bother me. I'm not the type of person that worries about that sort of thing. That had nothing to do with our decision [not to move to Elliot Lake]. It doesn't scare me.

> I'm sure that it can be very hazardous to my health, but no more so than what Inco [mining company operating in Sudbury] has produced.... I think pollution is everywhere. If it's not uranium in one place, then it will be something somewhere else.

> Maybe I should be concerned. But if you're always concerned

about all of these different things that could happen to you, you're going to drive yourself crazy.

Non-hazard concepts. During the non-directive phase of the interview, many of the concepts produced were unrelated to uranium mining and tailings wastes. As noted earlier, six main non-hazard themes were identified (these are summarized in Table 3).

Table 3. Non-hazard concepts relevant to retirees' relocation decisions

Concept	Proportion *
Positive	
Inexpensive housing	.80
Recreational activities	.75
Beautiful scenery	.60
Negative	
Lack of facilities	.50
Isolation from family and friends	.45
Leaving present medical care	.25

* Proportion of respondents who mentioned the concept at least once

Most respondents mentioned that they considered moving to Elliot Lake because of the inexpensive housing, diverse selection of recreational activities, and beautiful scenery. The following quotations are representative:

This is the biggest and most important thing right now — a fixed income. The rent is affordable. I could live there for pretty near half the money we have to spend in Sudbury.

A real nice town in the summertime. Lots of fishing. Economical rent for older people.
I've always liked the area. I like the hardwood trees and the rough rocky and hilly terrain. It's very appealing with the lakes and so on.

They have a golf course and a curling rink. They have swimming. There are two beaches there. I also hunt, and it's in the bush.

Aside from the tailings-related concepts, only three negative themes occurred with any regularity during the non-directive phase. Half of the sample indicated that they were concerned about the adequacy of the

A group of Elliot Lake residetns hiking in Mississagi Provincial Park, 25 kilometres north of the city.
City of Elliot Lake

community's facilities. Concerns related to shopping and medical facilities were mentioned most frequently.

> It's very nice, very clean. But once they started closing the stores, this is one of the reasons we hesitated. Woolco closed. That leaves you nothing. I lived in the bush for 26 years and I wasn't going to go do that again.

> I guess they can give you emergency treatment. But here [in Sudbury] we have a heart hospital right here. A cancer hospital is here. All these things they don't have there. They have to travel two to three hours to get the same treatment that we have right on our doorstep.

Being isolated from family and friends was another relatively common concern, mentioned by 45 percent of the sample.

> My family, that was the main one. I didn't want to be that far away from my kids.... To go for a weekend, they'd be driving all weekend.

> My mother is still living and I just couldn't see myself leaving her.... We're a close family and this would have meant a lot of separation, so no. We'll stay here.

Finally, one-quarter of the respondents indicated that they were reluctant to relocate to Elliot Lake because moving would entail leaving or distancing themselves from their present doctor and other medical caregivers.

> When you get to be my age — I'll be 73 next month — a doctor becomes sort of important in your life. Especially a doctor you've been going to for 20 years. They know everything about you.... If I want to go anywhere, I have to start again with somebody who doesn't even know me.

> I'm not too well and I need to be close to the doctor, which means that I would have to travel back and forth. You can't change doctors every time you turn around.

> I don't know what the doctors are like there. They're probably just as efficient as they are anywhere. But why take a calculated risk if you don't have to.

Discussion

This study was designed to determine whether Elliot Lake's efforts to attract new residents is being undermined by inflated risk perceptions about the uranium mine tailings stored near the community. If knowledge gaps and misperceptions about the tailings are biasing relocation decisions, a risk communication program could be developed by the community to help prospective residents make more informed decisions. Counter to previously reported findings in the risk perception literature, which suggested that laypersons often overestimate radiation-related risks (for example, Cohen 1983 and Slovic 1993), most of the respondents in this study indicated that they were unconcerned about the hazards posed by Elliot Lake tailings. Although over half of the sample believed there might be health risks associated with the tailings, most indicated these risks were minimal and that the presence of the tailings had not affected (or was unlikely to affect) their decision to retire in Elliot Lake. Other factors, such as the perceived lack of shopping and medical facilities, isolation from family and friends, and a reluctance to change medical caregivers, were listed as more important reasons for not moving to the community.

There are several plausible explanations to account for the low level of concern displayed by the respondents in this study about being adversely affected by the tailings. The first involves the age of the respondents. Most of the individuals interviewed were retired or were contemplating retirement. Given that low-level radiation generally acts slowly, most would likely die from other ailments before the radiation would have an effect. Had the respondents been younger or had young children, they might have been more worried about possible health consequences.

A second possibility is that living in Sudbury, also a major mining centre, may have desensitized the residents to the potential risks posed by the Elliot Lake tailings. Several subjects mentioned that they found it hard to believe that the risks in Elliot Lake could be any worse than those associated with the mines and smelters operating in Sudbury. Respondents living in less industrialized settings might have been more sensitive to the potential risks posed by the tailings.

Finally, it is possible that the respondents simply did not know enough about possible exposure paths and effects to be concerned about the tailings. Recall that one-quarter of the sample was unable to identify any mining-related hazards associated with living in Elliot Lake, and of those who could, most mentioned only a small proportion of the risk concepts in the expert influence diagram. Had they known more, they might have perceived the risks to be higher.

Past research on nuclear power suggests that there is often an inverse relation between knowledge and risk perceptions; individuals who know more (for example, experts) fear radiation and nuclear technology less (Pidgeon et al. 1992). The present study raises the interesting possibility that the relation between knowledge and perceived radiation risks might best be represented visually by an inverted u or horseshoe shape. Individuals with extremely low or extremely high knowledge of radiation hazards may perceive the risks to be minimal, whereas individuals with a moderate amount of information may have much stronger risk perceptions. We are currently conducting research to test this possibility, as well as the desensitization hypothesis outlined earlier.

Implications for risk communication. In general, low levels of hazard knowledge suggests the need for a risk communication program to increase public awareness and knowledge (Bostrom et al. 1992). In order to make responsible relocation decisions, retirees need to be aware of hazards present in potential retirement destinations. When one considers the best interests of the individual decision-maker, few would disagree with the claim that having more information on which to base a decision is better than having less information, assuming of course that the information is accurate and relevant. However, whether providing information of this sort is in the best interests of the risk communicator depends on a variety of factors, including the communicator's goals and base-line levels of knowledge and fear in the target population. For example, in the present case, one of Elliot Lake's primary goals is to attract more residents. If our results had suggested that retirees were choosing not to move to the community because of inflated risk perceptions associated with the mine tailings, a community-sponsored risk communication program might have been very effective in allaying public fears and increasing migration to the region. However, our analysis suggests that inflated risk perceptions do not appear to be a problem, at least among our sample of Sudbury residents. Given that the base-line fear is already so low, a risk communication program would likely do little to help the community to achieve its objective of attracting new residents. In fact, as we speculated earlier, educating the public about possible exposure paths and effects might hurt the community, increasing risk perceptions among prospective residents rather than decreasing them.

This raises an important ethical issue: to what extent is a community responsible for providing residents and/or prospective residents with information about the hazards that may be present in the community? On the surface, it seems reasonable that Elliot Lake should be forthright about the potential hazards posed by the mine tailings. However, there appears to be no strong precedent for this type of informed consent in other cities and towns. New residents of Toronto, for example, are not warned about all the potential risks associated with living in large urban centres. Furthermore, even if communities were legally obligated to provide hazard information, it is unclear to which hazards this law should apply. During the next 50 years in Elliot Lake, more people will likely die in motor vehicle accidents than from tailings-related cancers. Does this mean that the community should be obligated to warn all prospective residents about the risks associated with driving in the region?

Another potential problem stems from the uncertainty of many hazards. In many instances, the precise probabilities associated with hazards are unknown or are of questionable validity. In the case of Elliot Lake, for example, there is general agreement among local stakeholder groups about the main exposure paths and effects associated with the mine tailings. However, there is considerable disagreement about the exact probabilities that should be assigned to each path and effect. The mining companies argue that the probabilities are extremely small, whereas other stakeholders (most notably environmentalist organizations and Native groups) estimate the probabilities to be much higher. Given this uncertainty about the true magnitude of the risks, it becomes even more difficult to ascertain Elliot Lake's ethical obligation to inform prospective residents about possible risks.

These matters are very complex and difficult to resolve, and we will not even pretend to have satisfactory answers. At present, all we can do is to point out that the public's right to know is an important and still unresolved issue in the risk communication literature, and requires further attention.

Note

[1] This study was supported by a grant from the Centre for Resource Studies at Queen's University. The Strategic Decisions Group of the Centre for Research in Human Development at Laurentian University would like to thank Deborah Berthelot, Al Chegini, Richard Brummer, Antoinette McKenzie-Richer, Faye Healey, Carolyn Blais, and the Retirement Living Program for their assistance with this project.

References

Bostrom, A., B. Fischhoff, and M.G. Morgan. (1992). "Characterizing mental models of hazardous processes: a methodology and an application to radon," *Journal of Social Issues* 48, 4: 85–100.

Brummer, R.K. and A. Chegini. (1995). "Benchmarks for risk-related decision making in mine decommissioning." Paper presented at the Second Biennial Canadian Conference on Process Safety and Loss Management held in Toronto in June.

Cohen, B.L. (1983). *Before It's Too Late: A Scientist's Case for Nuclear Energy.* New York: Plenum Press.

Denison Mines Limited. (1993). *Project Description for the Decommissioning of the Denison Mine Tailings Management Areas TMA–1 and TMA–2.*

Denison Mines Limited. (1995). *Environmental Impact Statement: Decommissioning of the Denison and Stanrock Tailings Management Areas.*

Halpern, M.T. and K.E. Warner. (1994). "Radon risk perception and testing: sociodemographic correlates," *Journal of Environmental Health* 56: 31–35.

Howard, R.A. (1989). "Knowledge maps," *Management Science* 35: 903–22.

Hutchinson, D. (November, 1995). "Presentation on behalf of the United Steel Workers of America," *Environmental Assessment Panel Reviewing Decommissioning Proposals for Elliot Lake Uranium Mine Tailings Management Areas (TMAS): Transcripts of Proceedings, Vol. 1,* 151–72.

Lloyd, B. (November, 1995). "Presentation on behalf of NorthWatch," *Environmental Assessment Panel Reviewing Decommissioning Proposals for Elliot Lake Uranium Mine Tailings Management Areas (TMAS): Transcripts of Proceedings, Vol. 1,* 188–216.

Maharik M. and B. Fischhoff. (1993). "Contrasting perceptions of the risk of using nuclear energy sources in space," *Journal of Environmental Psychology* 13: 243–50.

Nightingale, J. and R. Payne. (November, 1995). "Presentation on behalf of Rio Algom," *Environmental Assessment Panel Reviewing Decommissioning Proposals for Elliot Lake Uranium Mine Tailings Management Areas (TMAS): Transcripts of Proceedings, Vol. 1*, 18.

Payne, R.A. (1995). "Decommissioning of Elliot Lake mining properties" in *Proceedings of Sudbury 95: Mining and the Environment Vol. 3*, ed. T.P. Hynes and M. C. Blanchette, 1199–1209. Ottawa: CANMET.

Pidgeon, N., C. Hood, D. Jones, B. Turner, and R. Gibson. (1992). "Risk perception" in *Risk: Analysis, Perception, and Management. Report of a Royal Society Study Group*, 89–134. London: Royal Society.

Rio Algom Limited. (1993). *An Overview of Environmental Effects of Extreme Natural Events on the Quirke and Panel Waste Management Areas.*

Rio Algom Limited. (1995). *Summary of the Environmental Impact Statement with Respect to Rio Algom's Application to the AECB to License the Decommissioning of the Quirke and Panel Waste Management Areas.*

SENES Consultants. (1993). *Environmental Impact Statement for the Decommissioning of the Quirke and Panel Waste Management Areas.* Prepared for Rio Algom Limited.

Slovic, P. (1987). "Perception of risk," *Science* 236: 280–85.

Slovic, P., M. Layman, N. Kraus, J. Flynn, J. Chalmers, G. Gesell, (1991). "Perceived risk, stigma, and potential economic impacts of a high-level nuclear waste facility in Nevada," *Risk Analysis* 11: 683–96.

U.S. National Research Council. (1988). *Health Risks of Radon and Other Internally Deposited Alpha-Emitters: BEIR IV.* Washington, DC: U.S. National Research Council.

Chapter 22
Establishment of Native Aquatic and Wetland Plants in Permanently Flooded Pyritic Uranium Tailings[1]

Peter Beckett, Sharon Pappin Willianen,
Albert Vivyurka, and Gerard Courtin

> *Rank weeds and lush, slimy water plants sent an odour of decay and a heavy miasmatic vapour onto our faces, while a false step plunged us more than once thigh-deep into the dark, quivering mire, which shook us for yards in soft undulations around our feet.*
>
> — Great Grimpen Mire in
> *The Hound of the Baskervilles,*
> by Sir Arthur Conan Doyle.

Wetlands (or areas with permanent or seasonal water with depths up to two metres) conjure up many feelings. In this chapter the value of utilizing wetland plants to "improve" the environment is discussed. Several options currently exist for the decommissioning of acid-generating tailings, including perpetual chemical treatment of effluent with a site remaining as deposited; a dry cover or cap consisting of soils, capillary breaks, or various waste materials; a revegetated terrestrial system; backfilling into mine or ventilation shafts; and finally, one of the most favourable options (provided the necessary site conditions exist or are created), the containment of tailings under a permanent, engineered water cover by flooding or subaqueous disposal.

Where sites allow, the flooding option has proven to be successful in eliminating acid mine drainage (AMD). Because soils are saturated in the case of flooded tailings, and wetlands require such hydrological conditions, these sites provide the opportunity to enhance the site through the establishment of wetland and aquatic vegetation. As an organic cover further impedes oxidation of the flooded tailings, this treatment would be suitable in conjunction with an already existing water cover. An organic cover and its associated plant roots should stabilize and bind the tailings' surface, preventing shoreline erosion and redistribution of the tailings in shallow areas during storms. In the case of drought, an organic layer would act as a saturated sponge, preventing oxygen diffusion into the tailings surface as water levels drop within the basin.

Acidic coal-mine and metal-mine drainage has been effectively treated with both laboratory and field-scale constructed and natural wetlands (Hedin 1989). Michelutti and Wiseman (1995) outline several operational wetlands, such as those of the Tennessee Valley Authority (constructed wetlands treating AMD), the Big Five Wetland in Idaho Springs (treating AMD, removing copper, zinc and iron, and increasing effluent pH from 3.0 to 6.2), and the wetlands below the Falconbridge Ltd. smelter in Falconbridge, Ontario. These traditional uses of constructed wetlands involve effluent or seepage interception and passive treatment.

More recent developments focus on plant establishment in tailings ponds (St-Germain, Larratt, and Prairie 1997) for biological treatment (significant removal of sulphate, nitrogen, phosphate, copper, dissolved solids, and molybdenum took place by submerged aquatic species and filamentous green algae) and development of self-sustaining organic covers in aquatic tailings environments (St-Germain and Kuyucak 1997), which results in the isolation of tailings material from the overlying water cover, with the added benefit of aesthetic enhancement.

Wetland vegetation, such as cattails, reeds, and sedges, has been shown to grow successfully in saturated and shallow water areas at the Quirke Mine Waste Management Area (WMA) and on other acid-generating tailings in Canada. However, flooded tailings sites require deeper water depths (>0.6 metres) in order to impede oxygen diffusion and prevent oxidation. In order to enhance the development of an organic oxygen barrier that is self-sustaining, deeper aquatic species that can thrive under the existing conditions have been planted to test their establishment and growth capabilities. The ability of the transplants to accumulate various metals and radionuclides was determined for the site and, once the plants were established, compared with their ability to do so at the uncontaminated source sites.

The Study

Objectives. The goal of the present research is to aid in the creation of self-sustaining plant communities and the formation of an organic layer within flooded, pyritic tailings ponds. The development of a self-sustaining aquatic plant community at the Quirke Mine WMA would prevent further oxidation of potentially exposed tailings through the development of an organic barrier by deposition of decaying plant matter. It would restore the basin to a more natural state by increasing potential habitat, and could contribute to effluent treatment through plant uptake of contaminants that would otherwise increase chemical treatment costs.

Study site. The Quirke Mine WMA contains 46 million tonnes of tailings and waste rock. It covers 192 hectares and includes 5 cells separated by internal dykes. Water is fed from a storage lake with oligotrophic characteristics into Cell 14. This cell is the first in the series and covers approximately 64 hectares (St-Germain and Kuyucak 1997). Subsequent cells are at gradually decreasing elevations, resulting in spillway flow from west to east and a drop of 14 metres at a grade of approximately 0.5 percent. Each cell is designed to maintain a permanent water cover 0.6 metres in depth or greater to effectively reduce acid generation. Currently, a range of water depths exists in the two study cells, from shallow shorelines to depths in excess of 5 metres. Water pH is between 6 and 7. Turbidity in Cell 15 in 1995 was high, as it was covered with water only a few months before introduction of plants. Currently, tailings surface discharge water is treated with barium chloride and lime at the eastern end of the WMA. The precipitates settle in a series of ponds and the treated effluent is discharged into the Serpent River which flows into the North Channel of Lake Huron.

Selection of species. Several criteria were used in the determination of aquatic and wetland species selected for transplant into the WMA ponds. The results of a study completed in British Columbia by St-Germain, Larratt, and Prairie (1997), involving aquatic species transplanting and an evaluation of species occurring in a local wetland that received a tailings spill in Elliot Lake (Rio Algom Limited 1995), were used to formulate a list of potentially suitable species. The biological characteristics of the potential species were considered by reference to standard monographs (Hutchinson 1975, Mitch and Gosselink 1993, and Sculthorpe 1967). Some species, for example pondweeds, have recently started to invade the Quirke Mine WMA naturally. Local water bodies were then examined as potential sources of plant material and approval was granted for the removal of six species from various lakes, wetlands, and creeks.

The six species chosen for introduction into water greater than 45 centimetres deep were: white or fragrant water lily (*Nymphaea odorata*), watershield (*Brasenia schreberi*), horned bladderwort (*Utricularia cornuta*), pondweeds (primarily *Potamogeton natans*), pickerel weed (*Pontederia cordata*) and hardstem bulrush (*Scirpus acutus*). All these species have to ability to grow in low-nutrient (oligotrophic) conditions, to survive in mineral or sandy habitats, and to tolerate some acidity. Other shoreline species were introduced into shallower water (see below).

Transplant techniques. All species were collected by hand from the source wetland. Vegetative parts, roots, rhizomes, and organic soil were removed from the site, transported, and kept moist until transplanted using the following methods. In each case not more than 10 percent of each species was removed from the donor site and all species were transplanted in August 1995. Forty locations were planted within Cell 14 and ten locations were planted in Cell 15.

Burlap was cut into pieces of approximately 30 centimetres by 60 centimetres, folded, and sewn together to make bags, which were then used to transplant white water lily, watershield, bladderwort, pondweed, and hardstem bulrush. With the exception of bladderwort, these species reproduce mainly by rhizome. Rhizomes and several litres of soil were placed in the burlap bags. Stems and leaves were left to float freely from

Students preparing material for transfer to tailings. Here, they put rhizomes of water lily, organic soil, and fertilizer into a burlap containment bag.

Peter Beckett

Planting water lily in the Quirke Waste Management Area tailings pond, October 1995.

Peter Beckett

the open top of the bag. Small rocks were placed in the bags for weight, and approximately 70 grams of bonemeal (2–11–0) was added to the soil.

The bags were then carefully lowered at each designated location into the flooded tailings cells from the edge of a boat or canoe. Where water levels were shallow enough, persons standing in the flooded tailings placed the bags in the proper location. Ten bags were grouped together as closely as possible at each location to avoid displacement due to wave action.

Pickerel weed was planted in shallower locations (<0.85 metres) by direct transplant of roots into the tailings. A cheesecloth bag containing approximately 70 grams of bonemeal was placed in close proximity to the roots of each plant at the time of planting. Where the physical properties of the tailings allowed, ten plants were planted at a density similar to the source sites.

In the fall of 1993, vegetation "islands" of several shoreline species were planted in Cell 14 in water depths of 30–60 cm. Among these were blue joint grass (*Calamagrostis canadensis*), beaked sedge (*Carex rostrata*), cattail (*Typha latifolia*), common reed (*Phragmites australis*), manna grass (*Glyceria borealis*), and wool rush (*Scirpus cyperinus*). Islands of approximately 10 square metres were planted; they included stems, rhizomes, and organic soil from the source wetland. This was done in order to gain information on transplant survival in species other than common cattail, which occurs frequently in acid-generating tailings. Annual estimates of surface area were calculated from diameters assuming the islands to be circular in shape.

Water, soil, and vegetation chemistry. Samples were taken for a variety of analyses including nutrients (nitrogen, potassium, and phosphorus), metals, and radium. Metal concentrations were determined using the atomic absorption spectrophotometer following an acid digestion. Tailings samples were analyzed for nitrogen with a specific ion electrode following acid digestion. Phosphorus analysis was determined by acid digestion followed by colorimetry with a spectrophotometer. Radium analyses were conducted using alpha spectroscopy.

Survival, growth, and biomass measurements. Initial survival was determined by looking for evidence of new growth from the bags or transplants. In June 1996, the number of bags or transplants with developing shoots (mostly leaves) was then counted at each location. The survival percentage was determined by the ratio of transplants showing new growth to the number of plants or bags planted. At mid-August (the time of maximum biomass production for the transplants), survival and leaf or stem count measurements were repeated. Corresponding leaf or culm dry weights were also determined for each species at the transplant locations and at the source sites by removing biomass from a small number of plants ($n = 3$–4) and drying at 80%C. The dried material was subsequently used for elemental analysis.

Results

Plants were obtained from soils and water with pH values generally greater than 6. This was similar to the water pH in Cell 14 and the surface pH of the tailings. There were minor changes in the plants in copper, nickel, iron, and manganese concentrations after one year. There was a slight increase in radium concentration, which was far less than amounts found in the tailings. The presence of phosphorus and nitrogen in the added bonemeal was reflected in the increase of these elements in the transplants. Vegetation samples taken from the islands that were established three years ago gave similar elemental concentrations compared with the more recent transplants. Soil at the source sites was low (below 10 percent) in organic matter with nitrogen amounts that reflect this amount of organic material. The low organic content of the tailings corresponded with the low nitrogen amounts. The tailings had a slight elevation in radium and other elements were similar at the tailings and source sites.

Initial results show the transplant technique of burlap containment bags to be effective in transporting source site organic matter and the accompanying rhizomes of several species to the transplant site. Observations showed that species not specifically requiring eutrophic water conditions for growth survived and grew into plants of similar size and vigour to those of the site from which they were harvested. Survival rates as high as 80 percent were recorded for fragrant water lily, 80 percent for pickerel weed, 30 percent for watershield, and 100 percent for hardstem bulrush (Figure 1). Bladderwort and pondweed transplants showed no survival, even when planted within an enclosure. There was little difference between the survey results obtained in June and those from August 1996 (Figure 1).

Figure 1. Survival rate (+ standard error) of species introduced into flooded tailings

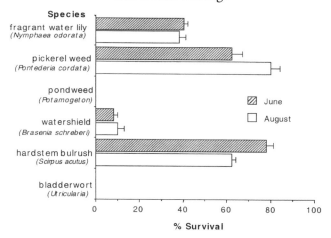

Performance was assessed by counting the number of leaves produced, or stems (clumps) in the case of bulrush. There was little difference in performance between plants in the donor sites and those in the tailing sites (Figure 2). However, with the exception of bulrush, biomass production was significantly less (Figure 3).

Figure 2. Leaf production (+ standard error) for species

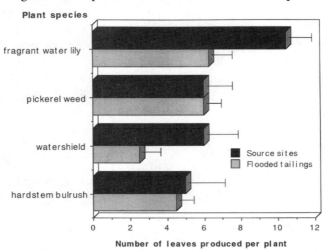

Figure 3. Mean biomass (+ standard error) produced by species

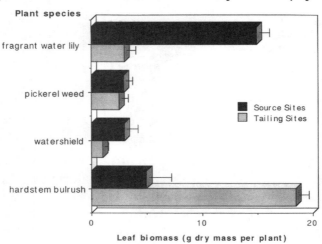

Most of the species used in creation of the vegetation islands grew, and over three years the size of the islands increased. Common reed produced numerous rhizomes that increased the diameter of the patch by 400 percent (Figure 4). Both wool rush and beaked sedge grew vigorously and formed denuded patches. A 2.5-centimetre layer of black organic detritus carpet developed on the tailings under the reeds.

Figure 4. Change in area of vegetation "islands" from 1993 to 1996

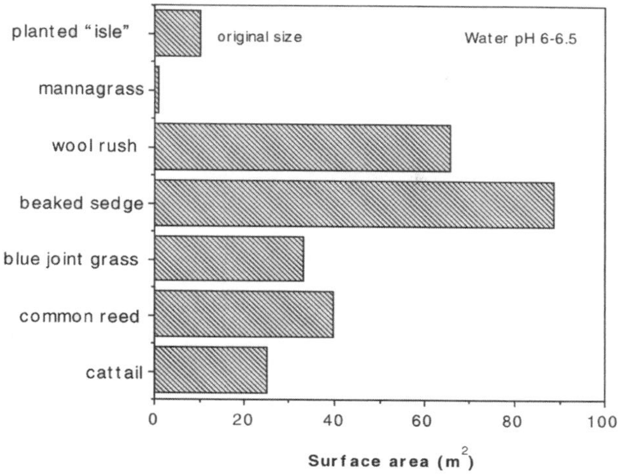

Discussion

One of the key features of any aquatic or wetland system is the number of species that are found. Each species has its special ecological requirements (niche) such as shoreline or shallow or deep water, so it is essential to transplant species into the correct microhabitat. It is also vital to ensure that in creating new wetland habitat, existing wetlands are not degraded. We ensured that a maximum of 10 percent of any population was removed from a site. In most cases, less than one percent was removed. Genetical considerations and local adaptation to climate dictate that plants from the same provenance should be used. In this investigation, species selection was based on the most widespread and abundant within a 30-kilometre radius from the mining operations.

Hardstem bulrush, pickerel weed and fragrant water lily gave the best survival rates (63 percent, 80 percent, and 38 percent respectively). There was no survival in Cell 15. With the transplanting season almost over, it became necessary to introduce plant material into the cell not long after it was flooded and treated with limestone. The high pH and turbidity appeared to have killed many of the plants, as they could not be relocated the following growing season.

Although the survey results were similar for July and August there was an increase in the number of pickerel weed observed (probably a reflection of the longer growing season). However, some of the bulrush died between June and August. These species possess rhizomes and

Vegetation island in Cell 14 near Dam K1, summer 1995.

Peter Beckett

aerenchyma (specialized cells for air transport) which may have given these species an advantage in transplanting and adapting to the flooded tailings environment. There was no survival of bladderwort, mostly because it was transplanted in deeper water than is normally found in the wild. Another significant factor is that bladderwort is also considered to be highly sensitive to pH and water-quality changes. Pondweed, despite having no survival of transplants, is becoming abundant in the WMA. It may have been partially spread through the formation of overwintering vegetative propagules from the introduced material, from seeds introduced in the soil used in the burlap bags, or from production of seeds by the introduced plants as a strategy to overcome adverse conditions.

Water lily and water shield both have a similar morphology and both produced about one-half to two-thirds the number of floating leaves compared to the plants at the source locations. The upright-growing pickerel weed and bulrush produced the same number. Some of the floating leaves may have been lost by wave action in the tailings pond, or some of the potential energy for shoot growth was perhaps consumed by new root production following transplanting. This diversion of energy resources, or transplant shock, could account for the smaller production of biomass. The use of stored starch and other carbohydrates for root growth during the early part of the year may have left few resources for the leaves.

It would seem that plants do better when transplanted with some organic matter. The small introduced island with plants and organic soils has led to a rapid increase of surface area of the majority of the species.

Peter Beckett stands in the vegetation island in Cell 14 near Dam K1, summer 1997. Since 1995, the vegetation has spread and there is a build-up of organic matter.

Peter Beckett

Several millimetres of new organic deposits have also built up. An active organic layer should start to play a role in decreasing oxygen passage to the underlying tailings.

Conclusion

Mining companies and society seek economical ways to reclaim landscapes that have suffered an impact from mining. New water bodies offer the potential to re-establish wetlands and recover some of the long-term economic and environmental costs. Successful transplantation of wetland plants into flooded tailings aids the rapid development of an active organic layer. This layer assists in the biological uptake of oxygen and the slowing of oxygen diffusion into the submerged tailings, with a subsequent decrease in acid generation. Longer-term assessment is required to ensure that contaminant uptake into plants and other components of the food web is not detrimental. Initial results showed little bioaccumulation of potential contaminants. Planned reclamation of flooded tailings into wetlands adds to the increasing knowledge, prospects and strategies for wetland restoration in temperate areas (Wheeler et al. 1995).

Note
[1] We thank NODA/Ontario Minerals and Rio Algom Limited for project funding and other assistance. Numerous summer assistants were employed through Ontario Ministry of Northern Development and Mines Youth

Corps grants. Tjoe-Pa Lim of CANMET (Elliot Lake) is thanked for technical advice. From the Elliot Lake Research Field Station, Doo- Hong Kim, Chief Chemist, performed the chemical analyses, and Deborah Berthelot provided administrative advice.

References

Hedin, R. (1989). "Treatment of coal mine drainage with constructed wetlands," in *Wetlands Ecology and Conservation: Emphasis in Pennsylvania*, ed. S. K. Majumdar, R. P. Brooks, F. J. Brenner and R. W. Tiner Jr. Philadelphia: The Pennsylvania Academy of Science, 349–62.

Hutchinson, G.E., (1975). *A Treatise on Limnology (Volume 3)*. New York: Wiley.

Michelutti, B. and M. Wiseman. (1995). "Engineered wetlands as a tailings rehabilitation strategy," in *Restoration and Recovery of an Industrial Region*, ed. John Gunn. New York: Springer-Verlag, 135–41.

Mitch, W.J. and J.K. Gosselink. (1993). *Wetlands,* 2nd edition. New York: Van Nostrand Reinhold.

Rio Algom Limited. (1995). *Summary of the Environmental Impact Statement With Respect to Rio Algom's Application to the AECB to License the Decommissioning of the Quirke and Panel Waste Management Areas.*

Sculthorpe, C.D. (1967). *The Biology of Aquatic Vascular Plants.* London: Edward Arnold.

St-Germain P., H. Larratt, and R. Prairie. (1997). "Field studies of biologically supported water covers at two Noranda tailings ponds," in *Proceedings of the 4th International Conference on Arid Rock Drainage*, Vancouver, June 1997.

St-Germain, P. and N. Kuyucak. (1997, in press). "Biologically supported water covers — a laboratory assessment," *Mineral Processing and Extractive Metallurgy Review*. Special Issue on the 3rd International Conference on Minerals Bioprocessing, Biorecovery/Bioremediation in Mining, 25–30 August 1996, Big Sky, Montana.

Wheeler, B.D, S.C. Shaw, W.J. Fojt, and R.A. Robertson. (1995). *Restoration of Temperate Wetlands.*Chichester, UK: Wiley.

Chapter 23
Reclamation Activities at the Pronto Copper Tailings Near Elliot Lake

Bryan Tisch, Peter Beckett, Gerard Courtin, and Roger Payne

The principal environmental concerns associated with the decommissioning of the Elliot Lake uranium mine tailings are acid generation, release of waterborne radioactive elements into downstream watersheds, and release of airborne radiation, while secondary concerns surround radiological effects (Rio Algom Limited 1995). However, it is acid-generating mine waste that generally represents the single most important aspect of mine decommissioning and is not specific to uranium mining (Rio Algom Limited 1995).

Tailings, which are the finely ground material remaining after extraction of the ore, are formed as a result of grinding the host rock to a consistency of sand (to expose desired minerals), followed by flotation (in metal mines) or acid leaching (in uranium mines).

The Elliot Lake tailings, along with those from most base-metal mines, contain various metal sulphides. When oxidized in the presence of water and oxygen, metal sulphides such as iron sulphide (pyrite) react (essentially rust) to produce drainage that is characteristically acidic and high in sulphate and dissolved metals, especially iron (Doyle and Mirza 1990, Skousen 1995). With tailings derived from uranium mining, the acidic drainage may also contain radionuclides such as uranium, thorium, lead, and polonium, which are soluble under acid conditions. Radium is of potential concern even if acid production is prevented in uranium tailings, as it is soluble even at neutral pH. Uranium tailings may also be sources of radioactive material such as radon gas, gamma radiation, and blowing dust, all of which may be eliminated through the application of a suitable cover (Rio Algom 1995).

305

Elliot Lake uranium deposits are classified as low grade, containing 0.1 percent or less uranium, and since approximately 95 percent of the uranium was removed through milling, uranium is generally present in low levels in the tailings (Rio Algom Limited 1995). Typically, Elliot Lake tailings are acid-generating, with an iron sulphide (pyrite) content of 5 percent (Golder Associates and SENES 1989). The oxidation of metal sulphides generally leads to two main environmental concerns: the creation of an environment that inhibits plant growth and the production of acid mine drainage (AMD). As tailings oxidize, a portion of the dissolved materials may remain on site, where they become part of the ion balance of the "soil" water and possibly affect plant establishment and growth (Gentry, Willis, and Halverson 1992), while the remainder may exert an effect on surrounding areas through addition to groundwater and surface runoff.

While most commonly associated with mine tailings and waste rock, AMD is also formed as a consequence of any activity that exposes sulphidic material, such as highway construction and other deep excavations (Skousen 1995). Acidic drainage waters generally represent a potential risk to the environment because low pH conditions are detrimental to aquatic life, because metals at high concentrations may be toxic to both aquatic and terrestrial life forms utilizing a contaminated source of drinking water, and because precipitates that form during neutralization of the leachate may adversely affect vegetation (Rio Algom Limited 1995).

Mine tailings are complex and offer barriers to revegetation that are not clearly understood. As a result, the Environmental Rehabilitation Research Group at the Elliot Lake Research Field Station was retained to identify problems and offer possible solutions for completing the revegetation of the Pronto Copper tailings. Specifically, this project was undertaken to determine both the past and present conditions on the tailings and to identify methods and materials of potential use in stabilizing and establishing a permanent vegetation cover on the tailings.

The Pronto Waste Management Area (WMA)

The Pronto WMA is located near Spragge, Ontario (see maps, p.4 and p. 262). The Pronto Mine was the first uranium mine to be opened in the Elliot Lake area, operating from 1955 to 1960. The property was then acquired by Rio Algom Limited, who modified the mill to process copper ore from nearby Pater Mine until 1970.

The eastern portion of the WMA, representing an area of approximately 80 hectares, is composed of uranium tailings covered by approximately 2 to 3 metres of copper tailings. This area can be further subdivided into areas of coarse copper tailings (near the original discharge points) and fine copper tailings (increasing with distance from the original discharge points). The western portion of the WMA is composed solely of uranium tailings. The present study is concerned with establishing vegetation on the eastern copper tailings only.

Attempts at establishing vegetation on the Pronto copper tailings during the late 1970s and early 1980s have included re-grading of the surface to enhance surface drainage and the application of lime (several applications), fertilizer (several applications), straw mulch, and seed. These attempts have been only partially successful, and until recently, no further measures had been undertaken. Vegetation on the coarse-grained copper tailings responded well to previous reclamation efforts, with 50 to 90 percent coverage. However, in some areas of the coarse tailings the vegetation is showing signs of stress, while in other areas distinct barren areas have developed. Vegetation on the fine-grained tailings areas remains limited to scattered islands and around the perimeter. Several factors were identified as contributing to the lack of vegetation, including acid-generation and seepage, compaction, erosion, high levels of soluble salts, poor nutritional status, toxic metals, and a lack of organic matter.

Site Assessment

Vegetation on the coarse-textured tailings of the Pronto Waste Management Area, July 1996. Mostly birdsfoot trefoil and vetch.

Bryan Tisch

An assessment of the existing site conditions was carried out by sampling the tailings along a precisely mapped grid. Tailings samples were obtained from the top 10 centimetres and from a depth of 20 to 35 centimetres.

Measurements included pH, conductivity, moisture content, and water-soluble metals. In addition, other parameters such as depth of oxidation, root penetration (if present), and litter layer (if present) were measured. Site characteristics were mapped using Arc/Info, ARCVIEW, and SPANS software. Vegetation cover for several different years was also assessed through aerial photographs, and mapped as above.

Historical pH data were obtained from Rio Algom Limited for the year 1979. This data showed a very uniform tailings surface pH, between 2.0 and 4.0, indicating that a significant degree of oxidation had already occurred. In 1995, the surface pH of the coarse copper tailings was generally between 6 and 8, corresponding to areas that have remained vegetated. The increased pH resulted from several limestone applications during the 1970s and early 1980s and also from downward leaching of acidic porewater. The bulk of the non-vegetated fine copper tailings generally had a pH of 4 or lower, indicating that the near-surface tailings in this area were still generating acid.

The present study found that the coarse tailings were typically oxidized to depths of at least 60 centimetres, and in fact Lakefield Research (1995), through core sampling, found that oxidation extended as deep as 1 metre. In the fine tailings area, oxidation was generally not noticeable below a depth of 30 centimetres. The coarse copper tailings appear to be completely oxidized, as only trace to minor amounts of pyrite were detected, even at depths of 4 metres (Lakefield Research 1995). This indicates that the near-surface coarse tailings — which comprise the majority of the grass rooting zone — are no longer generating acid and are therefore much more amenable to sustaining vegetation. However, much of the acid that has been generated in this area over the past 20 to 25 years has drained down into the tailings, where it eventually resurfaces as acid mine drainage. This has been confirmed by Lakefield Research (1995), who found through core sampling that the porewater pH in the coarse tailings was below 4, even deep within the tailings. In contrast, porewater pH within the fine tailings was above 7.5, even at depth. This suggests that the coarse tailings are responsible for the production of much of the contaminated seepage reporting to the effluent treatment plant. The small particle size (silt size) of the fine copper tailings results in a low hydraulic conductivity, which, combined with a shallow water table and high capillary fringe (Lakefield Research 1995), suggests that very little infiltration occurs, so that most of the precipitation in this area leaves the site as surface runoff.

Both surface and sub-surface moisture were generally lower in the coarse copper tailings areas, at around 15 to 20 percent moisture, compared to the fine copper tailings area, which generally contained approximately 20 to 30 percent moisture. The level of the water table was found to be at 2 metres in the coarse tailings, and between 1.2 and 1.8 metres in the fine tailings (Lakefield Research 1995). It is the shallow water table and high capillary fringe of the fine tailings that has prevented oxidation from occurring at depth over the last 20 to 25 years. The water table in the fine tailings area is subject to fluctuation, however, and it is during times when the water table lowers (during summer dry spells) that oxidation may occur to greater depths. When this occurs, the resulting acid- and metal-contaminated porewater is brought to the surface through surface evaporation as the water table is restored to its usual depth (during fall rain).

Thus, surface applications of acid neutralizers such as limestone, while initially increasing the tailings pH to a level adequate for plant growth, may be overcome in the long term by the continuous production of acidic porewater, unless limestone is repeatedly applied. It follows then, that vegetation established during periods when the pH remains high may be subsequently killed off if the pH declines.

While oxidation in the fine tailings area is decreased by the high moisture content, higher moisture and low pH result in an increase in the quantity of dissolved materials in the porewater. This was reflected in the measurement of electrical conductivity, which indicated lower levels of dissolved ions in the coarse tailings area as compared to the fine tailings area. The coarse tailings area generally showed conductivities in the 100 to 1000 S/cm^2 range compared to values of 1000 to 4000 S/cm^2 generally encountered in the fine tailings area. Values reach as high as 8000 S/cm^2 in the wetter regions of the fine tailings. Higher electrical conductivities are indicative of increased metal concentration, which can have a variety of detrimental effects on vegetation, including osmotic effects and metal toxicity.

While a complete suite of water-soluble metals was analyzed for the Pronto tailings, only aluminum and copper were mapped to show the general trends. Both these metals inhibit vegetation growth as concentrations increase, usually exerting their influence on root development. The analyses indicated that, as expected, levels for both these metals were higher in the fine tailings area than in the coarse tailings. This provides further evidence that the fine tailings are still reactive, and that it is this reactivity that is the main cause of difficulty in establishing vegetation.

Vegetation cover was mapped using air photographs from the years 1977, 1989, and 1995. From this data, the change in vegetation cover

over the various time intervals was also mapped. These data confirmed that vegetation cover on the coarse copper tailings has remained quite good since the revegetation measures undertaken in the late 1970s and early 1980s, and that vegetation on the fine copper tailings has remained sparse at best. While these maps merely indicate the presence or absence of vegetation and provide no indication of the degree of coverage present, they do provide good background data for assessing the effectiveness of future rehabilitation measures.

Treatment Options

Rio Algom has indicated that long-term plans for the Pronto WMA include collection and treatment of drainage/seepage. For this reason, rehabilitation measures being tested by the Elliot Lake Research Field Station do not specifically include provisions aimed at eliminating further oxidation of exposed tailings, but focus instead on establishing a sustainable vegetation cover. Four main treatment scenarios have been identified for the establishment of vegetation.

First, they could "do nothing," that is, leave the tailings undisturbed, in the hope that vegetation will eventually colonize naturally. But because colonization has been very slow over the 15 or so years since limestone and fertilizer were last applied, this option has essentially been dismissed from further consideration.

Second, a neutralizer, fertilizer, and seed could be incorporated. A neutralizing material and fertilizer would be worked directly into the tailings, with the hope of modifying the tailings sufficiently that seeded species will thrive and natural invasion by local plant species will be encouraged. This method is potentially the most cost-effective and simple from an operational standpoint.

The third option is to apply a soil cover. A material is placed on top of the tailings, with limestone and fertilizer added as required, and seeded. The thickness of the cover depends on its expected function, because a relatively thin cover may be all that is required for vegetation establishment, whereas a much thicker cover is needed to control oxidation of the underlying tailings. This is a more expensive and complicated process than the second option, as attention must be given to maintaining existing slopes and drainage pathways. Covers applied directly onto tailings are also prone to contamination from the underlying tailings.

The final possibility is the application of a soil cover/capillary break. This involves placing a layer of coarser material between the existing tailings and the cover, in order to prevent the upward migration (through capillary action) of acid- and metal-contaminated porewater originating from the underlying tailings. This is the most expensive and complicated of the options, as it requires a greater volume of material and careful placement of the layers. As with the third option, the thickness of the layers depends on the intended function of the cover.

In general, it may be years before the application of a cover to oxidized tailings has a noticeable impact on seepage quality, because of the oxidation products already present in the tailings mass. Water moves through tailings at a very slow rate, such that acidic and metal-contaminated water that is now near the surface of the tailings may not appear as seepage for 10 to 20 years or more. Hence the effect of current surface practices may not be observed for an equally long period of time. Also, once oxidation has occurred and large quantities of ferric iron have been generated, the iron sulphides may continue to be oxidized by ferric iron in the absence of oxygen, even after a cover has been applied.

Use of Waste Materials

The use of waste materials as a cover for the tailings not only eliminates or decreases the need for a storage site of their own, but eliminates the need for large volumes of imported borrow materials such as sand or gravel. This is only economical if the source of the waste material is located fairly close to the minesite. Many waste materials can be obtained free of charge, but transportation costs represent a serious potential obstacle, with distances generally limited to 50 to 100 kilometres (SENES 1993).

As a result of the SENES (1993) report, Ontario Ministry of Environment information, and telephone inquiries, waste materials from two locations were identified as the most promising candidates for use in the reclamation of the Pronto tailings: E.B. Eddy Forest Products Limited, a bleached kraft pulp and paper mill in Espanola, and Algoma Steel Limited in Sault Ste. Marie, Ontario. The materials and their potential benefits are indicated in Table 1.

Table 1. Identification of waste materials and their potential benefits
for reclamation of the Pronto tailings

Source/Material	Potential Benefits
E.B. Eddy Forest Products Limited	
Settling basin sludge	Neutralizer/growth medium
Composting bark	Growth medium/oxygen consumer
Spent lime (lime mud)	Neutralizer
Algoma Steel Limited	
Granulated blast furnace slag	Neutral/growth medium/capillary break

Settling basin sludge is classified as a non-hazardous solids waste. The sludge is produced as a result of primary treatment of the mill effluent. Mill effluent containing fibre, lime mud, and boiler ash enters a settling basin, where wood fibre, unreacted lime mud, and boiler ash settle out (E.B. Eddy 1987). The sludge is removed on a yearly basis and landfilled at E.B. Eddy in Espanola. The high calcium carbonate content, along with the boiler ash, provides the sludge with a pH of approximately 7.3 and neutralizing potential half that of limestone. The high organic matter content (about 19 percent, whole sludge sample) is expected to help control the release of both phytotoxic metals and nutrient ions from the tailings, thereby decreasing salinity effects normally associated with oxidizing tailings. In addition to these qualities, the sludge has a nitrogen content of approximately 3.4 percent and a low carbon/nitrogen ratio (5.8:1), which suggests that this material might be a potentially excellent growth substrate. The sludge contains trace levels of dioxin, which are well below government limits.

The composting bark consists of wood wastes generated during processing of the logs, and includes bark, wood scraps, and soil. This material was being considered for use as a growth medium and/or oxygen-consuming component of a cover system.

Spent lime consists of finely divided calcium carbonate ($CaCO_3$), and it was thought that this material might offer an alternative to agricultural grade limestone. However, because of the very small particle size, it was anticipated that spent lime might be a difficult material to spread, but that in the short term it might be more effective than limestone at generating alkalinity.

Blast furnace slag is produced as a byproduct of the steelmaking process. Chemical analysis indicated that silicon dioxide, calcium oxide, and magnesium oxide account for 90 percent of the chemical composition of the slag. It has a pH slightly greater than 10, and was chosen for its potential use as an acid-neutralizing capillary break.

Laboratory Studies

Pot trial in March 1996. Redtop growth in settling basin sludge and loam applied as covers over Pronto tailings, showing response to limestone and fertilizer.

Bryan Tisch

Laboratory growth studies conducted at the Elliot Lake Research Field Station revealed that grass growth in settling basin sludge was far superior to that in bark compost, slag, and a locally obtained loam (used as a control growth medium). In addition, lime and fertilizer were not required for growth in the sludge, but were absolutely necessary to achieve growth in all of the other materials.

Growth studies also revealed, surprisingly, that standard agricultural practices of adding lime and fertilizer directly to the fine copper tailings produced little or no growth, but that the incorporation of settling basin sludge or granulated slag did establish vegetation. Further, laboratory column weathering tests revealed that certain size fractions of blast furnace slag could be used in place of gravel as a capillary break. These weathering tests also showed that the granulated form of blast furnace slag, while not effective as a capillary break, acted as a chemical "filter." Conductivity measurements indicated that the high pH (approximately 10.5) conditions within the granulated slag seemed to cause the precipitation of metals dissolved in the porewater, as the porewater moved from the underlying tailings through the granulated slag. This effect resulted in the transfer of relatively uncontaminated water to the cover, an effect not observed with a similar-size fraction of gravel.

While this appears very promising, the filter effect would need to be investigated further. Also, concerns over the potential leaching of metals from the slag — especially under reducing (anaerobic) conditions and combined with transportation costs — has greatly decreased the possibility of utilizing blast furnace slag specifically at the Pronto site.

Following the initial testing of the materials, E.B. Eddy Forest Products Limited announced that the composted bark would no longer be available in quantity, as they may now be utilizing this material for energy production. Thus, this material was dropped from further study. In addition, it was felt that spent lime was not going to be a particularly useful material at the Pronto site because of its relatively limited availability and handling difficulties caused by its very small particle size. The settling basin sludge and granulated slag were therefore deemed the materials most worthy of further study.

Field Plots

Construction of capillary break sludge plot on fine tailings of Pronto Waste Management Area, October 1996.

Bryan Tisch

As a result of the laboratory experiments, small-scale (2 metres by 2 metres) field plots were constructed in triplicate during the fall of 1995 using gravel and loam to test for the necessity of a capillary break. Plots were constructed both with and without gravel capillary breaks under the loam covers, then limed and fertilized, and seeded with a grass/legume mixture. Thus far, vegetation growth on the loam plots has been rather poor regardless of the presence of a capillary break, and illustrates the rather poor nutritional status of the loam that was used. However, electrical conductivity measurements have indicated that metal-contaminated porewater from the tailings is moving into the loam cover in the absence of a capillary barrier. This effect is not occurring when the capillary barrier is present.

Plots (3 metres by 3 metres) on fine tailings of Pronto Waste Management Area, June 1997 (seeded early July 1996). From left to right, sludge directly on tailings, sludge with capillary barrier gravel, and gravel.

Bryan Tisch

In the spring of 1996, the Ontario Ministry of Environment granted approval for the transport of small volumes of settling basin sludge and granulated slag to the Pronto WMA. Additional small-scale field plots were constructed in triplicate, using granulated slag as the capillary barrier and settling basin sludge as the cover (growth medium). Plots were constructed both with the sludge applied directly to the tailings, and also with a slag capillary break between the tailings and the sludge. Vegetation growth in the sludge during the first summer has been excellent, regardless of the presence of the capillary break. However, no data are currently available regarding water movement into the covers.

In the fall of 1996, Ontario Ministry of Environment approval was obtained for the transport of a larger volume of settling basin sludge to the Pronto WMA. Three quarter-acre, semi-operational plots were established on the fine copper tailings area. One was treated with the incorporation of a sludge/sand mixture directly into the tailings, the second with the application of a thin cover of a sludge/sand mixture on top of the tailings, and the third with the application of a gravel capillary barrier between the tailings and a thin cover of a sludge/sand mixture. All three plots were fertilized and seeded with a grass/legume mixture. These plots were designed not only to determine potential problems on an operational level, but also to test the ability of the plots to support vegetation. Equipment and method of placement of the capillary break will be critical factors on an operational level, especially if a cover is to be applied on a large scale. Repeated passes by heavy equipment during placement of the gravel capillary break resulted in liquefaction of the fine-grained copper tailings, causing much of the capillary break to sink into the tailings. Alternate methods of placement need to be evaluated should further trials be undertaken.

First-year results indicate better vegetation cover (approximately 45 percent) when sludge was applied over the tailings with or without a capillary break, compared with 5 percent cover when the sludge was incorporated. A vegetation cover of 45 percent is considered satisfactory first-year growth in many reclamation projects on tailings. Better vegetation performance may be realized with the incorporation of sludge if a higher application rate is used. Typically, it takes several years of assessment to reach a final decision on the best method.

Approval is currently being sought from government regulatory agencies for the large-scale use of settling basin sludge in the entire fine tailings area. Should approval be granted, it is expected that this would be undertaken during July and August, when tailings are driest, with seeding occurring in late August or early September. It is expected that the addition of the settling basin sludge will have no detrimental impact on water quality emanating from the WMA. Should vegetation establishment not be successful, the surface of the tailings should, at the very least, have a neutral pH. This change in pH results in decreased metal solubility and therefore lower metal amounts in drainage water leaving the site.

Summary

The Pronto tailings are very complex, and represent two very different sets of conditions within the same site. An assessment was undertaken to establish the present chemical condition of the tailings and showed that over a period of approximately 16 years, the area of coarse copper tailings had oxidized to depths of around 1 metre, while the area of fine copper tailings had oxidized only to a depth of around 30 centimetres. Because of the differences in the rate of oxidation between the coarse and fine tailings, chemical conditions in the two areas are vastly different and have resulted in the establishment of a good vegetation cover on the coarse tailings and a sparse vegetation cover on the fine tailings. Lack of vegetation in the fine tailings has been attributed to the continuing reactive nature of these tailings with associated high levels of soluble salts (metals). The tailings in this area have not responded to standard reclamation practices such as the addition of lime and fertilizer, but have responded to applications of settling basin sludge and granulated slag.

Semi-operational field plots have been constructed on the tailings to determine the best method of revegetating the fine tailings, both from the standpoint of vegetation establishment and on an operational level.

References

Doyle, F.M. and A.B. Mirza. (1990). "Understanding the mechanisms and kinetics of acid and heavy metals release from pyritic wastes," in *Proceedings of the Western Regional Symposium on Mining and Mineral Processing Wastes,* Berkeley, CA, 43–51.

E.B. Eddy Forest Products Limited. (1987). *The Espanola Mill Story.* Espanola: E.B. Eddy Forest Products Limited.

Gentry, C.E., R.B. Willis, and H.G. Halverson. (1992). "Chemical and pedogenetic effects of simulated precipitation on strip mine spoil," in *Proceedings, Ninth Annual National Meeting of the American Society for Surface Mining and Reclamation,* Duluth, MN, June 1992, 61–67.

Golder Associates Limited and SENES Consultants Limited. (1989). *Phase 2 Status Report on the Evaluation of Decommissioning Alternatives, Quirke and Panel Tailings Impoundments,* prepared for Rio Algom Limited.

Lakefield Research. (1995). *Report on Chemical Analyses of Pronto WMA,* prepared for Rio Algom Limited, Elliot Lake.

Rio Algom Limited. (1995). *Summary of the Environmental Impact Statement With Respect to Rio Algom's Application to the AECB to License the Decommissioning of the Quirke and Panel Waste Management Areas.*

SENES Consultants Limited. (1993). *Evaluation of alternate dry covers for the prevention of acid mine drainage from tailings,* Draft Final Report, prepared for the MEND program and CANMET.

Skousen, Jeff. (1995). "Acid mine drainage," in *Acid Mine Drainage — Control and Treatment* compiled by J.G. Skousen and P.F. Ziemkiewicz. Morgantown, WV: West Virginia University and the National Mine Land Reclamation Center, 9–12.

Chapter 24
Respect and Responsibility: Community-Based Options for Perpetual Care in the Serpent River Watershed
Sharon Gow

Little White River on the Deer Trail north of Elliot Lake.
City of Elliot Lake

I want to touch upon a number of issues that can contribute to the successful transition of the Elliot Lake area from a resource-based, single-industry community into a diverse and healthy place in which to live and work. The challenge, as I see it, is to find ways to honour and respect the past while developing a realistic and respectful understanding of the future, to best serve the needs of present and future generations. "How can we foster opportunities where mutualism, co-operation, or reciprocity can take root so that insight into common ground will be discovered?" (Karlberg 1997).

I want to provide testimony about alternatives to the status quo model for public involvement and planning that we in Elliot Lake are accustomed to using in our local government structure as well as in our vocational and volunteer experiences. This same "stakeholder" model is suggested in *Decommissioning of Uranium Mine Tailings Management Areas in the Elliot Lake Area* (Canadian Environmental Assessment Agency [CEAA] 1996), which is the final report of the Environmental Assessment Panel that reviewed for Environment Canada the Elliot Lake decommissioning proposals for four of the five licensed uranium mines in the Elliot Lake area.

Background

In the fall of 1993, I became directly involved in the Ad Hoc Environmental Monitoring Committee of the Elliot Lake Women's Group that decided to submit an application for participant funding so that we could participate in the Federal Environmental Review Process into Decommissioning Proposals. The review process was set up to consider. We held community meetings and information workshops on the proposed plans to help inform the public, and we also conducted a questionnaire to gauge existing levels of understanding about the issues and to gather together a list of community concerns and solutions. In the process we met many men and women, both "newcomers" and "old-timers," from around the region. At the time, there was still one mine operating in the community, but quite a few people, women especially, were expressing relief that the mining era was drawing to a close. Similarly, many appeared "freer" to criticize the mining operations.

Our findings were incorporated into a report that we presented and submitted to the Environmental Assessment Panel during "scoping sessions" in early December 1993. We reported on the major findings from the 450 surveys that had been completed and analyzed, and presented our review of the environmental impact statements provided by each of the proponents. We also made a number of recommendations to the panel concerning the importance of continuing to involve the public in the ongoing care and maintenance requirements of the waste management areas. We also suggested ways of doing this. A familiar comment we encountered in the surveys was: "We benefited from the mines opening up, so we'll assume some of the responsibility for the cleanup."

During the actual hearings (December 1995 to January 1996), I made my submission to the panel as a concerned citizen and echoed many of the women's group's findings. On behalf of Northwatch, a coalition of environmental groups and citizens from around northeastern Ontario, I helped to coordinate local events and presentations to the panel.

Because of my participation in the entire environmental assessment process from December 1993 through to January 1996, I am able to detail some of the information presented to the panel and comment on their findings, especially as these relate to ways in which public participation can be encouraged.

The Experience

The Elliot Lake Women's Group proposed a community-driven initiative to address the waste sites and protect the Serpent River Watershed. We identified a need in our community for education about the waste sites and an interest in exploring options for containing uranium tailings as well as for their disposal. We suggested establishing a community-based information centre that would contribute to policy development and research on community re-development, environmental restoration, and emergency planning.

During a workshop at the local women's drop-in centre, many women expressed an interest in working towards reducing the risk of any adverse impact on the Serpent River Watershed, including all downstream communities. They realized that the people of Elliot Lake will be held accountable for a long time to come for whatever choices are made in the decommissioning stage. Many people explained that the only way they would feel confident that an acceptable, safe decommissioning plan would be implemented was by way of a transparent public process that would include the timely provision of "plain language" information and opportunity for *meaningful* involvement in every aspect of decision-making.

This demand for democratic participation has been encountered by others involved in environmental protection work, and it appears to be increasing. In fact, it is rooted in our understanding of democracy: "Access to information and participation in decision making touch upon key democratic rights. The credibility of the system of environmental protection and its consequent ability to inspire respect and commitment are fundamentally affected by the transparency and fairness of the decisions made by that system" (Burrell 1996, 54).

Community involvement in whatever processes are adopted is critical. We know that sooner or later responsibility for these sites will rest with us — both as the community left in charge and as the taxpayers most likely to have to cover some or all costs. The more that ordinary citizens become involved, the better informed the general population will be. We need to be able to explain what's going on about the tailings to *anyone* who asks! We need to have confidence, not just hope, that everything that can be done to ensure a secure and healthy future is being done, and that we are sharing our knowledge with the outside world in an open manner.

We already know a great deal about the tailings, both in content and amount. Some of us know better than others precisely how toxic the contents are or could become, and we realize that there is an obligation to ensure that the monitoring and maintenance requirements at these impoundments is performed with diligence for a very, very long time. This is why respect and responsibility must be factored into the stewardship of the watershed in the future.

The Panel's Report

Some of the details contained in the panel's final report (CEAA 1996) are not well known in our community or in the north. There was scant mention of the report's existence in the local media at the time it was released. It took Rio Algom Limited over four months to comment publicly to the local community through their occasional newsletter *Rio Report ... dialogue on decommissioning* (November 1996). A total of four paragraphs appeared under the heading "FEARO final report." The name FEARO appears here because the three-member panel was originally established by Environment Canada through its Federal Environmental Assessment Review Office (FEARO). When the Canadian Environmental Assessment Act was implemented in January 1995, the new Canadian Environmental Assessment Agency (CEAA) replaced FEARO.

The choice of language and the overall tone and brevity of the panel's report itself are positive, because they make the report accessible. Unfortunately, the recommendations are non-binding. But I hope that the citizens of Elliot Lake will be able to compel the proponents to consider seriously the content of this report and to provide the necessary funds to implement the recommendations. This seems unlikely because of the unenforceable nature of the report, and because we have heard so little in the way of reaction from either the proponents or the government. I guess this is also why we find ourselves waiting — waiting for a reaction from Ottawa, waiting for a reaction from mayor and council. But perhaps we should be taking a more proactive stance, especially with the Atomic Energy Control Board (AECB), and start asking some questions: What is the community's strategy at this point?

Can ordinary citizens participate in its development?

The biggest surprise for me in the report, and likely for others, is the recognition that "the tailings of the Elliot Lake uranium mines present a perpetual environmental hazard" (CEAA 1996, 1). This was a very significant and totally unexpected victory for the environment. Throughout the scoping and hearing process, I and others laboured under AECB regulation R-104 (AECB 1987), which required that the companies design "a walk-away solution." By acknowledging the perpetual hazards of the tailings, the panel was able to establish that "no walk-away arrangement is in fact possible for tailings having these characteristics" (CEAA 1996, 10). From this point of departure, they proceeded to set out a number of recommendations:

> that effective containment is established for the tailings; that an extensive monitoring, maintenance and research program is developed to ensure proper operation and safety *in perpetuity*; and that an appropriate management regime is established that includes adequate financial support for the care and maintenance programs, with significant involvement of the local community (italics added). (CEAA 1996, 1)

The report also recommends that "curiosity-driven research be supported as a central and critical element of the long-term monitoring approach, to provide early insights into actual behaviour," that would be supported by "the creation of a permanent endowment fund to support research associated with the Elliot Lake mine waste facilities" (CEAA 1996, 1). Another recommendation is "that there should be hard financial assurances made by the proponents" in order to ensure "that the contain-and-manage programs at each site will be effectively maintained in perpetuity" (CEAA 1996, 2). All of these recommendations affect the proposed timing for the decommissioning process itself — specifically the granting of various licences. Therefore the panel also recommends that "there be a number of conditions that should be incorporated into the licensing process" itself (CEAA 1996, 1). For instance, on the subject of funding for these activities the panel makes a strong case that "creating a separate, dedicated and protected endowment fund to support curiosity-driven research into aspects of uranium mine waste storage be a condition to be met before a decommissioning program is licensed" (CEAA 1996, 17).

In its analysis of the decommissioning proposals, the panel explains its concerns about the timeline for the decommissioning process because of "concerns about robustness and flexibility, and the limited extent of our present knowledge about the long-term behaviour of ecosystems involving saturated uranium mine tailings" (CEAA 1996, 28). The report continues, "what the panel sees as the short term includes *both* the short and transitional phases of the approach outlined in the proponents' Environmental Impact Statements" (italics added). And the panel sees a need "for a subsequent period, that could turn out to be relatively extended, in which the robustness of the systems can be tested and verified" (CEAA 1996, 28).

The panel's recommendation in this regard is that

> the final or long-term phase at each site *should not begin* until such time as the containment systems have met their design objectives for a sufficiently long time, and under sufficiently varied conditions, to provide convincing evidence that they are as effective and durable as predicted. *Only then should the proponents be authorized to negotiate the transfer to government of their responsibilities relating to these tailings sites* (italics added). (CEAA 1996, 28)

Finally, the panel asserts that "community involvement is a fundamental part of the perpetual care system," recommending that the proponents "take the lead in bringing about the creation of a not-for-profit organization that will focus on matters related to the impact of the tailings areas on the conservation of the Serpent River Basin environment" (CEAA 1996, 2).

The panel recommends three major elements, each to be considered separately, that need to be in place: 1) a fully funded plan, including schedules, facilities, monitoring, and maintenance; 2) the establishment of a community-based research endowment fund to support curiosity-driven research on issues related to the waste facilities; and 3) an emergency-response plan with necessary resources to deal with unanticipated events and disasters.

There is one other technical issue I want to draw attention to here, and that involves the panel's recommendations concerning the development of active ecological systems associated with the tailings areas. The report explains that "the fundamental question that arises is whether the development of active ecological systems associated with the Waste Management Areas will be beneficial or detrimental to their containment performance" (CEAA 1996, 36). And the panel recommends strongly that the issue of potential biological uptake of contaminants must receive more extensive and more careful attention, through adequate programs of sampling, analysis and interpretation, than has been suggested in the proponents' Environmental Impact Statement submissions. It is imperative not only that public concerns in this regard are addressed, but also that invaluable information that will become available through this 'very long experiment' is gathered and disseminated. (CEAA 1996, 36)

What to Do

The panel presents a number of suggestions — about funding, for example — for all three elements of facility operations and management during each stage of the decommissioning process. For instance, they recommend "that the surrounding community should be used as much as possible in the long-term care and maintenance activities," and "that the case is equally strong for involving the community in the development of the associated research program" that has been proposed (CEAA 1996, 44).

Finally, they also recommend "that an organization be created, which might be called the Serpent River Basin Conservation Council," and whose governing board would include "representatives of the two proponents, the City of Elliot Lake, the Serpent River First Nation, the research community, and, possibly, other communities in the area" (CEAA 1996, 44). They also suggest that the AECB should have a non-voting representative. Sadly, they appear to assume that interested citizen constituencies will naturally be represented by the stakeholders listed above, instead of insisting that the level of direct public participation begun during the hearings be continued on the council as well.

Some of the duties that the panel believe the council would be responsible for include managing the research endowment fund and using earnings from the fund to finance projects proposed by a research program committee. It also suggests the council "would review annual reports on the operation, monitoring, maintenance and repair of the Waste Management Area facilities, thereby providing a mechanism for keeping the local communities informed" (CEAA 1996, 45).

I find there are some significant shortcomings in the panel's proposed management structure, because I do not think the panel has outlined an organization capable of functioning as a truly independent, transparent entity. How can you have representatives of the proponents with voting rights on the governing board of an organization that they have endowed?

A Bigger Picture

Based on my understanding of area residents' concerns about the continued viability of the City of Elliot Lake and the North Shore region, there are many issues confronting the community that would benefit from an immediate, direct, and honest appraisal of the perpetual care and maintenance issues for the Waste Management Areas. The "family secret" is also compounded by real or perceived concerns (which abound, in every arena, and exist in every community) about the elitism that is contributing to a mounting apathy and does a great disservice to the community pioneers — young and old.

It seems to many, newcomers especially, that it is time for this legacy from the past mining glory to be discussed in a frank and honest way, and to become an integral part of *all* the planning exercises going on in the community. Until that happens, the dark clouds of misinformation and disinformation will continue threatening rain on the residents' otherwise very successful attempts to transform their single-industry town into a more diversified, thriving northern community.

A Return to the Commons

In Canadian law, our Crown lands are a modern-day vestige of the old European "Commons." I suggest that the "Conservation Council" reflect on the following description when attempting to draft its goals and objectives and formalize its constitution and bylaws.

> The Commons could be described as a specific local natural area adopted and protected by a specific local, human community. The Commons provides resources for the community and its individual members — now and in the future — while in return the community and its individual members protect the continued productivity, diversity, and long-term integrity of this particular natural area. (Brandt 1995, 207)

It is this kind of respect that appears to be lacking in so many of our planning decisions, past and present. Perhaps with more inclusiveness and more diversity we could begin to plan for the responsible management of funds and research which are needed to continue the modern-day traditions first carved out of the bush now almost 40 years ago.

The first steps along this path could involve delivering certain training initiatives to people and groups in the community, to enable local people to develop expertise and improve our ability to participate in the various decision-making activities. The requisite expertise to guide us in this process is readily available at reasonable cost.

Telling Stories about Our Homeplaces

One tool in particular is well suited to a principle-centred discourse in which we show mutual respect and engage in lively and inclusive debate while working towards our common goal; that tool is storytelling. Telling our stories about the past, as well as about the present, can help us articulate our region's historical ecology. It "remains an important cultural practice by which we, as individuals, transmit our knowledge of nature-as-lived-experience to our children and neighbours.... As an ancient strategy of survival, storytelling connects a society to its own history and its own place" (Bowerbank 1997). We would then be able to "trace the historical changes in individual and communal uses of [the watershed] through the stories of the people who experienced, and continue to experience, those changes" (Bowerbank 1997).

It would be important for the researchers involved in collecting these stories to seek out both historical and contemporary narratives in order to document personal and communal memories of people's activities, habits, and feelings relating to this particular local natural environment. To understand the linkages between people's lives and the condition of their environment, we would need to develop a multi-layered sense of the place as something co-created by generations of diverse peoples that have lived here, and still live here (Bowerbank 1997). The local mining companies and other agencies are able to "map" many types of information. Using this same technology we can now weave together the cultural and the physical components of any given place with the help of Geographical Information Systems (GIS) technology. We could add many interesting layers to their existing databases and create a very special community atlas in the process.

My challenge to the community, researchers, technicians, and policy-makers is to start implementing a participatory methodology for the creation of a conservation council that would respect people, not only as sources but as co-producers of bioregional knowledge

(Bowerbank 1997). I believe that Laurentian University has begun that kind of process with the work to date on the Elliot Lake Tracking and Adjustment Study, and also with the natural sciences, the "field research" being carried out around the area and based here in Elliot Lake. We need to both broaden these initiatives and integrate them into other studies in Elliot Lake.

Some Good Questions

- How do we, as citizens, learn to tell good stories that exemplify our expertise and responsibilities as inhabitants of the local environment?
- By what process can public servants and researchers learn to listen and to interpret these stories justly without imposing their own meta-narratives?
- How might the positive, and often intangible, values found in local stories get translated into community-directed and community-implemented environmental policy?
- By what criteria do we as citizens even begin to sort out what constitutes a "positive" as opposed to a "suspect" value?
- And ultimately, how do we, as local citizens and powerless communities, translate our stories, which often reflect diverse and conflicting desires, activities, interests, and philosophies, into a coherent approach to environmental caretaking? (See Bowerbank 1997.)

The sooner we start addressing these kinds of questions, the sooner this community and this region will begin to heal and move forward with true confidence.

How This Fits Our Experience

Those of us who told our stories at scoping or during the actual hearings were, I suspect, not that confident our words would be heard or that our experiences would matter when set against the science of the experts. I think many of us have been pleasantly surprised to discover that we can influence decision making, and that we can interject ethical considerations into a discourse ultimately dominated by cost-benefit analyses and risk-assessment reasoning.

Many people in other communities have come to conclusions similar to ours, and they are also seeking new ways of negotiating collective relationships with nature. We, too, can seek to create effective opportunities that will legitimize, rather than discredit, the knowledge and stories of ordinary people as co-producers of environmentally sound knowledge and behaviour. I think telling our stories in an open and respectful way might be a good option in this regard.

This kind of inclusive effort requires "the conscious invention and deployment of appropriate cultural as well as material and social technologies" (Bowerbank 1997). We will likely need help from "outsiders" if we decide to try to fashion the conservation council with these kinds of values. But experts are there, waiting and willing to help.

To listen and to honour the stories of our neighbours is to respect and nurture local knowledge and initiatives (Bowerbank 1997). I believe that inhabitants of the Serpent River Watershed have a shared interest in knowing about the natural, cultural, and industrial history of our homeplace. It matters to me and all my relations that we try to develop ways of life, as well as scientific projects, that will ensure the return of the pickerel to the Serpent River and will endeavour to protect us all from the toxic legacy of our past. At this moment, I don't feel that we have a very tangible grasp on how to search for the common ground we will need in order to meet our obligations to future generations of inhabitants throughout our local ecosystem.

We need to stop seeing the environment as "a series of problems which are disconnected from each other and, more importantly from the way we live and do business" (Keating 1997). This kind of local responsibility is not mere self-interest either. There is growing recognition that the global commons is shrinking rapidly and is severely threatened. In fact, the president of the Canadian Institute for Business and the Environment, Gary Gallon, has indicated that while the last 20 years of environmental activism were dominated by local flashpoints, "the next 20 years will be driven by international environmental agreements to protect the global commons" (Gallon 1997).

The Écomusée Idea

In 1997 we are honouring 40 years of intense human activity and settlement within the Serpent River Watershed at the same time as we struggle with changing demographic patterns and cuts to government programs and staffing levels. Perhaps we can borrow an idea from France called the "écomusée." It derives from the concept that a community is like a museum without walls, that everything within the community is a treasure that can be explored.

The Ecowise Project at McMaster University, a multi-disciplinary rehabilitation of Cootes Paradise in Hamilton, includes an écomusée. It is the intention of researchers to study the relation between the human/cultural environment and the natural environment (for a brief description, see Bowerbank 1997). The Ecowise Project aims to be "interdisciplinary and participatory in its methodology: it includes researchers from the humanities as well as from the natural and social sciences, *and* it actively seeks to involve the Hamilton community. The final goal is to provide a comprehensive framework for future planning decisions" (Bowerbank 1997).

As part of the Ecowise Project, a diverse group of historians, geographers, naturalists, outdoor enthusiasts, teachers, and students have started "Our Shared Home: An Écomusée Initiative" from a desire to provide free programming that will promote the active exploration of the natural, cultural, and historical areas of their community. Everyone is invited to lead a tour about some part of their community, thereby sharing their story about a particular part of their "homeplace" with their neighbours.

In conjunction with our pre-existing and ever-expanding local expertise in the above-mentioned disciplines, we also have a long history in the arts in Elliot Lake, and an especially exciting future in this regard with the recent announcement about the opening of the White Mountain Academy of the Arts. There is a wealth of life experience and creative talent to draw upon for any endeavour. And since we cannot count on Ottawa or Toronto to help us out as they have in the past, it is up to us to set the direction and find the leadership that will be able to navigate with respect through all the new responsibilities being passed down to our local governments and citizen groups.

References

Atomic Energy Control Board. (1987). *Regulatory Objectives, Requirements and Guidelines for the Disposal of Radioactive Wastes — Long-Term Aspects.* Regulation R–104, June 1987.

Brandt, Barbara. (1995). *Whole Life Economics: Revaluing Daily Life.* Gabriola Island, BC: New Society Publishers.

Bowerbank, Sylvia. (1997). "Telling stories about places: local knowledge and narratives can improve decisions about the environment," *Alternatives* 23 (Winter): 28–33.

Burrell, Terry. (1996). "Shrinking government and the protection of Ontario's environment," Paper commissioned for "Law for the Public Interest," a conference sponsored by the Canadian Environmental Law Association, November 1996.

Canadian Environmental Assessment Agency. (1996). *Decommissioning of*

Uranium Mine Tailings Management Areas in the Elliot Lake Area.
Report of the Environmental Assessment Panel (June 1996) of the
Canadian Environmental Assessment Agency of Environment Canada.

Gallon, Gary. (1997). "Looking backward (and forward)," *Alternatives* 23, 1
(Winter): 12.

Karlberg, Michael. (1997). "News and conflict: how adversarial news frames
limit public understanding of environmental issues," *Alternatives* 23, 1
(Winter): 22–27.

Keating, Michael. (1997). "Three decades on the green beat," *Alternatives* 23, 1
(Winter): 13.

Epilogue

Chapter 25
From Patchwork to Pro-Active Policies for Single-Industry Communities[1]
Anne-Marie Mawhiney

Canada's Policy Patchwork

In many ways, the stories of the mining families in Elliot Lake represent a best-case scenario, given the recent federal government's devolution of social programs, including training, education, and health, to provinces, as well as the Province of Ontario's downloading this year of a variety of services onto local municipalities. Except for those laid off from the Stanleigh Mine in 1996, most mining families in Elliot Lake made the layoff transition prior to the erosion of the Canadian safety net over the last three years. Although they were far from perfect in terms of their ability to respond adequately to the needs of people who are unemployed, disabled, elderly, or otherwise socially dependent, there is little doubt that past policies were better able than the current patchwork to ease the lives of Canadians, and especially of Canadian women, who for whatever reasons — including being victim to mass layoffs — depended on the safety net to meet basic human needs.

Until the recent devolution and downloading of services, the Canadian social welfare system was based on a division of society that rewarded the importance of paid, productive work of those in the labour market by providing an unemployment *insurance* — intended to buffer workers in poorer economic periods — and a government *pension* when the worker reached a certain age. Although the division between insurance and pensions on the one hand, and public assistance on the other, was intended to divide society between those making "valued" contributions to society and those unable or unwilling to do so, in fact the division followed more closely along gendered lines. Women — who made their contributions to the economy in unpaid, social, productive activities — were more likely than men to be among those receiving the residual benefits of old age security and (in Ontario) general welfare assistance and family benefits allowance. To a larger extent now than previously, unemployed workers are told that their contributions to society through unpaid work and former paid work will no longer be compensated through anything other than residual, short-term, and inadequate kinds of social programs. This changes the division of society so that it is no longer across gender lines, but across lines between those fewer people who are engaged in paid production and those not, even though this latter group is likely engaged in unpaid activities that make important contributions to the well-being of families, communities, and Canadian society as a whole.

The current policy context ensures that the burden of the transition from layoff to other paid or unpaid activities is now more difficult for families than it was even a few years ago; and the former social programs were less than ideal, as has already been pointed out throughout this book. This shift of federal and Ontario social policy so that social support programs are increasingly residual in nature is in contradiction to the globalization of the economy; it seems incongruent that we would establish economic policies at the federal level that are predicated on higher rates of permanent unemployment and yet fragment even further the safety net intended to buffer the transition from industrial to post-industrial society. Surely, more than ever before, the federal government should now retain national responsibility for the social consequences of its recent economic policies.

Historically, federal labour adjustment policies and programs have had as their primary goal assisting individual workers to find new employment. Employment insurance, social assistance, publicly funded programs to help workers with job-search skills, education and retraining programs, and even many personal counselling services have assumed that alternative jobs existed and were readily accessible to all, if only the worker would try hard enough, acquire the proper skills and education, and present him or herself well before and during job interviews. The underlying assumption for such a policy was that standard (full-time, permanent, and long-term) paid work is the only valued (in monetary ways) productive contribution to our society, in spite of the fact that by 1992 non-standard work accounted for four of every ten jobs in Canada (Donner et al. 1994, 27). The failure to shift our views of productivity has meant that social policies and programs have ignored other essential paid and unpaid activities that support our economic and social conditions. They have also ignored the skills, education, and productive experience of other family members who may, in some cases, have been more employable than the person who was laid off, because of particular local and regional labour demands or because of the educational attainment of these other family members. Finally, because these policies and programs were conceived in the postwar era, when the traditional, gendered division of labour was common, they have tended to be gender-blind and therefore structured to be more responsive to work traditionally viewed as men's. Thus, such policies and programs do not take into account the realities and work experiences of women workers who have always had multiple roles in paid and unpaid work.

Mass layoffs are often the result of major changes in the Canadian economy, yet we have been providing services to unemployed, non-employed, and laid-off workers as if the postwar boom were still happening. Thus, the response by the federal government, through its policies and programs, to post-industrial unemployment — when plants close, machines replace workers, or plants relocate (Perrucci et al.1988, 5) — has been to presume that individuals are merely undergoing cyclical or frictional unemployment. Individual workers are treated as though the next job is just around the corner, if only they would try hard enough to find it and present themselves in suitable ways for interviews. Such approaches are not appropriate for today's context, especially within the mining sector. What is needed instead is an approach to labour adjustment that is consistent with contemporary ways of thinking and living. If our economic priorities are to promote efficiency, productivity, and wealth in the economy (Picot, Lin, and Piper 1996, 1), then our orientation to work shifts in comparable ways so that the labour force becomes smaller and employers hire on short-term contracts and use flexible work arrangements. This is also true for mining companies, where the trend now is fly-in operations, which separate families and provide less job security. These shifts are partnered with higher unemployment and non-employment rates, which are structured into public policies and government planning. By focusing on individual weakness or lack of skills as the reasons for unemployment, decision-makers "divert attention away from the societal and political task of reducing unemployment by societal measures" (Frese 1987, 215).

Given current shifts in work policies and practices, it no longer makes sense after mass layoffs of miners or workers from other sectors to pretend that other work is easily accessible. Instead, innovative ways of addressing unemployment and non-employment are needed to allow

Canada's economic priorities to be maximized without placing the burden on individuals, families, and communities.

Implications of Post-Industrial Unemployment for Policy

Policy context for layoffs in the mining sector. In the specific case of the mining industry in Canada, post-industrial unemployment presents some unique differences in comparison with other sectors of the economy. For instance, manufacturing companies have moved outside Canada at least in part because labour is substantially cheaper and less protected by labour laws in developing countries. In the case of manufacturing, labour cost is a main factor in a decision to move offshore. The mining industry, in contrast, is limited in the extent to which it can easily move offshore because there are still rich and cost-effective mineral bodies remaining here. Thus, while mining companies are certainly investing in mineral exploration outside Canada, there is still ongoing interest in new discoveries within Canada as well. However, as more established Canadian mining sites approach the last stages of their life cycle, international and northern mineral exploration maximizes the likelihood of finding replacement ore bodies and also provides the companies with the potential of a cheaper labour pool, which would decrease production costs in comparison with existing mining sites. An example comes immediately to mind: the decision by Ontario Hydro to terminate its contracts in Elliot Lake, Ontario, and to buy uranium in Saskatchewan was made because of lower production costs. Shifts in mining locations by companies, along with the resultant mass layoffs, are part of the tradition of mining. The boom-bust cycles within the mining sector have occurred because of fluctuations in prices, market demands, and the finite nature of ore bodies. Mining companies have always sought new locations, and it is likely that they will continue to do so for as long as there are minerals to be found. Globalization only broadens the field for mining and mineral exploration, and certain sites offer the added incentive of a cheaper labour pool. Given the known cyclical nature of mining, the idea of planning proactively for the inevitable bust phase is perhaps even more important than for other sectors. The mining sector, therefore, would be an appropriate place to initiate and evaluate a new policy direction. However, this policy direction could and should apply to other sectors as well.

Ideas from the literature. Unemployment has traditionally been discussed in relation to its consequences for individuals (most often men) who have been laid off, and government policies and programs have targeted this group for assistance. However, once we broaden the perspective of unemployment to include its post-industrial causes and implications, we need also to extend the ways that we think about policies and programs. Briar (1988), for instance, suggests that

> unemployment is neither a static nor episodic state but, rather, a continuously compounding condition that cannot be understood solely by examining its human consequences. The dynamics of the unravelling of the capacity of workers, families, and communities to function effectively may involve the corrosive effects of declining resources, the discounting by policymakers of their problems and needs, and their consequent self-recrimination and immobilization (28).

Frese (1987) points out that those targeting individuals for employment opportunities fail to redress the overall picture:

> If such programs geared toward the individual are effective for those participating in them, it only means that *other* people stay unemployed longer. These programs only change one's position in the "line of the unemployed" waiting for a job; they do not change the length of the line itself (215).

Sherraden (1985) recommends a mixed (public and private) approach to employment policy (9) and points out that an

> implicit assumption in employment policy in the modern era has been that jobs are available in the traditional labor market for properly trained workers, at least during good times. Chronic unemployment has not, to any significant extent, been acknowledged in public policy since World War II, though an increasing proportion of total unemployment is apparently due to chronic demand deficiency (11).

Ternowetsky (1988) suggests that

> the persistence of unemployment and changes in work opportunities are leading to an increasingly divided society. This division is characterized by a growth in low income workers, falling levels of middle class income and a shrinking, yet increasingly affluent top tier of income earners (31).

These researchers point to the consequences of global policies intended to restructure the economy at the expense of people's well-being. In all cases, they are suggesting that unemployment can no longer be considered in isolation, ignoring global social and economic forces. Nor can it be considered the result of personal failings of individual workers. Yet we persist in providing employment services and incentives for employment insurance and public assistance as though this were the case. Our analyses of labour adjustment continue to focus on a narrow definition of productivity and to define "successful" adjustment as occurring only when the unemployed worker returns to the paid work force. We need to reconstruct our ways of helping all people through the inevitable transition from an industrial to a post-industrial economy. A federal strategy is required.

Characteristics of Proactive Policies

One conceptualization of a successful transition to a post-industrial economy specifies four groups of constituent elements of well-being as necessary for a minimum acceptable level of provisioning. These four groups of elements are productivity, equity, sustainability, and empowerment (United Nations Development Programme 1995, cited in Neitzert, Mawhiney, and Porter 1997). Neitzert, Mawhiney, and Porter argue that most labour adjustment studies have focused too narrowly on paid labour activities related to provisioning, and that all four elements are required for personal and collective (or social) well-being and successful adjustment after layoffs.

The views presented here of ways in which federal government and industrial policies and practices can respond to the consequences of globalization and downsizing follow this framework. The main recommendation presented in this chapter is that the costs of the labour adjustment process should be borne by industry and the federal government rather than by individuals, families or households, and communities.

The most obvious element of well-being is productivity; we need to satisfy a certain standard of living in order to survive and an even higher standard to live adequately or even well. In our society, productivity has been traditionally viewed as limited to paid economic activities outside the home. However, Neitzert, Mawhiney, and Porter (1997) view productivity as also including social and biological production, intellectual self-actualization and achievement, and social, cultural, and leisure activities that improve quality of life within any collective grouping, such as a family, neighbourhood, community, or district. Underpinning the more limited view of productivity are beliefs about individual and familial self-sufficiency and a gendered division of labour. In this limited view, the value of productive activities outside the labour market — let alone the necessity of social reproductive activities — remains invisible, unacknowledged, and therefore unvalued in any tangible way. When individuals and families have not supported themselves by way of paid economic activities, the State has provided minimal assistance, the goal of which is to help people to realize a minimal level of sustenance so that they can provide for themselves and their family members, although only at a very basic level. The goal of government assistance is always to help the person achieve self-sufficiency. However, this goal is often unrealistic. "The belief that hard work will ensure self-sufficiency persists despite centuries of evidence to the contrary. Women work extraordinarily hard at family care-giving, performing two-thirds of the world's work; yet it is estimated that they receive only five to ten percent of the world's income" (Briar 1988, 157, citing D. Bonnar 1987).

The capacity to sustain and replenish for the present and future generations — sustainability — is also an essential element of well-being and is braided closely with productivity. Our ability to produce for the immediate needs of ourselves, our families, and our community needs to be balanced with the ability to replenish resources for future generations. However, until recently, western economic practices have been oriented towards profit rather than the capacity to sustain. Instead of considering the results of production as a collective benefit for now and the future, our actions have been based on competition and social Darwinism, with the accumulation of wealth remaining in the hands of very few. As for sustaining our society over the longer term, this individualistic competitiveness has been very shortsighted, indeed. Sustainability includes activities in other spheres of production, as well. Our family's and society's abilities to support and sustain the pursuit of intellectual self-actualization and achievements have operated in our society during the twentieth century through social institutions such as schools, religious organizations, print materials, and the media. Most recently, intellectual self-actualization is also starting to occur through technological advances such as the world wide web and virtual libraries. Social, cultural, and leisure activities that sustain collectivities, such as families, neighbourhoods, communities, or society are also important to consider as ways of self-actualization and social support. These activities are the glue that binds people together; they create an environment that promotes interdependence and common goals among present and future generations.

Considering individual and communal well-being without also understanding power dynamics in our society is impossible. Empowerment refers to a process where people retain or regain control over decisions about their own lives and their society. Empowerment, then, encompasses both self-determination and democratization (Roeher Institute 1993), and "makes connections between social and economic justice and individual pain and suffering" (Lee 1996, 225). The extent to which people have control over their own lives has been related to people's health status and to their ability to draw on resources to cope with major live events (Turner, Kessler, and House 1991). At the individual level, a personal sense of power translates into an ability to deal effectively with externally driven events. The absence of this sense of personal power is a feeling of hopelessness that "leads to destruction of self and others, despair, apathy, internalized rage, and false beliefs about the worth of the self" (Harris 1993, cited in Lee 1996, 228).

However, power dynamics are often most influential at the structural — economic and political — rather than the personal level. With layoffs and plant closures, for example, industrial leaders and government officials have control over the decision, its timing, who benefits, and who assumes the costs. Then the social safety net, in whatever form it exists at the time, is assumed to help in picking up the pieces of those for whom the closure and layoffs have had the most devastating consequences. Without a feeling of control over their lives, people's well-being is seriously affected and their overall productivity diminishes.

> As global economic interdependence has increased, with concomitant social and economic changes at the national level, the problem of poverty has intensified in many countries of both South and North, including certain populations in many industrialized nations. Families, women and children often bear this intensification. Structures at international, national, state or provincial and local governments levels affect neighbourhoods, families and children (Vosler and Nair 1993, 159).

Equity issues are embedded in the different starting places of people who are laid off. For instance, at least in the short term, a family that has accumulated personal assets and effects may feel the effects of being laid off differently than a family that does not have the basic financial resources to sustain the family beyond the breadwinner's last pay cheque. The difference between these two families may be explained by a variety of arbitrary factors such as "family size and composition and the family's life cycle stage" (Voydanoff 1983, 95) as well as the family's world-view and planning priorities (Neitzert, Mawhiney, and Porter 1997). Equity is also an issue in the case of re-entry into the workforce after a layoff, as the literature tells us that women, people of colour, First Nations people, and older workers are less likely to find re-employment — regardless of their experience, skills, and education — than younger, white men (Neitzert, Mawhiney, and Porter 1997; Voydanoff 1983; Moen 1982).

By positioning productivity within the broader notion of well-being, I have crafted a way of looking at contributions that people make to our society that is more comprehensive than the one presently allowed in federal and provincial policies and programs. I suggest that this comprehensive approach is proactive and more reflective of today's socioeconomic context than is the patchwork approach that has been used over the last half of this century and that is presently unravelling. By broadening the definition of "productivity" to "well-being," we are reflecting the true nature of the Canadian reality, where much work has remained invisible, ignored, and unvalued in our society — work that has most often been done by women, people of colour, First Nations people, and others on the margins of the economic sphere of society.

A New Partnership

In February 1995 the Raglan Agreement (unpublished) was made among the Makivik Corporation, Qarqalik Landholding Corporation of Salluit, Northern Village Corporation of Salluit, Nunaturlik Landholding Corporation of Kangiqsujuaq, Northern Village Corporation of Kangiqsujuaq, and the Société Minière Raglan du Québec Limitée. This agreement presents the terms and conditions for the Raglan Project, a mining project to produce nickel, copper, and cobalt within the Nunavik area under the James Bay and Northern Quebec Agreement. I recognize that the social, economic, and political contexts for agreements to develop mining projects are vastly different between Euro-Canadian communities and communities of Aboriginal peoples. There are, however, elements of the Raglan Agreement from which leaders from Euro-Canadian communities and governments can learn, and that can promote more sustainable solutions for mining communities over the long term.

Two objectives of the Raglan Agreement are: that "Inuit Beneficiaries and, in particular, the Inuit Beneficiaries of Salluit and Kangiqsujuaq, derive direct and indirect social and/or economic benefits during" the various phases of the Raglan Project; and that the project "facilitate equitable and meaningful participation for Inuit Beneficiaries ... with respect to the Raglan Project" (12). Economic benefits to the communities of Salluit and Kangiqsujuaq include money transfers of $10 million over the first year, $800,000 for each year thereafter of the project, and an additional "4.5 percent of the Annual Operating Cash Flow from the Raglan Project" (37). The agreement gives priority in hiring for the Raglan Project in the following order: Inuit residing in Salluit and Kangiqsujuaq, Inuit residing in other northern villages, Inuit residing elsewhere besides in a northern village, persons of Inuit ancestry, and others not of Inuit ancestry (23). In the event of layoffs, consideration would be given to Inuit employees first rather than on the basis of seniority, and the Société Minière commits to striving to find new employment elsewhere for Inuit employees after the permanent closing of the Raglan Project (28). The Raglan Committee, which consists of three Inuit members appointed by the relevant Inuit stakeholders and three Société Minière members, make decisions based on a majority vote that requires at least one vote from each of the two cultural groups. The committee is chaired alternately by an Inuit representative and a Société Minière representative (49).

Several principles emerge from the Raglan Agreement that were lacking in the Elliot Lake situation and are relevant for other non-Aboriginal communities where mining development may be taking place in the future. The first is a long-term employment commitment to local workers that gives priority to hiring locally and to striving to find work elsewhere for local workers after the life of the project. Given the very high human costs the are presently borne by mining families from Elliot Lake (see Leaderbeater, Chapter 11 in this volume), it would seem that the primary burden for job search should be carried by the company and by government rather than by the individual workers.

A second principle in the Raglan Agreement is profit-sharing: the community and its citizens share in the profits with the company. One model that has been proposed elsewhere for non-Aboriginal communities is the establishment of a Community Economic Development Fund that could be used by the community towards the end of the mining cycle so that the community could diversify its economic base. The tradition in Northern Ontario communities has been for the mining company to provide donations for specific projects such as recreation centres and hospital equipment. But perhaps it would be more appropriate to have, in addition to a share in profits, annual payments to a community-directed fund, whereby the community could determine the best use of the profits rather than receiving "benevolent donations" prioritized by the company.

A third principle from the Raglan Agreement is that community leaders have an equitable say in decisions made by the mining company that would have an impact on the community and mining families. This moves the community away from being economically dependent on the company to a relationship of interdependence among the community and the company (and the union). Such a partnership would mark a radical shift from the present situation in mining communities throughout Canada, with the few exceptions of some on Aboriginal lands. However, in order for community, family, and personal well-being to become core to decision-making, this radical shift is needed.

The company's commitment to seeking employment for workers after the mining cycle is complete could have a negative impact on the community's viability. However, with funds to build a diversified economic base, the community might be able to ensure that mining families have viable choices of finding new employment within the community or moving to a new mine site elsewhere. In this way, the community's viability could be maintained for future generations.

Summary and Conclusions

We need to consider ways of living in our society so that families and communities no longer have to bear the brunt of global economic restructuring, and the natural boom-bust cycles of Canadian resource industries. In order to accomplish this, we need to consider more effective ways to restructure our society socially so that individuals, families, and communities are able to be productive — in the wider sense of the term, to sustain themselves and future generations, to feel control over their own lives, and to enjoy equitable shares in resources and opportunities. Change efforts need to occur in the following ways:

- focus change efforts at the macro-level to emphasize equity, so that all citizens have an equitable share in society's rewards, and productivity in its broader sense, so that our society values these alternative forms of productivity. Policies and programs need to be reformulated so that industry and government are responsible for ensuring that families have the necessary resources to sustain themselves over the long term, whether or not paid work is a viable option for a family.
- ensure that the costs and burden for post-industrial unemployment are shared equitably by government and industry so

that individuals, families and communities do not carry the undue burden of economic policies and practices outside their control;
• support people's change efforts and decreasing the negative effects of their so-called private troubles by helping them understand these in the wider socio-economic context;
• empower people to develop meaningful and valued ways of shifting their personal and family activities so that other, non-monetary forms of productivity are valued.

There is a danger of establishing or maintaining inappropriate policies and programs whenever we fail to recognize the true costs and consequences of mass layoffs. By maintaining social and economic policies and practices that do not address the hidden and long-term implications of inadequate resources, dislocation, deprivation, and personal and social isolation, we risk incurring even larger social costs to present and future generations (Briar 1988, 5) than has been the case until recently in Canada. On the other hand, if we learn from the lessons of Elliot Lake and other cases of mass layoffs, we can formulate policies and practices that genuinely address structural inequities in our society by restitching the fabric of our society so that the well-being of society, of all its members and its institutions, is sustained in ways that are valued as productive. Policies and practices that focus on these approaches to social restructuring are much more likely to support families and communities, and they reflect an important investment in the well-being of present and future generations.

Note

[1] The author has benefited from discussions at the ELTAS policy workshop, September 1997, with Greg Albo, Erling Christensen, Ursule Critoph, Kevin Hayes, Andrew King, Meg Luxton, Martha MacDonald, Sharon Gow, Richard Hamilton, Dan Hutchinson, and Jan Lewis. Brad McKenzie, Monica Neitzert, and Patrick Barnholden have made insightful comments on earlier drafts.

References

Briar, Katherine Hooper. (1988). *Social Work and Unemployment*. National Association of Social Workers: Silver Spring, MD.

Donner, Arthur et al. (1994). *Working Time and the Distribution of Work*. Ottawa: Minister of Supply and Services Canada.

Frese, Michael. (1987). "Alleviating depression in the unemployed: adequate financial support, hope and early retirement," *Social Science and Medicine* 25, 2: 213–14.

Lee, Judith. (1996). "The empowerment approach to social work practice," in *Social Work Treatment*, 4th edition, ed. Francis Turner. London: The Free Press, 218–49.

Moen, Phyllis. (1982). "Preventing financial hardship: coping strategies of families of the unemployed," in *Family Stress, Coping and Social Support*, ed. Hamilton McCubbin, A.E. Cauble, and J. Patterson. Springfield, IL: Charles C. Thomas Publisher.

Neitzert, Monica, Anne-Marie Mawhiney, and Elaine Porter. (1997). *Stitching the Equilibria: A Feminist Tapestry of Labour Adjustment.* ELTAS Analysis Series #1A1. Sudbury, ON: INORD, Laurentian University.

Perrucci, Carolyn, R. Perrucci, D. Targ, and Harry Targ. (1988). *Plant Closings: International Context and Social Costs.* Hawthorne, NY: Aldine de Gruyter.

Picot, Garnett, Z. Lin, and Wendy Pyper. (1996). *Permanent Layoffs in Canada: Overview and Longitudinal Analysis.* Ottawa: Statistics Canada.

Roeher Institute. (1993). *Social Well-Being: A Paradigm for Reform.* North York, ON: York University.

Sherraden, Michael. (1985). "Employment policy: a conceptual framework," *Journal of Social Work Education* 21, 2: 5–14.

Ternowetsky, Gordon. (1988). "Unemployment, employment, the declining middle and the expanding bottom: the challenge for social work," *Canadian Review of Social Policy* 22: 20–35.

Turner, J. Blake, R. Kessler, and James House. (1991). "Factors facilitating adjustment to unemployment: implications for intervention," *American Journal of Community Psychology* 19, 4: 521–42.

United Nations Development Programme. (1995). *Human Development Report 1995.* New York: Oxford University Press.

Vosler, Nancy. (1994). "Displaced manufacturing workers and their families: a research-based practice model," *Families in Society: The Journal of Contemporary Human Services* 75, 2: 105–15.

Vosler, Nancy and Sudha Nair. (1993). "Families, children, poverty: education for social work practice at multiple systems levels," *International Social Work,* 36: 159–72.

Voydanoff, Patricia. (1983). "Unemployment: family strategies for adaptation," in *Stress and the Family, Volume II,* ed. Charles Figley and Hamilton McCubbin. New York: Brunner/Mazel, 90–102.

Mystère économique
Paroles d'Alex Berthelot Jr.

À dix-sept ans, j'ai été me faire éduquer,
La secondaire complète, c'était l'temps pour l'université.
Nos bagages faites, bien j'étais prêt à m'faire expliquer
Ce monde de toute complexité.

On m'a dit dans ma classe d'économie
Que les ressources naturelles, c'est la richesse garantie,
Mais si c'est l'cas, dis-moi pourquoi, j'ai peut-être mal compris,
Ce n'est pas c'que j'ai vu dans ma vie.

Né dans le Nord de l'Ontario,
Ressources naturelles abondantes comme l'eau,
Fourrures, forêts, pouvoir hydro, toutes sortes de minéraux,
Donc la richesse se trouve à Toronto.

Un d'ces jours il va falloir réveiller nos gens,
Malgré l'exploitation notre richesse reste grande.
Prenons donc charge de notre futur, c'est à peu près l'temps
Qu'on y participe intelligemment. (bis)

Used with permission

344

Contributors

PETER BECKETT — associate professor of biology at Laurentian University and a principal investigator with Environmental Services at the Elliot Lake Research Field Station in Elliot Lake.

ALEX BERTHELOT, JR. — business owner in Elliot Lake, who has taken leadership roles with the Elliot Lake and District Chamber of Commerce, the Elliot Lake Economic Diversification Committee (ELEDC), and the Elliot Lake and North Shore Corporation for Business Development (ELNOS).

DEBORAH BERTHELOT — Former facility manager of the Elliot Lake Research Field Station. She is currently compliance supervisor, Mine Waste Management Inc., in Elliot Lake.

MERLYN BISHOP — treasurer of the City of Elliot Lake.

CARRIE CHENIER — senior compensation officer for Local 5417 of the United Steelworkers of America in Elliot Lake.

GERARD COURTIN — associate professor of biology at Laurentian University.

MAYOR GEORGE FARKOUH — mayor of the City of Elliot Lake.

BARRY FERGUSON — manager of administration for the Elliot Lake Division of Rio Algom Limited.

SHARON GOW — community-based environmental activist and grassroots economic development proponent in the Elliot Lake and North Shore areas.

SHAWN HEARD — research associate at Laurentian University and program manager, Human Ecology, at the Elliot Lake Research Field Station, Elliot Lake. Among other research projects, he conducted the Elliot Lake Seniors' Needs Assessment.

DONALD W. HINE — formerly at Laurentian University, now lecturer in cognitive psychology at the University of New England in Armidale, New South Wales, Australia.

DAVID LEADBEATER — associate professor of economics at Laurentian University and a researcher with the Elliot Lake Tracking and Adjustment Study.

JAN LEWIS — former manager of the Training Access Centre and the Workforce Development Centre in Elliot Lake and a community-based research associate with the Elliot Lake Tracking and Adjustment Study.

JOHN LEWKO — director of the Centre for Research in Human Development at Laurentian University.

MICK LOWE — freelance journalist and author based in the Sudbury region.

ANNE-MARIE MAWHINEY — professor of social work at Laurentian University, former director of of the Institute of Northern Ontario Research and Development (INORD), and a researcher with the Elliot Lake Tracking and Adjustment Study.

MONICA NEITZERT — associate professor of economics at Laurentian University and a researcher with the Elliot Lake Tracking and Adjustment Study.

ROGER PAYNE — general manager, Elliot Lake Division and East Kemptville Division of Rio Algom Limited.

JANE PITBLADO — projects coordinator/editor for INORD at Laurentian

University.

RAYMOND W. PONG — research director of the Centre for Rural and Northern Health Research at Laurentian University.

ELAINE PORTER — associate professor of sociology at Laurentian University and a researcher with the Elliot Lake Tracking and Adjustment Study.

MARK PRYSTUPA — formerly assistant professor of geography at Laurentian University, now manager, Land Claims and Self-Government, Department of Resources, Wildlife and Economic Development, Government of the Northwest Territories.

PEGGY QUINN — executive director of the Elliot Lake Family Life Centre.

DAVID ROBINSON — associate professor of economics at Laurentian University and a researcher with the Elliot Lake Tracking and Adjustment Study.

GARRY ROMAIN — executive director of the Elliot Lake Men's Support Centre.

ALAN SALMONI — professor of human kinetics at Laurentian University.

CRAIG SUMMERS — associate professor of psychology at Laurentian University.

BRYAN TISCH — program manager, Environmental Services, at the Elliot Lake Research Field Station in Elliot Lake.

ALBERT VIVYURKA — senior environmental engineer (now retired) at the Elliot Lake Division of Rio Algom Limited.

DEREK WILKINSON — associate professor of sociology at Laurentian University and a researcher with the Elliot Lake Tracking and Adjustment Study.

SHARON PAPPIN WILLIANEN — former research associate of the Environmental Rehabilitation Group at the Elliot Lake Research Field Station in Elliot Lake.

STEPHEN WITHERS — volunteer coordinator at the Elliot Lake Men's Support Centre.

Denison Mines #2 shaft, May 1972.
City of Elliot Lake